Digital Transformation with AI and Smart Servicing Technologies for Sustainable Rural Development

This book introduces and demonstrates the state-of-the-art research and development in tackling sustainable urban and rural integration, supported by digitalization and digital transformation in rural areas with Industry 4.0/5.0 technologies. *Digital Transformation with AI and Smart Servicing Technologies for Sustainable Rural Development* is centered around how to deal with the sustainable urban and rural integration with advanced digital technologies such as artificial intelligence (AI), Big Data, Crowdsourcing, Crowdsensing, and digital twin applications.

The main content of this book comes from the authors' international collaborative projects funded by British Council and National Sciences Foundation of China and our Newton Prize Winning project founded by UK Department for Business, Energy & Industrial Strategy. It covers digital platform design with integrated crowdsourcing, crowdsensing, and digital twin technologies for smart community services and governing. The authors discuss smart textile design for health and social care and VR/AR-based telehealth care services for plants, livestock, and people. It also presents smart building technologies and integrated services for remote rural areas.

This book will be a valuable reference for multidisciplinary researchers, policy makers, urban and rural development engineers, and university students to support their research and work in AI and smart technology applications.

Digital Transformation with AI and Smart Servicing Technologies for Sustainable Rural Development

Edited by
Shengfeng Qin, Hongan Wang, and Cuixia Ma

CRC Press
Taylor & Francis Group
Boca Raton London New York

CRC Press is an imprint of the
Taylor & Francis Group, an **informa** business

Designed cover image: ©Shutterstock

First edition published 2024
by CRC Press
2385 NW Executive Center Drive, Suite 320, Boca Raton FL 33431

and by CRC Press
4 Park Square, Milton Park, Abingdon, Oxon, OX14 4RN

CRC Press is an imprint of Taylor & Francis Group, LLC

© 2024 selection and editorial matter, Shengfeng Qin, Hongan Wang, and Cuixia Ma; individual chapters, the contributors

ISBN: 978-1-032-68667-7 (hbk)
ISBN: 978-1-032-68668-4 (pbk)
ISBN: 978-1-032-68669-1 (ebk)

DOI: 10.1201/9781032686691

Typeset in Times
by codeMantra

Contents

About the Editors

Dr Shengfeng Qin is currently a Professor in Design in Northumbria School of Design at Northumbria University, UK. Prior to Northumbria University, he was a Lecturer/Senior Lecturer in Product Design in the Department of Design at Brunel University, UK. He received his Ph.D. degree in design from the University of Wales, UK, in 2000. He was the 2019 Newton Prize recipient based on his collaborative research work with Professor Cuixia Ma at the Institute of Software of Chinese Academy of Sciences on Transforming Service Design and Big Data Technologies into Sustainable Urbanization. Professor Qin has established the Smart Design Lab (SDL) at Northumbria School of Design, leading design research into future smart products, services, and interconnected systems design by applying cutting-edge smart technologies and smart multidisciplinary design research methods/tools. He is currently the Editor-in-Chief of the *International Journal of Advanced Design Research* and Editor-in-Chief of the *International Journal of Rapid Manufacturing*.

Hongan Wang is currently a Professor with the Institute of Software, Chinese Academy of Sciences. He is also the Director of Beijing Key Laboratory of Human Computer Interaction. He received his Ph.D. degree from the Institute of Software, Chinese Academy of Sciences, Beijing, China, in 1999. He has published over 120 papers on important journals and conferences. Prof. Wang won the Second Prize of the 2018 National Science and Technology Progress Award and the First Prize of the 2015 Beijing Science and Technology Award. His research interests include human–computer interaction, real-time intelligence, and real-time database.

Cuixia Ma is currently a Professor with the University of Chinese Academy of Science and the Institute of Software, Chinese Academy of Sciences. She received her B.S. and M.S. degrees from Shandong University, China, in 1997 and 2000, respectively, and her Ph.D. degree from the Institute of Software, Chinese Academy of Sciences, Beijing, China, in 2003. She was the 2019 Newton Prize recipient and received the First Prize of the 2015 Beijing Science and Technology Award. Her research interests include natural user interface, sketch interaction, multimodal fusion, and visual analysis.

List of Contributors

Cuixia Ma
Institute of Software
Chinese Academy of Sciences
Beijing, China

Xiaojing Niu
Department of Industrial Design
Northwestern Polytechnical University
Xi'an, China

Kun Qian
School of Biomedical Engineering &
 Imaging Sciences
King's College London
London, United Kingdom

Shengfeng Qin
School of Design
Northumbria University
Newcastle, United Kingdom

Song Qiu
Academy of Arts and Design
Tsinghua University
Beijing, China

Hongan Wang
Institute of Software
Chinese Academy of Sciences
Beijing, China

Meili Wang
College of Information Engineering
Northwest A&F University
Xianyang, China

Shan Wang
Winchester School of Art
University of Southampton
Southampton, United Kingdom

Xiao Wei
Winchester School of Art
University of Southampton
Southampton, United Kingdom

Yuanyuan Yin
Winchester School of Art
University of Southampton
Southampton, United Kingdom

Xiao Zhang
Academy of Arts and Design
Tsinghua University
Beijing, China

Guozhen Zhao
Institute of Psychology
Chinese Academy of Sciences
Beijing, China

1 Introduction to Sustainable Urban and Rural Integration

Shengfeng Qin

1.1 THE RAPID URBANIZATION AND SUSTAINABILITY ISSUES

Cities continue to attract people in search of a better life and greater job prospects and services. Urbanization is the process of more and more people living in towns and cities, mainly moved from rural areas (countryside), when towns and cities are still in developing stages, thus offering more opportunities for people's development. The term migration is used to describe this truly global phenomenon with people movements both within nations (internal migration) and internationally across borders (international migration). The internal migration includes rural to urban, urban to urban, rural to rural, or urban to rural. In this book, we focus our discussion on internal rural to urban migration because it is a main form of migration in developing countries.

The two common causes for urbanization are natural population increase and rural to urban migration. According to the United Nation's The World Urbanization Prospects 2022 report (United Nations Department of Economic and Social Affairs, 2022), the world's population continues to grow although the pace of growth is slowing down, and it is projected to reach 8 billion on 15 November 2022, around 8.5 billion in 2030, 9.7 billion in 2050, and 10.4 billion in 2100. The population growth is partly due to the declining levels of mortality, resulting in an average longevity of around 77.2 years globally in 2050. This in turn makes the population of older persons aged 65 years or above increasing both in numbers and as a share of the total rising from 10% in 2022 to projected 16% in 2050. In 2022, the two most populous regions were both in Asia: Eastern and South-Eastern Asia (29% of the global population) and Central and Southern Asia (26%). China and India, with a population of more than 1.4 billion each, account for the most populous countries (OpenLearn create, 2022).

The key impacts of urbanization include:

- Growth in the size of urban population and the extent of urban areas;
- Changes in land use, economic activity, and culture;
- Significant economic and social transformation;

- Greater access to social services and enhanced opportunities for urban migration;
- Increased pressures on providing good services in housing, water and sanitation, transportation, and educational and health care services caused by rapid and unplanned urban growth.

With a high volume of migrants arriving in cities from rural areas (called internal rural to urban migration), municipal authorities or city leaders are faced with the challenge in managing migration and cities, alongside the recognition that well-managed migration can be an asset for economics and societies, particularly in the long term. As reported in "Migration and Its Impact on Cities" (World Economic Forum, 2017), the rural to urban migration has various impacts on cities. These impacts include economic impact, social impact, political impact, and urban infrastructure and services. City leaders are faced with the challenge of providing vital urban infrastructure and services to meet the needs of the migrant population. This includes affordable social housing, quality education and health services, simple access to basic utilities (water, power, etc.), robust and congestion-free roads and transportation infrastructure, and, finally, ensuring integration and social cohesion for the increased diversity.

On the other hand, with the influx of migrant workers (usually young males) to cities, the internal rural to urban migration also has great impacts on the rural areas. The rural areas become "hollow" villages as appeared in China (Sun et al., 2011). What's left in the village are the elderly, the young ones, and females. "Hollow" villages phenomenon contains two essential features: (1) a significant loss of land resources in rural areas due to housing developments annexed massive amounts of land and (2) a decrease in the number of residents in the village due to urbanization. The problems brought about by "hollowing" of villages are twofold. First, food security becomes a big challenge due to the loss of a big amount of farming land to housing development. Second, the social problem of stay-at-home children in rural areas appears. Stay-at-home children are children who live in the village usually with their grandparents when their parents have already moved to cities to work. More than 70% of stay-at-home children show signs of unhealthy mental states such as depression, anxiety, and emotional instability due to the lack of proper care and love from their parents. This also leads to higher dropout rate of stay-at-home children from schools, and without further studies, their whole future will be put at risk. This will in turn contribute to sustainability issues by the widening of urban–rural income disparity and the worsening of rural poverty (Chinapedia, 2014).

For better management of migration in cities, data on migration and urbanization are essential (Migration Data Portal, 2022). However, these data are not always available (Migration Data Portal, 2022). While data could improve urban planning and delivery of public services, they could help measure progress toward Sustainable Development Goals (SDGs) as well, and thus toward the UN Habitat's New Urban Agenda (UN Habitat III, 2016), which was adopted at the United Nations Conferences on Housing and Sustainable Urban Development (Habitat III) in 2016. The New Urban Agenda represents a shared vision for a better and more sustainable future in which all people have equal rights and access to the benefits and opportunities that cities can offer. All these issues affect sustainable development.

1.2 NEED FOR INTEGRATING URBAN AND RURAL DEVELOPMENT FOR ALL AGES AND SOCIAL CLASSES

In order to harvest the long-term benefits of both urbanization and migration, there is a need to integrate urban and rural development for all ages such as the young and the old and social classes such as the poor and the rich. The rapid population growth presents challenges of achieving SDGs, as the growing proportion of older persons requires improvements in sustainable social security, pension systems, universal health care, and long-term care systems and services. Integration of urban and rural development is regarded as the key to implement SDGs at various levels (Stafford-Smith et al., 2017).

The imbalanced development of urban and rural areas or the rural–urban transformation process is one of the most important issues developing countries confront today, which poses serious challenges to the ecosystem of these countries (McGee, 2008). To address this issue, coordinated and integrated rural and urban development policies and implementation means are both needed (McGee, 2008). But how to implement integrated rural and urban development policies is a great and ambiguous challenge; it may vary from region to region and country to country due to differences in their cultural, political, and economical systems.

For example, China is one of the strongest developing countries in the world over the last 40 years. China began to experiment with integrated urban and rural development in 2016 (Cheng Xiang Yi Ti Hua) to coordinate the process of urban and rural development and improve the relationship between city and countryside with stated purposes of creating more efficient and equitable urbanization that benefits both urban and rural areas by facilitating the movement of people, goods, capital, and services and narrowing gaps in urban–rural income, public services, infrastructure, and productivity. It is intended to fundamentally restructure economic and social relations between city and countryside to produce a more equitable and harmonious society (Chen et al., 2019).

During the process of integrated urban and rural development in China, cities and the countryside are viewed as an inseparable organic whole, requiring integrated urban and rural development and rural vitalization (Fang, 2022). The problems faced in integrated urban and rural development are coupled "urban–rural problems" (Fang, 2022). Problems inherent to urban areas are caused by those inherent to rural areas and vice versa. Thus, new theories (models) and methods of integrated urban and rural development are needed to create desirable urban and rural areas with greater synchronization, deeper integration, and mutual success between the new model of urbanization and rural vitalization. Although China has made tremendous achievements in the integration of urban and rural populations, industry, infrastructure and public service facilities, pensions, and ecological and environmental protection, its integrated urban and rural development still faces problems such as persistent disparity and unequal public services.

1.3　KEY CHALLENGES IN SUSTAINABLE URBAN AND RURAL INTEGRATION

The challenges in sustainable urban and rural integration lie on how to sustainably reduce various rural–urban disparities and inequalities during urbanization.

Urban and rural disparity is a global phenomenon, inequalities have been growing in many countries in recent decades, and COVID-19 pandemic has further heightened these disparities. Apart from well-known income inequality (Federico and OECD, 2014), most noticeable urban and rural disparity is in public service coverage.

Inequalities in public service coverage (United Nations, 2021) include land tenure services; banking and financial services; infrastructure such as roads, irrigation systems, water and sanitation systems, and electricity; ICT and telecommunications; health services; education and lifelong learning opportunities; social protection, including food security; and agricultural and market-oriented services, among other services. This in turn results in a lack of access to markets and job opportunities.

For example, an estimated 2 billion people living in rural and remote areas across the world do not have adequate access to the essential health services they need within their communities. Even, in the United States, significant differences in health care access between rural and urban areas exist (Douthit et al., 2015). Compared to urban residents, rural ones have lower access to primary care providers, specialist doctors, and health information (Chen et al., 2019). According to the study (Dong and Simon, 2010) in China, rural aging people (aged 60 years or greater) have significantly lower overall health status and lower quality of life. In addition, they have a significantly higher proportion of depressive symptomatology, feelings of loneliness, and lower levels of social support measures.

As far as education is concerned, it is estimated that in 2019, in low-income countries where every 100 urban residents complete secondary school, only 23 rural residents do so. In the context of COVID-19, nearly 500 million students from prep-rimary to upper secondary school level did not have any access to remote learning, three-quarters of whom lived in rural areas (United Nations, 2021).

It is well understood that available, affordable, and reliable energy is pivotal for achieving rural development. However, it is estimated that in 2019, 759 million people globally still lacked access to electricity, 84% of whom lived in rural areas.

1.4　STRATEGIC SOLUTIONS

In order to reduce urban and rural disparity in public service coverage, rural development needs to adopt a smart rural area/smart village strategy (Cowie et al., 2020; Adamowicz and Zwolinska-Ligaj, 2020) to solve rural problems through innovative ways enabled by new digital and information technology such as Industry 4.0 and 5.0, including big data analytics, Internet of Things, crowdsourcing, blockchain, and digital twins (Adel, 2022; EC, 2021) so that rural communities can identify local problems (sensing), understand the context and conditions (understanding), and solve problems via various existing resources and smart services effectively and efficiently.

The key to smart rural area/smart village is the involvement of the local community and the digitalization and digital transformation in rural areas enabling those local communities to use digital technologies and innovations in their daily life, thus improving their access to public services and ensuring better use of resources (Smart villages (europa.eu)). Giving people easier access to essential goods and services is more important than the ownership of most material goods. New digital technology can improve public service delivery through, for example, e-government, telemedicine and telecare, remote teaching, and service sourcing.

In the implementation of the rural development strategy of the digitalization and digital transformation of rural areas, the development of digital services could particularly benefit people in rural areas by connecting various people, businesses, and services in both urban and rural areas on a digital platform. Of course, in order to make the digital platform accessible, first, it is to reduce the digital divide by building basic digital infrastructures such as Internet and 4G/5G connections in rural areas to make a universal minimum broadband service and mobile data services available in rural areas. Second, a well-designed and -managed digital service platform is key to provide various rural development services needed to rural people and businesses. Third, it is to engage potential digital service providers and develop various digital services, which can meet different rural development needs and user-experience requirements.

1.5 HIGHLIGHTS OF THE BOOK FEATURES

Our world is facing a number of sustainable development issues such as aging, climate change, and inequality. How to tackle these sustainable development issues to achieve SDGs set by the United Nations is a challenge all of us are facing across the globe. In recent years, a great deal of efforts are made to address development issues in sustainable urbanization and smart cities. While the sustainable urban and rural integration is understudied, it is very important for achieving the overall SDGs.

This book focuses on how to deal with unequal urban–rural infrastructure and services by applying smart rural area/village/community strategy with smart service design and service delivery technologies into various service provision and delivery. More specifically, in this book, we assume that a universal minimum broadband service and mobile data services are increasingly available, and this is supported by the facts that mobile phones are used worldwide and mobile connectivity is increasing to reach complete spatial coverage in many rural areas such as in China. Thus, the focus of this book is on the digital platform development techniques and digital service development techniques.

The main content of this book comes from our international collaborative projects funded by British Council and National Sciences Foundation of China and our 2019 Newton Prize Winning project founded by the UK Department for Business, Energy & Industrial Strategy. China as a fast-developing country is facing the sustainable urban and rural integration issue, while its technological development status in AI and smart digital technology is advanced. This book is coauthored by key researchers on our collaborative projects, with most of the case studies from China.

This book first introduces the key issues in sustainable urban and rural integration, which need for better integral developments in both urban and rural areas, and novel and practical ways to tackle the issues with AI, big data, and smart technologies such as Industry 4.0 and 5.0. The following specific urban and rural integration issues are addressed in each chapter. Chapters 2 and 3 mainly focus on the rural service digital platform development technologies and demonstrations, and this digital platform provides a digital market role enabling good accesses to various digitalized services. While the remaining chapters pay more attention to various specific digital service development techniques and demonstrations with case studies, these digital services have a potential to be integrated in the digital platform developed in Chapters 2 and 3. Putting them together demonstrates how AI, big data, and Industry 4.0 and 5.0 technologies can be utilized to support the digitalization and digital transformation of rural areas for addressing integrated urban and rural development issues.

Chapter 2 focuses on a rural service digital platform development based on crowdsourcing and crowdsensing technologies. First, the crowdsourcing and crowdsensing (a subtype of crowdsourcing) technologies and their roles in cocreating and delivering various services for rural areas are discussed. Second, the digital service platform development process and technology are introduced via a digital prototype. Finally, a case study of how this platform can support a rural service (plant disease diagnostics and treatment) is demonstrated. Finally, crowdsensing technology for better service decision-making is explored.

Chapter 3 presents sustainable and smart service design and servicing technologies. In general, people in rural areas have less access to various services for their daily life, for example, healthy aging services discussed in Chapter 4; livestock and medical care services presented in Chapter 5; and mental health services in rural areas addressed in Chapter 6. In this chapter, researchers aim to address the general service shortage issues in rural areas with smart technologies such as crowdsourcing and digital twin by looking at (1) how to design or adapt city services for rural areas and (2) how to efficiently deliver the rural services in a timely fashion and traceable way. The authors first introduce the concepts of digital twin, digital shadow, and digital thread technologies. Then, they demonstrate with a case study of how to integrate crowdsourcing technology and digital twin technologies in both the service design and service delivering (service outsourcing) processes. This integrated platform can support smart servicing ecosystem development involving the use of product DTs, service DTs, and human DTs, mirrored to the service supply chains in the physical world. This new system can support better service traceability and optimal service recommendations with less CO_2 footprint.

In Chapter 4, the focus is on the issues in population aging and healthy aging. Population aging associated with digital divide has been identified as one of the most significant social transformations impacting nearly all sectors in our society. The authors from the University of Southampton, UK, demonstrated how inclusive design can play a role in healthy aging through three case studies. Case 1 shows a case study of smart retail service design for older customers. This case study introduces how smart retail service can support and improve older customers' supermarket shopping experience so that they have equal and better access to healthy foods. Case 2 demonstrates how smart textile design is used for health and social care. Smart textiles are textile materials that can sense and respond to changes in their environment and adapt to them by the integration of functionalities into the textile structure. This case study discovers the health care needs of people aged 65+ who live alone and challenges they face when they use health care–related products, identifies their unmet needs, and develops inclusive smart textiles design insights to address their needs. Case 3 presents an inclusive home design for older people by investigating older people's life experience of their living room at home and related risks and challenges they face in their day-to-day life.

Chapter 5 addresses the rural area development issues in plant diseases, livestock management, and medical care. The importance of balanced development of urban–rural areas is first emphasized, and then, plant diseases management, livestock management, and medical care (technology) management are chosen as representative areas to be addressed in imbalanced urban and rural development. Digital agriculture and rural area are promoted as a future development direction. In livestock management, the researchers have focused on cashmere goat management in a farmer land with images-based deep learning for cashmere goat identification, outperforming the traditional approach of individual animal tagging. In the plant disease management, plant disease detection is studied with YOLOv5 deep learning algorithm because precise prevention and control of plant pests and diseases are highly dependent on timely plant disease detection according to the local geographical location, climate, natural enemies, monitoring, and early warning and other information. In medical care, researchers present a virtual surgery training system based on high-fidelity visualization of the organ anatomy models and interactive simulation with operational actions. The doctors in rural areas can benefit from this virtual training system greatly by saving their time, traveling, and widening their access to advanced training from experts in cities.

In Chapter 6, the authors present sustainable mental health service models for rural schools. Adolescents' mental health status in urban and rural areas of China has been investigated, and it is found that adolescents in rural areas are more vulnerable to mental problems, and the overall level of positive mental health of rural students is lower than that of urban students. On the other hand, the researchers found the shortage of rural mental health resources; for instance, the mental health education in rural schools lags behind that in urban schools, which in turn contributes to poorer mental health status of rural students. By taking all these issues into account, the authors first proposed a sustainable mental health service model with three key components: classical mental health screening, multimodal observation, and group intervention for teachers and students. The applicability of the sustainable mental health service model has been demonstrated with case studies in China. Second, smart mental health serving with advanced virtual assessment technologies has been investigated and tested in Guangdong Province in China. Going beyond the mental health status assessment, multimodal mental health intervention tools are explored and tested with a telepsychology method.

In Chapter 7, the authors present a study on smart building technology – the basic element of the urban smartness. A smart building as a place for implementing smart and integrated services and green economy enables users to achieve optimum efficiency, while managing their resources most effectively and with minimum maintenance costs, to enable users to achieve their business quickly. The concept, structure, and key technologies of smart building are first discussed, followed by the study on a more perceptive smart building design and implementation technologies. Finally, a case study on National Speed Skating Oval in Beijing is demonstrated with DT model and smart services. A miniversion of smart building is a smart home for rural areas, which shares the similar principles and implementation techniques.

Chapter 8 presents a user-centered smart service interaction research. Researchers from the Institute of Software, Chinese Academy of Sciences, discuss human–computer interaction, especially natural interaction for various smart services to enable common unskilled computer users supported by emotional design and user-experience design principles. The user-oriented services with affective computing capability are first studied with user's intent and emotional recognition, followed by a case study on emotion regulation services. Furthermore, sketch-based interfaces for smart information retrieval services are investigated and demonstrated with examples.

In Chapter 9, researchers from Tsinghua University of China address the electric energy shortage issues in remote rural areas by designing a home-based electric generator based on thermoelectric generation technology. The modern energy security issues to support the living habits of remote ethnic minorities in a sustainable way are first discussed, and then a home-based thermoelectric power generation furnace design with morphological form design and phase change materials is studied and showcased. In addition, the design of an associated stove heating system is studied and presented.

Miss Ziwen Zhu, a PhD student at Northumbria University, provided great help in this book's editing, and her help is very much appreciated by all authors.

REFERENCES

Adamowicz, M. & Zwolinska-Ligaj, M. (2020). The "smart village" as a way to achieve sustainable development in rural areas of Poland. *Sustainability*, 12(16), 6503. https://doi.org/10.3390/su12166503.

Adel, A. (2022). Future of industry 5.0 in society: Human-centric solutions, challenges and prospective research areas. *Journal of Cloud Computing*, 11, 40.

Chen, C., LeGates, R., & Fang, C. (2019). From coordinated to integrated urban and rural development in China's megacity regions. *Journal of Urban Affairs*, 41(2), 150–169. https://doi.org/10.1080/07352166.2017.1413285.

Chen, X., Orom, H., Hay, J. L., Waters, E. A., Schofield, E., Li, Y., & Kiviniemi, M. T. (2019). Differences in rural and urban health information access and use. *The Journal of Rural Health*, 35(3), 405–417. https://doi.org/10.1111/jrh.12335.

Chinapedia. (2014). "Hollow" Villages Phenomenon. https://chinapedia406.weebly.com/hollow-villages-phenomenon.html.

Cowie, P., Townsend, L., & Salemink, K. (2020). Smart rural futures: Will rural areas be left behind in the 4th industrial revolution? *Journal of Rural Studies*, 79, 169–176.

Dong, X. & Simon, M. A. (2010). Health and ageing in a Chinese population: Urban and rural disparities. *Geriatrics & Gerontology International*, 10(1), 85–93. https://doi.org/10.1111/j.1447-0594.2009.00563.x.

Douthit, N., Kiv, S., Dwolatzky, T., & Biswas, S. (2015). Exposing some important barriers to health care access in the rural USA. *Public Health*, 129(6), 611–620. https://doi.org/10.1016/j.puhe.2015.04.001.

European Commission, Directorate-General for Research and Innovation, Breque, M., De Nul, L., & Petridis, A. (2021). Industry 5.0: Towards a Sustainable, Human-Centric and Resilient European Industry, Publications Office. https://data.europa.eu/doi/10.2777/308407.

European Parliament, Martinez Juan, A., & McEldowney, J. (2021). Briefing: Smart Villages: Concept, Issues and Prospects for EU Rural Areas, Smart Villages. https://www.europarl.europa.eu/thinktank/en/document/EPRS_BRI(2021)689349.

Fang, C. (2022). On integrated urban and rural development. *Journal of Geographical Sciences*, 32(8), 1411–1426. https://doi.org/10.1007/s11442-022-2003-8.

Federico, C. & OECD. (2014). Trends in Income Inequality and its Impact on Economic Growth. https://www.oecd-ilibrary.org/social-issues-migration-health/trends-in-income-inequality-and-its-impact-on-economic-growth_5jxrjncwxv6j-en.

McGee, T. G. (2008). Managing the rural-urban transformation in East Asia in the 21st century. *Sustainability Science*, 3(1), 155–167. https://doi.org/10.1007/s11625-007-0040-y.

Migration Data Portal. (2022). Urbanization and Migration. https://www.migrationdataportal.org/themes/urbanization-and-migration.

OpenLearn create. (2022). Urbanisation: Trends, Causes and Effects. https://www.open.edu/openlearncreate/mod/oucontent/view.php?id=79940&printable=1#:~:text=The%20two%20causes%20of%20urbanisation,more%20than%20ten%20million%20people.

Stafford-Smith, M., Griggs, D., Gaffney, O., Ullah, F., Reyers, B., Kanie, N., Stigson, B., Shrivastava, P., Leach, M., & O'Connell, D. (2017). Integration: The key to implementing the sustainable development goals. *Sustainability Science*, 12(6), 911–919. https://doi.org/10.1007/s11625-016-0383-3.

Sun, H., Liu, Y., & Xu, K. (2011). Hollow villages and rural restructuring in major rural regions of China: A case study of Yucheng City, Shandong Province. *Chinese Geographical Science*, 21(3), 354–363. https://doi.org/10.1007/s11769-011-0474-0.

UN Habitat III. (2016). New Urban Agenda. *UN Habitat III*. https://habitat3.org/wp-content/uploads/NUA-English.pdf.

United Nations. (2021). Tackling inequalities in public service coverage to "build forward better" for the rural poor. In *Policy Brief by the HLCP Inequalities Task Team*. New York: United Nations. https://unsceb.org/sites/default/files/2021-12/HLCP%20ITT%20Policy%20Brief%20Rural%20Inequalities%202021.pdf.

United Nations Department of Economic and Social Affairs (UN DESA). (2022). World Population Prospects 2022: Summary of Results. https://www.un.org/development/desa/pd/sites/www.un.org.development.desa.pd/files/wpp2022_summary_of_results.pdf.

World Economic Forum. (2017). Migration and Its Impact on Cities. https://www.weforum.org/reports/migration-and-its-impact-on-cities.

2 Crowdsourcing and Crowdsensing as Smart Rural Service Platform Technology

Shengfeng Qin and Xiaojing Niu

2.1 INTRODUCTION

2.1.1 Needs for Smart Rural Service Platform

The rural areas with many families or village-based businesses play a vital role in the economy by meeting employment needs in both urban and rural areas. As discussed in Chapter 1, people in rural areas who live farther away from physical services in general have less access to various services, comparing the city residents, especially information services and digital services.

In order to support smart rural areas/village development and digital transformation of rural areas, many governments and public organizations have created development policy and implementation guides. For example, The Central Office of State Council of China in 2021 issued the 'Digital Rural Development Strategy Outline' (www.gov.cn, 2019). The Office of the Central Cyberspace Affairs Commission of China in 2022 published the 'Guidelines for the Construction of the Digital Village Standard System' (www.cac.gov.cn, 2022). The three key parts are agricultural informatization, rural digitalization, and information and digital service management platform development to support sustainable agricultural information services and village digital services innovation and delivery. However, how to identify rural areas' service needs, design new services with participation from rural people and businesses, and deliver these services is a challenging problem. What kind of the smart rural digital service platform can serve this development requirement?

2.1.2 Definitions of Service Design and Smart Servicing

As a relatively new research area, there is no universally agreed definition of service design. For example, Interaction Design Foundation defines it as 'a process where designers create sustainable solutions and optimal experiences for both customers in unique contexts and any service providers involved' (Interaction Design Foundation, 2022). Nielsen Norman Group defines it as 'the activity of planning

DOI: 10.1201/9781032686691-2

and organizing a business's resources (people, props, and processes) in order to (1) directly improve the employee's experience, and (2) indirectly, the customer's experience' (Gibbons, 2017). While the most generally accepted definition of service design is 'the activity of planning and organizing people, infrastructure, communication and material components of a service in order to improve its quality and the interaction between the service provider and its customers' (Wikipedia, 2023). Service design can be both tangible and intangible. Its ultimate goal is to improve service quality and user experience of all involved users.

In this book, we consider smart servicing as the process of designing and delivering services via smart platforms. The smart platform is the core as it is the place where services are processed.

2.1.3 CROWDSOURCING AND CROWDSENSING AS SMART RURAL SERVICE PLATFORM

Based on our previous research (Niu et al., 2019), we propose to explore online crowdsourcing and crowdsensing platform technologies as the basis for developing the smart rural service platform. Crowdsourcing is a business model for participative online activity in which an individual, an institution, a nonprofit organization, or a company can outsource a task/service or data collection activity to a heterogeneous group of people (the contributors or participants) via a flexible open call to voluntarily undertaking a task. The crowdsourcing models also apply to crowd wisdom, crowdfunding, crowd voting, and crowdsensing tools (Staletić et al., 2020). Crowdsensing is a subtype of crowdsourcing for data collection, often denominated as community-based monitoring, citizen sensing, or citizen monitoring. Staletić et al. (2020) found that citizens in developing countries are ready to accept crowdsourcing services related to their most concerned services.

Crowdsourcing is increasingly used in scientific research and operational applications as participatory approaches. It has already been applied in both agricultural research and farming applications (Minet et al., 2017). Current crowdsourcing initiatives are always mediated by Internet platforms, which are accessible on desktop and laptop computers, pads, and mobile phones. Crowdsourcing applications in agriculture and rural areas are increasingly used in both industrialized and developing countries because mobile phones are used worldwide, and mobile connectivity can reach many rural areas.

Crowdsourcing and crowdsensing applications in agriculture (Minet et al., 2017) have been classified as crowdsourcing of (1) tasks such as plant disease image identification or weed identification, (2) local visual observation such as community-based environmental monitoring, (3) data from disseminated sensor measurements such as using mobile phones to measure crop height in a maize field, and (4) knowledge via Questions & Answers (Q&A) forums to establish a two-way relationship between researchers and farmers. Minet et al. (2017) also summarized what information can be collected from crowdsourcing, which include (1) agriculture land-use data, (2) soil data, (3) weather data, (4) phenology and crop calendar information, (5) weeds, pests, and diseases, (6) yield and vegetation status, (7) prices of agricultural products, and (8) general agriculture knowledge, concerning agricultural machinery, crop and animal productions, pests and diseases, trade and market, information about regulations, etc. The majority of crowdsensing initiatives aim at collecting environmental, field, and wildlife observations by volunteers. The contributors include non-experts, inexpensive crowds and experts, and professional extension agents (Wiggins and Crowton, 2011). Thus, in general, crowdsourcing applications in agriculture and village can not only foster farmer-to-famer and service providers-to-service recipients' interaction but also help policy makers and researchers closing information and knowledge dissemination loop between researchers and practitioners. For example, in rural areas of Poland, crowdsourcing has been used in land consolidation process (Krupowicz et al., 2020) as a tool of local communities' activation.

2.1.4   MOBILE CROWDSENSING APPLICATIONS

Smart handheld devices such as smart phones are capable of sensing and interacting with the surrounding environments. Smart devices with unique multisensing proficiency and context-aware capability will be able to utilize the full potential of crowdsourcing for crowdsensing or mobile crowdsensing (MCS), which utilizes the different sensors in the smart devices to sense data from the surroundings and then transmit large amount of data to a crowdsourcing platform for analytics and extension services/applications benefiting the society for a better standard of life (Ray et al., 2022). The most used sensors are GPS, camera, accelerometer, gyroscope, temperature sensor, microphone, and humans. The MCS applications in smart city include environmental monitoring, traffic management, urban sensing, social networking services, health care, and public safety (Ray et al., 2022). The MCS also has the potential applications in smart agriculture (Sun et al., 2022) including (1) measuring cultivated area, (2) collecting meteorological disaster information, (3) collecting pest and disease images, (4) planning for production, (5) cooperative sensing with intelligent agricultural machinery, (6) identifying the quality of fruits, and (7) maintaining SILs.

In our research, we take a service-centered view to regard the crowdsourcing of either tasks or data as crowdsourcing of an end-to-end service. In this way, we can integrate the identification of users' service needs via crowdsensing, new service codesign with online participants as a task crowdsourcing, and service delivery as a service outsourcing/crowdsourcing into a single digital platform. For example, for public transportation, transportation service operators/providers are exploring various technologies in order to understand where, when, and how there is a service demand and be able to provide passengers accurate real-time information (service) to plan their journeys. In this application scenario, crowdsourcing or participatory sensing can be thought of as a service platform by which information can be collected, augmented, and used for better planning as well as a mode to deliver real-time information to commuters (Nandan et al., 2014). Also, crowdsourcing can be used as a mode to verify the accuracy and obtain feedback on the performance of such systems for further service (design) improvement.

In this chapter, we discuss and present our research on (1) what crowdsourcing technologies can enable service design in rural areas and (2) how to integrate crowdsourcing/crowdsensing in designing and developing a digital platform to effectively support various services innovation and delivery in a digital way for rural areas based on assumed available broadband and mobile data services. Such a digital platform can help a family business offer services flexibly and dynamically based on residents' current needs. Furthermore, rural residents also benefit from such a digital platform in quick responses for their service requests and improved user experience.

This chapter mainly introduces crowdsourcing and crowdsensing as smart rural service platform technologies so that readers have a comprehensive understanding of the roles crowdsourcing and crowdsensing play in smart cities/villages. Its remaining part is structured as follows. Section 2.2 describes crowdsourcing technologies in terms of its concept, key components, crowdsourcing system, and key techniques. Section 2.3 illustrates crowdsourcing and crowdsensing for smart city with a case study 'remote diagnosis of crop disease'. Section 2.4 summarizes this chapter.

2.2 CROWDSOURCING TECHNOLOGY FOR SERVICE DESIGN AND CROWD-BASED SERVICE OUTSOURCING

2.2.1 CROWDSOURCING CONCEPT

The term crowdsourcing is a combination of crowds and outsourcing. It is coined by Jeff Howe in 2006 as the practice of turning to a body of people to obtain needed knowledge, goods, or services (Howe, 2006). It is usually adopted to solve tasks that cannot be processed by sophisticated computer programs but trivial for humans, such as image labeling and basic data collections (Yuen et al., 2011). Since then, it is widely adopted by enterprises as an effective tool to get crowds involved in their business practices for open innovation, problem solving, collective intelligence, and marketing (Sammie, 2014). For manufacturers, it is expected to help reduce the production costs and make more efficient use of labor and resources (Yuen et al., 2011). From the perspective of manufacturers, crowdsourcing is an innovative business model that helps them obtain needed services, ideas, or contents by soliciting contributions from a large group of people (the crowd).

Crowdsourcing has also been leveraged in many areas, such as health care, smart business solutions, social innovation, software/web development, multimedia data annotation, and social innovation. To make crowdsourcing appliable to specific application area, diverse crowdsourcing definitions have emerged. Some crowdsourcing definitions are listed in Table 2.1. More additional definitions of crowdsourcing can be found in 'Towards an Integrated Crowdsourcing Definition' (Estellés-Arolas and González-Ladrón-De-Guevara, 2012) and 'The four pillars of crowdsourcing: A reference model' (Hosseini et al., 2014). Correspondingly, various crowdsourcing models have been proposed, such as intermediary model, citizen media production model, collaborative software development model, digital goods sales model, product design model, consumer report model, knowledge base-building model, and collaborative science project model (Saxton et al., 2013).

TABLE 2.1

The Definitions of Crowdsourcing

Reference	Crowdsourcing Definition
Howe (2006)	The act of taking a job traditionally performed by a designated agent (individual, institution, nonprofit organization, or enterprise) and outsourcing it to an undefined, generally large group of people in the form of an open call.
Alonso and Lease (2011)	The outsourcing of tasks to a large group of people instead of assigning such tasks to an in-house employee or contractor.
Brabham (2009)	A legitimate, complex problem-solving model.
Pedersen et al. (2013)	A collaboration model enabled by people-centric web technologies to solve individual, organizational, and societal problems using a dynamically formed crowd of interested people who respond to an open call for participation.
Brabham (2008)	An online, distributed problem-solving and production model already in use by profit organizations such as Threadless and iStock.
La Vecchia and Cisternino (2010)	A tool for addressing problems in organizations and businesses.
Estellés-Arolas and González-Ladrón-De-Guevara (2012)	A type of participative online activity in which an individual, an institution, a nonprofit organization, or a company proposes to a group of individuals of varying knowledge, heterogeneity, and number, via a flexible open call, the voluntary undertaking of a task.
Saxton et al. (2013)	A sourcing model in which organizations use predominantly advanced Internet technologies to harness the efforts of a virtual crowd to perform specific organizational tasks.
Bhatti et al. (2020)	An online distributed problem-solving paradigm in which an individual, a company, or an organization publishes defined task(s) to the dynamic crowd through a flexible open call to leverage human intelligence, knowledge, skill, work, and experience.

Regardless of the application area of crowdsourcing, the identified key elements of a crowdsourcing process include the crowd, the task, the crowdsourcer/requester, and the process based on a platform (Hosseini et al., 2014; Saxton et al., 2013).

2.2.1.1 The Crowd

In Howe's (2006) definition to crowdsourcing, the crowd is an undefined online community that is expected to play the role of service providers as producers, innovators, and problem solvers. In practice, to ensure the output quality, the crowdsourcer/requester usually selects the crowd with specific skills and qualifications to participate in the crowdsourced task.

2.2.1.2   The Crowdsourcer/Requester

In the crowdsourcing process, the crowdsourcer refers to the person or institution seeking knowledge, creativity, innovative ideas, and solutions for their business problems from the crowd. Generally, crowdsourcer also acts as solution evaluators who are responsible for evaluating and selecting winner solutions to the crowdsourced task.

2.2.1.3   The Task

There is a broad array of activities that can be crowdsourced. It can be products, services, or parts of products. And the complexity varies from task to task. And according to the complexity of the task, different crowdsourcing platforms will be utilized (Saxton et al., 2013). During a crowdsourcing process, only when the crowdsourcing task is well defined, the proper crowds with specific knowledge and skills can be identified. The crowdsourcing task proposed by the requester needs to be mapped from the high-level goal to specific subtasks to be completed by the crowd.

2.2.1.4   The Process

The crowdsourcing process is controlled by the platform. It provides a virtual space where the initiator can crowdsource his/her task to the crowd. Both social media platforms, such as Twitter and Facebook, and purposely developed platforms, such as 99designs and Amazon MTurk, can be used in this process. The platform provides the crowdsourcer a way to get access to tons of crowds conveniently and involve them into their production process and decision-making process, and organizes the crowd structure and manages workflows to enable the crowdsourcing process.

2.2.1.5   Crowdsourcing Forms

The crowdsourcing form depends on the nature of crowdsourcing tasks. Before crowdsourcing of the task, an open call including the specific task and its evaluation criteria need to be defined first. The evaluation criteria can be provided by the requester directly or be collected from the cloud. According to the board of innovation and the guidelines to effective crowdsourcing (Simperl, 2015), there are a lot of types of crowdsourcing a task, which are shown in Table 2.2. The crowdsourcing forms could be used for classifying crowdsourcing platforms.

In these crowdsourcing types, micro- and macrotasks are classified by the granularity of tasks. Compared to macrotasks, microtasks are highly parallelizable and can be divided into smaller pieces, which can be completed by taking seconds to minutes. Microtasks are always the tasks that are simple and easy to be accomplished by humans but are challenging for computers, such as recognizing things in images. Macrotasks are difficult to be decomposed straightforward, and the resolutions for macrotasks require a great share of contextual information or dependencies to intermediary results.

In addition to micro- and macrotasks, other crowdsourcing types could be classified into the same category as neither can they be divided into microtasks nor do they depend on the context information and intermediary results. How the task will be crowdsourced depends on the task nature.

TABLE 2.2
Types of Crowdsourcing a Task

Form	Description	Platform Examples
Microtasks	The crowdsourced routine work is broken down into smaller and independent units	Amazon MTurk, microtask.com, Clickworker
Macrotasks	Close to classical outsourcing	Quirky, InnoCentive
Challenges	Competitions targeting grand scientific, technology, business, or social questions	OpenIDEO, InnoCentive
Volunteer campaigns	Initiatives seeking ideas and contributions for the public good	Crowd4U
Contests	Asking crowds to work and only providing compensation to the winner	99designs, Crowdspring

2.2.2 CROWDSOURCING SYSTEM

Crowdsourcing is firstly adopted mainly because of the way it provides access to a large pool of community to address business problems with potentially reduced time and monetary cost. With the extensive application of crowdsourcing, more benefits have been brought, and crowdsourcing is being used in many situations as a powerful and flexible tool. The benefits brought by crowdsourcing can be divided into process- and results-based (Wazny, 2017), as shown in Table 2.3.

Due to the advantages of crowdsourcing, many organizations are developing their own crowdsourcing systems. However, the development of a crowdsourcing platform

TABLE 2.3
Benefits of Using Crowdsourcing (Wazny, 2017)

Process-Based Crowdsourcing Benefits	Results-Based Crowdsourcing Benefits
• Large potential scale of participants involved	• Increased accuracy over or when results combined with machine learning tasks
• Large scale of coverage of potential intervention	• Enabling high speed of research progression
• Raising public awareness	• Novel discoveries
• Transcending borders and boundaries	• Data produced previously unattainable
• High social robustness	• Ability to complete tasks otherwise not possible, including digitizing medical artifacts or notes
• High mobility	• Rewards may accrue more directly
• Ability to 'tap into' untapped expertise	• Possibility to detect and respond to disease outbreaks earlier
• Ability to cover unpredictable events	• Result accuracy has been shown to be equal to or more accurate than traditional research
• Widespread software available to enable feasibility	

and its integration into the existing enterprise innovation platforms are risky and hardly undertaken without theoretical foundation (Hetmank, 2013). Furthermore, the design of any crowdsourcing system is deeply related to the answers to three questions: what the required data are, how to obtain it through crowdsourcing, and how to use it in the specific application scenario? The features of the required data usually determine the complexity of the whole system. Next, we introduce the research development in crowdsourcing process models and the components of crowdsourcing systems.

2.2.2.1 Crowdsourcing Process Models

Since the existing crowdsourcing platforms have their own logic of how to crowdsource tasks, e.g., marketplace, contest, or bid, the activities conducted in a crowdsourcing process vary from project to project (Amrollahi, 2016; Tranquillini et al., 2015). Tranquillini et al. (2015) considered that the typical steps involved in crowdsourcing a task are task publication, worker preselection, task execution, validation, and rewarding, while Amrollahi (2016) regarded the preparation stage before crowdsourcing and poststage after crowdsourcing as necessary parts of a crowdsourcing process. To generally describe a crowdsourcing process (Tranquillini et al., 2015), Amrollahi (2016) extracted common crowdsourcing phases and identified the key activities at each phase. Table 2.4 shows the key phases and the corresponding activities in a crowdsourcing model from the perspective of the crowdsourcer.

TABLE 2.4

Key Phases and Corresponding Activities in a Crowdsourcing Model

Crowdsourcing Phase	Definition	Phase Activities Identified from the Literature
Technical design	Design and development of the crowdsourcing platform	Platform selection, platform design and development
Conceptual design	Activities that should be performed before start of the technical development of the project	Definition of tasks, qualification requirements of participants, timeline
Participant selection	Selection of the crowd that will participate in the crowdsourcing task	User selection, team formation
Communication	Communication with the selected crowd	Contact the crowd, crowdsourcer broadcasting, communication
Idea generation	The crowds start their interactions with the system to submit their ideas	Task choice, idea generation, collection of ideas from crowd, job execution
Idea evaluation	Checking the appropriateness of the crowd's inputs/ideas, then ranking, filtering, and commenting on the crowd's inputs/ideas	Crowd's inputs evaluation, result analysis, competitive and judging process

(Continued)

TABLE 2.4 (*Continued*)
Key Phases and Corresponding Activities in a Crowdsourcing Model

Crowdsourcing Phase	Definition	Phase Activities Identified from the Literature
Monitor	Organization of the team during the implementation	Coordination, manage concurrency/input and output/time, workflow management
Grant award	Identification of the best entry and awarding related incentive	Prize for winning ideas, reward
Process evaluation and documentation	Reviewing the project and documenting the lesson learned for future improvements	Knowledge retrieval and capture, knowledge evaluation, deciding on future crowdsourcing arrangements, project evaluation, train models
Implementation	Implementation of the results of the crowdsourcing	Collaborative discussion, presentation of results, collective action, results and analysis, implementation actions

2.2.2.2 Components of a Crowdsourcing System

Because of the diversity of crowdsourcing models, it is difficult to define crowdsourcing systems and to derive a unified crowdsourcing process that should be implemented in a crowdsourcing system. However, the key components of crowdsourcing systems are the same. They are the requester, the crowd (workers), the task, and the platform (Bhatti et al., 2020; Hetmank, 2013). After analyzing the diverse definitions of crowdsourcing systems, Bhatti et al. (2020) proposed the components and processes in crowdsourcing systems (Figure 2.1) that should be implemented. In addition to the proposed key components of a crowdsourcing system, Hetmank (2013) classified the crowdsourcer and the crowd into the user category and considered that contribution/solution submitted by the crowd was also an important part because it connected the crowdsourcer and the crowd.

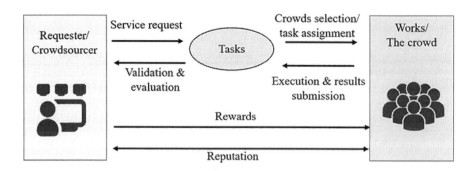

FIGURE 2.1   Components and processes in crowdsourcing systems (Bhatti et al., 2020).

TABLE 2.5

Functions in Each Component of a Crowdsourcing Platform (Hetmank, 2013)

Crowdsourcing System Component	Functions
User (including the crowdsourcer and the crowd)	Register user, evaluate user, form user group, and enable coordination
The task	Design and assign task
Contribution/outputs from the crowd	Represent contribution, evaluate contribution, and select contribution
The platform	Define workflow, manage workflow, and organize the structure of the crowd

Around the key components of a crowdsourcing system, the key functions that should be implemented in each component have been identified (Hetmank, 2013). In addition to the basic functions, such as user registration and task broadcasting, additional functions to support the activities listed in Table 2.5 should be implemented as well.

With the identified system components, the system entities can be extracted as they refer to the individual or organization interacting with the platform to generate and process data. To ensure the management and effective sharing of information and the output quality during a crowdsourcing process, the system entities must be well defined (Evans et al., 2016).

2.2.3 CROWDSOURCING TECHNOLOGIES FOR SERVICE DESIGN

Service design can be applied to many services along the product lifecycle such as product design services, manufacturing services, and maintenance services by designing service interactions between service providers and service requesters. This chapter mainly focuses on crowdsourcing technologies that enable the collaboration and interaction of actors from which the service is designed and delivered. Next, we explore some key techniques that work together to enable requesters to reach the crowds at the scale and the speed needed for service crowdsourcing.

2.2.3.1 Incentive Mechanism Techniques

Incentive mechanism motivates crowds to get involved in performing the crowd-sourced task. Since the existing crowdsourcing platforms are typically open to the public and do not rely on contracts, certain measures must be adopted to compel crowds to participate in the task; otherwise, they cannot be performed. The ways to attract crowds could be categorized into two distinct categories: extrinsic (e.g., reward and building of their personal reputation) and intrinsic (e.g., enjoyment and being part of the common good) (Simula and Ahola, 2014).

Reward, enjoyment, and reputation are the three main incentives adopted by a crowdsourcing platform. According to the type of a crowdsourced task, the platform can adopt more than one incentive.

2.2.3.2   Crowds' Qualification Techniques

Different crowdsourced tasks have different skill and qualification requirements for their participants, such as open to all and reputation- and credential-based. Therefore, the evaluation of crowds' qualification is vital for a crowdsourcing platform to ensure the crowds' quality. To assess a crowd's quality, gold data were integrated seamlessly to learn the quality of crowds when the crowds are asked to answer a multiple choice question to complete a task (Ipeirotis et al., 2010).

Existing crowdsourcing platforms rely on the crowds to fill in their profiles, leading to a possibility of mismatching to their actual qualifications. To avoid such cheating behaviors, the most often adopted measure is verification questions (gold questions) (Bragg et al., 2016; Chang and Chen, 2015) that are inserted to test the performance of crowds, especially when crowdsourcing microtasks.

Besides cheating behaviors, some crowds do not perform the task carefully as a result of poor platform control on the submissions. To ensure the quality of work submitted by crowds, worker agreement is usually signed before participating in the task. This measure is adopted by most of the crowdsourcing platforms, but it works little on the final output. A promising approach for ensuring the reliability of submissions is to recommend crowds that have strong points in desired skills and capabilities. Although this method is powerful, the cold-start question (Sedhain et al., 2014) that is common in recommender system cannot be neglected.

2.2.3.3   Task Assignment Techniques

The aim of task assignment is to assign the requested tasks to suitable crowds on the platform to get tasks finished within a fixed time and budget. In a formalized task assignment problem, the requester owns a fixed set of tasks of different types and a budget that specifies how many crowds are required and how soon the requester would like the task to be accomplished. Before assigning the task, many matches about reputations and interests will be carried out to guarantee that all employed crowd workers have the potential to accomplish the tasks with high quality.

There are two different assignment types: worker selected and server assigned. In worker-selected-task mode, the server publishes tasks, and it is totally the crowd's call to choose any tasks they are interested in. One drawback of this mode is that the server does not have control over the allocation of tasks, which may cause some tasks not to be assigned while others do. Differently, in server-assigned-task mode, the task is totally assigned by the server according to certain rules. This mode has a global picture of the tasks. The three basic algorithms that are used to assign tasks in the server-assigned-task mode are greedy algorithm (Gao et al., 2020), online primal dual framework (Ho and Vaughan, 2012), and least popular priority (To et al., 2015).

2.2.3.4   Crowd's Structure Techniques

In crowdsourcing environments, hierarchy structure is the most popular organization structure. Since the crowds have various professional skills and experience, they are good at in one or some specific domains but not in others. As a result, they play different roles in different crowdsourcing tasks. In a hierarchy structure with many layers, the position of a crowd depends on his/her capability. The hierarchy structure is more suitable for performing microtasks. The crowds at the lowest level perform subtasks with the smallest granularity, while those at higher level integrate the results submitted by the crowds at the lower layer.

As for tasks that are not easy to be decomposed, the hierarchy structure is useless as all employees work collaboratively targeted at the same goal, and their work may have dependency on others. Taking software design and development consisting of various functional modules as an example, the task of software design and development is a microtask on the whole, but when focusing on the lowest level of decomposition (module), it is a macrotask, as each module is still complex and cannot be decomposed anymore, which will be realized by the collaboration of a group of individuals with various specialties. In this occasion, a team structure with different expertise should be more effective and efficient. Thus, the traditional team structure can be applied in the virtual environment if it can be well organized and controlled.

2.2.3.5 Workflow Management Techniques

Enabling more complex workflows on a crowdsourcing platform can result in large differences in output quality even with small differences in rewards and task order (Kittur et al., 2008; Shaw et al., 2011). Workflow management involves where the data come from and where they go as well as the integration of data steams coming from various sources. It is affected by many factors, such as the organization structure of crowds, the volume of submitted solutions, and task integration mechanism (Pedersen et al., 2013).

Generally, the structured workflow (Xu et al., 2015) is usually used to provide interpretative and diverse feedback. Additionally, decision theory was used to model the iterative workflows and define equations that govern the various steps of the crowdsourcing process (Dai and Weld, 2010). Kittur et al. (2013) indicated that existing workflows should be improved on a large space of parameters, instructions, incentives, and decompositions so that they can be able to support the execution of complex tasks.

2.2.3.6 Quality Control Techniques

The quality control approaches could be classified into two categories (Allahbakhsh et al., 2013): design time and runtime. The design-time approaches include the open call generation and crowds' qualification, as described previously. There are a lot of runtime quality control approaches, for example, workflow management, expert review, output agreement, ground truth, and majority voting (Allahbakhsh et al., 2013). These approaches can be adopted together for better quality as using one approach alone may contribute to cheating behaviors.

2.2.3.7 Techniques for Information Communication and Sharing

In a crowdsourcing process, all participated crowd workers must be teamed structurally such as hierarchical structure and team structure in traditional in-house design environments so that they could collaborate effectively. Effective communication approaches could enable crowds to spend less time on understanding their tasks and improve the work efficiency.

Currently, discussion forums, blogs, and microblogs (e.g., Sina Weibo (Zhang et al., 2014)) are commonly used by crowds as their communication medium, which is not real time and may lead to some delays. Also, such kind of communication is not suitable in a large scale (Girotto, 2016; Zhai et al., 2009). Social media, such as Facebook, Twitter, and WeChat, are real time, but they only support the sharing of information and asynchronous edition of documents. In order to satisfy the increasing need of synchronous collaboration, Tencent Instant Messenger (TIM) is developed as a free cloud-based and platform-independent office software. It not only supports instant messaging and the synchronous edition of simple documents, such as Word and Excel, but also integrates social interaction functions. However, when it is applied to product design and development, the platform can only support the sharing of documents in various formats, but it is inconvenient for users to view and edit them unless the corresponding software or tool is installed.

To facilitate communication in expert crowdsourcing, a structured handoff method was proposed to use (Embiricos et al., 2014), where participants were asked in live (live conference and screen share are used) and recorded scenarios (short screen capture video with voiceover), respectively. Their experiments indicated that higher work quality could be resulted in by the structured handoff approach. Since crowds are located at various places and are not available to participate in the task at any time, the structured handoff approach may be useful for them to know the working process.

2.3   CROWDSENSING AND CROWDSOURCING FOR SMART CITY/VILLAGE—CASE STUDY

Smart city is an effective way to realize the efficient and scientific management of urbanization, creating new productive forces and lifestyles and promoting the sustainable development of business and society. The development of Internet of Things (IoT), Big Data, Artificial Intelligence, 5G, and Augmented Reality has provided effective support for smart cities. However, in the development process of smart cities, collaboration with citizens is one of the issues for real smart cities. This issue is particularly incisive in rural areas where the level of information and industry development is far lower than that of urban areas.

In rural areas, investing in IoT facilities is effective to realize the smartness of traffic and energy networks, but it is challenging for the management of farm lands, remote diagnosis of crop disease and animal illness, etc. due to their distribution diversity and complexity. Based on the current information and communication technology (ICT), crowdsourcing and crowdsensing offer a cost-effective way to address the aforementioned issues. Crowdsensing and crowdsourcing can enable intelligent citizens for smart cities as they can provide appropriate feedback and useful ideas. Especially with the development of advanced mobile devices, crowdsensing has emerged as a tool for fostering collaboration between citizens and smart cities, enabling the utilization of citizens' potential for various tasks. Accordingly, crowdsensing, also known as participatory sensing or MCS, is a means of collecting people's surrounding information via mobile sensing devices (such as smartphones, tablet computers, and wearables). Its highly expressive and powerful sensing capabilities can carry out a big sensing project by fragmenting tasks into small pieces.

In recent years, in order to meet the communication needs in rural areas, communication infrastructures have been well established. However, due to the limited cultural level and entertainment time, the residents in rural areas have not fully utilized the convenience brought by the Internet. This leads to a heavy dependence on third parties when they require some services, such as the sale of agricultural products and the diagnosis of crop diseases. Without third parties, it is impossible for residents in rural areas to get access to product buyers and consumers. Because of the opacity of the transaction process, the third party not only charges commissions but also lowers the price of agricultural products, resulting in lower income for product producers. Therefore, the direct connections between product producer and consumer and the transparency of the transaction process are important. To our knowledge, the best solution to build the dynamic relationship among humans is the platform-based ecosystem, which involves all key actors in a service process, corresponding smart products, and services.

Here, we take 'remote diagnosis of crop disease' as an example to investigate how crowdsourcing coordinates experts to deliver services in urban rural integration during urbanization process.

2.3.1 CASE STUDY—CROWDSOURCING PLATFORM FOR RURAL FARMING

2.3.1.1 Background

To understand the real service requirements in rural areas, we conducted interviews with local farmers, pesticides wholesalers, agricultural experts, etc. in Sanquan Village, Shandong Province, China. We found that the farmers do not have direct communication with the corresponding experts. When the crop disease occurs, they will only ask for help from pesticides wholesalers who can give some suggestions based on their experience. However, this mode works well only when the crop disease is universal. For crop diseases that have never occurred before, the wholesaler and farmers will try to treat it with different pesticides that are used to treat similar diseases. The key disadvantages include (1) the high monetary cost spent in treating crop disease and (2) the possibility of missing the best treatment time and then lowering the harvest. These service needs highlight the importance of direct connections between key role players in a service process.

2.3.1.2 Integrated Crowdsourcing Platform Design and Evaluation

An all-in-one service platform prototype for smart services is developed for the service coordination and delivery in 'the diagnosis of crop disease'. Firstly, we explored the service process in the service concept 'the diagnosis of crop disease' to identify the key actors in typical service processes and their interactions. The key actors involved in a service process include farmers (service requesters), experts in crop disease diagnosis and treatment, salesmen on various farming tools and pesticides, and regional managers. In traditional environment, salesmen on various farming tools

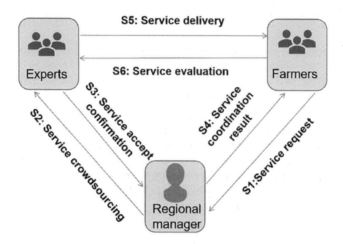

FIGURE 2.2   The interactions in a typical disease diagnosis service.

and pesticides act as experts, while in the platform-based environment, experts in the field of agriculture located all around the world will get involved in the service process. The key interactions among farmers, experts, and regional manager in a typical disease diagnosis service are shown in Figure 2.2.

To make the platform-based service process meet the needs of farmers in crop health management and disease diagnosis, we designed it closely collaborating with local farmers. The service process includes four steps: service request initialized by the farmer, expert matching controlled by the regional manager, service delivery by the expert, and service evaluation made by the corresponding farmer. The detailed service process is described as follows:

a. When some diseases occur in crops, the farmer is required to initialize the service request by submitting the requested topic, the disease symptoms, and the corresponding pictures. These information form the basis for expert matching, and the disease symptoms and pictures will help experts identify the disease type and provide corresponding solutions. When the service request is submitted successfully, the farmer can directly view the service progress from the 'status' column in his/her personal interface. Before the service request is processed by the regional manager, the farmers can update the information he/she submitted via the first operation in the 'operation' column. When the service request is closed, the farmers can view the corresponding solution to his/her request from the second operation in the 'operation' column. Figure 2.3 shows a list of simulated service requests submitted by farmers.

b. When the service request is submitted, it will go to the to-do list of the regional managers. Currently, it is the regional manager who is responsible for matching the most suitable expert to a specific service request.

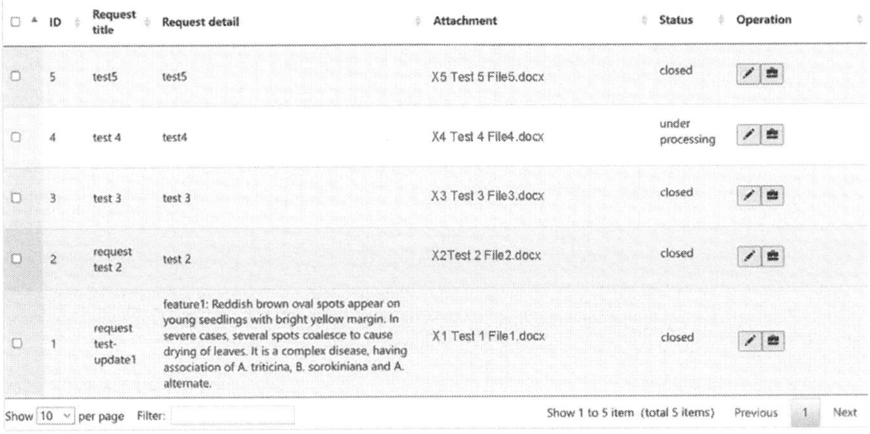

	ID	Request title	Request detail	Attachment	Status	Operation
	5	test5	test5	X5 Test 5 File5.docx	closed	✎ 🗑
	4	test 4	test4	X4 Test 4 File4.docx	under processing	✎ 🗑
	3	test 3	test 3	X3 Test 3 File3.docx	closed	✎ 🗑
	2	request test 2	test 2	X2Test 2 File2.docx	closed	✎ 🗑
	1	request test-update1	feature1: Reddish brown oval spots appear on young seedlings with bright yellow margin. In severe cases, several spots coalesce to cause drying of leaves. It is a complex disease, having association of A. triticina, B. sorokiniana and A. alternate.	X1 Test 1 File1.docx	closed	✎ 🗑

Show 10 ∨ per page   Filter: _____   Show 1 to 5 item (total 5 items)   Previous 1 Next

FIGURE 2.3   A list of simulated service requests submitted by farmers.

When there are enough data on the platform, the machine-learning-based method will be adopted to learn how to match suitable expert to service request automatically. Figure 2.4 shows the interface of manual matching of experts and service requests. To choose the most suitable expert for a specific service request, the regional manager needs to read the crop disease information submitted by farmers in the first step, thus identifying the professional area category the service request belongs to. At the simulation stage, the key categories we provide include crop disease, crop planting, crop management, spray crops by UAV, and mechanical crops harvesting. In our crop disease diagnosis example, the crop disease categories are selected, and then the experts who have corresponding professional knowledge will be listed based on their historical service satisfaction. When the experts listed in the interface are fewer than three, all of them will receive a service invitation from the regional manager, or only the top three will receive a service invitation.

c. When experts receive the service invitation, he/she will accept or decline the service request by just clicking the corresponding button. Figure 2.5 shows the invitation confirmation interface from the expert personal portal. The key information in the service invitation includes invitation

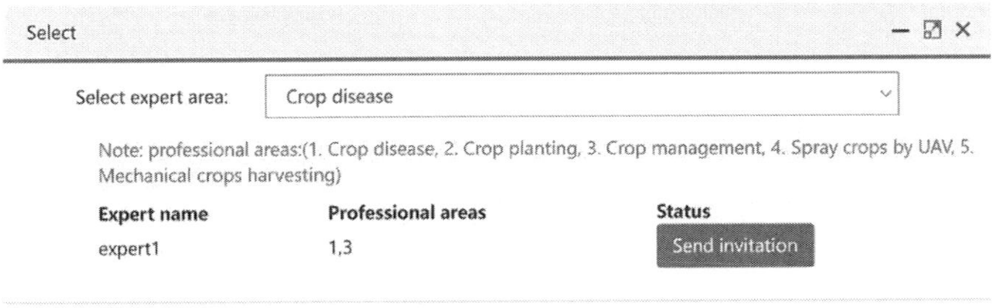

Select   — ☑ ✕

Select expert area: | Crop disease   ∨ |

Note: professional areas:(1. Crop disease, 2. Crop planting, 3. Crop management, 4. Spray crops by UAV, 5. Mechanical crops harvesting)

Expert name   **Professional areas**   **Status**
expert1   1,3   Send invitation

FIGURE 2.4   Interface of manual matching of experts and service requests.

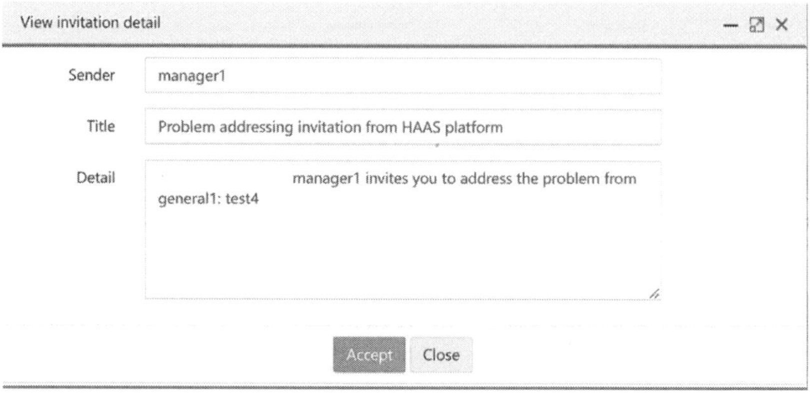

View invitation detail   — ⬚ ✕

Sender   manager1

Title   Problem addressing invitation from HAAS platform

Detail   manager1 invites you to address the problem from general1: test4

Accept   Close

FIGURE 2.5 Invitation confirmation interface from the expert personal portal: (a) maize smut and (b) maize rust.

sender, the service requester, and the service request topic. Only when the expert confirms the invitation, and he/she is ultimately selected for the service request, he/she can view the detailed description of the crop disease symptoms and pictures (example pictures of maize smut and rust are given in Figure 2.6; these pictures are uploaded to the platform as attachments).

(a)   (b)

FIGURE 2.6 Example pictures of universal maize diseases.

	ID	Request title	Request detail	Attachment	Status	Operation
	4	test 4	test4	X4 Test 4 File4.docx	under processing	
	3	test 3	test 3	X3 Test 3 File3.docx	closed	
	1	request test-update1	feature1: Reddish brown oval spots appear on young seedlings with bright yellow margin. In severe cases, several spots coalesce to cause drying of leaves. It is a complex disease, having association of A. triticina, B. sorokiniana and A. alternate.	X1 Test 1 File1.docx	closed	

Show 10 ∨ per page Filter: [   ]   Show 1 to 3 item (total 3 items)   Previous 1 Next

FIGURE 2.7   A list of service requests to be processed or already processed in the expert personal portal.

d. When an expert is selected for a specific service request, the service request will go to the expert's to-do list. Figure 2.7 shows a list of the service requests to be processed and already processed in the expert personal portal. The status column is used to distinguish the to-do service request list and the processed ones. The expert can view the detailed service request including the detailed disease symptom description and supporting pictures and then propose his/her solutions via the first operation in the operation column. The interface of solution submission is shown in Figure 2.8. When he/she submits the solution, the service request will be closed and he/she can view the solution detail via the second operation in the operation column.

e. When the service request is closed, the farmer will be invited automatically to mark or evaluate the service delivered by the expert in terms of customer satisfaction and service quality. The service evaluation results will be written into the service requests, and the reputation of the expert will be updated accordingly. The service evaluation results will affect the qualification of the selected expert for later service requests on the platform.

Expert solution   — ⊡ ×

Request title: request test-update1

Request detail: feature1: Reddish brown oval spots appear on young seedlings with bright yellow margin. In severe cases, several spots coalesce to cause drying of leaves.
It is a complex disease, having association of A. triticina, B. sorokiniana and A. alternate.

Supporting document: X1 Test 1 File1.docx

Solution detail: Your solution

FIGURE 2.8   Solution submission interface from the expert personal portal.

2.3.1.3   Evaluation of the Integrated Crowdsourcing Platform

To evaluate the effectiveness of the developed integrated crowdsourcing platform, we form a focus group mainly with the local farmers and pesticides wholesalers. In the focus group, we first show the platform and the service process to the participants and then we discuss around three key questions: (1) Is the developed platform effective and efficient in diagnosing crop disease remotely? (2) What changes should be made to improve the developed platform? (3) What's your key concerns in utilizing the developed platform?

In the focus group, all of them consider that the platform is theoretically effective and efficient in diagnosing crop disease remotely. The involvement of agricultural experts will diagnose crop disease more accurately and teach them some scientific farming methods and preventive measures against pests and diseases. However, the concerns for farmers are if their service request will be processed timely and the cost they should pay using the platform. Pesticide wholesalers hope that the platform is not put in use because they think the involvement of agricultural experts will decrease the sales of pesticides, largely affecting their earnings. Regarding the necessary changes to enhance the platform, it is believed that the local government should take charge of its management, otherwise, its widespread adoption and utilization may be hindered.

2.3.1.4   The Benefits of the Integrated Crowdsourcing Platform

The benefits of this service-centered platform solution include (1) the digitization of the service process. The platform realizes the online coordination and offline delivery of services. On the one hand, the online coordination of services makes it possible to track every step of the service process; on the other hand, it breaks through the limitation of time and space, thus greatly improving the service efficiency. After service coordination, the corresponding service provider (in the selected example, the service provider means agricultural experts) will deliver the requested service and then update the online service status. (2) The service platform makes it possible for farmers to communicate directly with agricultural experts. (3) The mutual evaluation mechanism in the platform could make the platform data credible to some extent and provide a reference for follow-up service coordination.

2.3.2   CROWDSENSING FOR COLLECTIVE DECISION-MAKING

Smart city integrates the physical world with the virtual world. This is achieved by providing additional capabilities such as environmental sensing and automatic behavior to common objects, allowing to capture and analyze the data from the real world to ensure a better operation of the virtual one (Alvear et al., 2018). In the urbanization process, without investing in any infrastructure, crowdsensing is introduced to make a large group of people actively participate in the data acquisition process through different devices and technologies. Once data are collected, they are sent to a central server for analysis, and feedback will eventually be returned to citizens through actions and services aimed at improving their life quality.

In urbanization process, crowdsensing can be classified into two categories. The first one is active crowdsensing. This means that the smart phones of the residents in both urban and rural areas act as sensors to gather data related to traffic, weather, energy, etc. and send them to a central server so that the local government can make real-time decisions based on these data. The second one is passive crowdsensing. This means that the service request is launched by the local government, and then the residents gather the requested data and send them back to the local government. For example, when natural disasters such as hailstone and frost occur, the government will count the affected area where crops are largely affected. In traditional way, the farmers are required to personally report the amount of affected area owned by them to the local government, which is time consuming. However, while adopting crowdsensing, in addition to the amount of the affected area owned by a specific farmer, data including the site of the affected area, severity of disaster, and crop type can be gathered as well, which enables the local government to have a big picture about the natural disaster and helps it make evidence-based decisions.

2.4 SUMMARY

This chapter first clarifies the urgent need for a smart rural service platform. Then, it describes crowdsourcing technologies for service design crowdsourcing and crowd-based service outsourcing including incentive mechanisms, crowds' qualification, task assignment, workflow management, quality control, crowds' structure, and information communication and sharing. After that, a crowdsourcing platform prototype for 'remote diagnosis of crop diseases' is developed. It integrates crowdsourcing mechanisms to create an all-in-one platform able to support the effective deliveries of requested services dynamically and flexibly. With information accumulation on the platform and AI technology, it can help optimize the allocation of local manufacturing/service/agricultural resources and capabilities and help create win–win service-centered business ecosystems with better service traceability.

The developed crowdsourcing platform was qualitatively evaluated through the case study 'remote diagnosis of crop diseases', and we found that it helped platform actors gain more values from personalized services with improved user experience although some improvements such as privacy protection are still required to be made.

REFERENCES

Allahbakhsh, M., Benatallah, B., Ignjatovic, A., Motahari-Nezhad, H. R., Bertino, E., & Dustdar, S. (2013). Quality control in crowdsourcing systems: Issues and directions. *IEEE Internet Computing*, 17(2), 76–81. https://doi.org/10.1109/MIC.2013.20.

Alonso, O. & Lease, M. (2011). Crowdsourcing 101: Putting the WSDM of crowds to work for you. *Proceedings of the 4th ACM International Conference on Web Search and Data Mining - WSDM 2011*, New York, USA, p. 1. https://doi.org/10.1145/1935826.1935831.

Alvear, O., Calafate, C. T., Cano, J. C., & Manzoni, P. (2018). Crowdsensing in smart cities: Overview, platforms, and environment sensing issues. *Sensors (Switzerland)*, 18(2), 460. https://doi.org/10.3390/s18020460.

Amrollahi, A. (2016). A process model for crowdsourcing: Insights from the literature on implementation. *Australasian Conference on Information Systems*, Adelaide, Australia, pp. 1–12. https://doi.org/10.48550/arXiv.1605.04695

Bhatti, S. S., Gao, X. F., & Chen, G. H. (2020). General framework, opportunities and challenges for crowdsourcing techniques: A comprehensive survey. *Journal of Systems and Software*, 167, 110611. https://doi.org/10.1016/j.jss.2020.110611.

Brabham, D. C. (2008). Moving the crowd at iStockphoto: The composition of the crowd and motivations for participation in a crowdsourcing application. *First Monday*, 13(6), 1–22. https://doi.org/10.5210/fm.v13i6.2159.

Brabham, D. C. (2009). Crowdsourcing the public participation process for planning projects. *Planning Theory*, 8(3), 242–262. https://doi.org/10.1177/1473095209104824.

Bragg, J., Mausam, M., & Weld, D. S. (2016). Optimal testing for crowd workers. *Proceedings of the 15th International Conference on Autonomous Agents & Multiagent Systems*, Singapore, pp. 966–974.

Chang, D. N. & Chen, C.-H. (2015). Product concept evaluation and selection using data mining and domain ontology in a crowdsourcing environment. *Advanced Engineering Informatics*, 29(4), 759–774. https://doi.org/10.1016/j.aei.2015.06.003.

Dai, P. & Weld, D. S. (2010). Decision-theoretic control of crowd-sourced workflows. *Proceedings of the Twenty-Fourth AAAI Conference on Artificial Intelligence*, Atlanta, Georgia, USA, pp. 1168–1174. https://doi.org/10.1609/aaai.v24i1.7760.

Embiricos, A., Rahmati, N., Zhu, N., & Bernstein, M. S. (2014). Structured handoffs in expert crowdsourcing improve communication and work output. *Proceedings of the Adjunct Publication of the 27th Annual ACM Symposium on User Interface Software and Technology - UIST'14 Adjunct*, New York, USA, pp. 99–100. https://doi.org/10.1145/2658779.2658795.

Estellés-Arolas, E. & González-Ladrón-De-Guevara, F. (2012). Towards an integrated crowdsourcing definition. *Journal of Information Science*, 38(2), 189–200. https://doi.org/10.1177/0165551512437638.

Evans, R. D., Gao, J. X., Mahdikhah, S., Messaadia, M., & Baudry, D. (2016). A review of crowdsourcing literature related to the manufacturing industry. *Journal of Advanced Management Science*, 4(3), 224–231. https://doi.org/10.12720/joams.4.3.224-231.

Gao, L., Gan, Y., Zhou, B. H., & Dong, M. Y. (2020). A user-knowledge crowdsourcing task assignment model and heuristic algorithm for expert knowledge recommendation systems. *Engineering Applications of Artificial Intelligence*, 96, 103959. https://doi.org/10.1016/j.engappai.2020.103959.

Gibbons, S. (2017). *Service Design 101*. California: Nielsen Norman Group. https://www.nngroup.com/articles/service-design-101/.

Girotto, V. (2016). Collective creativity through a micro-tasks crowdsourcing approach. *Proceedings of the 19th ACM Conference on Computer Supported Cooperative Work and Social Computing Companion - CSCW '16 Companion*, New York, USA, pp. 143–146. https://doi.org/10.1145/2818052.2874356.

Hetmank, L. (2013). Components and functions of crowdsourcing systems - A systematic literature review. *Proceedings of the 11th International Conference on Wirtschaftsinformatik*, Leipzig, Germany, pp. 55–69. https://doi.org/10.13140/2.1.3836.4166.

Ho, C. & Vaughan, J. W. (2012). Online task assignment in crowdsourcing markets. *Proceedings of the Twenty-Sixth AAAI Conference on Artificial Intelligence*, Toronto, Ontario, Canada, pp. 45–51. https://doi.org/10.1609/aaai.v26i1.8120.

Hosseini, M., Phalp, K., Taylor, J., & Ali, R. (2014). The four pillars of crowdsourcing: A reference model. *Proceedings of the 8th IEEE International Conference on Research Challenges in Information Science*, Marrakech, Morocco, pp. 1–12. https://doi.org/10.1109/RCIS.2014.6861072.

Howe, J. (2006). The rise of crowdsourcing. *Wired Magazine*, 14(6), 1–5. https://doi.org/10.1086/599595.

Interaction Design Foundation. (2022) Service Design. https://www.interaction-design.org/literature/topics/service-design.

Ipeirotis, P. G., Provost, F., & Wang, J. (2010). Quality management on amazon mechanical turk. *Proceedings of the ACM SIGKDD Workshop on Human Computation - HCOMP '10*, New York, USA, pp. 64–67. https://doi.org/10.1145/1837885.1837906.

Kittur, A., Chi, E. H., & Suh, B. (2008). Crowdsourcing user studies with mechanical turk. *Proceedings of the Twenty-Sixth Annual CHI Conference on Human Factors in Computing Systems - CHI '08*, New York, USA, pp. 453–456. https://doi.org/10.1145/1357054.1357127

Krupowicz, W., Czarnecka, A., & Grus, M. (2020). Implementing crowdsourcing initiatives in land consolidation procedures in Poland, *Land Use Policy*, 99, 105015.

La Vecchia, G. & Cisternino, A. (2010). Collaborative workforce, business process crowdsourcing as an alternative of BPO. *In: Daniel, F., Facca, F.M. (eds) Current Trends in Web Engineering. ICWE 2010. Lecture Notes in Computer Science, vol 6385. Springer, Berlin, Heidelberg*, pp. 425–430. https://doi.org/10.1007/978-3-642-16985-4_40

Minet, J., Curnel, Y., Gobin, A., Goffart, J-P., s Mélard, F., Tychon, B., Wellens, J., & Defourny, P. (2017), Crowdsourcing for agricultural applications: A review of uses and opportunities for a farmsourcing approach, *Computers and Electronics in Agriculuture*, 142(2017), 126–138.

Nandan, N., Pursche, A., & Zhe, X. (2014). Challenges in crowdsourcing real-time information for public transportation. *Proceedings of the 2014 IEEE 15th International Conference on Mobile Data Management, Brisbane, QLD, Australia*, pp. 67–72. https://doi.org/10.1109/MDM.2014.70.

Niu, X., Qin, S., Vines, J., Wong, R., & Lu, H. (2019). Key crowdsourcing Technologies for Product Design and Development. *International Journal of Automation and Computing*, 16(1), 1–15. https://doi.org/10.1007/s11633-018-1138-7.

Pedersen, J., Kocsis, D., Tripathi, A., Tarrell, A., Weerakoon, A., Tahmasbi, N., Xiong, J., Deng, W., Oh, O., & de Vreede, G.-J. (2013). Conceptual foundations of crowdsourcing: A review of IS research. *Proceedings of the 46th Hawaii International Conference on System Sciences*, Wailea, HI, USA, pp. 579–588. https://doi.org/10.1109/HICSS.2013.143.

Ray, A., Chowdhury, C., Bhattacharya, S., & Roy, S. (2022). A survey of mobile crowdsensing and crowdsourcing strategies for smart mobile device users. *CCF Transactions on Pervasive Computing and Interaction*, 5, 98–123. https://doi.org/10.1007/s42486-022-00110-9.

Sammie, S. (2014). Crowdsourcing Industry Trends: Unique Ways Companies are Leverageing the Crowd. https://www.crowdsource.com/blog/2014/05/crowdsourcing-industry-trends-unique-ways-companies-are-leverageing-crowd-will-impact-future-job-markets/.

Saxton, G. D., Oh, O., & Kishore, R. (2013). Rules of crowdsourcing: Models, issues, and systems of control. *Information Systems Management*, 30(1), 2–10.

Sedhain, S., Sanner, S., Braziunas, D., Xie, L. X., & Christensen, J. (2014). Social collaborative filtering for cold-start recommendations. *Proceedings of the 8th ACM Conference on Recommender Systems - RecSys '14*, New York, USA, pp. 345–348. https://doi.org/10.1145/2645710.2645772.

Shaw, A. D., Horton, J. J., & Chen, D. L. (2011). Designing incentives for inexpert human raters. *Proceedings of the ACM 2011 Conference on Computer Supported Cooperative Work - CSCW '11*, New York, USA, pp. 275–284. https://doi.org/10.1145/1958824.1958865.

Simperl, E. (2015). How to use crowdsourcing effectively: Guidelines and examples. *LIBER Quarterly*, 25(1), 18-39. https://doi.org/10.18352/lq.9948.

Simula, H. & Ahola, T. (2014). A network perspective on idea and innovation crowdsourcing in industrial firms. *Industrial Marketing Management*, 43(3), 400–408. https://doi.org/10.1016/j.indmarman.2013.12.008.

Staletić, N., Labus, A., Bogdanović, Z., Despotović-Zrakić, M., & Radenković, B. (2020). Citizens' readiness to crowdsource smart city services: A developing country perspective. *Cities*, 107, 102883. https://doi.org/10.1016/j.cities.2020.102883

Sun, Y., Ding, W., Shu, L., Li, K., Zhang, Y., Zhou, Z., & Han, G. (2022). On enabling mobile crowd sensing for data collection in smart agriculture: A vision. *IEEE Sytems Journal*, 16(1), 132–143. https://doi.org/10.1109/JSYST.2021.3104107.

To, H., Shahabi, C., & Kazemi, L. (2015). A server-assigned spatial crowdsourcing framework. *ACM Transactions on Spatial Algorithms and Systems*, 1(1), 1–28. https://doi.org/10.1145/2729713.

Tranquillini, S., Daniel, F., Kucherbaev, P., & Casati, F. (2015). Modeling, enacting, and integrating custom crowdsourcing processes. *ACM Transactions on the Web*, 9(2), 1–43. https://doi.org/10.1145/2746353.

Wazny, K. (2017). Crowdsourcing's ten years in: A review. *Journal of Global Health*, 7(2), 020602. https://doi.org/10.7189/jogh.07.020601.

Wiggins, A., & Crowston, K. (2011). From conservation to crowdsourcing: A typology of citizen science. *Proceedings of the Annual Hawaii International Conference on System Sciences*, Kauai, HI, USA, pp. 1–10. http://doi.org/10.1109/HICSS.2011.207

Wikipedia. (2023). Service Design. https://en.wikipedia.org/wiki/Service_design.

www.gov.cn. (2019). "Digital Rural Development Strategy Outline" issued by The General Office of the Central Committee of the Communist Party of China and the General Office of the State Council. https://www.gov.cn/zhengce/2019-05/16/content_5392269.htm.

www.cac.gov.cn. (2022). "Guidelines for the Construction of the Digital Rural Standard System" issued by the Central Network Information Office and other four departments. https://www.cac.gov.cn/2022-09/01/c_1663666394684797.htm.

Xu, A. B., Rao, H. M., Dow, S. P., & Bailey, B. P. (2015). A classroom study of using crowd feedback in the iterative design process. *Proceedings of the 18th ACM Conference on Computer Supported Cooperative Work & Social Computing - CSCW '15*, Vancouver, BC, Canada, pp. 1637–1648. https://doi.org/10.1145/2675133.2675140.

Yuen, M.-C., King, I., & Leung, K.-S. (2011). A survey of crowdsourcing systems. *Proceedings of the 3rd IEEE International Conference on Privacy, Security, Risk and Trust and the 3rd IEEE International Conference on Social Computing*, Boston, MA, USA, pp. 766–773. https://doi.org/10.1109/PASSAT/SocialCom.2011.203.

Zhai, L. Y., Khoo, L.-P., & Zhong, Z. W. (2009). Design concept evaluation in product development using rough sets and grey relation analysis. *Expert Systems with Applications*, 36(3), 7072–7079. https://doi.org/10.1016/j.eswa.2008.08.068.

Zhang, H. P., Zhang, R. Q., Zhao, Y. P., & Ma, B. J. (2014). Big data modeling and analysis of microblog ecosystem. *International Journal of Automation and Computing*, 11(2), 119–127. https://doi.org/10.1007/s11633-014-0774-9.

3 Integrating Crowdsourcing and Digital Twin Technologies for Smart Service Design and Servicing Platform

Shengfeng Qin and Xiaojing Niu

3.1 INTRODUCTION

Smart cities and villages face sustainable development challenges in providing various services in the fields of health care, wellness, security, safety transportation, energy, mobility, and communications. In order to make these services sustainable, there is a need to make participative service design, service delivery, and service innovation into a product/service-life-cycle management ecosystem. One promising solution is that of Digital Twins (DTs) (El Saddick et al., 2021) technology. DTs are defined as digital replicas or virtual models of living as well as nonliving entities such as a product, process, or service that enable any interaction happening in the real world to be transmitted to the digital world and vice versa (El Saddick et al., 2021), allowing for participatory and collaborative processes to empower citizens (Dembski et al., 2020).

DTs for smart cities or city DTs are a virtual representation of a city's physical assets, using data, data analytics, and machine learning to build simulation models that can be updated and changed in real time to support city data management, urban planning and decision-making (Dembski et al., 2020), visualization, situational awareness, and citizen engagement (Ketzler et al., 2020; Shahat et al., 2021) and for improving health and well-being (El Saddik, 2018).

DTs and data analytics can also enable the design and development of new commercial activities and services based on data. There is a growing interest in using DTs as interactive tools to support (shared and augmented) decision-making, codesign, simulation, and training. Cities never stop changing, and therefore, city DTs need to be constantly updated with data from both smart IoT sensors and human sensors. Thus, crowdsourced and crowdsensed data can enable the automated updating of the city DTs, service cocreation, and service delivery (Lehtola et al., 2022). Thus, we propose an integral solution of integrating crowdsourcing and digital twin technologies for smart city applications in this chapter.

DOI: 10.1201/9781032686691-3

3.2 DIGITAL TWIN AND ITS RELATIONSHIP TO DIGITAL SHADOW AND DIGITAL TREAD

DT is a possible option for the global expansion of smart cities (Waqar et al., 2023). Underpinned by Internet of Things (IoT), Cyber-Physical System (CPS), Big-Data Analytics, and other Industry 4.0/5.0 technologies, DT is potentially applicable for many fields that involve the mapping, bidirectional interaction, and coevolution of physical and virtual spaces. Currently, DTs are mainly applied in construction, aerospace, automobile, manufacturing, etc. (Tao et al., 2018; Qi et al., 2021).

Benefited from the increasing connectivity and amount of usable data, DTs are shifting the businesses from analyzing the past to predicting the future, achieving data-driven development of innovative product and services (Tao et al., 2019) and diversifying value creation and business models in an iterative manner (Zheng et al., 2018). With the product–service integration in all aspects of modern society, the importance of service is recognized by more and more enterprises under the paradigm of Everything-as-a-service (XaaS). To meet the increasing service demands from different application fields, different levels of users, and different businesses, a product–service system consisting of various DTs of products, services, customers, and stakeholders on the supply chain shows great potential for supporting and speeding up this servitization process (Tao et al., 2014; Catarci et al., 2019).

DT is considered to consist of three crucial parts: physical products, virtual products, and the connections between them. It exhibits the following characteristics (Zheng et al., 2019): (1) integrating various types of data of physical objects; (2) existing in the entire life cycle of physical objects, coevolving with them, and continuously accumulating relevant knowledge; and (3) describing and optimizing physical objects. In 2021, Qi et al. (2021) proposed a five-dimensional DT model, consisting of five components: data, physical model, virtual model, service, and relationships. The link among the digital and physical equivalents is a crucial component of the digital twin. Here, two similar concepts, digital thread and digital shadow, are inevitable to be mentioned. Both of them can be treated as key enablers for DT (Wohlfeld et al., 2017; Dertien et al., 2019). Figure 3.1 shows DT, digital thread, and digital shadow relationship.

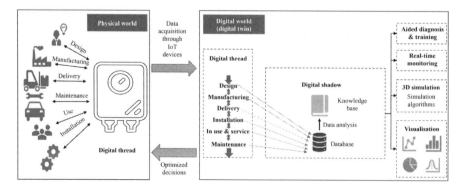

FIGURE 3.1 The relationship of DT, digital thread, and digital shadow.

Digital thread can create access channels to diverse but interrelated data sets so that the upstream and downstream are consistent and available to all users involved in a product life cycle (Dertien et al., 2019). It can maintain data associativity and traceability in a smart manufacturing/production process. Digital thread is a prerequisite to true DTs as it enables the evolution of DTs by enabling bidirectional communication between DTs. Currently, the research on digital thread mainly focuses on linking different life cycle data in a digital thread to support life cycle decision-making. For example, Kwon et al. (2020) proposed an approach to fuse as-designed data represented in STEP (STandard for Exchange of Product model data) and as-inspected data represented in QIF (Quality Information Framework) in a standards-based digital thread based on ontology with knowledge graphs. Implementing digital thread in manufacturing systems plays a significant role in enhancing cross-functional collaboration, enabling efficient change management in manufacturing and service processes, eliminating rework, and reducing lead times (Dertien et al., 2019). Digital thread makes it possible to deliver the right information to the right place at the right time (Kwon et al., 2020).

Digital shadow can be described as 'an always up-to-date information system, which integrates data from all available sensors and IT systems into one virtual representation including seamless interfaces and visualization for all connected services' (Wohlfeld et al., 2017). It only supports one way real-time data communication from physical to digital space (Teisserenc et al., 2021), reflecting changes in physical objects in corresponding digital models. In practice, digital shadow is mainly implemented at product operation stage to collect product working data (Ladj et al., 2021). As a core component of DTs, digital shadow enables the management and analysis of real-time data coming from the physical space (Schuh et al., 2019). In the manufacturing context, the data profiles of any product or component including operation, condition, and process data can be depicted as digital shadows. Digital shadow can achieve a comprehensive structuring of heterogeneous kinds of data available and connect them to their respective semantics and context for later retrieval and interpretation. Digital shadow can be subsets of data from production process according to the specified purpose (Liebenberg et al., 2020).

Compared to digital thread and digital shadow, DT supports bidirectional interactions between physical and virtual models. In service-oriented digital systems, there already exist studies to develop digital shadow for data management and analytics, laying foundation for the development of DT in the future (Ladj et al., 2021). And digital thread has been adopted to enable connectivity throughout the system's life cycle and to collect data from the physical twin for updating the corresponding digital representation in the virtual space (Madni et al., 2019). However, little existing research has been focused on the communications/interactions between DTs in service process (Lu et al., 2020). Implementing service DTs enabled by digital thread and digital shadow can help enterprises deliver experiences and outcomes to customers prescriptively rather than reactively (Dertien et al., 2019).

3.3　DIGITAL TWIN FRAMEWORK FOR SMART CITY

Digital twin-supported transformation of cities and villages is an essential choice of urban governance (Deng et al., 2021). In a digital twin city, all entities will exist simultaneously in parallel with historical records that can be traced, a present state that can be checked, and a future state that can be predicted.

With support from edge computing, cloud computing, 5G, IoT, etc., Deng et al. (2021) proposed a three-layered framework for digital twin city. The first layer is infrastructure that is the touchpoint and handler for building cities. It provides data support for the platform layer, analyzes and executes data, and offers feedback to the real-time physical world. The second layer is platform that is the intelligence hub for the operation of cities. It can perceive information from the first layer and provides feedback to it, thus connecting the digital cities and the physical ones. Meanwhile, it can enable the data by utilizing AI, big data, operations optimization algorithms, and simulation capabilities, providing data support to the third application layer. The application layer is a modular application collection. It invokes city data to deliver scenario services, data services, and simulation services. The scenario services include the provision of real-time data on urban architecture, geospace, and environments. The data services include tracing and tracking the past behaviors of physical entities, monitoring current behaviors, and predicting future behaviors. The simulation service includes the simulation of time, events, and scenarios.

Different from the three-layered smart city digital twin framework, this book presents a four-layered digital twin framework for smart cities with reference to that for manufacturing (ISO 23247). The lowest layer describes the smart city elements by describing all the items that constitute the city and need to be modeled. In manufacturing, it is officially not part of the framework because it already exists. The second layer is the device communication entity. This layer collates all the state changes of the smart city elements and sends control programs to those elements when adjustments become necessary. The third layer is the digital twin entity. This layer models the digital twins. It reads the data collated by the device communication entity and uses the information to update its models. The fourth layer contains user entities.

3.4　SERVICE-ORIENTED PLATFORM DEVELOPMENT SUPPORTED BY DIGITAL TWIN—CASE STUDY

3.4.1　INDUSTRIAL BACKGROUND AND REQUIREMENTS

Our industrial research partner is a residential/domestic boiler manufacturer. Currently, a domestic boiler, typically a gas boiler, is used widely in huge number of homes for heating purpose. For example, in the UK domestic sector, around 85% of energy is used for heating purpose. Typically, a boiler as a product can be owned by a householder or a landlord based on the product-centered business model. Regardless of what the product ownerships are, a boiler itself needs a regular annual maintenance service for reasons including safety check, identifying potential faults, and efficiency. For example, landlords in the United Kingdom who rent out their property are legally required to have their gas appliances and flues serviced on an annual basis by a certified Gas Safe heating engineer with a visual inspection and prescribed tests.

To facilitate the servitization, our research partner has made the boiler product smart with embedded SIM (Subscriber Identity Module) card so that it can transmit real-time product status data back. However, there is still a long way to implement manufacturing digital servitization. On this digital transformation journey, the core is an approach centered on the DT that is used for collecting data from product design, manufacturing, operations, maintenance, operating environments, and user experience and utilize these data to create a corresponding model of each specific asset.

From two workshops, it is found that there are two key challenges our research partner faces in digital servitization. The first challenge is the lack of product operation data (including product performance, maintenance, user interaction, and experience information) for advanced service innovation. Our research partner hopes to have a big picture of its product usage throughout the life cycle and based on that to offer advanced service provisions to increase revenues while enhancing user experience. In this process, in addition to product design and as-built manufacturing data that have been owned by the business, product operation data play an important role in uncovering insights on advanced manufacturing services innovation as well. Nevertheless, our partner usually adopts fixed contracts with its business partners for product installation and maintenance in the traditional product-centric business model, leading to the fragmented product operation data belonging to its business partners. In the current scenario, it is important to collect product operation data, and this should be the starting point of advanced service innovation. The second challenge is the low efficiency in delivering services. The traditional service delivery ensured by fixed contracts is costly and inflexible. After customers request a service, they usually need to wait for a certain period of time before getting serviced, greatly reducing the user experience. Our research partner hopes to find a new way to dynamically coordinate service providers such as installers and maintenance engineers to serve customers in a flexible and timely way. In the servitization process, the ownership of product could change to a product provider such as a manufacturer or jointly with householders or landlords, while the heating services including basic, intermediate, and advanced services (Ishizaka et al., 2019) need to be provided to the end users such as home residents or tenants by various service providers. Better connectivity is also required at the service level to connect the smart product to its owners such as landlords, end users (residents or tenants), and service providers.

Overall, the servitization goal of our research partner is to develop outcome- and performance-based advanced services such as 'heat as a service' and coordinate service providers to deliver them to customers based on product operation data in product use and maintenance stages by integrating crowdsourcing into DTs. Therefore, we design and prototype the DT platform based on the hybrid DT and digital thread conceptual model for evaluating the feasibility of using a smart product and service DTs to support this business concept.

3.4.2　THE SERVICE-ORIENTED HYBRID DT AND DIGITAL THREAD CONCEPTUAL MODEL

Drawing from the industrial application context, we designed a service-oriented hybrid DT and digital thread conceptual model (see Figure 3.2) aimed at revolutionizing advanced manufacturing services. This model is underpinned by innovative business models, service-/crowdsourcing, and DTs encompassing products, services, and users. This is enabled by the integration of the IoT, IoU, and IoS. It not only integrates existing smart products with smart services but also engages all stakeholders such as customers and service providers along the whole product and service life cycle.

In Figure 3.2, in the physical world side, real-world products, services, and human participants have their corresponding DTs in the virtual world. A service process could start from either the smart product-generated data such as an annual service notice to landlords or householders or customer-generated data such as a repairing or training service request in the physical world. Once these data generated from either physical sensors or human participants (or human sensors) are communicated to its digital counterparts via digital threads, they will be analyzed by the platform for generating proper new service requests (or offers) and creating the corresponding service DTs. For each service under request, crowdsourcing-based service sourcing is adopted to dynamically coordinate service providers to deliver the requested service. It is performed in the virtual space based on the profile of the product, the service requested, and service providers DTs, and as a result, a certain number of competent service providers in the physical world will be invited to act on the crowdsourcing and compete for the service job. As a result of the crowdsourcing, the best suitable ones will be shortlisted for landlords or householders to choose from. Once they select a service provider, a contract containing requester (landlords or householders)

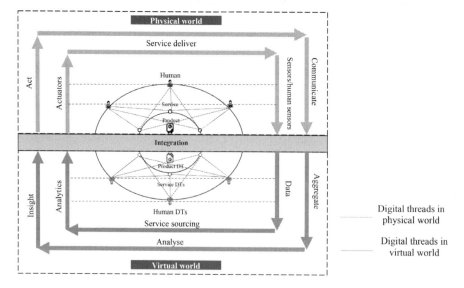

FIGURE 3.2　The service-oriented hybrid DT and digital thread conceptual model.

address, service date and time, requested service type, selected service provider, etc. will be formed. Finally, the selected service provider will be actuated to deliver the service in the physical space according to the contract, resulting in the physical product status changes as virtual-to-physical twining. In this loop, all data associated with the service and generated by both the boiler and the human users will be recorded, and the associated databases will be updated. Thus, when a service is delivered physically, the changes in user-generated data are combined with the product-generated data via IoT, IoU, and IoS to trigger a physical-to-virtual twinning that updates their corresponding DTs of the product, service, and users. These updated DTs will feedforward to the next round service sourcing and service recommendation for delivering next round services.

To describe a service process at product-in-use and maintenance stages under the conceptual model (see Figure 3.2), the key assets in the process such as products, services, and human actors (including customers, service providers, and other stakeholders on the supply chain) have their corresponding DTs (digital representations) in the virtual space. Each of them is identified (or identifiable) by a unique identifier and refers to the digital representation/model of a particular asset. A basic DT unit (see Figure 3.3) in this paper consists of the physical asset and its digital counterpart. In the DT unit, there are four types of communications: physical-to-physical, physical-to-virtual, virtual-to-physical, and virtual-to-virtual. All these communications are enabled by digital threads represented by arrow lines (the arrow direction indicates data communication direction) with different arrow line types in Figure 3.3. The internal communications within the DT unit including physical-to-virtual and virtual-to-physical ones represented by dash-dot arrow lines are supported by IoT infrastructures such as sensors and smart devices. The physical asset in a DT unit can only communicate with its digital representation via dash-dot arrow line channels and with other physical assets that are connected to it via dash arrow line channels. Similarly, the digital representation in a DT unit can only communicate with its physical asset and other digital representations connected to it via dot arrow line

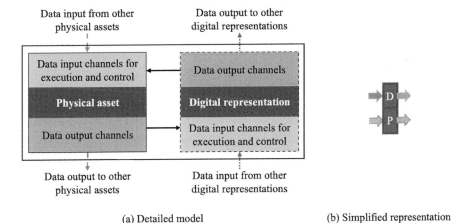

(a) Detailed model   (b) Simplified representation

FIGURE 3.3   The basic DT unit.

channels. There must exist at least two DTs that are channeled together by digital threads in order to communicate with each other for servicing. As illustrated in Figure 3.3a, a simplest service on the product can be performed automatically by the product itself such as self-diagnostics. The digital threads among physical assets are represented by dash arrow lines, while those among digital representations are dot ones. If we take the communication between the physical asset and its digital twin as default, the simplified representation of a basic DT unit is as shown in Figure 3.3b.

Around a specific physical product in a DT unit, there are many different services such as product installation, annual safety check, operation training, and other maintenance services that are bound to it (one-to-many relationship). These services have their unique codes/identifiers. The combination of a product identifier and a service code could form an integrated service identifier to indicate the product and the service that are connected. For a product DT, its simplest digital representation could be just an ID (identity) for service-oriented applications. Of course, the digital representation can be further improved with 2D (two-dimensional) and 3D (three-dimensional) simulation models when needed.

In the virtual space, DTs are developed in an incremental way in terms of representation detail and interaction complexity. A DT could be just a predefined object with a unique identifier at the very beginning. Then, with the collection of more product operation data, the DT can be continuously improved with higher fidelity and ultimately to be a perfect copy/DT to the physical asset. In interaction complexity, DTs including product DT, customer DT, and service provider DTs are independent at the starting point. Then, with interactions between the product and customer or service providers happening, service DTs and digital threads are developed incrementally. Service DTs are secondary and associated with initially independent product, customer, and service provider DTs.

Taking a boiler repair service as an example to demonstrate the incremental development process of DTs:

1. When a physical boiler runs normally at a home, the home user (consumer) can interact with it normally and receive right feedback from the boiler digital representation. The routine interaction process between the boiler and the consumer is shown in Figure 3.4, with dash-dot, dash, and dot arrow lines representing interactions within the DT unit, between physical assets, and between digital representations, respectively. The closed-loop digital thread in the routine interaction process is marked by solid arrow lines connecting the dash-dot, dash, and dot arrow lines. For example, the boiler can send its sensor data to its digital representation, and according to the incoming data analysis, the boiler's DT can send a 'healthy' boiler information to the consumer DT. Upon receiving this information, the consumer can continue to use the boiler normally.

2. When the physical boiler breaks down, it will send the breakdown information to the consumer through its DT and the consumer DT, and the home consumer will then request a repair service along the following key process. The key interactions between DT units and the incremental development of the service DT and digital threads in the process are represented in Figure 3.5.

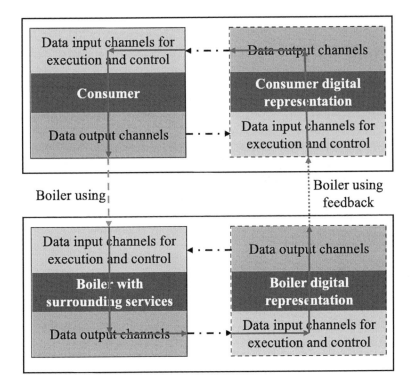

FIGURE 3.4   The routine interaction process between a boiler product and the consumer.

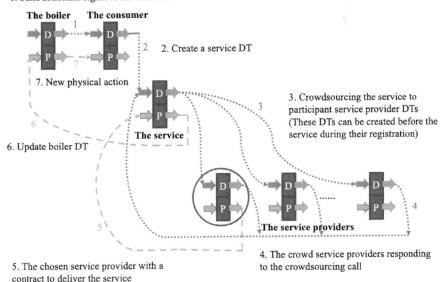

FIGURE 3.5   The interaction process in a typical repair service process.

Step 1: Start with two DTs as shown in Figure 3.4. In Figure 3.5, the two DTs, namely, 'The boiler' and 'The consumer', are represented in their simplified forms. The physical boiler reports the problem to its digital representation, and then, abnormal feedback will be sent to the smart home consumer via digital thread 1.

Step 2: With the abnormal feedback, the consumer will make a service request for the corresponding service from the boiler-bounded service list with his/her expected service date and time. This request will create a new service DT 'The service' connected to the consumer via a new thread 2.

Step 3: The requested service will be crowdsourced to a group of service providers. A group of new service sourcing threads 3 will be created to connect the service in request and the crowd service providers. For each service provider, its DT has already been created when they registered on the platform.

Step 4: At this step, digital threads between the digital representation of the service and any service providers that can provide the requested service are developed so that they can confirm their availability at the requested date and time. They will send their responses back to the service DT via thread 4.

Step 5: After receiving responses among the available service providers, only the most suitable one based on low-carbon footprint principle or quality priority principle will be chosen to carry on the service job. Let's assume that the first service provider highlighted by a circle is selected. The serviceman will provide the requested repairing service in physical world via interaction 5, and then, the communication between the serviceman DT and the service DT can be through a new thread like 4 to complete the service DT with all information involved.

Step 6. After the selected service provider delivers the requested service in the physical space, the physical boiler product will be updated from the repairing service via interaction 6 and will send real-time status to its digital representation. In this way, the boiler, the consumer, the service, and the service provider DTs are connected in a loop. The service provider is also required to update the formed service in his/her digital representation so that the service completion status can be cross-validated, enabling a new physical action 7 such as a 'Restart' to resume the boiler use.

In the service interaction process, the digital thread-based connectivity around the product itself and associated human users will enable the collection of operation data at product-in-use and maintenance stages. Once the operation data are sufficiently rich, they will be able to drive both the updates of existing products/services and the development of new products/services from a data-driven product/service design perspective. In this way, the accumulation of operation data and DT updates are happening in turn to support a gradual and incremental digital twinning process along the product/service life cycle, making the manufacturing system into an ecosystem.

3.4.3 THE ARCHITECTURE OF THE DT PLATFORM PROTOTYPE

Inspired by the DT Reference Architecture Model (Madni et al., 2019), the service-oriented hybrid DT and digital thread conceptual model in Figure 3.2 can be realized by its four-layered computational architecture as shown in Figure 3.6. The four layers are the perception layer, application layer, digital layer, and storage layer.

The application layer packages capacities and resources as services to serve stakeholders involved in the product–service ecosystem. The perception layer perceives the real-time status of smart products in physical space enabled by IoT infrastructure. These two layers form the network of humans and products, respectively. The digital layer is the DT-based crowdsourcing platform that implements not only the DTs (virtual models) of users, products, and services but also the connections among platform users and between physical product and its virtual counterpart enabled by IoT devices. The key role players involved in the product–service ecosystem including requesters, crowd workers acting as designers, evaluators, installers, and other stakeholders interact with the platform through predefined web-based user portal/interface. When requesters post tasks through their personal portals, the platform will design the tasks, and then, the platform crowdsources them to crowd workers with expected skills. To improve the capability of data storage in the platform, MongoDB (a NoSQL database that stores data in the form of 'key-value pairs') is used to store the very large amount of raw data with various formats collected from users, products, and services in the storage layer.

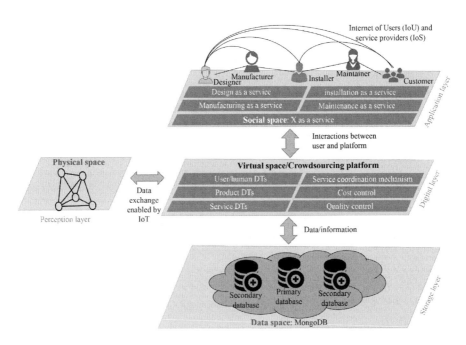

FIGURE 3.6 The overall architecture of the hybrid DT and the digital thread platform.

3.4.4 IMPLEMENTATION OF SERVICE PROVIDER COORDINATION MECHANISM ON THE PLATFORM

This section details the coordination of service providers for delivering a requested service. The coordination process includes two steps: service-/crowdsourcing and service provider recommendation.

3.4.4.1 Service-/Crowdsourcing

Posting a service request is regarded as a start point of the ecosystem evolution. Crowdsourcing integrating with service recommendation is considered as a tool to find the right service providers (crowd workers) with the best value for the tasks/ services required. Therefore, we formulate the service crowdsourcing problem into a combinatorial optimization one. The goal is to find a small set of service providers from a big crowd pool based on a requested service (task) profile by broadcasting the service request with highest possibility of finding at least one qualified service provider and the minimum unnecessary information burden to the rest of service providers in the pool.

Before proceeding further, we start with the following definitions from an overall perspective of the product–service ecosystem based on ordinary crowdsourcing (Blohm et al., 2018).

Definition 1: A product–service ecosystem based on a crowdsourcing platform can be described as a time-related state system with a 5-tuple (M, O, W, C, S).

1. $M = \{m_a | a = 1, 2, \ldots, M_N\}$ is a set of machines on the crowdsourcing platform, and M_N is the total number of machines. Assuming that a machine is only used by one end user and owned by an owner at time t, the corresponding end users (such as tenants) set is donated by $C = \{c_b | b = 1, 2, \ldots, M_N\}$, and the owners (such as landlords) set by $O = \{o_x | x = 1, 2, \ldots, O_N\}$, where $O_N \leq M_N$. A new service request could be initiated by a machine m_i's owner o_x, $x \in [1, O_N]$ after receiving the system remainder and problem report from the corresponding end user c_i.
2. $W = \{W_y | y = 1, 2, \ldots W_M\}$ is a set (pool) of service providers who work on service requests on the crowdsourcing platform, and W_M is the total number of service providers.
3. $S = \{s_i | i = 1, 2, \ldots, S_N\}$ is a set of service packages around machines, and S_N is the total number of service packages.

In the product–service ecosystem, each key element can be regarded as a live being-B such as a machine, and its states at time t can be described as triple (B^{t-}, B^t, B^{t+}). B^{t-} represents its history state, B^t represents its current state, and B^{t+} represents its future state. The exemplar data to describe each state for each element are shown in Table 3.1. In this ecosystem, B^{t-} is used for service-/crowdsourcing, B^t is used for service provider recommendation, and B^{t+} is used for representing the updated states of beings after contracts end.

Definition 2: A service task T_i related to M_i and the inputting request R_i by O_i. With a service analysis tool f, T_i can be defined with five dimensions: complexity

TABLE 3.1
Being State

Symbol	History State B^{t-}	Current State B^t	Future State B^{t+}
M	Design and manufacturing related data, service history record data, historical performance data, etc.	Machine's current performance data, warning information or codes and/or faulty codes transmitted by IoT devices, etc.	Predictive maintenance or scheduled annual service/check, etc.
O	Location and contact information, the machine ownership history and the machine service management history, etc.	A service request, urgency, current availability, etc.	Appointments for scheduled machine service and planned the ownership change, etc.
C	Location and contact information, the machine usership history and the machine service management history, etc.	A service request, urgency, current availability, etc.	Appointments for scheduled machine service and planned the usership change, etc.
W	Location and contact information, his/her qualifications, professional training and certifications, experience, and quality of the previous services on M, pricing history for the services, etc.	Current location, availability, pricing expectation, etc.	Appointments for delivering services, etc.
S	Service design and associated business models, service quality and associated user experience, service history data, etc.	Service requests to be processed with current resource constraints, etc.	The follow-up service scheduling, etc.

(P), required skills (K), estimated service cost (SC), urgency level (SL), and detailed service request description $(\$)$:

$$T_i = f(M_i, R_i, O_i) = T_i \langle P, K, SC, SL, \$ \rangle \qquad (3.1)$$

Based on the previous definition, given a service task T_i around machine M_i, broadcasting T_i on the crowdsourcing platform to a subset of W who are qualified to take the service job. For each candidate $W_j (j = 1, 2, \ldots, \phi)$, the following constraints must be met. ϕ can be a predefined small number such as 10 for crowdsourcing in order to minimize the unnecessary interruption to most of the members in W.

Constraint 1: potential service provider w_j must have the task-requested skills. Denoting the threshold for measuring the minimum value between two skills as ε_1, constraint 1 can be formulated as

$$\text{dis1}(w_j) = \text{distance}(w_j(K), T_i(K)) \geq \varepsilon_1 \qquad (3.2)$$

Constraint 2: the estimated service cost is close to the service provider's historical average price for similar services. Denoting the cost threshold as ε_2, constraint 2 can be formulated as

$$\text{dis2}(w_j) = \text{distance}\left(\overline{w_j(\text{Cost})}, T_i(SC)\right) \le \varepsilon_2 \tag{3.3}$$

Constraint 3: the potential service providers must be locationally close to machine M_i to have a shorter traveling distance for lower CO_2 footprints from the service. Denoting the distance threshold as ε_3, constraint 3 can be formulated as

$$\text{dis3}(w_j) = \text{distance}\left(w_j(\text{location}), M_i(\text{location})\right) \le \varepsilon_3 \tag{3.4}$$

Constraint 4: the performance of the potential service providers must be accepted by the service requester. Assuming that the accepted performance and performance threshold are denoted by θ_p and ε_4, constraint 4 can be formulated as

$$\text{dis4}(w_j) = \text{distance}\left(w_j(\text{performance}), \theta_p\right) \le \varepsilon_4 \tag{3.5}$$

To measure the performance of a service provider W_j in constraint 4, we quantitively describe it by a 3-tuple (AR, CS, SQ), where AR, CS, and SQ denote the acceptance rate, customer satisfaction, and service quality, respectively.

1. *Acceptance rate* $AR(w_j)$ of service provider w_i:

$$AR(w_j) = \frac{\text{Num}\left(T_{\text{accepted}}(w_j)\right)}{\text{Num}\left(T_{\text{all}}(w_j)\right)} *100\% \tag{3.6}$$

   where $\text{Num}\left(T_{\text{all}}(w_j)\right)$ and $\text{Num}\left(T_{\text{accepted}}(w_j)\right)$ denote the overall and accepted number of service tasks taken by w_j.
2. *Customer satisfaction* $(CS(w_j))$. Assuming that service provider w_j has taken N service tasks, and the customer satisfaction scores marked by end users are denoted by $CS_i, i \in [1, N]$, the average customer satisfaction of w_j is calculated by

$$\overline{CS(w_j)} = \frac{\sum_{i=1}^{N} CS_i(w_j)}{N} \tag{3.7}$$

3. *Service quality* $(SQ(w_j))$. Assuming that service provider w_j has taken N service tasks, and the service quality scores marked by end users are denoted by $SQ_i, i \in [1, N]$, the average service quality of w_j is calculated by

$$\overline{SQ(w_j)} = \frac{\sum_{i=1}^{N} SQ_i(w_j)}{N} \tag{3.8}$$

Then, normalize $\overline{CS(w_j)}$ and $\overline{SQ(w_j)}$ through Min–Max Normalization to make them belong to [0, 1], and the normalized customer satisfaction and service quality are denoted by $\overline{CS(w_j)}^*$ and $\overline{SQ(w_j)}^*$. If the weightings of acceptance rate, customer satisfaction, and service quality are denoted by q_{AR}, q_{CS}, and q_{SQ}, respectively, then the historical performance of w_j is formulated as

$$W_j(\text{performance}) = AR(w_j)*q_{AR} + \overline{CS(w_j)}^**q_{CS} + \overline{SQ(w_j)}^**q_{SQ} \qquad (3.9)$$

Constraint 5: the selected ϕ service providers must have the maximum skills, best performance, and the minimum service cost and distance. Assuming that the weighting functions for constraints 1, 2, 3, and 4 are donated by f_1, f_2, f_3, and f_4, respectively, constraint 5 can be formulated as

$$\min \sum_{j=1}^{\varnothing} \frac{\text{dis}2(w_j)*f_2 + \text{dis}3(w_j)*f_3}{\text{dis}1(w_j)*f_1 + \text{dis}4(w_j)*f_4}, \varnothing \in [1, W_M] \qquad (3.10)$$

With Equations (3.2)–(3.10), ϕ service providers satisfying constraints will be screened out as candidates that will receive the broadcasting of the requested service.

3.4.4.2 Service Provider Recommendation

Service provider recommendation or personalized task recommendation (Blohm et al., 2018) is an AI agent, one typical application scenario of recommendation algorithms that have been one of the research hotspots for many years to suggest relevant items to users. On a crowdsourcing platform, recommendation principles such as low footprint, superior quality, and whole life cycle principles are usually adopted (Mountney et al., 2020), and they should be balanced during the recommendation process to provide high-quality services around products to customers/end users while bringing maximum benefits to involved actors. For worker recommendation in crowdsourcing context, the jointly considered factors include a worker's capabilities and his/her external assessment of capabilities (Blohm et al., 2018). Besides these factors, we also consider their availability and location at the expected service time and their real quote for providing the requested service to calculate their recommendation priorities denoted by Rank.

When the ϕ service providers receive the crowdsourcing call, they are required to confirm their availability and provide their quotes for the requested services. Assume that their availability, locations, and quotes are donated by A, L, and Q, respectively. If w_j is not available at the expected service time, then $\text{Rank}(w_j) = 0$, or the rank of w_j, should be recalculated.

When w_j provides his real quote $Q(w_j)$ and current location $L(w_j)$, the dis2 and dis3will be updated as

$$\text{dis}2'(w_i) = \text{distance}\left(Q(w_j), T_i(SC)\right) \qquad (3.11)$$

$$\text{dis3}'(w_i) = \text{distance}\big(L(w_j),\ M_i(\text{Location})\big) \tag{3.12}$$

Then, based on low-cost recommendation principle, the rank of w_j is

$$\text{Rank}(w_j) = \frac{\text{dis2}'(wi) - \text{dis2}_{\min}}{\text{dis2}_{\max} - \text{dis2}_{\min}} * 100\% \tag{3.13}$$

where $\text{dis2}_{\max}$ and $\text{dis2}_{\min}$ denote the maximum and minimum distances from the quotes to estimated service cost, respectively.

Based on low-carbon footprint recommendation principle, the rank of w_j is

$$\text{Rank}(w_i) = \frac{\text{dis3}'(w_j) - \text{dis3}_{\min}}{\text{dis3}_{\max} - \text{dis3}_{\min}} * 100\% \tag{3.14}$$

where $\text{dis3}_{\max}$ and $\text{dis3}_{\min}$ denote the maximum and minimum distances from the locations to machine location, respectively.

Although the ranks of the $\varnothing$ service providers have been calculated, which one will be chosen for performing the requested service is determined by the service requester.

When a requested service T_i is finished, the product status and the profile of the selected service provider w_i, primarily the acceptance rate, customer satisfaction score, and service quality score, will be updated automatically. Denoting the service satisfaction score and service quality score given by the end user as Score_{CS} and Score_{SQ}, the updated customer satisfaction $CS(w_i)^+$ and service quality $SQ(w_i)^+$ are calculated by

$$CS(w_i)^+ = \frac{\overline{CS(w_i)} * \text{Num}\big(T_{\text{all}}(w_i)\big) + \text{Score}_{CS}}{\text{Num}\big(T_{\text{all}}(w_i)\big) + 1} \tag{3.15}$$

$$SQ(w_i)^+ = \frac{\overline{SQ(w_i)} * \text{Num}\big(T_{\text{all}}(w_i)\big) + \text{Score}_{SQ}}{\text{Num}\big(T_{\text{all}}(w_i)\big) + 1} \tag{3.16}$$

The updated acceptance rate $AR(w_i)^+$ is updated by

$$AR(w_i)^+ = \begin{cases} \dfrac{\text{Num}\big(T_{\text{accepted}}(w_i)\big)}{\text{Num}\big(T_{\text{all}}(w_i)\big) + 1} * 100\%, & T_i \text{ is not accepted} \\[4mm] \dfrac{\text{Num}\big(T_{\text{accepted}}(w_i)\big) + 1}{\text{Num}\big(T_{\text{all}}(w_i)\big) + 1} * 100\%, & T_i \text{ is accepted} \end{cases} \tag{3.17}$$

3.5 EVALUATION OF THE DEVELOPED PLATFORM BASED ON THE CASE STUDY 'HEAT AS A SERVICE'

The primary goal of the DT platform is to build an ecosystem involving not only the network of smart products but also the network of users and stakeholders. In the case study, 10 service concepts (Mountney et al., 2020) have been identified after the boilers have been installed and in use. Taking 'maintenance as a service' (SC2 proposed in Mountney et al. (2020), shown in Table 3.2) as an example, we implemented a software prototype consisting of the frontend user portal and backend DT-based crowdsourcing platform to simulate the service process. The user portal was developed based on HTML, Bootstrap, and JavaScript, and the DT-based crowdsourcing platform is developed based on Django framework. For a specific boiler in SC2, the tenant and the landlord act as the end user and the authorizer, respectively. Servicemen/engineers act as service providers/crowd workers.

Under SC2, annual machine check is one of the typical scenarios formed by these identified advanced services listed in Table 3.2. Taking the annual machine check service in social housing segment as an example, the DT unit involved in this service process includes boiler, landlord, tenant, and service providers offering annual machine check service. In order to illustrate the interactions among DTs in the service process, the sequential interaction diagram with information flow in the service digital thread is provided in Figure 3.7 where the physical and virtual parts in the boiler and the selected service provider DT units are separated to, respectively, represent interactions in physical and virtual space with dash and dot line arrows. The service digital thread has four steps/subservices: service appointment, crowdsourcing and service recommendation, contract generation, and service evaluation. This service process mainly involves the update of boiler DT and the selected service provider DT. The key interface for boiler DT, crowdsourcing results, and service evaluation are also provided in Figure 3.7.

TABLE 3.2
Key Features of SC2 and Its Corresponding Advanced Services

Service Concept	Key Features	Advanced Services Under the Concept
SC2-Managing access around the annual gas safety check	Opening up communication channels with the tenant and scheduling inspection visits based on engineer locations and availability	1. Service engineers' training and certification as a service 2. Crowdsourcing or service outsourcing as a service 3. Contract-enabled 'warm hours' as a service 4. User Experience as a Service (UXaaS) embedded in the smart service recommendation

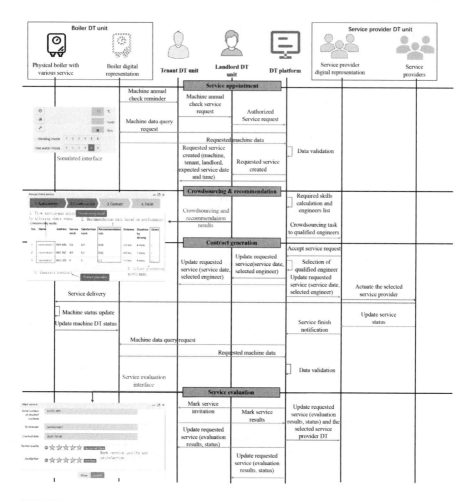

FIGURE 3.7 The sequential interaction process with information flow in annual machine check service and interface examples.

3.5.1 SERVICE APPOINTMENT

The annual check date is determined by the installation date of the machine. Before a given period of the expected machine check date, such as 2 weeks, the machine DT automatically reminds the tenant to request annual machine check with the landlord. When the machine DT notifies the tenant to check the machine, the tenant is required to request the service from the landlord. After the landlord authorizes the service request, the DT-based crowdsourcing platform requests the historical data from the machine DT to diagnose machine problem and calculate the required skills to solve the problem. How to diagnose machine problem and calculate the required skills are out of the scope of this paper. The key output from authorized service request is the requested service type, i.e., machine annual check. When the DT platform validates the service request to be true, a requested service is created, which contains the information of the machine that needs service, the information about the requested service, the machine end user, the machine owner (landlord), the expected service date and time, etc.

3.5.2 Service Crowdsourcing and Recommendation

Notice that all indicators measuring the qualification of an engineer, namely, AR, CS, and SQ, are initially set as 0. With the increase of performed services in the past, these indicators are calculated by Equations (3.6)–(3.8) and will be updated automatically according to Equations (3.15)–(3.17) when a new service is performed by the engineer. Before broadcasting the service request, the platform calculates CS, SQ, the recommendation rate based on engineer's performance with Equation (3.9), distance-to-machine address, and duration by driving of each engineer registered in the ecosystem. In recommendation rate calculation, the weighting parameters to AR, SQ, and CS are 0.5, 0.3, and 0.2, respectively. Based on the calculation results, the top three engineers with higher recommendation rate are shortlisted to broadcast the service request to. The engineers who receive the broadcast service request can decide whether to accept the service request or not. Among those who accepted, low-cost or low-carbon footprint principle can be applied to shortlist them. In our simulation, low-carbon footprint (shortest distance to destination address) principle is adopted. In this process, the landlord can decide which engineer is eventually selected for the requested service. An example of service crowdsourcing and recommendation results is shown in Figure 3.7.

3.5.3 Service Contract

When the landlord selects an engineer for the requested service, the service request will be updated automatically, and the tenant, the landlord, and the selected engineer/service provider notified about the service date and time. Then, at the expected date, the engineer will perform the service physically and then tell the service results to the DT platform. After DT platform verifies the service results by cross-checking it with the real-time machine data, the platform will ask the machine end user to mark the service provided by the selected engineer.

3.5.4 Service Evaluation

After the requested service is performed by the engineer, the tenant will be asked to mark or evaluate the service experience and quality. The service evaluation results will be written into the service request, and the reputation of the engineer (the selected service provider DT) will be updated accordingly. The service evaluation interface is shown in the service evaluation part in Figure 3.7. The service evaluation results will affect the qualification of the selected engineer for later service requests on the platform.

3.6 SUMMARY

This chapter first clarifies that DT is one of the key enablers for smart servicing. Then, it describes the DT concept and its relationship with digital thread and digital shadow. Then, a four-layered DT framework for smart city is proposed. After that, it presents the service-oriented platform development supported by digital twin, including industrial requirements for a service-oriented platform and the development of the service-oriented hybrid DT and digital thread platform in terms of its conceptual model and the overall architecture, and the implementation of service provider coordination mechanism on the hybrid DT and digital thread platform. Finally, it evaluates the feasibility of coordinating service providers to deliver the requested service and the evolutionary updating of DTs around the 'maintenance as a service' concept.

REFERENCES

Blohm, I., Zogaj, S., Bretschneider, U., & Leimeister, J. M. (2018). How to manage crowdsourcing platforms effectively?. *California Management Review*, 60(2), 122–149. https://doi.org/10.1177/0008125617738255.

Catarci, T., Firmani, D., Leotta, F., Mandreoli, F., Mecella, M., & Sapio, F. (2019). A conceptual architecture and model for smart manufacturing relying on service-based digital twins. In *2019 IEEE International Conference on Web Services (ICWS)* (pp. 229–236). Milan, Italy: IEEE. https://doi.org/10.1109/ICWS.2019.00047.

Dembski, F., Wössner, U., Letzgus, M., Ruddat, M.,& Yamu, C. (2020). Urban digital twins for smart cities and citizens: The case study of Herrenberg, Germany. *Sustainability*, 12, 2307. https://doi.org/10.3390/su12062307.

Deng, T., Zhang, K., & Shen, Z. J. M. (2021). A systematic review of a digital twin city: A new pattern of urban governance toward smart cities. *Journal of Management Science and Engineering*, 6(2), 125–134. https://doi.org/10.1016/j.jmse.2021.03.003.

Dertien, S., Lang, J., & Immerman, D. (2019). *Digital Twin: A Primer for Industrial Enterprises*. Boston, MA: PTC Inc.

El Saddik, A. (2018). *Digital Twins: The Convergence of Multimedia Technologies*. Milan, Italy: IEEE MultiMedia, pp. 87–92. https://doi.org/10.1109/MMUL.2018.023121167.

El Saddik, A., Laamarti, F., & Alja'Afreh, M. (2021). The potential of digital twins. *IEEE Instrumentation & Measurement Magazine*, 24(3), 36–41. https://doi.org/10.1109/MIM.2021.9436090.

Ishizaka, A., Bhattacharya, A., Gunasekaran, A., Dekkers, R., & Pereira, V. (2019). Outsourcing and offshoring decision making. *International Journal of Production Research*, 57(13), 4187–4193. https://doi.org/10.1080/00207543.2019.1603698.

ISO 23247. Digital Twin Framework for Manufacturing. https://www.ap238.org/iso23247/#:~:text=The%20digital%20twin%20framework%20for,products%2C%20more%20quickly%20and%20efficiently.

Ketzler, B., Naserentin, V., Latino, F., Zangelidis, C., Thuvander, L., &Logg, A. (2020). Digital twins for cities: A state of the art review. *Built Environment*, 46(4), 547–573. https://doi.org/10.2148/benv.46.4.547.

Kwon, S., Monnier, L. V., Barbau, R., & Bernstein, W. Z. (2020). Enriching standards-based digital thread by fusing as-designed and as-inspected data using knowledge graphs. *Advanced Engineering Informatics*, 46, 101102. https://doi.org/10.1016/j.aei.2020.101102.

Ladj, A., Wang, Z., Meski, O., Belkadi, F., Ritou, M., & Da Cunha, C. (2021). A knowledge-based digital shadow for machining industry in a digital twin perspective. *Journal of Manufacturing Systems*, 58, 168–179. https://doi.org/10.1016/j.jmsy.2020.07.018.

Lehtola, V., Koeva, M., Elberink, S., Raposo, P., Virtanen, J., Vahdatikhaki, F., & Borsci, S. (2022). Digital twin of a city: Review of technology serving city needs. *International Journal of Applied Earth Observation and Geoinformation*, 114, 102915. https://doi.org/10.1016/j.jag.2022.102915.

Liebenberg, M. & Jarke, M. (2020). Information systems engineering with digital shadows: concept and case studies: an exploratory paper. In *Advanced Information Systems Engineering: 32nd International Conference, CAiSE 2020, Grenoble, France, June 8–12, 2020, Proceedings* (pp. 70–84). Cham: Springer International Publishing. https://doi.org/10.1007/978-3-030-49435-3_5.

Lu, Y., Liu, C., Kevin, I., Wang, K., Huang, H., & Xu, X. (2020). Digital Twin-driven smart manufacturing: Connotation, reference model, applications and research issues. *Robotics and Computer-Integrated Manufacturing*, 61, 101837. https://doi.org/10.1016/j.rcim.2019.101837.

Madni, A. M., Madni, C. C., & Lucero, S. D. (2019). Leveraging digital twin technology in model-based systems engineering. *Systems*, 7(1), 7. https://doi.org/10.3390/systems7010007.

Mountney, S., Ross, T., May, A., Qin, S. F., Niu, X., King, M., ... & Burton, J. (2020). *Digitally Supporting the Co-creation of Future Advanced Services for 'Heat As A Service'*. In Bigdeli, A and Baines, T (ed) *The Spring Servitization Conference 2020; Proceedings of the The Spring Servitization Conference 2020*, Birmingham, UK, pp. 64-71. ISBN: 9781854494290.

Qi, Q., Tao, F., Hu, T., Anwer, N., Liu, A., Wei, Y., ... & Nee, A. Y. C. (2021). Enabling technologies and tools for digital twin. *Journal of Manufacturing Systems*, 58, 3–21. https://doi.org/10.1016/j.jmsy.2019.10.001.

Schuh, G., Kelzenberg, C., Wiese, J., & Ochel, T. (2019). Data structure of the digital shadow for systematic knowledge management systems in single and small batch production. *Procedia CIRP*, 84, 1094–1100. https://doi.org/10.1016/j.procir.2019.04.210.

Shahat, E., Hyun, C., & Yeom, C. (2021). City digital twin potentials: A review and research agenda. *Sustainability*, 13(6), 3386. https://doi.org/10.3390/su13063386.

Tao, F., Cheng, Y., Da Xu, L., Zhang, L., & Li, B. H. (2014). CCIoT-CMfg: Cloud computing and internet of things-based cloud manufacturing service system. *IEEE Transactions on Industrial Informatics*, 10(2), 1435–1442. https://doi.org/10.1109/TII.2014.2306383.

Tao, F., Sui, F., Liu, A., Qi, Q., Zhang, M., Song, B., & Nee, A. Y. (2019). Digital twin-driven product design framework. *International Journal of Production Research*, 57(12), 3935–3953. https://doi.org/10.1080/00207543.2018.1443229.

Tao, F., Zhang, H., Liu, A., & Nee, A. Y. (2018). Digital twin in industry: State-of-the-art. *IEEE Transactions on Industrial Informatics*, 15(4), 2405–2415. https://doi.org/10.1109/TII.2018.2873186.

Teisserenc, B. & Sepasgozar, S. (2021). Adoption of blockchain technology through digital twins in the construction industry 4.0: a PESTELS approach. *Buildings*, 11(12), 670. https://doi.org/10.3390/buildings11120670.

Waqar, A., Othman, I., Almujibah, H., Khan, M. B., Alotaibi, S., & Elhassan, A. A. (2023). Factors influencing adoption of digital twin advanced technologies for smart city development: Evidence from Malaysia. *Buildings*, 13(3), 775. https://doi.org/10.3390/buildings13030775.

Wohlfeld, D., Weiss, V., & Becker, B. (2017, April). Digital Shadow-From production to product. In: *Bargende, M., Reuss, HC., Wiedemann, J. (eds) 17. Internationales Stuttgarter Symposium. Proceedings*. Springer Vieweg, Wiesbaden, pp. 783–794. https://doi.org/10.1007/978-3-658-16988-6_61.

Zheng, P., Lin, T. J., Chen, C. H., & Xu, X. (2018). A systematic design approach for service innovation of smart product-service systems. *Journal of Cleaner Production*, 201, 657–667. https://doi.org/10.1016/j.jclepro.2018.08.101.

Zheng, Y., Yang, S., & Cheng, H. (2019). An application framework of digital twin and its case study. *Journal of Ambient Intelligence and Humanized Computing*, 10, 1141–1153. https://doi.org/10.1007/s12652-018-0911-3.

4 Digital Technologies for Inclusive Healthy Ageing

Yuanyuan Yin, Shan Wang, and Xiao Wei

4.1 INTRODUCTION

Population ageing has been identified as one of the most significant social transformations which has impacted nearly all sectors of our society (United Nations, 2022). By 2050, the global population aged 65 years or over is projected to rise from 10% in 2022 to 16% (UNDESA, 2022). The Office for National Statistics predicts that there will be 19.8 million people aged 65 years and over by 2069 in the United Kingdom. This is about 26.2% of the projected UK population (ONS, 2021). Due to such a substantial demographic shift, many researchers have highlighted the importance of healthy ageing and are keen to contribute to the UKRI's Challenge Mission to *'ensure that people can enjoy at least five extra healthy independent, years of life by 2035, while narrowing the gap between the experience of the richest and poorest'*. A key challenge to achieving healthy ageing is recognising the diversity of ageing groups and their unmet needs for healthy ageing. Social and economic inequalities in later life are associated with a similar inequality in health status. These inequalities often arise in middle age and may be amplified by transitions into retirement and then from 'younger old' age to 'older old' age (Fors et al., 2012). Older people with low income, living in poor housing, living with disabilities or long-term health conditions, primary caregivers, and people from ethnic minority or immigrant backgrounds are underserved groups, which often suffer from poor health and unequal access to health and social care (Adams et al., 2013). Thus, inclusive, affordable, and ageing friend products/services that better meet the health-related (or healthcare) needs of the elderly are urgently required.

Apart from the global ageing trend, another significant revolution in our community is digital transformation. With the increasing digitisation in our society, digital technologies have changed people's living behaviour and will continue to shape the way how we communicate with each other, access information, think, work, and live (Nanda et al., 2020). For example, social media and smart devices have enabled people with more social opportunities, which has led to a wider range of channels and forms for receiving and sharing information, establishing relationships, and interacting with others (Siddiqui and Singh, 2016). Likewise, technologies such as artificial intelligence (AI), big data, and the Internet of Things have had a significant impact on public healthcare (Harris, 2013). As a result of technological advancements, medical and health services have become more convenient for patients, such as personal alarm devices, fall detection devices, activity monitoring devices, and telehealthcare services (Lu et al., 2016; Syed et al., 2019). Although new design interventions have

DOI: 10.1201/9781032686691-4

been developed to support older people in their later life, older people have diverse attitudes towards using these assistive interventions: reported limitations include uncomfortable or inconvenient implementation of interventions and perceived stigma associated with obtrusive wearable devices (Song et al., 2019). It is important to note that older people's experiences of these health-related digital interventions differ due to their social and economic statuses, health conditions, education levels, and prior experience with technology. Designers should therefore not only focus on the functionality of new products and services to promote healthy ageing but also make them affordable, accessible, inclusive, and age-friendly in order to combat this new form of social inequality – the 'Digital Divide'.

The digital divide refers to the disparities between individuals, organisations, and nations in their ability to access, use, and benefit from digital technologies (Castell, 2002; Wei et al., 2011; Scheerder et al., 2017). Scholars believe that the unbalanced distribution of economic, social, and cultural resources and capital owned by individuals and ageing are the basis of digital inequality (Ragnedda et al., 2019; Van Deursen et al., 2015; Scheerder et al., 2017; Livingstone et al., 2005). The elderly groups face greater challenges and injustices in the digital age due to their age, education, income, and regional economic development, which shapes the so-called 'grey digital divide' – the inequalities and differences in the use of digital technologies between the elderly and the young people (Friemel, 2014; Morris and Brading, 2007). Some studies show that 'age' is negatively correlated with one's online performance including information and communications technologies access and digital literacy (e.g., Friemel, 2014; Scheerder et al., 2017). Limited knowledge of information and communications technologies and physical constraints such as deterioration of memory, vision, and hearing can lead to difficulties when using digital technologies (Friemel, 2014; Pan and Jordan-Marsh, 2010). Perception of risk and complexity, cost and affordability, value proposition, and low expectations will also obstacle seniors' use of digital technologies (Knowles and Hanson, 2018; Blok et al., 2020; Orellano-Coló, 2015). Many elderly people reject or abandon digital technologies due to these subjective and objective factors. In contrast, other studies have shown that appropriate digital engagement can positively impact the happiness of the elderly in their later years, by enhancing people's social participation, maintaining social relations, and providing them with additional social support (Sum et al., 2008; Lifshitz-Assaf et al., 2017; Li et al., 2019). Hence, it is vital to examine how inclusive design can contribute to improving older people's interactions and experiences with digital technologies for healthy ageing in their daily lives.

Therefore, this chapter reviews related research on inclusive design for healthy ageing and presents three case studies to demonstrate how inclusive design has contributed to the improvement in older individuals' quality of life towards healthy ageing.

4.1.1 CASE STUDY 1: SMART RETAIL SERVICE DESIGN FOR OLDER CUSTOMERS

This case study introduces how smart retail services can support and improve older customers' supermarket shopping experience so that they have equal and better access to healthy foods. In this case study, key supermarket shopping-related issues have been explored, which include difficulties finding items in the store; design issues of a trolley, basket, and shelf; checkout, trust issues of online payment; and issues of online shopping interaction and interface design. Based on the identified shopping issues, the authors developed a Smart Shopping App prototype to support older customers to receive a tailored shopping service based on their specific needs, such as providing product suggestions for improved health outcomes related to aggregated data on the shopper's health, budget, independence and skills level (e.g., cooking ability), cognitive ability, mobility, and any forthcoming calendar events. The App also provides support for shopping plans, in-store navigation, call for staff help, and easy checkout.

4.1.2   CASE STUDY 2: SMART TEXTILE DESIGN FOR HEALTH AND SOCIAL CARE

Smart textiles are textiles that can sense and respond to changes in their environment and adapt to them through the integration of functionalities into the textile structure. This case study aims to discover the healthcare needs of people aged 65+ who live alone and the challenges they face when they use healthcare-related products, identify their unmet needs, and develop inclusive smart textile design insights to address their needs. Interviews and questionnaires were conducted to understand older people's experience of healthcare and social care at home and their attitude towards inclusive smart textiles to support and improve existing healthcare and social care services. Finally, insights into how smart textile technologies can be applied to improve health and social care services have been developed.

4.1.3   CASE STUDY 3: AN INCLUSIVE HOME DESIGN FOR OLDER PEOPLE

A number of researchers have examined and contributed to improving the quality of life for older individuals by focusing on ageing in place. In spite of the fact that the living room has been identified as one of the most frequently used spaces in the home due to its multifunctional features, there remains a lack of research on living room design for the elderly. Thus, this case study presents an investigation of older people's experience of their living room at home and the related risks and challenges they face in their day-to-day life. A 9-week ethnographic user study approach was employed to explore older people's natural behaviour with multiple activities in their living room through video-based observation, in-depth interviews, and cultural probes with 11 households. Based on the research findings, design insights were developed for improving living room space design, furniture and furniture arrangement, and atmosphere design to improve older people's standard of living in the United Kingdom.

4.2   OVERVIEW

4.2.1   DEMOGRAPHIC CHANGE

Globally, there will be approximately 727 million people aged 65 and over by 2020, representing 9.3% of the world's population. By 2050, this number will have increased to 1.5 billion or 16% of the population (United Nations, 2022). In terms of the United

Kingdom, there are almost 11 million people aged 65 and over, which represent 19% of the total population in the country in 2022, and it is projected to rise by over 40% (40.77%) by 2040, which means nearly one in four people in the country will be aged 65 or over (Centre for Ageing Better, 2022). Due to such significant demographic change, the costs for social care and healthcare have increased dramatically in the United Kingdom for older people. This includes the provision of pensions and public infrastructure. Wittenberg and Hu (2015) projected that the annual costs of social care would rise from £6.9 billion in 2015 to £17.5 billion in 2035.

4.2.2 Features of Older People

According to the World Confederation for Physical Therapy (WCPT, 2001), older people may be defined by a variety of characteristics, such as chronological age, social role change (such as retirement), and functional ability change (such as disability). Most studies define the elderly population as those aged 65 and over (OECD, 2018). Accordingly, the authors will use the term 'old person' as a general definition of an individual over the age of 65 in this chapter.

During ageing, people experience declines in visual function, hand function, body mobility, balance, and memory. As a result, older individuals may have different requirements when requesting a service or utilising a product in their daily lives (Farage et al., 2012). For instance, 20% of individuals over 75, and 50% of individuals over 90, suffer from visual impairment in the United Kingdom (Rotheroe et al., 2013), including decreased visual acuity (such as near-focus or presbyopia) and contrast sensitivity (Sinclair et al., 2015), problems with glare and low light (Pattison and Stedmon, 2006; Schmall, 1991), and age-related colour perception loss. These visual impairment issues can cause many limitations with regard to mobility, balance, and activities of daily living (Salvi et al., 2006; Sinclair et al., 2015; Salive et al., 1994; Tobis et al., 1985). For instance, Brawley (2008) reported that up to half of all nursing home residents in San Francisco had difficulty navigating around their home environment because of vision problems. Meanwhile, quality of life in old age is also related to mobility (Metz, 2000; Fisk et al., 2009), and muscle strength declines and flexibility reduces (Kalyani et al., 2014). Mobility changes can present physical challenges for living independently (Metz, 2000), and unsuitable living environment design might cause safety issues for older people (e.g., stairs present a high risk at home) (Robson et al., 2005). Previous research also confirms that reduced body movement for older people limited the control of their bodies, such as creating difficulty transferring from a wheelchair to an armchair, or losing body balance when bending, stooping, and stretching (Czaja et al., 2019; Metz, 2000). These features and limitations of older people have great impacts on their use, interaction, and engagement with health-related products and services. Therefore, if we want to design and develop inclusive, ageing-friendly products and services, these features and characteristics of older people have to be considered and accommodated during the product/service design and development process (Wilkinson and De Angeli, 2014). An inclusive design for ageing has attracted more and more attention from designers, researchers, policymakers, and other key stakeholders.

4.2.3 Inclusive Design for Ageing

The goal of inclusive design is to provide a service that is accessible to as many people as possible (Pattison and Stedmon, 2006). Inclusive design recognises the importance of acknowledging individual wants and needs, personalisation in products and services design, and ever-changing people's needs in order to be flexible and adaptable (Manthorpe and Samsi, 2016). It considers the full range of human diversity in the areas of ability, language, culture, gender, age, and other forms of human difference in the ageing population group (Inclusive Design Research Centre, 2022). There have been many studies in the field of inclusive design that focus on the ageing challenge and place older people at the centre of the design and development of products and services. A variety of assistive products are designed to enhance and support older individuals' daily competencies (Wahl et al., 2009). For instance, adjustable chairs can help to reduce prolonged stress on the neck and back when older people have a habit of sitting for long periods (Pinto et al., 2000). Adjustable beds were designed to change the position and height level of a mattress to relieve pressure and prevent muscle contractions. Other design-for-ageing–related studies highlight the concept of ergonomics, giving specific attention to exploring how the experience of 'ageing in place' might differ between different groups of older people (Harrington and Harrington, 2000; Yu et al., 2011; Wills et al., 2013). For instance, Pinto et al. (2000) explored the use of the entrance and kitchen environment at home, analysing living behaviour and observing collision issues among older people with furniture. Moreover, some simple monitoring devices designed to facilitate communication between older people and their caregivers, such as intercoms (Milligan et al., 2011), have been used for maintaining older people living independently at home. Although results from existing inclusive design research are notable, most of these studies mainly focus on functionality and usability. Few of them have systematically considered possible environments and the circumstances in which end users (older people) may use or operate the products. For example, older people might not be able to use installed handrails and walking aids due to a narrow hallway at home or discomfort with new technologies (National Research Council, 2011). Thus, the challenge for design inclusivity for healthy ageing is that it is difficult to design products, services, or environments that fit every older people every time (Rouzet et al., 2019). Especially, due to the social, economic, and health inequalities, it is crucial to explore how to create a supportive environment of buildings, products, services, and interfaces that makes it possible for every older people to live independent and fulfilling lives for as long as possible (Phillips et al., 2004; Russo et al., 2004).

4.2.4 Digital Transformation

Our social lives and entertaining activities increasingly took place online and got virtualised. In this digital era, people do not have to take a long-distance trip to meet their long-lost friends, relatives, and loved ones since video calls can easily ease their feelings of missing each other with a tap. Technologies such as AI, big data, and the Internet of Things have brought a huge boost to public healthcare. With the help of technologies, medical and health services have become more convenient for patients. WhatsApp or WeChat, as widely used applications, became healthcare platforms for they could facilitate the exchange of patients' medical information via smartphones (Murero, 2019). With just a smartphone, patients can register, make appointments, check the blood test results, and make payments, which undoubtedly saves the resources of medical services to a large extent (Hao and Wang, 2018). The application of technologies such as AI and big data has also dramatically improved the possibility of predicting and diagnosing diseases, preventing risks, giving better treatments, and extending life expectancy (Kaur et al., 2018; Saravana kumar et al., 2015). The Fourth Industrial Revolution led by digitalisation process has brought with significant implications in industry, economy, science, and society (Diaconu, 2019). The ways people work, socialise, think, and act have taken on new characteristics of the new digital age since digital technologies are being integrated into all aspects of our lives (Musik and Bogner, 2019).

4.2.5 DIGITAL TECHNOLOGIES FOR HEALTHY AGEING

Within the past decade, a variety of new product and service concepts have been developed for supporting older people in remaining active, healthy, independent, and staying as long as possible. Electronic Assistive Technology (EAT) products and Ambient Assisted Living (AAL) technology have played important roles in improving the physical and mental well-being of older adults at home (Song et al., 2019). These technologies have been used in a range of healthcare-related products and services within the home environment to assess older people's health conditions and prevent accidents at home (Song and van der Cammen, 2019), for example, voice-controlled intelligent personal assistants to support ageing in place in terms of entertainment, companionship, control of the home, reminders, and emergency communication (O'Brien et al., 2019), such as Amazon Alexa and Google Home (Ermolina and Tiberius, 2021); health-monitoring technology and wearable smart healthcare products, such as Smart Watch, Personal Alarm Devices, Falls Detection Devices, Activity Monitoring Devices, Wearable Technology, and Smart textile products (Lu et al., 2016), used to track older people's activities to provide real-time monitoring and detected emergencies (such as asthma attacks, heart attack, diabetes, and fall) by adding intelligent and wearable sensors (Sindhwani et al., 2021); and Internet of Things devices, such as telehealthcare (Syed et al., 2019), consist of a network of sensors in the human's body which sends to a hub and receives data to track health. It can assist older people to manage and prevent chronic conditions (Whitley et al., 2021) and assist remote healthcare providers to take care of their patients with the continuous transmission of physiological information (Syed et al., 2019).

While these digital technologies in the healthy ageing field have been widely used to support older people living independently in recent decades, especially during COVID-19 (Hamblin, 2022), issues of ageing-friendly product design and older people's receptivity to using technology remain (Buyl et al., 2020). For example, they may forget to take some medicines (Milligan et al., 2022), and they may forget to use prevention devices, such as heart rate monitors or fall alarms (El-Bendary et al., 2013). Seniors also feel struggle with telehealth products to book appointments with physicians (Graham, 2020). Moreover, some older people indicated that communication products, such as Zoom, family chats on FaceTime, and WhatsApp messaging, are difficult to use due to vision or hearing issues (Graham, 2020). Therefore, it is important to continually explore new methods to develop innovative and ageing-friendly products and services to support older people in achieving the healthy ageing goal.

In the following sections, the authors present three case studies that illustrate the use of inclusive design to promote healthy ageing for older people through the lenses of inclusive smart grocery shopping, smart textiles, and home space design.

4.3   CAST STUDY

4.3.1   INCLUSIVE SMART RETAIL SERVICE DESIGN FOR OLDER PEOPLE

4.3.1.1   Research Background

One in five (19%) people aged 80–84 have difficulty shopping for groceries, and this rises to 60% for those aged over 90 (Age UK, 2021). In addition to contributing to the basic need to access nutritious foods, grocery shopping also serves as a vital aspect of social interaction for older adults. Several researchers have recognised the importance of elderly consumers (grey pound) to retailers as a result of the substantial global ageing trend and focused their research on improving ageing people's shopping experiences in a variety of ways, including the design of stores, transportation services, and social community services. Despite the notable results of the existing research, very few studies have examined in depth how smart retail technologies can support older customers in having a more enjoyable grocery shopping experience as well as enhancing their independence.

A smart retail system integrates multiple intelligent retail technologies in order to revolutionise the customer experience using big data, AI, and other technologies. Previous studies have shown that smart retail reduces operating costs, improves profitability, and facilitates a seamless, integrated customer experience. AI has been identified as the most promising information technology in the field of smart retail since it can be applied both on the backend (from the perspective of the retail business) and on the frontend (from the perspective of the customers) of the smart retail process. Using deep learning algorithms, AI programs enable retailers to provide customised offers based on their customers' preferences and needs, thus providing a human-like experience without involving human interaction (Lu et al., 2019). The Intelligent Retail Lab (IRL) at Walmart, for example, is testing AI and analytics to determine whether the store can restock an item quickly after a customer picks up the last item. Increasingly, AI is used in customer service environments as a primary source of innovation. Such interaction takes place on a virtual platform such as online shopping or via face-to-face interactions for in-store shopping. From a frontend perspective, AI also adds value to retailers by influencing customer engagement and purchasing decisions (including health-based decision-making) and can be varyingly implemented in-store and out-of-store including at home (Välkkynen et al., 2011). Therefore, this case study presents an exploratory study of Smart Retail Service design to improve ageing customers' supermarket shopping experience through smart retail technologies.

4.3.1.2 Aim and Objectives

This study aims to explore the challenges and difficulties that elderly consumers currently face during their supermarket shopping and in turn to understand how smart retail technology can be applied to improve elderly consumers' supermarket experience in the United Kingdom. The objectives are:

- To investigate the difficulties and challenges that elderly supermarket consumers face in the United Kingdom.
- To study how smart retail technologies can be applied to improve the supermarket shopping experience for older customers.
- To design and develop smart retail service concepts and prototypes.
- To evaluate the smart retail service concepts and prototypes.

4.3.1.3 Methodology

In order to achieve the research objectives, two focus groups were formed with elderly shoppers to learn about their supermarket shopping experiences across multiple user groups based on their experience with smart retail technologies, including online shopping, mobile shopping, and self-checkout in-store. Group 1 participants have some experience with technology, including the use of online services through computers and tablets, but have limited experience with smart retail services, including online shopping and self-checkout. We examined the reasons why people do not use smart retail services in this group. The participants in group 2 have a good understanding of technology and use smart retail services daily. In this group, we focused on the experience of older customers when shopping in supermarkets using current smart retail services. There were six participants in each of the focus groups. Audio–video recordings were made of both focus groups with the consent of the participants for data analysis. Content analysis was chosen as the analytical method for this study because it emphasises natural and empirical content rather than interpretative arguments.

4.3.1.4 Key Findings

Based on the focus group study, key challenges that older people face during grocery shopping can be summarised as (1) difficulties in finding items, (2) issues with store facilities design (such as trolley, shelf, and checkout), and (3) concerns about smart retail services (such as online shopping and self-checkout). Firstly, most participants indicated difficulty finding items in a supermarket. It was associated with issues relating to store layout design, signage, display of products on shelves, packaging design, and customer service. For instance, many of the participants reported feeling frustrated when their familiar items could not be found in the new store layout. Additionally, participants found it difficult and confusing to find products if the packaging had been altered, or if different products in the same category were packaged similarly (for example, flour). Secondly, participants expressed their unmet needs regarding the design of store facilities. For example, some participants indicated that it was difficult to put their shopping baskets or wheelie trolleys in the supermarket trolley. Therefore, they have to leave them at the customer service desk and pick them up upon completion of their shopping. Other participants would like a list holder on the trolley as well as compartments for holding fresh flowers and other items separate from the main shop. There were some concerns that the baskets and trolleys were found to be dirty or littered with receipts from previous customers, and the trolleys outside were left to get wet and/or cold. For shelf design, participants found that it was difficult to reach items at the back of shelves as well as determining whether or not there is any stock available. Regarding the store aisle, a wide or slow lane would be useful if the participant was in a mobility scooter or wheelchair. Finally, many participants indicated their concerns and worries about smart retail services such as online shopping and self-checkout services. Most of those who have never used online shopping expressed concern about online payment security, and they were concerned that their bank account information may be compromised. The participants who used online shopping services expressed similar concerns and said that they only used their credit cards to make online purchases. Aside from information related to online payments, some participants also raised data privacy and protection concerns in general with regard to online-based services. Approximately two-thirds of the participants do not use self-checkouts for a variety of reasons. Some of them were intimidated by the self-checkout technology because they had too much shopping to do, they found it a nuisance, or they were unable to see the screen. Others felt it was important for them to interact with staff and to keep their jobs protected at the same time.

4.3.1.5   Development of a Smart Shopping App Prototype

Based on the findings of the focus groups, a Smart Shopping App prototype was designed and developed. Designed as a virtual assistant, the Smart Shopping App allows older customers to improve their shopping experience through a variety of features, including autoshopping list generation, in-store navigation, easy checkout, call for help, and smart shopping guidance for healthy ageing.

When older customers use the Smart Shopping App in a store, they can log in to the system by tapping their customer loyalty card. Based on the customers' shopping transaction data, the system generates a shopping list based on the items they frequently purchase (Figure 4.1). After that, the customer will be able to edit the shopping list by adding new items or removing those that are already listed.

The Smart Shopping App creates a shopping route map based on older customers' shopping lists and the supermarket store's latest layout and product display so that older customers are able to pick up all the shopping items in an efficient and effective manner. The in-store navigation guide will assist the customer in finding the closest item to his/her shopping list. The App will confirm the scanning of an item by

FIGURE 4.1   Autoshopping list generation.

FIGURE 4.2 In-store navigation.

showing a green tick beside it on the interface (Figure 4.2), and the map will show the route to the next shopping item. Once the customer clicks the 'Go to checkout' button, the App will display a route to the checkout counter. For checkout, staff can scan a QR code from the App to transfer shopping information for payment.

To promote healthy ageing, the Smart Shopping App can assist older customers in receiving customised shopping services that are tailored to meet their specific needs, such as recommending products based on aggregated information regarding a shopper's health, budget, independence, and level of skills (e.g., cooking abilities), cognitive abilities, mobility, and upcoming calendar events in order to improve health outcomes. For instance, the App may recommend cheaper or special-priced coffee products based on the user's budget setting. Additionally, older customers can ask for assistance by clicking the 'I need help' button in the upper right corner of the App during the shopping process. In the following steps, a member of the customer service department will find the customer and provide in-store support (Figure 4.3).

4.3.1.6 Evaluation and Conclusions

The Smart Shopping App prototype has been tested by 11 older customers. The participants were given a pre-designed shopping list as their shopping task for them to complete in the user test study. Using the Smart Shopping App prototype and the pre-designed shopping list, they were instructed to collect all shopping items from shelves and take them to the checkout point in a local store. Depending on the participant, the user tests took between 20 and 40 minutes. Following the user test, they were invited to participate in an interview to provide feedback on the Smart

FIGURE 4.3 Smart shopping guidance and call for staff help functions.

Shopping App prototype. All participants completed the shopping tasks using the Smart Shopping App prototype and provided positive feedback on the App design. In general, participants found the App's workflow to be easy to comprehend, and they felt confident in using it for shopping purposes. There were some participants who indicated that they would be willing to use the App once they became familiar with it. Most participants found the characters on the App to be easy to read and the App's interface to be intuitive and easy to understand. Ten out of eleven participants in the user study indicated that they found the in-store navigation function very helpful during their shopping. The participants were pleased with the smart shopping guidance function. Participants also provided suggestions for improving the App design, including improving the accuracy of the placement of the targeted item on the shelf, designing icons with a larger size, and adjustable colour settings for older customers with visual impairments. The evaluation feedback indicates that the Smart Shopping App is able to assist older consumers with their shopping plan, in-store navigation, calling staff for assistance, easy checkout, and smart shopping guidance, ultimately fulfilling their unmet shopping needs. At the same time, the Smart Shopping App needs further R&D to enhance its interface design and functionalities.

4.3.2   Smart Textile Design for Healthy Ageing

4.3.2.1   Research Background

Smart textiles have been widely used in healthcare and reached maturity in the past decade (Schaar and Ziefle, 2011; Brauner et al., 2017; van Heek et al., 2018). It could access a person's physiological state and body activities through the integration of invisible sensors, actuators, and the development of a Wireless Body Area Network (WBAN) (Libanori et al., 2022; Esfahani, 2021). Communication and sensor technologies have been integrated into garments for monitoring people's health consistently and accurately, such as smart textile shirts, belts, and shoes (Romagnoli et al., 2014; Okss, 2016; Pham and Phuong, 2017). Meanwhile, smart textile jewellery, wristwatches, and fitness trackers are popularly used for medical and wellness purposes (Capalbo et al., 2019).

Smart textile technology has highlighted interventions for physical and mental health. In terms of physical intervention, previous research emphasised how to use smart textile technology to monitor one's activities (Mokhlespour et al., 2019), gait analysis, and falling (Wang et al., 2019; Mokhlespour et al., 2019). Moreover, smart textiles have also applicated successfully in rehabilitation (Lorussi et al., 2013). In terms of mental health, smart textile can help recognise one's emotions by analysing related activities. For example, the smart cushion has been developed as an approach to analysing activities from the user's sitting postures and upper limb gestures and to provide emotional regulation (Gravina and Li, 2019). This development is crucial for older people's physiological and psychological well-being (DeSteno et al., 2013).

Although these miniaturised smart textile systems open potential opportunities to improve older people's quality of life, some wearable devices still have many usability issues. For instance, visibility and privacy issues are presented on some attached devices to garments and bodies. Users may feel they are vulnerable, therefore compromising their privacy (Schaar and Ziefle, 2011). Meanwhile, due to the issues of technology barriers of older people, technology-oriented research has focused on reducing the digital barriers (Wilson et al., 2021), but there is a scarcity of research that investigates older people's real needs for using smart textile and smart healthcare products at home from the user's perspective.

4.3.2.2 Aim and Objectives

Therefore, this study aims to investigate smart healthcare product needs of people aged 65+ who live independently at home, to explore challenges that they face when they use healthcare-related products, identify their unmet needs, and develop inclusive smart textile design insights to address their needs. The main objectives are:

- To explore state-of-the-art studies on older people living alone, smart textiles, smart healthcare products, inclusive design, and service design.
- To discover aged 65+ and living alone users' experience with healthcare products and define the unmet needs.
- To explore and develop inclusive smart textile design insights for improving healthcare products.

4.3.2.3 Methodology

Semi-structured interviews and questionnaires have been used in this research to address the above research objectives from April to July 2021, during the COVID lockdown in the United Kingdom. Participants were recruited from local ageing organisations such as Age UK and MHA. This study involved 12 participants over 60 for interviews and collected 43 valid questionnaires. Research ethics approval was applied for first-hand data collection through the University of Southampton ethics committee (Ethics/ERGO Number: 64221).

Data collected from interviews is intended to understand 60+ aged people's perception of healthy ageing, unmet healthcare-related needs at home, experiences with home-based health and well-being–related products and services, and their attitudes and needs towards smart textiles in healthcare applications, and their attitude towards smart healthcare technologies applications to support and improve older people's health and well-being at home.

Data collected from questionnaires examine the priority of older people's healthcare needs at home, verify findings from interviews, and explore new design insights into smart textiles to promote healthy ageing at home.

4.3.2.4 Key Findings

Four key research findings have been discussed in this research project. One of these issues is the decrease in physical exercise among older people due to COVID-19. Second, hand arthritis affects the daily activities of older individuals. A third finding is that older people have increased their use of technology during COVID. The final finding relates to the current healthcare products used by older people at home in order to identify future development opportunities.

4.3.2.5 Decrease Physical Exercise Issues

The finding shows older people's physical exercise situation during the COVID-19 lockdown period; 81% ($N=43$) of the participants felt that they did not have enough exercise every day, though 98% ($N=43$) of the participants have noticed the importance of doing exercises. This issue has more impact on male participants (31%, $N=13$) than on females (13%, $N=30$). Half of the female participants (50%, $N=30$) reported that they preferred to exercise at home even without COVID due to the convenience of exercising indoors. Male participants pointed the opposite opinion that they preferred outdoor exercise (77%, $N=13$).

Another reason for the decrease in physical exercise at home is the challenge to do home-based exercise for participants who had knee surgery, back pain, mobility issues, or balance issues. Some of them relied on home physio to assist them to do home exercises for rehabilitation after surgery. The participant stated that doing exercises with physiotherapy made her feel more confident and safer because the exercise program was tailored to her specific needs and desires, and she felt well protected during exercise. As a result of the COVID-19 lockdown, she was no longer able to receive physiotherapy at home, affecting her mobility significantly.

In order to ensure that older people have adequate exercise at home in an independent manner, it is worth exploring how smart textiles can be applied for home-based exercise, physiotherapy, and rehabilitation. Furthermore, it is necessary to tailor exercise programs to older individuals based on their gender, health conditions, and physical capabilities.

4.3.2.6 Hand Impacts Daily Activities

Millions of people have arthritis in the United Kingdom (NHS, 2022). The results indicate that 63% ($n=43$) of the participants had arthritis. From them, 82% ($n=27$) of participants had hand arthritis, which impacts their daily activities at home, such as they felt difficulty opening bottles and jars and difficulty pressing small buttons on devices. A participant with hand arthritis reported that although gadgets could provide some support, it was still difficult for her to use some of them due to limitations in her finger flexibility.

Keeping personal hygiene and keeping the home clean are other challenges for older people who suffer from hand arthritis. Some participants with hand arthritis had difficulty using heavy cleaning equipment (such as vacuum cleaners) and ironing. Therefore, it is important to take into consideration the use of easy-to-maintain materials in smart textile products, such as smart clothes, smart cushions, and smart shoes. Furthermore, hand arthritis has also affected the way older people dress. There were some participants who needed garments that could be easily put on and taken off, such as those without zippers at the back, without tightness getting over their heads, and with easily openable buttons. According to the findings, hand arthritic older people require simple, easy-to-use, easy-to-wear, and easy-to-clean smart textile products.

4.3.2.7 Technology Engagement Has Increased

According to the findings of the study, the majority of participants had a positive attitude towards technology in their day-to-day lives. It also indicates that the level of acceptance of technology has increased during COVID-19. For example, one participant highlighted that technology, such as FaceTime or WhatsApp, helped them to maintain a good relationship with their family and friends during the lockdown period as well as online exercise sessions via Zoom meetings or YouTube live sessions, which may motivate them to engage in physical activity.

Moreover, another popular approach for older people to engage with technology is playing games; 49% of the participants ($n=43$) indicated that they played digital games on digital devices such as iPads and tablets to maintain their mental health. The majority of respondents (86%, $n=21$) found it easy to play digital games. They also had a positive attitude towards learning new things and acknowledged the significance of preserving cognitive health through engaging in activities that stimulate their brains. This study also found that current digital games designed for older people are more popular among female players (60%, $n=30$) than male players (23%, $n=13$). This may be due to the fact that most digital games designed for older adults are geared towards female audiences with features such as puzzles, explorations, role playing, social interaction, cooperative play, and flexibility in choosing and making decisions (Marston and Graner-Ray, 2016). Moreover, male participants indicated that they preferred to spend their time watching TV or doing gardening rather than playing games. As a result, gaming-related products for males require further development to meet their preferences and characteristics. While male participants were not particularly engaged with game-related technologies, they demonstrated a willingness to explore other fields of technology in the future. A participant believed that smart textiles would have a tremendous impact on the medical and health services industry. Another participant mentioned that smart textiles can be used to generate health data through their continuous monitoring functions. 'If we had something that was attached to us or even embedded that could monitor certain aspects of blood that would be revolutionary'. However, some participants expressed concern about the use of technology in their daily lives, particularly the fear that technology might override their lives. In the future, if they become too dependent on technology, they might not be able to perform daily activities independently.

Boost their brain activity (83%, $n=21$).

Therefore, when designing and developing smart textile products and services for older people, designers, researchers, and technicians should take older people's features, preferences, and technology acceptance levels into account.

4.3.2.8 Current Healthcare-Related Products Used at Home

Weight scales were found to be the most frequently used health-related product at home, as weight is an important indicator of healthy ageing (Gill et al., 2015). Among the participants, 81% ($N=43$) measure their weight regularly in order to maintain a healthy body weight. Other popular health-related products at home include blood pressure monitoring (63%), water reminders (26%), blood oxygen monitoring (23%), sleep trackers (16%), electric pads to relieve pain (12%), blood glucose monitoring (9%), stand reminders (9%), personal alarms (7%), and circulation boosters (5%). The main concerns with these products were their functionality and comfort. One participant mentioned the accurate problem of blood pressure monitoring as he needed to monitor four or five times and then take the average index. Another participant pointed out the design problems of her personal alarms, such as comfortable wearable materials, easily forgotten to wear, and the emergency button being too sensitive causing the wrong emergency call. Therefore, designing an ageing-friendly interface and user-centred design should be considered in smart textiles-related products or service designs for older people.

4.3.2.9 Conclusion

In recent decades, considerable research and resources have been devoted to the development of smart textiles that monitor, engage, entertain, and ultimately enhance safety and quality of life. In the ageing context, smart textiles can be used in wearable devices (shoe insoles and wrist braces) to track older people's daily activity data and monitor their health conditions, such as weight, heartbeat, and blood pressure. However, few of them explored the smart healthcare products and smart textiles needs of older people in the home environment from a user perspective. Therefore, though the research found that older people's attitudes towards technology have improved during COVID-19, the usage of smart textile products is still problematic. Due to the differences between health conditions and personal requirements, smart textiles and healthcare-related products need to provide personalised services for individuals. Moreover, designing ageing-friendly applications to present health data to older people needs to be considered. Therefore, it is necessary to conduct multidisciplinary research and collaborate with researchers, engineers, designers, and relevant stakeholders to understand older people's real needs, challenges, and motivations while designing smart healthcare products and using smart textiles.

4.3.3 Inclusive Home Design for Healthy Ageing

4.3.3.1 Research Background

Most older people wish to remain at home as long as possible (Severinsen et al., 2015). With age increasing, the living environment is not always fit for older people's needs and expectations. The functions of their sight, hand, mobility, balance, and memory decrease as they age (Farage et al., 2012). Their bodies become increasingly less mobile and less capable of adjusting to their reduced mobility (Metz, 2000; Arthur et al., 2009). These changes can affect older people's living ability in a physical environment (Renaut et al., 2014; Pinto et al., 2000; Schmall, 1991), which leads to difficulties doing daily activities or everyday household tasks at home. In order to support older people, researchers have developed a variety of strategies and solutions to improve the home environment, including inclusive kitchens, bedrooms, and bathrooms (Maguire et al., 2014; Booranrom et al., 2014; Chuah et al., 2016), assistive lighting (Fisk and Raynham, 2013), and monitoring assisted fall-prevention services (Tchalla et al., 2012). Space-related inclusive design has been researched from the perspective of floor surface design and carpet design to protect older people from falls (Pynoos et al., 1989; Clemson et al., 1997). Housing planners, commissioners, and designers have considered the special needs of older people with physical and mental health issues and focused on inclusive design for improving the home environment for an ageing society (CABE, 2009; Williams, 1990). Researchers have highlighted that accessible space is important for older people's safety. The need for accessible space has been discussed from the aspects of a wide doorway, a clear floor, and an accessible furniture arrangement (Demirkan and Olguntürk, 2013). Structural changes or adaptations in the environment also take into consideration inclusive space design (Mohammad et al., 2014), which includes the installation of handrails to support older people when standing or walking and the adaptation of wider living room entrance doors for wheelchair users. Additionally, research also indicates that inclusive space can affect indoor atmospheres, such as illumination, air quality, and temperature (Harrington and Harington; 2000; Rowles et al., 2003; Andersson, 2011; Gitlin et al., 2001; Farage et al., 2012).

Although the existing research is notable, there is a paucity of research exploring living room design for older people. The living room has been identified as one of the most frequently used spaces for older people, which conduct different activities, such as daily activities, leisure activities (Pirker and Bernhaupt, 2011; Rechavi, 2009), and socialisation activities (Wiles et al., 2011). Different activities require a variety of furniture arrangements to suit older people's specific needs (Saruwono et al., 2012). Thus, it is necessary to explore older peoples' interactions with spaces, furniture, and people in the living room at home so as to identify risks and challenges that older people face and develop solutions.

4.3.3.2   Aim and Objectives

With the intention of improving elderly living room experience, the aim of this research is to investigate the experiences of older people in the United Kingdom with their living room at home so as to identify risks and challenges they face in their day-to-day life and develop design insights for improving living room space design, furniture and furniture arrangement, and atmosphere design so as to improve their living room experience. In order to achieve the research aim, three objectives are considered:

- Investigate older people's living experience with their living room at home in the United Kingdom.
- Identify the challenges and needs that older people face in their living room at home under different scenarios and analyse the reasons behind these challenges.
- Develop design insights and recommendations for improving living room environment design for older people in the United Kingdom.

4.3.3.3   Methodology

This research used an ethnographic approach, which includes interviews, video observation, and culture probe research methods, to establish an in-depth understanding of the challenges and needs that older people face in the living room and the reasons behind those challenges. Data was collected between Jul 2017 and Dec 2017 from 12 households aged 65+ from southwest and southeast England. Five households lived in flats, four in bungalows, and three in houses. Collected materials from the research include audio data (from interviews), video data (from observation), and text data (from culture probe). All data were transcribed into text data and then analysed via a content analysis method.

4.3.3.4 Key Findings

The key results from this study can be divided into five aspects of the living room environment design, which are (1) size and structure, (2) floor and wall, (3) door and window, (4) sockets and switches, and (5) furniture, such as sitting facilities and tables.

   Size and structure: The size of the living room limited the way older people selected furniture, and the limited-sized living room made it difficult to select furniture to entertain visitors. Due to the size of the space, some participants felt limited in their ability to entertain friends in their living room. How to maximise the use of space with furniture to allow for socialisation should thus be a key consideration when designing older people's living rooms. The size of the living room also limited participants' use of adaptation products, such as wheelchairs and walking support frames. One participant had restructured their living room and changed to a wider living room doorway to allow for easier access with wheelchairs. However, for small living spaces, it still poses a problem. This led some participants to worry that the living room size could limit their accessibility to adaptation products in the future. Moreover, the living room structure limited how older people positioned their furniture. Consequently, some furniture was positioned in an inappropriate place to satisfy older people's accessibility needs. The irregular shape (such as the window bay) and the narrow-sized living room might cause poor access for elderly people to use their furniture.
   Floor and wall: The findings showed that the floor design was directly relevant to the safety issues of the participants, particularly how older people (1) walked around in the living room, (2) moved furniture in the living room, (3) cleaned the living room, and (4) negotiated uneven floors. A few participants mentioned that their carpets were not flat and had been a trip hazard (such as rippling or buckling areas). As an alternative, they put rugs to cover the wrinkled points. However, the rugs were not stable on the top of the carpet even though they had a non-slip mat liner. Moreover, five participants mentioned that a carpeted floor made it easier to move their furniture (such as a settee, coffee table, or side table). Several participants pointed out that due to their curled corners, rugs made it difficult to move the furniture. Additionally, uneven and bumpy carpets and rugs might cause potential risks when older people clean and vacuum the floor of the living room. Wall-related key findings are the colour usage of the wall. The wall colour had an impact on how the elderly felt about their living room in terms of brightness and size. In addition, the items on the wall also influenced the perception of the size of the living room. For example, for a small-sized

living room, putting a mirror on the wall could make the space feel larger. However, if too many decorative items were on the wall, it could make the space feel crowded and messy.

Door and window: The issues related to the living room door could be divided into two aspects, door access and door-opening direction issues. According to our findings, individuals who use walking frames, walking aids, and wheelchairs have a reduced ability to negotiate living room doors due to mobility issues. Their door was designed to be of a normal width but did not allow them to easily pass through. Furthermore, poor access may be caused by the handle design of the door. There was no difficulty opening the door with the knob, according to participants. The knob door handle users found it less user-friendly. One participant realised the issue with her living room door, which blocked her way into the living room. Moreover, if she opened the door, as the door was not against the wall, it made her living room even smaller. During the middle of the user study, she changed the swing direction of her door and felt very satisfied with the revised opening direction. Access issues for windows in this study can be divided into two aspects. The first is the window design itself, which includes (1) the opening direction of the window and (2) the position, height, and design style of the window handle. The second aspect is the furniture planning around the window that influenced older people's access.

Sockets and switches: Switches and sockets are important for older people because they are in continual use. During the user study, the author found issues related to (1) socket position; (2) hazards of adaptors (lack of sockets linked to hazards with adapters), and (3) colour usage and design style of switches. Some participants pointed out that their sockets were too low to access. Some participants pointed out that they wanted their sockets positioned at waist height on the wall for easier access. For a short-term solution, a few participants used adaptors to solve this problem. Another problem related to the position of the sockets and switches was that they were often positioned behind the furniture, so they were hard to access. Due to the limited range of motion of the shoulder joint, two of the participants had reduced ability to reach distant objects and objects on the floor. Although some participants used adapters to solve this problem, this caused other new issues: (1) The adaptors did not match the existing style of the living room. (2) The wires of the adaptors caused tripping issues. Furthermore, one participant indicated that he could not clearly see the switch on the wall with his reduced eyesight, especially in a dim environment. This is due to the low colour contrast between the wall and the switches (they were both white, without edges). Moreover, one participant indicated that the large rocker-type light switches were easier to control. He had problems wrapping his hand around objects, which affected his ability to turn and manipulate sockets and switches.

Sitting facilities and tables: The author has observed and discussed the challenges and demands of sitting facilities and tables in the living room. In this case study, the sitting facilities in the living room include a sofa, chair, and settee. Based on the observation and interviews, most of the participants have their favourite sitting areas in their living rooms. Those areas were designed and created by themselves and often not shared with anyone else, even their spouses. As older people spend more time in the living room every day than younger groups, the sitting facilities are one of the most important pieces of furniture. Participants mentioned that the chair or sofa must be comfortable and have proper support for their arms and heads. Based on the research findings, five key requirements for sitting facilities have been identified. Older people need (1) a suitable size to sit, (2) a good firmness and highness to sit, (3) a suitable height to sit and have an armrest to let them easily get up from the chair or sofa, (4) a multifunctional seating area to meet different requirements (such as massage, sleep, or easy to move), and (5) good-quality materials to maintain the chair or sofa. Table-related issues focused on the table furniture that is used by older people themselves, such as a coffee table, a side table, a chair table, or a dinner table. Based on the observations and interviews, all the participants have more than one type of table in their living room and combine them to use in different circumstances. Based on the research findings, three key requirements for table furniture have been identified: (1) the need for a suitably-sized table to fit the available space, (2) the need for a suitable height table to reach, and (3) the need for a safe table leg and surface.

4.3.3.5   Insights for Inclusive Living Space Design

Based on the key findings, the authors have developed several design insights for interior designers, architects, and service providers to improve living room space design for older people.

Designers need to consider how to let older people use a wheelchair or walking cane easily and flexibly in a small- or narrow-sized living room. There should be a wider pathway between each piece of furniture to make sure they can place their wheelchair in front of or beside the furniture. The space should ensure that the wheelchair can turn around without bumping. Meanwhile, if the structure of the living room could not be changed, consider designing smaller and more flexible walking support products.

For a smaller-sized living room, folded or multifunctional furniture, such as a folded dining table, can be used for entertaining visitors. This furniture should be easy to move and light enough to carry from the other room to the living room. Meanwhile, it needs to be easy to store. In addition, small-size furniture should be used for a narrow-width living room to make sure older people have enough empty space to walk comfortably between the furniture.

Consider designing a flat floor for older people. Rearrange furniture to create clear and wide floor space and remove unnecessary mats and rugs to prevent tripping and slipping accidents in the living room. Especially for older people who use mobility walking aid products, such as a walker or cane, uneven and unflat floors might cause hazards. If older people want to use the mats or rugs for decoration reasons, they should stick double-sided tape onto the mats or rugs to make sure they don't move.

Use a warm colour on the wall to promote a sense of security and harmony in the living room, such as soft yellow and soft orange. For smaller-sized living rooms, a mirror can be fitted to the wall to make the space feel larger.

Make sure that the width of the living room door is wide enough to walk through with a wheelchair, a walker, or a cane (minimum 80 cm). Extend the door frame if necessary. For those small-sized living rooms that cannot extend their door width, the designer should consider designing a smaller-sized wheelchair that can move easily inside.

The opening direction of the door should lay flush against the wall to ensure that there is a wider view from the hallway to the living room. Consider removing the door if necessary to make a wider doorway. Meanwhile, the layout should consider the ventilation and energy problem. Removing the door will have better ventilation but will lose warm energy during winter. Alternately, consider installing a sliding living room door.

Lever door handles are much easier to open than round doorknobs, especially for older people who have arthritis or reduced strength in their hands. Lever handles are also easier to manage if older people are carrying something, as they can use their elbows to open the door.

Consider installing blinds on windows or French doors in the living rooms. The blinds can avoid the strong sunshine that may damage furniture and the carpet colour. The installed blinds should not be too heavy and thick and should be easy to open and use. If an older person's window faces a public footpath, the blind should also provide privacy.

Avoid fitting top-hung windows that open from the bottom out, as they might open too far for older people to reach the handle of the window to close. Meanwhile, ensure that the French door is easy to slide open, as older people's hand muscles are not strong enough to slide heavy French doors.

Place the handles for windows at a suitable height to facilitate their easy use (recommended height is 114–125 cm from the door). The handle should be a lever design, to make sure older people can easily grasp and pinch.

Ensure that the number of sockets is enough for older people to use in the living room, and that they are placed in an easily accessible location that avoids bending the body to reach them. Dwelling access requirements from England building regulations (GovUK, 2014) suggest placing the sockets between 45 and 1,200 mm from the floor. However, for older people, it is better to place the sockets between 600 and 1,200 mm, as they might feel difficulty bending their bodies down. Meanwhile, avoid placing sockets behind furniture as this is hard to access. If using adaptors, avoid loose wires that might cause tripping issues. If older people use an adaptor, make sure the wires are covered with tape to stick securely to the floor.

Ensure that the colour of the switches on the wall has a high colour contrast and the switches have a night light function that can be found easily in the evening. As older people's vision reduces, it is necessary to use high contrasting colours and night lights to enhance safety and accessibility among older people to use switches and sockets in the living room.

When designing or selecting a sofa or armchair for older people, ensure that the chair/sofa is of suitable size to fit their body size, and that the chair/sofa has good firmness to sit and supports their sitting posture, including when eating on the sofa. Meanwhile, the height of the sofa/chair and the armrest of the sofa/chair are important to allow older people to get up from the sofa/chair safely.

A multifunctional sofa/chair is necessary for older people. A useful feature is a foot-lift and raising-up function. Ensure that the foot lift of the chair is easy to pull out and back to avoid using a footstool as it might cause tripping issues, and that the chair has a raising-up function to let older people get up from the chair easily.

Ensure that dining chairs are designed with arms, as older people have reduced strength of leg muscles and they need to use their arms to support their body weight; the table legs and arms are steady and solid; and the table surface is safe (no glass surface).

In addition, smart home devices and assisted care facilities are necessary to support older people's daily activities at home, which include:

- Telecare systems (to communicate with doctors).
- Robotic vacuum cleaners (to support home cleaning).
- Medical alert bracelets (to track health data and prevent accidents).
- Voice assistants (to use voice control other smart facilities).
- Smart pillbox (to help people take the right medicine at the right time).
- Automated lighting and smart bulbs (to open and close light by phone or by voice without bending body down to the floor to reach some lamp switches).
- Automatic home climate control (to control the home environment by heating or cooling the home without bending down).
- Smart door locks (to improve safety and security at home).

4.3.3.6 Conclusion

This study focuses on older people's living room design in the United Kingdom. It is important to explore relationships between space, products, and older people in the living room environment in order to gain a systematic understanding of how older people use their living rooms. For example, the lack of space in an older person's living room may make it impossible for them to comfortably use a well-designed ergometric table. The results of this study develop coherent living room design insights that will (1) help interior designers, architects, and service providers to enhance their thinking of design and develop details in the current design guidelines for older people's living room design, and (2) provide inclusive design insights that are interlinked with other formats of older people's living environments.

4.4 SUMMARY

In 2022, there were almost 11 million people aged 65+, which represent 19% of the working population (ONS, 2022). Because of the substantial global demographic shift, numerous studies have been conducted to improve ageing people's quality of life from multiple perspectives such as public service, transportation services, health and social care, product and service design, and the pension system (Stewart, et al., 2014; Iparraguirre, 2014; Li et al., 2012; Pattison and Stedmon, 2006). Among the different types of research on ageing, healthy ageing has attracted more and more attention in the research field. In 2015, healthy ageing was promoted by the World Health Organization (WHO) and aimed to support older people to be able to develop and maintain functional ability and enable well-being in their later life (World Health Organization, 2015). In 2018, as part of the UK's Industrial Strategy, £300 million was announced for a landmark ageing society grand challenge that aims to promote innovative products, services, and business models that can support the ageing population.

This chapter discusses how inclusive design has contributed to promoting healthy ageing, especially in a rapidly transforming digital world. Related theories of inclusive design, older people and their features, digital transformation, digital divide, and smart design for healthy ageing have been reviewed and discussed. Three case studies demonstrated how inclusive design can support older people from retail design, healthcare design, and home design perspectives, which contributed to two of the UKRI-identified healthy ageing challenges 'design for ageing-friendly homes' and 'managing common complaints from ageing' (Figure 4.4). In the future, the authors will extend their research to explore how inclusive design can be applied to promote healthy ageing from the other aspects of the healthy ageing challenge framework.

Supporting social connections
Increasing the quantity and quality of social connectivity means better mental and physical health.

Design for age-friendly homes
Homes designed and adapted to make everyday life work best for older people keeps us living independently for longer.

Creating healthy, active places
Easy access to outdoor places in any weather can help keep us active.

Managing common complaints of ageing
Simple changes and clever innovations can help us manage common problems associated with ageing.

Sustaining physical activity
Regular exercise keeps many health conditions at bay as we get older.

Living well with cognitive impairment
Innovations and tailored support can improve quality of life for people with cognitive impairment and their carers, extending independent living.

Maintaining health at work
Helping people to keep working, by providing adaptations and workplace support, increases financial wellbeing and independence.

FIGURE 4.4 Healthy ageing challenges framework (UKRI, 2022).

REFERENCES

Adams, R. J., Piantadosi, C., Ettridge, K., Miller, C., Wilson, C., Tucker, G., & Hill, C. L. (2013). Functional health literacy mediates the relationship between socio-economic status, perceptions and lifestyle behaviors related to cancer risk in an Australian population. *Patient Education and Counseling, 91*(2), 206–212. https://doi.org/10.1016/j. pec.2012.12.001

Andersson, J. E. (2011). Architecture for the silver generation: Exploring the meaning of appropriate space for ageing in a Swedish municipality. *Health & Place, 17*(2), 572–587. https://doi.org/10.1016/j.healthplace.2010.12.015

Arthur, W., Glaze, R. M., Villado, A. J., & Taylor, J. E. (2009). Unproctored internet-based tests of cognitive ability and personality: Magnitude of cheating and response distortion. *Industrial and Organizational Psychology, 2*(1), 39–45. https://doi. org/10.1111/j.1754-9434.2008.01105.x

Blok, M., Van Ingen, E., De Boer, A. H., & Slootman, M. (2020). The use of information and communication technologies by older people with cognitive impairments: From barriers to benefits. *Computers in Human Behavior, 104*, 106173. https://doi.org/10.1016/j. chb.2019.106173

Booranrom, Y., Watanapa, B., & Mongkolnam, P. (2014). Smart bedroom for elderly using Kinect. *2014 International Computer Science and Engineering Conference (ICSEC)*, Khon Kaen, Thailand. https://doi.org/10.1109/icsec.2014.6978235

Brauner, P., Van Heek, J., & Ziefle, M. (2017). Age, gender, and technology attitude as factors for acceptance of smart interactive textiles in home environments - towards a smart textile technology acceptance model. *Proceedings of the 3rd International Conference on Information and Communication Technologies for Ageing Well and E-Health*, Porto, Portugal. https://doi.org/10.5220/0006255600130024

Brawley, E. C. (2008). *Design Innovations for Ageing and Alzheimer's: Creating Caring Environments*. Hoboken, NJ: John Wiley & Sons.

Buyl, R., Beogo, I., Fobelets, M., Deletroz, C., Van Landuyt, P., Dequanter, S., & Gagnon, M. (2020). E-health interventions for healthy ageing: A systematic review. *Systematic Reviews, 9*(1), 128. https://doi.org/10.1186/s13643-020-01385-8

CABE. (2009). *Home for Our Old Age: Independent Living by Design (Rep.)*. Retrieved November 20, 2022, from Commission for Architecture and the Built Environment website: https://www.housinglin.org.uk/_assets/Resources/Housing/Support_materials/ Reports/Homes-for-our-old-age.pdf

Capalbo, I., Penhaker, M., Peter, L., & Proto, A. (2019). Consumer perceptions on smart wearable devices for medical and wellness purposes. *2019 IEEE Technology & Engineering Management Conference (TEMSCON)*, Atlanta, GA, USA. https://doi.org/10.1109/ temscon.2019.8813685

Castells, M. (2002). *The Internet Galaxy: Reflections on the Internet, Business, and Society*. Oxford: Oxford University Press.

Center for Ageing Better. (2022). *Summary: The State of Ageing 2022*. Retrieved November 20, 2022, from https://ageing-better.org.uk/summary-state-ageing-2022

Chuah, Y. D., Lee, J. V., Ganasan, D., Chong, Y. S., Lum, W. Q., Nor, N. M., & Soong, W. Y. (2016). Fall detection of elderly people in bathroom: A complement method of wearable device. *International Journal of Applied Engineering Research, 11*(6), 4184–4186.

Clemson, L., Roland, M., & Cumming, R. G. (1997). Types of hazards in the homes of elderly people. *The Occupational Therapy Journal of Research, 17*(3), 200–213. https://doi. org/10.1177/153944929701700304

Czaja, S. J., Boot, W. R., Charness, N., & Rogers, W. A. (2019). *Designing for Older Adults: Principles and Creative Human Factors Approaches*. Boca Raton, FL: CRC Press.

Demirkan, H. & Olguntürk, N. (2013). A priority-based 'design for all' approach to guide home designers for independent living. *Architectural Science Review*, *57*(2), 90–104. https://doi.org/10.1080/00038628.2013.832141

DeSteno, D., Gross, J. J., & Kubzansky, L. (2013). Affective science and health: The importance of emotion and emotion regulation. *Health Psychology*, *32*(5), 474–486. https://doi.org/10.1037/a0030259

Diaconu, A. I. (2019). Increasing economic competitiveness through the contribution of digitalization. *Logos Universality Mentality Education Novelty: Economics & Administrative Sciences*, *4*(1), 33–42. https://doi.org/10.18662/lumeneas/11

El-Bendary, N., Tan, Q., Pivot, F. C., & Lam, A. (2013). Fall detection and prevention for the elderly: A review of trends and challenges. *International Journal on Smart Sensing and Intelligent Systems*, *6*(3), 1230–1266. https://doi.org/10.21307/ijssis-2017-588

Ermolina, A. & Tiberius, V. (2021). Voice-controlled intelligent personal assistants in health care: International Delphi Study. *Journal of Medical Internet Research*, *23*(4), e25312. https://doi.org/10.2196/25312

Esfahani, I. M. (2021). Smart textiles in healthcare: A summary of history, types, applications, challenges, and future trends. In *Nanosensors and Nanodevices for Smart Multifunctional Textiles* (pp. 93–107). Netherlands: Elsevier Publishing.

Farage, M. A., Miller, K. W., Ajayi, F., & Hutchins, D. (2012). Design principles to accommodate older adults. *Global Journal of Health Science*, *4*(2), 2–25. https://doi.org/10.5539/gjhs.v4n2p2

Fisk, M. J. & Raynham, P. (2013). Assistive lighting for people with sight loss. *Disability and Rehabilitation: Assistive Technology*, *9*(2), 128–135. https://doi.org/10.3109/17483107.2013.781235

Fors, S., Modin, B., Koupil, I., & Vågerö, D. (2012). Socioeconomic inequalities in circulatory and all-cause mortality after retirement: The impact of mid-life income and old-age pension. Evidence from the Uppsala Birth Cohort Study. *Journal of Epidemiology and Community Health*, *66*(7), e16. https://doi.org/10.1136/jech.2010.131177

Friemel, T. N. (2014). The digital divide has grown old: Determinants of a digital divide among seniors. *New Media & Society*, *18*(2), 313–331. https://doi.org/10.1177/1461444814538648

Gill, L. E., Bartels, S. J., & Batsis, J. A. (2015). Weight management in older adults. *Current Obesity Reports*, *4*(3), 379–388. https://doi.org/10.1007/s13679-015-0161-z

Gitlin, L. N., Corcoran, M., Winter, L., Boyce, A., & Hauck, W. W. (2001). A randomized, controlled trial of a home environmental intervention. *The Gerontologist*, *41*(1), 4–14. https://doi.org/10.1093/geront/41.1.4

GOV. UK. (2014). *Approved Document M: Part M Access to and Use of Buildings - Volume 1 Dwellings*. Retrieved November 20, 2022, from GOV.UK website: https://assets.publishing.service.gov.uk/government/uploads/system/uploads/attachment_data/file/354091/02__140731__HSR_Supporting_Doc1__Access.pdf

Graham, J. (2020, July 23). *Seniors Who Struggle with Technology Face Telehealth Challenges and Social Isolation*. Retrieved November 20, 2022, from https://edition.cnn.com/2020/07/23/health/seniors-technology-telehealth-wellness-partner/index.html

Gravina, R. & Li, Q. (2019). Emotion-relevant activity recognition based on smart cushion using multi-sensor fusion. *Information Fusion*, *48*, 1–10. https://doi.org/10.1016/j.inffus.2018.08.001

Hamblin, K. A. (2022). Technology in care systems: Displacing, reshaping, reinstating or degrading roles? *New Technology, Work and Employment*, *37*(1), 41–58. https://doi.org/10.1111/ntwe.12229

Hao, F. & Wang, S. (2018). Construction of wechat public patient service platform in cancer hospital. *Proceedings of the 8th International Conference on Management and Computer Science (ICMCS 2018)*, Shenyang, China. https://doi.org/10.2991/icmcs-18.2018.41

Harrington, T. L. & Harrington, M. K. (2000). *Geotechnology: Why and How.* Netherlands: Shaker Maastricht

Harris, L. M. (Ed.). (2013). *Health and the New Media: Technologies Transforming Personal and Public Health (Lea's communication series).* London: Routledge.

Inclusive Design Research Centre. (2022). Retrieved November 20, 2022, from https://idrc. ocadu.ca/

Iparraguirre, C. (2014). Hacia una definición del español neutro. *Síntesis, 5,* 232-252.

Kalyani, R. R., Corriere, M., & Ferrucci, L. (2014). Age-related and disease-related muscle loss: The effect of diabetes, obesity, and other diseases. *The Lancet Diabetes & Endocrinology, 2*(10), 819–829. https://doi.org/10.1016/s2213-8587(14)70034-8

Kaur, P., Sharma, M., & Mittal, M. (2018). Big data and machine learning based secure healthcare framework. *Procedia Computer Science, 132,* 1049–1059. https://doi.org/10.1016/j. procs.2018.05.020

Knowles, B. & Hanson, V. L. (2018). The wisdom of older technology (non) users. *Communications of the ACM, 61*(3), 72–77. https://doi.org/10.1145/3179995

Li, Y., Wu, Q., Xu, L., Legge, D., Hao, Y., Gao, L., & Wan, G. (2012). Factors affecting catastrophic health expenditure and impoverishment from medical expenses in China: Policy implications of universal health insurance. *Bulletin of the World Health Organization, 90*(9), 664–671. https://doi.org/10.2471/blt.12.102178

Li, Z., Tang, J., & Mei, T. (2019). Deep collaborative embedding for social image understanding. *IEEE Transactions on Pattern Analysis and Machine Intelligence, 41*(9), 2070–2083. https://doi.org/10.1109/tpami.2018.2852750

Libanori, A., Chen, G., Zhao, X., Zhou, Y., & Chen, J. (2022). Smart textiles for personalized healthcare. *Nature Electronics, 5*(3), 142–156. https://doi.org/10.1038/s41928-022-00723-z

Lifshitz-Assaf, H. (2017). Dismantling knowledge boundaries at NASA: The critical role of professional identity in open innovation. *Administrative Science Quarterly, 63*(4), 746–782. https://doi.org/10.1177/0001839217747876

Livingstone, S., Van Couvering, E., & Thumim, N. (2005). *Adult Media Literacy a Review of the Research Literature on Behalf of Ofcom.* Retrieved November 20, 2022, from https://www. academia.edu/6346518/Adult_Media_Literacy_A_review_of_the_research_literature_ on_behalf_of_Ofcom

Lorussi, F., Galatolo, S., Bartalesi, R., & De Rossi, D. (2013). Modeling and characterization of extensible wearable textile-based electrogoniometers. *IEEE Sensors Journal, 13*(1), 217–228. https://doi.org/10.1109/jsen.2012.2211099

Lu, T., Fu, C., Ma, M., Fang, C., & Turner, A. (2016). Healthcare applications of smart watches. *Applied Clinical Informatics, 7*(3), 850–869. https://doi.org/10.4338/aci-2016-03-r-0042

Maguire, M., Peace, S., Nicolle, C., Marshall, R., Sims, R., Percival, J., & Lawton, C. (2014). Kitchen living in later life: Exploring ergonomic problems, coping strategies and design solutions. *International Journal of Design, 8*(1), 73–91.

Manthorpe, J. & Samsi, K. (2016). Person-centered dementia care: Current perspectives. *Clinical Interventions in Ageing, 11,* 1733–1740. https://doi.org/10.2147/cia.s104618

Marston, H. & Graner-Ray, S. (2016). Older women on the game: Understanding Digital Game Perspectives from an ageing cohort. *Ageing and Technology, 2016,* 67–92. https://doi. org/10.1515/9783839429570-004

Metz, D. (2000). Mobility of older people and their quality of life. *Transport Policy, 7*(2), 149–152. https://doi.org/10.1016/s0967-070x(00)00004-4

Milligan, C., Roberts, C., & Mort, M. (2011). Telecare and older people: Who cares where? *Social Science & Medicine, 72*(3), 347–354. https://doi.org/10.1016/j.socscimed.2010.08.014

Milligan, M. A., Hoyt, D. L., Gold, A. K., Hiserodt, M., & Otto, M. W. (2022). Covid-19 vaccine acceptance: Influential roles of political party and religiosity. *Psychology, Health & Medicine, 27*(9), 1907–1917. https://doi.org/10.1080/13548506.2021.1969026

Mohammad, M. P., Ahmad, A. S., Mursib, G., Roshan, M., & Torabi, M. (2014). Interior layout design parameters affecting user comfort in EE buildings. *Global Science Publication*, *16*(3), 1–9.

Mokhlespour Esfahani, M. I. & Nussbaum, M. A. (2019). Classifying diverse physical activities using "smart garments". *Sensors*, *19*(14), 3133. https://doi.org/10.3390/s19143133

Morris, A. & Brading, H. (2007). E-literacy and the grey digital divide: A review with recommendations. *Journal of Information Literacy*, *1*(3), 13. https://doi.org/10.11645/1.3.14

Murero, M. S. (2019). *The Role of Domestic Politics in Influencing Foreign Policy Formulation: A Case of Kenya's 'Look East' Economic Diplomacy 2002–2016* (Unpublished doctoral dissertation). United States International University-Africa. Retrieved November 22, 2022, from https://erepo.usiu.ac.ke/handle/11732/4984

Musik, C. & Bogner, A. (2019). Book title: Digitalization & society. *Österreichische Zeitschrift Für Soziologie*, *44*(S1), 1–14. https://doi.org/10.1007/s11614-019-00344-5

Nanda, S., & Berruti, F. (2020). Municipal solid waste management and landfilling technologies: A Review. *Environmental Chemistry Letters*, *19*(2), 1433–1456. https://doi.org/10.1007/s10311-020-01100-y

National Research Council. (2011). *The Home Environment. In Health Care Comes Home: The Human Factors*. Chapter 6. Retrieved November 22, 2022, from https://www.nap.edu/read/13149/chapter/8

NHS. (2022). *Overview-Arthritis*. Retrieved November 22, 2022, from https://www.nhs.uk/conditions/arthritis/

O'Brien, K., Liggett, A., Ramirez-Zohfeld, V., Sunkara, P., & Lindquist, L. A. (2019). Voice-controlled intelligent personal assistants to support ageing in place. *Journal of the American Geriatrics Society*, *68*(1), 176–179. https://doi.org/10.1111/jgs.16217

OECD. (2018). *Elderly Population*. Retrieved November 22, 2022, from https://data.oecd.org/pop/elderly-population.htm

Okss, A., Katashev, A., Mantyla, J., & Coffeng, R. (2016). Smart textile garment for breathing volume monitoring. *Biomedical Engineering*, *20*(1), 167–170.

ONS. (2021, January 14). *Overview of the UK Population: January 2021*. Retrieved November 22, 2022, from https://www.ons.gov.uk/peoplepopulationandcommunity/populationandmigration/populationestimates/articles/overviewoftheukpopulation/january2021

ONS. (2022, January 12). *National Population Projections: 2020-based Interim*. Retrieved November 22, 2022, from https://www.ons.gov.uk/peoplepopulationandcommunity/populationandmigration/populationprojections/bulletins/nationalpopulationprojections/2020basedinterim#changing-age-structure

Orellano-Colón, E. M., Mann, W. C., Rivero, M., Torres, M., Jutai, J., Santiago, A., & Varas, N. (2015). Hispanic older adult's perceptions of personal, contextual and technology-related barriers for using assistive technology devices. *Journal of Racial and Ethnic Health Disparities*, *3*(4), 676–686. https://doi.org/10.1007/s40615-015-0186-8

Pan, S. & Jordan-Marsh, M. (2010). Internet use intention and adoption among Chinese older adults: From the expanded technology acceptance model perspective. *Computers in Human Behavior*, *26*(5), 1111–1119. https://doi.org/10.1016/j.chb.2010.03.015

Pattison, M. & Stedmon, A. W. (2006). Inclusive design and human factors: Designing mobile phones for older users. *Psychology Journal*, *4*(3), 267–284.

Pham, C., Diep, N. N., & Phuong, T. M. (2017). E-shoes: Smart Shoes for unobtrusive human activity recognition. *2017 9th International Conference on Knowledge and Systems Engineering (KSE)*, Hue, Vietnam. https://doi.org/10.1109/kse.2017.8119470

Phillips, D. R., Siu, O., Yeh, A. G., & Cheng, K. H. (2004). Ageing and the urban environment. In *Ageing and the Urban* (1st ed., pp. 163–179). London: Routledge.

Pinto, M. R., De Medici, S., Van Sant, C., Bianchi, A., Zlotnicki, A., & Napoli, C. (2000). Technical note: Ergonomics, geotechnology, and design for the home-environment. *Applied Ergonomics*, *31*(3), 317–322. https://doi.org/10.1016/s0003-6870(99)00058-7

Pirker, M. M. & Bernhaupt, R. (2011). Measuring user experience in the Living Room. *Proceddings of the 9th International Interactive Conference on Interactive Television - EuroITV '11*, Lisbon, Portugal. https://doi.org/10.1145/2000119.2000133

Pynoos, J., Cohen, E., & Lucas, C. (1989). Environmental coping strategies for alzheimer's caregivers. *American Journal of Alzheimer's Care and Related Disorders & Research*, *4*(6), 4–8. https://doi.org/10.1177/153331758900400603

Ragnedda, M., Ruiu, M. L., & Addeo, F. (2019). Measuring digital capital: An empirical investigation. *New Media & Society*, *22*(5), 793–816. https://doi.org/10.1177/1461444819869604

Rechavi, T. B. (2009). A room for living: Private and public aspects in the experience of the living room. *Journal of Environmental Psychology*, *29*(1), 133–143. https://doi.org/10.1016/j.jenvp.2008.05.001

Renaut, S., Ogg, J., Petite, S., & Chamahian, A.(2014). Home environments and adaptations in the context of ageing. *Ageing and Society,* 35(6), 1278–1303. https://doi.org/10.1017/s0144686x14000221

Robson, D., Nicholson, A., & Barker, N. (2005). *Homes for the Third Age: A Design Guide for Extra Care Sheltered Housing*. London: E & FN Spon.

Romagnoli, M., Alis, R., Guillen, J., Basterra, J., Villacastin, J. P., & Guillen, S. (2014). A novel device based on smart textile to control heart's activity during exercise. *Australasian Physical & Engineering Sciences in Medicine*, *37*(2), 377–384. https://doi.org/10.1007/s13246-014-0271-z

Rotheroe, A., Bagwell, S., & Joy, I. (2013). *In Sight: A Review of the Visual Impairment Sector* (Rep.). Retrieved November 22, 2022, from NPC website: https://www.thinknpc.org/resource-hub/in-sight-a-review-of-the-visual-impairment-sector/

Rouzet, D., Sánchez, A. C., Renault, T., & Roehn, O. (2019). *Fiscal Challenges and Inclusive Growth in Ageing Societies*. Paris: OECD Publishing.

Rowles, G. D., Oswald, F., & Hunter, E. G. (2003). Interior living environments in old age. *Annual Review of Gerontology and Geriatrics*, *23*(1), 167–194. https://doi.org/10.1891/0198-8794.23.1.167

Russo, J., Sukojo, A., Helal, A. S., Davenport, R., & Mann, W. C. (2004). *SmartWave -Intelligent Meal Preparation System to Help Older People Live Independently*. Retrieved November 22, 2022, from https://www.cise.ufl.edu/~helal/projects/publications/Russo-ICOST2004-SmartWave-final.pdf

Salive, M. E., Guralnik, J., Glynn, R. J., Christen, W., Wallace, R. B., & Ostfeld, A. M. (1994). Association of visual impairment with mobility and physical function. *Journal of the American Geriatrics Society*, *42*(3), 287–292. https://doi.org/10.1111/j.1532-5415.1994.tb01753.x

Salvi, S. M. (2006). Ageing changes in the eye. *Postgraduate Medical Journal*, *82*(971), 581–587. https://doi.org/10.1136/pgmj.2005.040857

Saravana kumar, N., Eswari, T., Sampath, P., & Lavanya, S. (2015). Predictive methodology for diabetic data analysis in big data. *Procedia Computer Science*, *50*, 203–208. https://doi.org/10.1016/j.procs.2015.04.069

Saruwono, M., Zulkiflin, N. F., & Mohammad, N. M. (2012). Living in living rooms: Furniture arrangement in apartment-type family housing. *Procedia - Social and Behavioral Sciences*, *50*, 909–919. https://doi.org/10.1016/j.sbspro.2012.08.092

Schaar, A. K, & Ziefle, M. (2011). Smart clothing: Perceived benefits vs. perceived fears. *Proceedings of the 5th International ICST Conference on Pervasive Computing Technologies for Healthcare,* Dublin, Ireland. https://doi.org/10.4108/icst.pervasivehealth.2011.246031

Scheerder, A., Van Deursen, A., & Van Dijk, J. (2017). Determinants of internet skills, uses and outcomes. A systematic review of the second- and third-level digital divide. *Telematics and Informatics*, *34*(8), 1607–1624. https://doi.org/10.1016/j.tele.2017.07.007

Schmall, V. L. (1991). *Sensory Changes in Later Life*. Corvallis, OR: Oregon State University Extension Service.

Severinsen, C., Breheny, M., & Stephens, C. (2015). Ageing in unsuitable places. *Housing Studies*, *31*(6), 714–728. https://doi.org/10.1080/02673037.2015.1122175

Siddiqui, S. & Singh, T. (2016). Social media its impact with positive and negative aspects. *International Journal of Computer Applications Technology and Research*, *5*(2), 71–75. https://doi.org/10.7753/ijcatr0502.1006

Sinclair, A., Ryan, B., & Hill, D. (2015). *Sight Loss in Older People: The Essential Guide for General Practice*. Retrieved November 22, 2022, from https://media.rnib.org.uk/documents/Sight_loss_in_older_people_-_Guide_for_GPs.pdf

Sindhwani, N., Maurya, V. P., Patel, A., Yadav, R. K., Krishna, S., & Anand, R. (2021). Implementation of intelligent plantation system using virtual IOT. *Internet of Things and Its Applications*, *38*, 305–322. https://doi.org/10.1007/978-3-030-77528-5_16

Song, S., Song, S., Zhao, Y., & Zhu, Q. (2019). Investigating the relationship between internet use and perceived loneliness among older Chinese. *Innovation in Ageing*, *3*(Supplement_1), S413. https://doi.org/10.1093/geroni/igz038.1538

Song, Y. & Van der Cammen, T. J. (2019). Electronic assistive technology for community-dwelling solo-living older adults: A systematic review. *Maturitas*, *125*, 50–56. https://doi.org/10.1016/j.maturitas.2019.04.211

Stewart, A. M., Grossman, L., Nguyen, M., Maximino, C., Rosemberg, D. B., Echevarria, D. J., & Kalueff, A. V. (2014). Aquatic toxicology of fluoxetine: Understanding the knowns and the unknowns. *Aquatic Toxicology*, *156*, 269–273. https://doi.org/10.1016/j.aquatox.2014.08.014

Sum, S., Mathews, R. M., Hughes, I., & Campbell, A. (2008). Internet use and loneliness in older adults. *CyberPsychology & Behavior*, *11*(2), 208–211. https://doi.org/10.1089/cpb.2007.0010

Syed, L., Jabeen, S., Manimala, S., & Alsaeedi, A. (2019). Smart healthcare framework for ambient assisted living using IOMT and big data analytics techniques. *Future Generation Computer Systems*, *101*, 136–151. https://doi.org/10.1016/j.future.2019.06.004

Tchalla, A. E., Lachal, F., Cardinaud, N., Saulnier, I., Bhalla, D., Roquejoffre, A., & Dantoine, T. (2012). Efficacy of simple home-based technologies combined with a monitoring assistive center in decreasing falls in a frail elderly population (results of the ESOPPE study). *Archives of Gerontology and Geriatrics*, *55*(3), 683–689. https://doi.org/10.1016/j.archger.2012.05.011

Tobis, J. S., Reinsch, S., Swanson, J. M., Byrd, M., & Scharf, T. (1985). Visual perception dominance of fallers among community-dwelling older adults. *Journal of the American Geriatrics Society*, *33*(5), 330–333. https://doi.org/10.1111/j.1532-5415.1985.tb07132.x

UKRI. (2022). *UKRI Healthy Ageing Challenge Our Story So Far Helping People to Remain Active, Productive, Independent and Socially Connected for Longer*. Retrieved November 22, 2022, from https://www.ukri.org/wp-content/uploads/2022/07/UKRI-030822-OurStorySoFarHACImpactReport2022.pdf

UNDESA. (2022). *World Population Prospects 2022: Summary of Results. United Nations Department of Economic and Social Affairs, Population*. Retrieved November 22, 2022, from https://www.un.org/development/desa/pd/content/World-Population-Prospects-2022

United Nations. (2022). *Peace, Dignity and Equality on a Healthy Planet: Ageing*. Retrieved November 22, 2022, from https://www.un.org/en/global-issues/ageing%20

Välkkynen, P., Boyer, A., Urhemaa, T., & Nieminen, R. (2011). Mobile augmented reality for retail environments. In *Proceedings of Workshop on Mobile Interaction in Retail Environments in Conjunction with MobileHCI*, pp. 1–4.

Van Deursen, A. J. & Helsper, E. J. (2015). The third-level digital divide: Who benefits most from being online? *Communication and Information Technologies Annual, 10*, 29–52. https://doi.org/10.1108/s2050-206020150000010002

Van Heek, J., Brauner, P., & Ziefle, M. (2018). What is hip? - classifying adopters and rejecters of interactive digital textiles in home environments. *Communications in Computer and Information Science, 869*, 1–20. https://doi.org/10.1007/978-3-319-93644-4_1

Wahl, H., Schilling, O., Oswald, F., & Iwarsson, S. (2009). The home environment and quality of life-related outcomes in advanced old age: Findings of the enable-age project. *European Journal of Ageing, 6*(2), 101–111. https://doi.org/10.1007/s10433-009-0114-z

Wang, C., Kim, Y., Shin, H., & Min, S. D. (2019). Preliminary clinical application of textile insole sensor for hemiparetic gait pattern analysis. *Sensors, 19*(18), 3950. https://doi.org/10.3390/s19183950

WCPT. (2001). *WCPT: The First 50 Years*. Retrieved November 22, 2022, from https://world.physio/sites/default/files/2020-06/50th-anniversary-2001.pdf

Wei, K., Teo, H., Chan, H. C., & Tan, B. C. (2011). Conceptualizing and testing a social cognitive model of the digital divide. *Information Systems Research, 22*(1), 170–187. https://doi.org/10.1287/isre.1090.0273

Whitley, M. (2021). *7 Best Innovative Products for the Elderly*. Retrieved November 22, 2022, from https://www.aplaceformom.com/caregiver-resources/articles/cutting-edge-products-for-seniors

Wiles, J. L., Leibing, A., Guberman, N., Reeve, J., & Allen, R. E. (2011). The meaning of "ageing in place" to older people. *The Gerontologist, 52*(3), 357–366. https://doi.org/10.1093/geront/gnr098

Wilkinson, C. R. & De Angeli, A. (2014). Applying user centred and participatory design approaches to commercial product development. *Design Studies, 35*(6), 614–631. https://doi.org/10.1016/j.destud.2014.06.001

Williams, G. (1990). Development niches and specialist housebuilders: An overview of private sheltered housing in Britain. *Housing Studies, 5*(1), 14–23. https://doi.org/10.1080/02673039008720669

Wills, W., Meah, A., Dickinson, A., & Short, F. (2013). *Domestic Kitchen Practices: Findings from the 'Kitchen Life' Study*. Retrieved November 22, 2022, from https://uhra.herts.ac.uk/handle/2299/19588

Wilson, J., Heinsch, M., Betts, D., Booth, D., & Kay-Lambkin, F. (2021). Barriers and facilitators to the use of e-health by older adults: A scoping review. *BMC Public Health, 21*(1), 1556. https://doi.org/10.1186/s12889-021-11623-w

Wittenberg, R. & Hu, B. (2015). *Projections of Demand for and Costs of Social Care for Older People and Younger Adults in England, 2015 to 2035*. Retrieved November 22, 2022, from https://www.pssru.ac.uk/pub/DP2900.pdf

World Health Organization. (2015). *World Health Statistics 2015*. Retrieved November 22, 2022, from https://www.who.int/publications-detail-redirect/9789240694439

Yu, L., Yeung, S., Tang, C., Terzopoulos, D., Chan, T. F., & Osher, S. J. (2011). Make it home: Automatic optimization of furniture arrangement. *ACM Transactions on Graphics, 30*(4), 1–12. https://doi.org/10.1145/2010324.1964981

5 Smart Rural Services for Managing Plant Diseases, Livestock, and Medical Care

Meili Wang and Kun Qian

5.1 INTRODUCTION TO RURAL DEVELOPMENT CHALLENGES AND SOLUTIONS

Plant diseases, livestock management, and medical technology are very important for the development of towns and cities, which are two equally important aspects of promoting the integration of urban and rural development and cannot be neglected, with towns and villages promoting each other and coexisting with each other. To build a modern country in all aspects, it is necessary to build both prosperous cities and prosperous countryside. No matter how far industrialization or urbanization goes, there will still be a large number of farmers in the countryside, and the basic position of agriculture still needs to be firmly established. In the process of modernization, the success or failure of modernization is determined, to a certain extent, by how well the relationship between industry and agriculture and between urban and rural areas is handled.

In the future, we will accelerate the application of new technologies such as the Internet of Things, 5G, and artificial intelligence in the field of agricultural machinery; create a digital planting scheme for the whole process of crops; constantly improve the mechanization, digitalization, and intelligence of agricultural production; promote industrial integration and upgrading; and help agricultural high-quality and sustainable development.

5.2 CASHMERE GOATS IDENTIFICATION AND MANAGEMENT

5.2.1 Overview

Modern livestock farming is developing in the direction of scale, high intensification, high efficiency, and ecological safety. Especially in recent years, with the development of artificial intelligence, intelligent farming has become a breakthrough in the reform of the animal husbandry industry. Building modern animal husbandry, providing information, automation, and intelligence, is an indispensable core content, the direction of industrial development today and in the future, and one of the important directions of effort for the current technological progress of the animal husbandry industry and industrial innovation drive. However, the overall level of development of intelligent animal husbandry in China still has a large gap compared with the developed countries, and the intelligent animal husbandry industry is still in the early-development stage. However, overall, the "Internet" + "intelligent animal husbandry" integration development momentum is strong, and R & D innovation has become the endogenous power and core competitiveness of the development of intelligent farming. Traditional farming methods are prone to high labor and material costs, while marking the identity of the goat, such as ear tagging and branding, can cause high damage to the sheep. Thus, it is important to study the identification of goat based on automation, intelligent equipment, and multimedia technology. Computer vision and image processing–based approaches are rapidly gaining attention as they require only the analysis of rich information in livestock images, are cost-effective, do not require contact with livestock, and can be replicated in large numbers.

This study addresses the current lack of relevant research on high-similarity sheep identification with vision technology, deep learning, and image processing fusion. This research aims to solve the problem of high-similarity goat identification continues to lay the foundation for exploring farming models such as intelligent animal husbandry and smart agriculture.

5.2.2 CASHMERE GOATS IDENTIFICATION WITH DEEP LEARNING

This study mainly consists of three stages: preprocessing of goat image data, goat recognition network model, and platform deployment. Firstly, the improved Cycle-GAN network model is used to perform nonlinear data enhancement on goat images, laying the foundation for subsequent data set balancing and high-quality image understanding tasks; secondly, the single-shot multibox detector (SSD) network is used to detect goat targets in images, segmenting them with bounding boxes to reduce background interference, and adopting a multibranch mode to fuse multidimensional features of goat achieved through joint loss optimization strategies, with the network backbone being a transfer learning model to develop algorithms in the context of goat using cascading deep learning; finally, based on the implementation of goat identification, a platform for individual goat identification was built using the Flask framework and PyTorch framework based on the Python language.

5.2.2.1 Deep Learning–Based Identification Method for Individual Cashmere Goats

In the stage of the rapid development of computer image processing technology, target recognition technology and related research have been mature, but the research in the field of individual animal recognition is still very limited. The triplet loss function (Schroff et al., 2015) is widely used in face recognition and pedestrian recognition. The main principle is that through training, the individual differences between different classes are significantly greater than those between individuals within the same class. Which means the distance between the anchor and the positive of images belonging to the same category decreases, while the distance between the negative and the anchor of images not belonging to the same category increases. What we need to do is reduce the distance of image samples of the same category in high-dimensional space by training the triplet loss function (anchor and positive) and make the distance of image samples of different categories larger in high-dimensional space (anchor and negative). CrossEntropy loss (Zhang and Sabuncu, 2018) function is a very common and effective classification loss function. Its main purpose is to measure the difference of different probability distributions of 24 species (24 cashmere goats in this study) in the same random variable through crossentropy, and the smaller the value of crossentropy, the better the effect of the model. However, due to the small amount of data, the smooth CrossEntropy loss function is used to prevent the overfitting problem.

Further, the characteristics of the goats are so similar that it is difficult to distinguish between individuals. The transfer learning method can learn more specific features from the goat's body images, which is necessary for accurate recognition. Transfer learning has a deep network structure which is effective for learning high-quality features. As an optimization, it can improve learning efficiency and save training time. Because of its better performance, it can also make up for the limitations of the data set, which not only solves the problem of data collection in the actual breeding process but also improves the accuracy of the experiment. We chose ResNet34 as the network structure. Compared with ResNet18, it not only solves the problem of network degradation but also greatly improves the depth of the network and further improves the measurement accuracy. The initial training parameters are not random but set to the default value.

Therefore, we selected cashmere goats with similar characteristics for identification. First, an SSD network (Berg et al., 2015) is used to process data settings. Next, transfer learning is used to build the backbone network for learning the features of goats, as follows: the loss function is composed of triplet loss function and labels smooth CrossEntropy loss function to achieve the multibranches mode for fusing the features in multidimension perspective. The use of the multibranch network is very novel. Its innovation is that we input three images (three images as a group, including anchor, positive example, and negative example) into three networks with the label smoothing CrossEntropy loss function branch network as the loss function for pretraining and then use their output as the input of the triplet loss function. Based on the data of each cashmere goat, we set a large number of parameter combinations for experimental model and then use the trained model with the best accuracy to find out the ID of goats with the lowest recognition accuracy. The Cycle-Consistent Generative Adversarial Network (Cycle-GAN) (Zhu et al., 2017) is used to learn as well as generate the goat image that is difficult to identify. Unlike previous studies using Cycle-GAN, we used a novel method to use this network to learn and integrate the features in the images of the same cashmere goat as the learned characteristics are observed in the same goat. Finally, we found that the data accuracy of this recognition can reach 93.75%. These results show that the recognition of individual cashmere goats based on deep learning is also of great value.

As shown in Figure 5.1, cashmere goats with a triple data pair are constructed based on the traditional triplet loss function. The purpose is that this structure helps to reduce the Euclidean distance between the same individual images and expand the

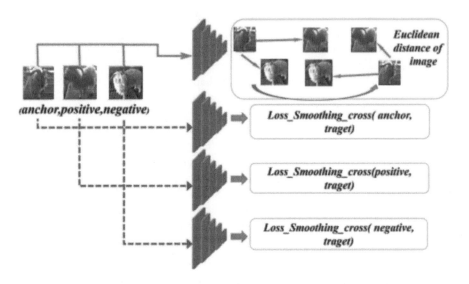

FIGURE 5.1   Multibranch loss function structure fusion in cashmere goat.

distance between different individuals. Secondly, the label smoothing CrossEntropy loss function can not only effectively complete the classification but also prevent the overfitting problem. To further integrate the features of goats for recognition and keep consistent with the optimized structure of triplet loss structure, a set of samples (anchored, positive and negative) input into the triplet loss function are also input into the label smoothing CrossEntropy loss. Finally, the values of the four loss functions of four branches are averaged.

As shown in Figure 5.2, for the triplet loss function, a small number of images of other goat and sheep breeds are mixed into the data of each cashmere goat data set. Based on the principle that the Euclidean distance of the goat image of different species is greater than that of the goat image of the same species, it can help to expand the distance between different individuals and recognition.

Data enhancement based on improved Cycle-GAN. As shown in Figure 5.3, Cycle-GAN can be used for style conversion without matching data. It can realize feature reorganization and generate data without establishing a one-to-one mapping between the input image and the target image to be generated. Unlike pix2pix, this network not only does not need to provide relevant pairing input data but also has better performance than the traditional GAN (Goodfellow et al., 2014).

5.2.2.2 Deep Learning–Based Identification Method for Key Body Part Detection of Cashmere Goats

An accurate and rapid recognition of cashmere goat posture including abnormal behavior has been very necessary to effectively prevent diseases in large-scale breeding, with the rapid development of intelligent agriculture and cashmere goat management. A cashmere goat skeleton key points detection model HRTF (HRNet-Transformer) is proposed, which consists of three parts: (1) a feature extractor that uses the convolutional neural network as the backbone to extract low-level

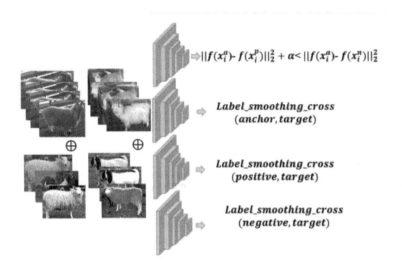

$$\Rightarrow \|f(x_i^a) - f(x_i^p)\|_2^2 + \alpha < \|f(x_i^a) - f(x_i^n)\|_2^2$$

Label_smoothing_cross
(anchor, target)

Label_smoothing_cross
(positive, target)

Label_smoothing_cross
(negative, target)

FIGURE 5.2 Multibranch loss function structure fusion in cashmere goat mixed with other goat image.

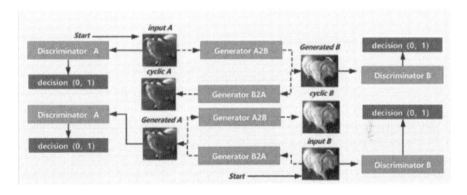

FIGURE 5.3 Schematic diagram of Cycle-GAN for cashmere goats.

features from images; (2) a transformer encoder that captures global cross-location information to model high-level semantic features; and (3) a regression key points heat map module that outputs the final prediction results. A variety of cashmere goat experiments were implemented to prove the cross-domain and generalization ability of the model. This finding can also provide effective technical support to accurately detect the key points of cashmere goat skeletons for the cashmere goat behavior in intelligent cashmere goat husbandry.

The parallel design of HRNet (Sun et al., 2019) facilitates feature fusion, which consists of several subnetworks connected in parallel, usually with four levels of subnetworks, where the resolution of the current subnet is half of the previous level. The network uses the high-resolution subnets as the first stage of the network and forms more stages by adding lower-resolution subnets. However, HRNet needs to

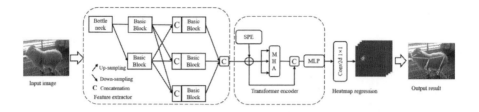

FIGURE 5.4   Framework of HRNet-Transformer (HRTF).

stack multiple layers to obtain global information, and it is also difficult to capture the constraint relationship between the key points. Its complex parallel structure and small number of downsampling lead to a slow inference speed, especially the last level of the subnetwork, because it needs to fuse the key point feature information of the first three levels of subnetwork, and the number of participants accounts for more than 70% of the whole network.

To improve the network performance, the first three levels of HRNet are designed in parallel to enhance the model's ability to acquire low-dimensional features of cashmere goat images. The transformer encoder is optimized to replace the last level of subnets to effectively extract high-dimensional features while reducing the parameter size. Then, the feature fusion module is used to fuse the high- and low-resolution feature information in multiple scales to improve the accuracy of locating the key points of cashmere goat bones. The overall design is shown in Figure 5.4.

The introduction of the transformer encoder can effectively solve the problems of a large number of HRNet parameters and poor extraction of high-dimensional features, which helps to localize key points in complex scenes such as occlusion and lying down. However, the conventional transformer encoder requires a large amount of training set data and converges slowly during training, and that is inconsistent with convenient and intelligent agriculture in practical farm application. Therefore, in this study, the transformer module is improved to reduce the amount of data required by the model and accelerate the convergence speed. The optimized transformer encoder consists of three parts: Sine Position Embedding (SPE), Multihead Self-Attention (MSA), and Multilayer Perceptron (MLP). The overall design is shown in Figure 5.5. In the transformer encoder, a sine position-embedding module was introduced to improve the utilization of spatial position relations, which is vital for the image of occlusion. The Hardswish activation function was used to improve the convergence speed of the training process. Secondly, a multiscale information fusion module was introduced to improve the learning ability of the model in the different dimensional features. As such, the improved model was also applied to the more practical scenarios. A distribution-aware coordinate representation strategy was adopted to reduce the quantization error in the conversion of coordinates and heat map when encoding and decoding from the small-scale heat map, where the mean square error was used as the loss function. Furthermore, the key point data set of goat skeletons was collected and annotated to verify the effectiveness and generalization of the model.

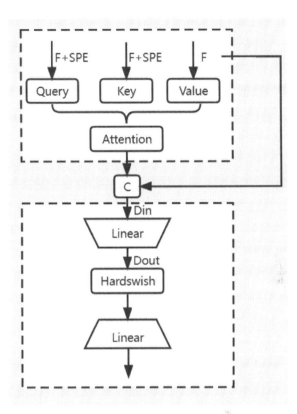

FIGURE 5.5 Framework of transformer encoder.

Cashmere goat skeletons have certain symmetries and domain correlations; for example, the key points of the leg skeleton are linked to each other. The optimized transformer can more accurately establish the dependencies between key point locations. To better show the intermediate output layer of the HRTF, we visualized heatmap in the attention module to reflect the aggregation and association between key points. The subsequent heatmap regression module further refines the key point positions and outputs the final predicted positions. This shows that the attention module can effectively discover these dynamic features without relying on image features, proving that the model is explainable and can be used to solve the problem of difficulty in locating key points in complex scenes such as occlusion and lying down, which has reference and application significance for other livestock.

5.2.3 DISCUSSIONS FOR FUTURE DEVELOPMENT

Inspired by the idea of introducing artificial intelligence and computer vision into the field of agricultural livestock breeding, and using cashmere goats as the research object, this study starts with data preprocessing, proposes a novel and effective model through experimental comparisons, fusing the multibranch fusion optimization structure of triplet loss and label smoothing CrossEntropy loss functions and an improved Cycle-GAN algorithm as well as a framework for integrating transfer learning and cascading deep learning. We compared and analyzed different experiments. From the experimental results, we find that this method is effective and can be applied to livestock breeding, especially for livestock with high similarity.

However, this method has its limitations: we can, for instance, only recognize the identity of the cashmere goat with a single image input–output method, but we cannot dynamically identify the identity of the cashmere goat through the real-time video stream of the goat farm. Additionally, the data set used in this study is not large enough. In the future, first, we will consider identifying and tracking goats or other livestock in groups and will look at a larger number of samples for individual identification. Cross-age recognition will be further studied to identify those characteristics that will change during the growth cycle of the animals, such as body shape. Then, we will apply our algorithm to large-scale goat farms or other animal husbandry farms to find the best robust and universal intelligent, deep learning–based animal husbandry recognition algorithm.

The algorithm in this study can provide a research basis for abnormal behavior warning of livestock, such as studying the individual recognition of cashmere goats with high similarity and recognizing the ID of cashmere goats with abnormal behaviors such as lying down for too long without eating and moving.

Finally, the algorithm model of this study can not only provide a research basis for livestock breeding in smart agriculture but also provide a great reference value for future research of virtual reality combined with smart agriculture and precision agriculture. What's more, the identification technology in this study can quickly understand the identity of livestock through virtual reality images or monitoring to view and manage livestock (taking goat as an example in this study), and then get the information of livestock through the database, to minimize the contact with livestock using virtual reality technology. In a word, this study can support intelligent precision breeding under virtual reality technology in the future, and it can provide an important reference value for virtual reality research combining intelligent agriculture and precision agriculture in the future.

5.2.4 Intelligent Management Platform for Goats

This study develops a platform for high-similarity goat identification. Firstly, it introduces the YOLOv4-based (Bochkovskiy et al., 2020) detection model, the deep SORT (Simple Online and Real-Time Tracking) (Wojke et al., 2017) based target tracking model, and uses jQuery, Ajax, and Flask technologies to integrate several intelligent modules with the high-similarity goat identification module.

In this platform application, users can take short videos of goats by themselves or capture short videos of goats using a camera and upload the short videos to the platform for high-similarity goat identification integrated into this study, which will use its intelligent module to process the videos and return the processed results. In addition, the platform supports real-time access by providing the IP address of the live camera on the goat farm, which is similar to the processing of the short video for goat identification in this study (Figure 5.6).

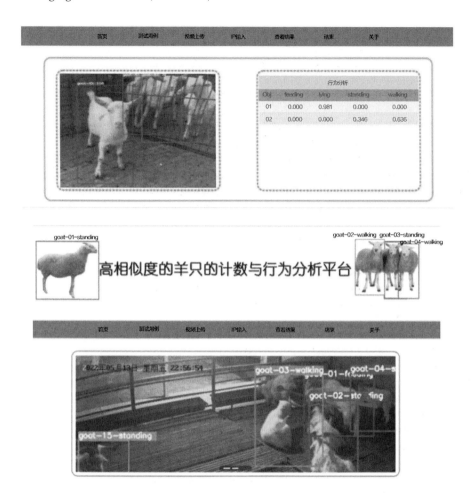

FIGURE 5.6 Identification, behavior recognition, and tracking management platform.

5.3 PLANT DISEASE DETECTION

5.3.1 Overview

Plant resources are the essential material basis for human survival and development. Protecting plants can provide sufficient resources for the development of various industries and maintain the balance of the ecological environment. The emergence of plant diseases hinders the process of normal growth and affects human economic benefits. Due to the characteristics of different diseases being similar and interference from the external environment, it makes it difficult to detect plant diseases. Therefore, this project proposed an improved algorithm for plant disease detection based on YOLOv5s. The CSP, FPN, and NMS modules in YOLOv5s are improved to eliminate the influence of the external environment, enhance the extraction capability of multiscale features, and improve the detection range and detection performance. To verify the effectiveness and generalization of the model, we conducted experiments on public data sets. Experiments show that the proposed algorithm effectively reduces missed detection and wrong detection caused by the complex background and improves detection and localization effects on small-scale diseases.

5.3.2 Deep Learning–Based Plant Disease Detection Methods

In the early stage, crop diseases were identified mainly through manual on-site inspection, measurement, statistics, and identification. However, artificial identification of crop diseases has strong subjectivity and poor efficiency (Bock et al., 2010). The more realistic problem is that for a vast crop area, it is far from enough to rely on limited human resources to complete a comprehensive and systematic detection task (Garciaab, 2013). With the revolution in the fields of computer vision and graphics processing units, disease detection is mainly divided into the following two categories: traditional machine vision technology and target detection technology based on deep learning.

Traditional machine vision methods mainly use high-sensitivity sensor cameras to capture images and image processing technology to enhance the image, segment disease spots, extract features, and optimize.

Target detection technology based on deep learning extracts complicated and abstract image feature information through complex network structures. Compared with traditional methods, this nondestructive recognition technology can identify crop diseases in the visible light range, with higher accuracy, faster detection speed, and better stability (Shaopeng et al., 2019). In the past 5 years, weed identification and disease detection of plants using deep learning techniques by convolutional neural networks (CNNs) have been widely used (Jiang et al., 2020; Qi et al., 2022; Sun et al., 2021; Wang et al., 2021; Zhang et al., 2022; Carion et al., 2020; Szegedy et al., 2016). Unlike traditional machine learning–based models that manually select features, CNNs automatically extract advanced and stable features through an end-to-end pipeline, thus significantly improving the utility of plant leaf detection. However, most of the CNN models for vegetable disease detection are implemented on images with simple backgrounds, which limits their application in practical production. In addition, natural scenes with diverse light conditions and varied backgrounds may increase the difficulty of detection and identification.

5.3.2.1 Target Detection Method Based on Deep Learning

Based on the advantages of the YOLOv5s algorithm, we propose an improved algorithm for plant disease detection and recognition, which improves the accuracy of the network in recognizing plant diseases in complex backgrounds while ensuring real-time performance. The proposed algorithm is improved mainly from three parts, CSP-TR, improved inception module, and confluence module. Figure 5.7 shows the overall framework of the plant disease detection model.

The global semantic information is very important in the target detection task, and the detection area is judged considering not only the current area but also the semantic information of the surrounding area to locate the target area accurately. The self-attentive mechanism is based on the human visual attention mechanism, which allocates corresponding resources according to the importance of visual objects

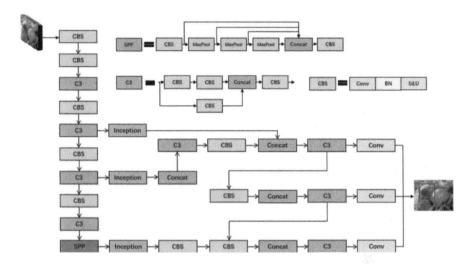

FIGURE 5.7 The overall structure of YOLOv5.

(Shepley et al., 2020). In the neural network, the self-attention mechanism assigns different weights according to the importance of image regions. The self-attention mechanism has a global sensory field, which can model long-range contextual information, capture rich global semantic information, and assign different weights to different semantic information so that the extracted features are more relevant to the target and the network focuses on key information. The self-attention mechanism contains three basic computational elements: query, key, and value, which are denoted by Q, K, and V. The semantic information weights are obtained by computing the similarity between Q and K. The module of self-attentive attention uses the scaled dot-product as the similarity calculation function. First, the similarity between Q and K is calculated using the scaled dot-product function; then, the similarity is scaled and normalized by Softmax to obtain the semantic weights; and finally, all the semantic weights are weighted and summed to obtain the final self-attentive features.

Based on the scaled self-attention network, we consider mapping Q, K, and V into several different subspaces by different linear transformation matrices, and after the self-attention features are calculated by different self-attention modules, multiple self-attention features are stitched together by vector stitching for linear transformation to output multiheaded attention features. The structure of the multiheaded attention network is shown in Figure 5.8. To optimize the detection effect, let N equal 4. Multihead attention improves the feature extraction capability without increasing the computational complexity, which can better capture long-range dependencies and improve the network model performance.

To effectively model and capture long-range global contextual semantic information and improve the accuracy of the detection network, the C3 module connected before the SPP structure of the original YOLOv5s network is replaced with the CSP-TR module shown in Figure 5.9. In the CSP-TR module, one branch feature is passed into the transformer module with a multiheaded attention mechanism module to extract global contextual semantic information and capture long-range

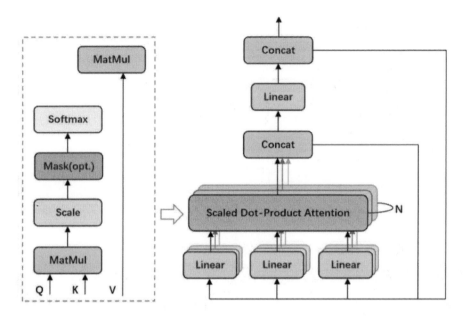

FIGURE 5.8   Structure of multihead attention.

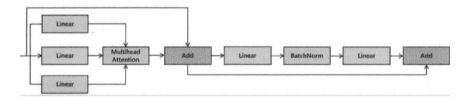

FIGURE 5.9   Structure of the CSP-TR module.

dependencies and rich contextual information. After stitching the output of the transformer module with the input feature map, the direct input to the fully connected layer generates a large number of parameters. The two branches perform different feature extraction tasks, respectively.

YOLOv5s adopts CSP_Darknet as the feature extraction network, improves the detection accuracy by fusing the features of high and low layers through upsampling and convolution operations, and predicts independently on three feature maps. However, the deepening of the feature network layers makes it difficult to extract small-scale target information and lacks diverse sensory fields for each scale of the feature map, thus leading to a weak network in detecting small-scale targets and easily clustered objects, especially in the detection of similar diseases and when the diseases are obscured from each other.

An improved Inception-A structure is proposed as shown in Figure 5.10. For the input feature map, three kinds of convolution kernels of different sizes, 1×1, 3×3, and 5×5, are used in parallel for feature extraction, and the results of feature extraction are fused and output. The convolution on the large scale can learn global

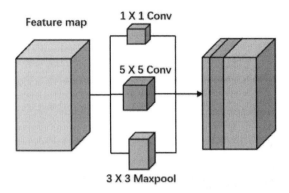

FIGURE 5.10   Structure of Inception-A module.

features; the convolution on small scale can extract local features; and the convolution with different sizes has different sizes of perceptual fields, which can extract rich features and improve the robustness of the network (Byungjoon et al., 2008). Adding 1×1 convolution before a big convolution can reduce the model parameters. In the experiment, two 3×3 convolution kernels are used instead of 5×5 convolution kernels, which is about 30% less than the former. The maximum pooling operation preserves the maximum value in the region, provides a form of translation without deformation, extracts the main features while compressing the feature map, and reduces the complexity of computation.

After adding the Inception-A module shown in Figure 5.10 behind the C3 and SPP structures, the feature maps are connected to the inception module before fusion, and multiscale feature extraction is performed on the same layer. The perceptual field of the convolutional layer becomes smaller; the network can perceive the small-scale disease features more accurately; and the multiscale feature fusion results are obtained and then spliced to obtain richer feature information, preserving the network's perception of large-scale diseases. Since the low-level feature map has more fine-grained feature information than the high-level feature map, more diverse features can be obtained through multiscale feature extraction, and more meaningful features can be retained for small objects and occluded parts to improve the detection accuracy of small-scale diseases and mutual occlusion of diseases in the natural environment.

5.3.2.2   Lightweight Plant Disease Detection Methods

The NMS in YOLOv5s is a greedy algorithm that uses the highest scoring box to suppress other overlapping boxes each time, so there is misdetection in disease-prone and overlapping areas. To improve the recognition accuracy and detection range of the network, and reduce the probability of misdetection, the confluence module replaces the original NMS.

The main idea of the confluence method is not to suppress a large number of detection results but to find a way to identify the optimal box from them, which is achieved by identifying the one that intersects the most with other boxes (Ben et al., 2006). Confluence is a two-stage method in which the first stage measures the correlation between frames by the Manhattan distance, weighting them according to the confidence score to obtain the optimal one, and the second stage removes the other frames by comparing the degree of intersection with the optimal one. The Manhattan distance is the L1 parametrization, which is the sum of the vertical and horizontal distances between two points.

NMS only considers the confidence score of the object, while confluence considers both the confidence score c and p values of the object. The biggest advantage is that it can preserve some of the detection frames that were suppressed by IoU when NMS was used and is more suitable for crowded detection scenarios, such as when there are multiple dense and mutually occluded diseased plants in a single image.

5.3.3 Mobile App-Based Disease Detection Application System

As shown in Figure 5.11, the trained network model is transformed into ONNX format, transplanted to the Android platform, and deployed to the device. Real-time reasoning is carried out using the images collected by the device; the detection results of pests and diseases are predicted; the corresponding prevention and control measures are provided to users; and then, the severity is graded.

Figure 5.12 provides an example of detecting tomato leaf disease on a mobile phone, which shows tomato gray mold. The first button at the bottom is to detect image defects. The second button is to view the corresponding prevention and control measures. The third button is for taking photos and uploading images. The last button represents disease detection through real-time video.

In terms of precise prevention and control of plant pests and diseases, when pests and diseases break out, timely push the occurrence of pests and diseases according to the local geographical location, climate, natural enemies, monitoring, and early warning and other information; provide farmers with precise pest and disease-prevention measures; and avoid farmers from indiscriminate use of pesticides.

The plant pest identification system is an important part of digital agriculture. In the future, the plant intelligent identification system will shift from a single plant pest identification to the identification and monitoring of growth, cultivation, and other aspects so as to integrate multiple functions into one system and improve the level of agricultural digital management.

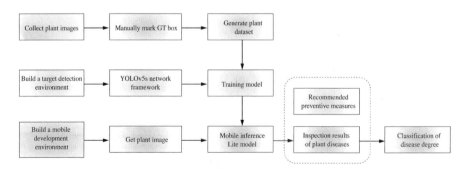

FIGURE 5.11   Technical route of plant pest detection based on deep learning.

FIGURE 5.12   Visualization of detection results on the mobile phone.

5.4 VIRTUAL SURGERY TRAINING SYSTEM

5.4.1 OVERVIEW

The virtual surgery training system is a platform that begins with medical imaging data. Through the use of computer graphics, it creates a detailed virtual model of human soft tissue. This system then simulates a realistic medical environment, allowing interaction through haptic devices. This proves invaluable for training doctors in remote areas. Central to this system is its ability to simulate surgical procedures, offering doctors a 3D virtual environment and an interactive platform that closely mirrors the real-life surgical process.

A realistic 3D anatomical model is vital for real-time medical applications such as surgery simulation. The visual quality hinges on the model's accuracy and the material realism needed for the physical-based rendering (PBR) pipeline. CT and MRI-derived models aren't directly suitable for PBR rendering due to a lack of surface parameterization, necessitating additional manual adjustments. While the digital market offers numerous 3D human anatomical models with detailed parameterization, these are often artistically designed for visual appeal. These artistic representations, especially by less-experienced artists, can introduce geometric irregularities. While these don't affect visual rendering, they hinder the model's use in physics-based simulations.

The main contribution of this work is a cutting-based surface parameterization transfer algorithm, which can be used to transfer the surface parameterization attribute, especially the boundary information (UV seam), from the source mesh to the new target mesh. It solves the parameterization space distortion problem in state-of-the-art tools when performing surface parameterization transfer.

5.4.2 VIRTUAL SURGERY THEORY AND TECHNIQUES

Our pipeline comprises two distinct stages. The initial stage entails a voxelization and remeshing-driven pipeline for generating simulation-ready models. This stage aims to preserve the shape of the original 3D surface model while simultaneously eliminating nonmanifold geometry. The second stage represents the primary contribution of this work, introducing a new algorithm for transferring surface parameterization using a cutting-based approach. This algorithm emphasizes transferring the original UV mapping and preserving UV seams to the simulation-ready model. We've conducted a thorough comparison with existing pipelines to showcase our pipeline's ability to preserve surface parameterization and its potential to improve the efficiency of virtual surgery production.

In the process of transferring surface parametrization (UV mapping) information from the source mesh to the target mesh, a common approach involves transferring the surface attribute from the source model to the nearest location on the target mesh. However, this method has the drawback of transferring the UV seam from the source mesh to the target mesh, leading to UV space stretching for polygons that intersect the UV seam on the target mesh. To address this issue, we propose a novel methodology. Our approach entails projecting the target mesh onto the source mesh and dissecting the target mesh based on how the intermediate mesh is dissected by the UV seam's corresponding edges (referred to as UV seam edges) on the source mesh. This approach effectively eliminates the UV space stretch artifact. Subsequently, the newly generated dissected edges are employed as hard edges, and the dissected target mesh undergoes a remeshing process to produce the final high-quality simulation-ready model. This final model seamlessly inherits the surface parameterization of the source mesh without any distortion.

5.4.2.1 Voxelization-Based Mesh Optimization Techniques

The traditional method for creating a volumetric representation involves transforming the explicit geometric representation into a signed distance function, referred to as $\varphi(x)$. This distance function calculates the minimum distance from a given point x to the mesh boundary, where $\varphi(x)$ equals zero. It assigns positive values to points outside the domain and negative values to points inside it. When dealing with input nonmanifold geometries characterized by self-intersections and degenerate elements, the initial step involves their conversion from the explicit polygonal representation into a signed distance function $\varphi(x)$, typically referred to as a level set, using scan conversion techniques (Denis et al., 2006) (Per-Olof, 2006). The gradient of this signed distance function serves as a valuable source of geometric information. The choice of resolution for sampling the Signed Distance Field (SDF) plays a critical role in accurately representing the shape of the input polygonal geometry. Within the center of each voxel data, a sampled value from the distance field is stored.

Following the establishment of the signed distance function for the input geometries (refer to the outcome depicted in algorithmic procedure description in Figure 5.13), the Signed Distance Field (SDF) can readily eliminate the self-intersections and degenerate elements present in the input geometries, which are referred to as the "source mesh." This is achieved through straightforward and efficient topological operations involving distance fields, including union, difference, and intersection.

Following the topological adjustments, we obtain the volumetric representation of the desired object's shape. Subsequently, it is necessary to convert the volumetric data back into a polygon mesh through an isosurfacing process using a specified iso value. However, two challenges are encountered when generating the output isosurface. Firstly, the quality of the isosurface relies on the resolution of the voxel size. Secondly, the new mesh loses the surface parameterization information (UV coordinate) present in the original mesh.

To address the first challenge, maintaining the shapes and details of the input polygon geometries from the source mesh often requires the use of small voxel sizes, which can lead to the creation of high-density polygons (as observed in Figure 5.13). To mitigate this, we employ a remeshing technique to reduce the polygon count

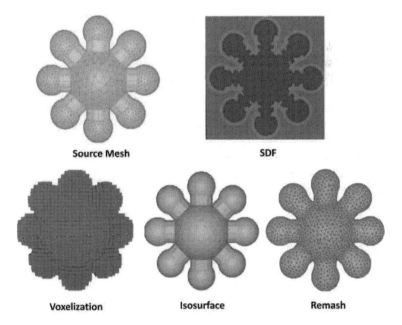

Source Mesh   **SDF**

Voxelization   **Isosurface**   **Remash**

FIGURE 5.13   First stage of voxelization and remesh-based simulation-ready model generation pipeline.

while preserving the isosurface's shape. This remeshed model can serve as a simulation-ready model and is referred to as the "target mesh."

As for the second challenge, unwrapping the target mesh and creating new surface parameterization for it is a computationally inefficient process, no less complicated than resolving mesh degeneracies on a piecewise basis. In the subsequent section, we propose a cutting-based surface parameterization transfer method that can transfer the surface parameterization information from the source mesh to the target mesh without introducing distortion.

5.4.2.2   UV Island-Based Surface Parameterization Transfer Technology

During the surface transfer operation, determining the precise location for transferring the surface attribute is crucial. Given that the shape of the target mesh conforms to that of the source mesh, it is logical to transfer the surface attribute from the source mesh to the closest corresponding location on the target mesh. This transfer process involves iterating through the vertices of the source mesh and systematically transferring attributes to each vertex on the target mesh. For a given vertex, say the ith vertex, on the target mesh, its corresponding point (denoted as x_i) is projected onto the surface of the source mesh, resulting in an intermediate point xp_i. This intermediate point (xp_i) serves as an intermediary for the attribute transfer process. In other words, the surface parameterization attribute is first transferred from the source mesh to the intermediate point xp_i, and subsequently, this attribute is copied to the corresponding vertex on the target mesh. The transfer operation is executed based on barycentric coordinates. For each intermediate point xp_i, a set of barycentric coordinates w_i is calculated relative to the host primitive it is projected onto. These coordinates are represented as $w_i \in Rk$, where k typically equals 3 or 4 (although if k exceeds 4, the source mesh may need to be triangulated or quadrangulated to meet this standard). Subsequently, the surface parameterization attribute ($uv_i \in R^2$) of xp_i is computed by barycentrically interpolating the parameterization attributes of the corresponding vertices on the source mesh. Finally, uv_i is assigned to the ith vertex on the target mesh.

Nevertheless, this approach introduces a specific artifact. As illustrated in Figure 5.14 (case 1, world space), the primitives of the intermediate mesh may intersect the UV seam of the source mesh within the world space. In scenarios where the UV seam divides the source mesh into several distinct UV islands, the primitives crossing this UV seam will undergo stretching in the UV space, as exemplified in Figure 5.14 (case 1, UV space). This issue arises because the vertices of the intermediate mesh within the same primitive belong to distinct UV islands. Consequently, the neighboring points on the surface of the intermediate mesh are widely separated from each other within the parameterization space (UV space). During the barycentric interpolation process for these primitives crossing the UV seam, their vertices are interpolated into different UV islands, leading to distortion or stretching artifacts.

To mitigate the artifact arising from the crossing UV islands, it is essential to ensure that each primitive of the intermediate mesh is consistently interpolated within the same UV island. To achieve this, the determination of which UV island each primitive should be interpolated into is a crucial step prior to the barycentric-based attribute transfer. For the intermediate mesh, each vertex is initially labeled with the UV island (kj) by assigning the UV island ID of the host primitive to it. In the case of

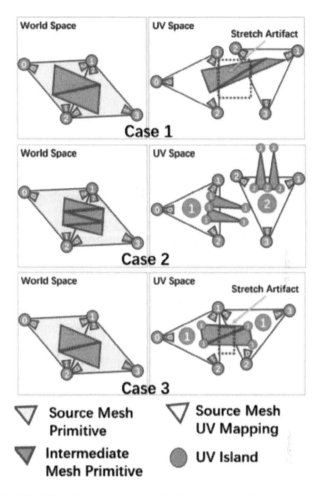

FIGURE 5.14   The UV artifact associated with UV space stretching.

primitives intersecting the UV seam, we calculate the area portion divided by the UV seam and assign the UV island ID of the largest portion to all the vertices within that primitive, as illustrated in Figure 5.14 (case 2). Although this method may be effective for certain models, it can still result in a zigzag UV pattern near the UV seam. However, when the UV seams do not entirely partition the mesh into two distinct UV islands, meaning that the area intersecting the UV seam shares the same UV island ID, the aforementioned method will still lead to UV space stretching artifacts near the UV seams, as depicted in Figure 5.14 (case 3).

5.4.2.3   UV Seam-Based Primitive Cutting Transfer

To address the issue of intersecting UV seams, we employ a UV seam cutting-based parameterization transfer technique. This method involves testing the intersection between the intermediate mesh's primitives and the corresponding UV seam edges from the source mesh. If an intermediate primitive intersects with UV seam edges, the corresponding primitive on the target mesh is dissected into refined primitives in a manner similar to how the intermediate primitive is dissected by the UV seam edges. This process is referred to as UV seam cutting-based parameterization transfer and is based on the approach proposed in (Nicolas et al., 2002). It combines vertex snapping with element refinement to ensure that small or poorly shaped primitives are avoided. When dealing with intermediate mesh primitives that cross the UV seam, we measure the polygon area on both sides of the UV seam and decide whether vertices should be snapped onto the seam or split, depending on the polygon area ratio.

Algorithm

Algorithm   1   Cutting   Based   Surface Parametrization Transfer

---

1: **Definition:** target mesh (**T**), source mesh (**S**), barycentric coordinate (**w**), uv coordinate (**uv**).

2: **procedure UVTRANSFER(T, S)**

3:     Project **T** onto **S** to get intermediate mesh **I**

4:     **for all** primitive $\pi_i \in$ **I do**

5:         **if** π_i intersect with UV seam **then**

6:             Split π_i into π_i^k $(k = 1, 2)$

7:         **if** π_i^k $(k = 1, 2)$ is ill shaped **then**

8:             Perform vertex snapping

9:         **for all** vertices $\mathbf{x}_j \in \pi_i^k(k = 1, 2)$ **do**

10:             Compute $\mathbf{w}_j$ for $\mathbf{x}_j$

11:             Interpolate $\mathbf{uv}_j$ using $\mathbf{w}_j$

12:             Transfer $\mathbf{uv}_j$ back to **T**

13:         **for all** edge $\mathbf{e}_m \in \pi_i^k(k = 1, 2)$ **do**

14:             **if** $\mathbf{e}_m$ coincides uv seam **then**

15:                 Mark $\mathbf{e}_m$ as hard edge

16:         Feed **T** and all $\mathbf{e}_m$ into remesher

17:         Return simulation ready model **T**

After this operation, there will be no primitives crossing the UV seam. Subsequently, we perform UV island-based surface parameterization transfer, resulting in no artifacts near the seam between two different UV islands (refer to Figure 5.15a). In cases where the seam splits the same UV island, we follow a rule during the computation of barycentric coordinates for the newly generated vertices that lie on the UV seam (as seen in Figure 5.15b). According to this rule, vertices in the same primitive (on the target mesh) should use the same host primitive (on the source mesh) to compute barycentric coordinates and transfer attributes. Not adhering to this rule would lead to vertices in the same primitive receiving attributes from two different primitives on the source mesh, resulting in UV space stretching.

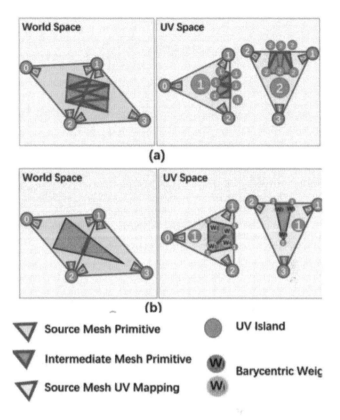

FIGURE 5.15 Cutting of primitives based on UV seams.

Finally, we apply remeshing techniques (Eftychios et al., 2012) to optimize the shape of polygons, utilizing the UV seam edge as a hard edge. Although the hard edge may be subdivided by the remesher based on user-specified edge length criteria, the overall shape of the hard edge is preserved, thus avoiding UV space stretching. With this pipeline, we can convert 3D anatomy models with self-intersections and degenerate elements into simulation-ready models while preserving the original mesh's surface parameterization. The entire procedure for cutting-based surface parameterization transfer is summarized in Algorithm 5.1.

5.4.3 Virtual Surgery Visualization and Interactive System

5.4.3.1 Voxelized Mesh Model Visualization and Analysis System

The anatomical model employed in this study represents a human kidney, encompassing various components such as the renal pelvis, adrenal gland, pyramid, arteries, and veins. While this kidney anatomy model is suitable for rendering purposes, it falls short of the prerequisites for physics simulation due to its inclusion of irregularly shaped polygons, self-intersections, and nonwatertight features, as illustrated in Figure 5.16.

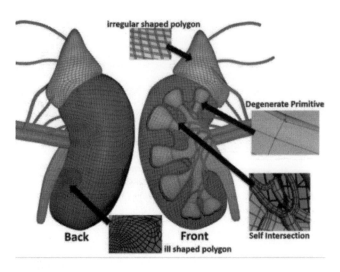

FIGURE 5.16   Visualization of the anomalies in the experimental model.

The voxelization process can be conducted separately for each component of the source mesh or applied to the entire mesh, depending on the simulation requirements. However, voxelizing the entire mesh may lead to the loss of intricate geometric details and alterations to the source mesh's geometry group information, potentially impacting the artistic pipeline. Voxelizing each component of the source mesh individually allows for capturing fine-grained details and ensures that each part of the model is ready for simulation. For clarity, the experiment was conducted on a single part of the mesh, specifically the renal pelvis, but similar operations can be applied to other mesh components.

In Figure 5.17, it is evident that high-resolution voxels effectively capture the mesh's intricate details, as demonstrated by the signed distance function (SDF) and the corresponding isosurface. The quality of the isosurface has a direct impact on the final outcome of the remesher. When sending the isosurface to the remesher, there is an option to set the remesher's edge length as either fixed or adaptive. In the case of adaptive remeshing, the result's quality is controlled by the gradation, which determines the rate at which edge lengths are allowed to change from one primitive to another. A more accurate isosurface results in the remeshed model better approximating the source model. The closeness of the remeshed model to the source mesh is quantified using relative surface distance (RSD), calculated as the surface distance (SD) divided by the source mesh's average edge length.

As seen in Figure 5.17, both fixed and adaptive edge lengths effectively capture the shape of the source mesh, even when using larger edge lengths for remeshing. While the remeshed model's shape may not be an exact match to the source mesh, the RSD of the high voxel resolution remeshing result in Figure 5.17 (bottom row) indicates that the distance between meshes is no greater than 16% of the source mesh's average edge length. Such a minor difference is sufficient to meet the requirements of most virtual surgery simulators designed for training purposes. Any subtle variations

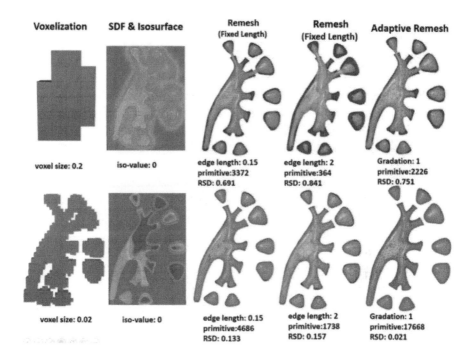

FIGURE 5.17 Pipeline utilizing voxelization for mesh enhancement and remeshing results. The comparison between the original source mesh's shape (depicted as a translucent purple layer) and the resulting remeshed model (represented as a solid pink layer) is presented.

in shape can be addressed using rendering techniques such as displacement mapping. Displacement mapping calculates the displacement from the target mesh to the source mesh along the local surface normal, ensuring that the target mesh is rendered to match the shape of the source mesh.

5.4.3.2 Simulation System Based on Surface Attribute Transfer

Observations from Figure 5.18b reveal that transferring the UV parameterization without incorporating UV island information leads to UV space stretching and noticeable object space artifacts. This proximity-based attribute transfer approach is commonly used in digital content creation software such as Houdini and Maya. By factoring in UV island information (as depicted in Figure 5.18c), the UV space stretching artifact can be mitigated, but the zigzag artifact near the UV seam and stretching artifact persist within the same UV island. However, Figure 5.18d illustrates that our method effectively eliminates UV space stretching.

In Figure 5.19, upon employing our approach for each segment of the kidney model, a simulation-ready model is produced, featuring high-quality polygon discretization and fully preserving the surface parameterization of the source model. Figure 5.19 also presents the outcome of simulating the target mesh utilizing the finite element method (Haase and Amthor, 2020).

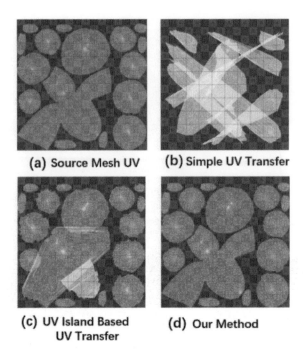

(a) Source Mesh UV   (b) Simple UV Transfer

(c) UV Island Based
UV Transfer   (d) Our Method

FIGURE 5.18 Surface attribute transfer results.

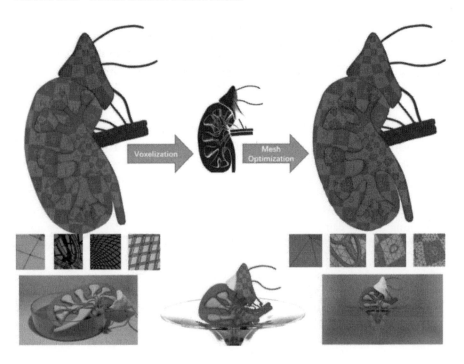

FIGURE 5.19 Kidney model conversion and the simulation result.

5.5 FACE DISEASE IDENTIFICATION AND DIAGNOSIS

5.5.1 OVERVIEW

In the new journey toward common prosperity, it is necessary to further strengthen the foundation of rural health care and to enhance the construction of rural health care systems to provide strong support for the concerted promotion of new urbanization and the comprehensive promotion of rural revitalization. Over the years, the state has vigorously promoted the construction of an "Internet + health care" service system, encouraging higher-level medical institutions to provide teleconsultation and other medical services to the grassroots, so that the grassroots can share quality medical resources and improve the capacity and efficiency of grassroots medical services. In addition, we are constantly improving our hardware facilities and software design, summarizing our experience and innovating applications in practice, so that we can continue to modernize our rural health care service system with information technology.

Skin diseases are one of the most common human diseases and place a huge nonfatal burden on the activities of daily life. They are caused by chemical, physical, and biological factors. Visual assessment combined with clinical information is a common disease diagnostic procedure. However, these procedures are manual, time consuming, and require experience and excellent visual perception. In this study, we present a face disease recognition analysis system that uses data from clinical images and patient information to identify and diagnose four common skin diseases using models trained by deep learning. Data is collected both online and offline, and different data preprocessing and enhancement techniques are applied to improve the performance of the model prior to training. To achieve the practicality of the model, we used the ShuffleNetV2 (Ma et al., 2018) module in our study and used blueprint separation convolution (BSConv) (Haase and Amthor, 2020) instead of the original Deep Separable Convolution (DSC) (Chollet, 2017) to improve the accuracy of the network while keeping the model lightweight. The results show that the developed system provides excellent diagnostic performance for these four dermatological conditions, and that it has the potential to be used as a decision support system in low-resource settings where dermatological expertise and tools are limited.

5.5.2 FACE DISEASE RECOGNITION THEORY TECHNOLOGY

5.5.2.1 Disease Recognition Model Building

To improve the accuracy of the model when the data set is limited, we add the pretrained convolutional neural network. The pretraining network is a well-preserved network, which has been trained on large data and before. We use the VGG16 architecture (Simonyan and Zisserman, 2014), which is a simple and widely used convolutional neural network architecture. The pretraining data set used is ImageNet, which has a large amount of data and of many kinds, and is widely used in the field of deep learning images. There are two methods to use the pretraining network: feature extraction and fine-tuning.

Feature extraction is to extract interesting features from new samples using the representation learned from the previous network and then put these features into a new classifier and train from scratch. Before compiling and training the model, one must "freeze" the convolution base. To "freeze" one or more layers means keeping its weight unchanged during the training process. Model fine-tuning and feature extraction complement each other. For the "frozen" model base used for feature extraction, fine-tuning refers to "thawing" the top layers of the model base and training the unfrozen layers and the newly added parts. The purpose of freezing convolution basis is to train a random initialization classifier on it.

In the training process, we iterated a total of 50 times, in each iteration process, the network will calculate the gradient of batch loss relative to the weight, and update the weight accordingly, so that the network loss value becomes small enough and the network can be classified with high accuracy. In the process of training and testing, we use the accuracy of the verification set as the monitoring index and draw the loss and accuracy change diagram of the model on the training data and validation data during the training process, as shown in Figure 5.20. Since the model is to achieve single label and multiclassification, in the process of training the model, we use the categorical_CrossEntropy as our loss function.

In the process of training, the phenomenon of overfitting often appears. The reason for overfitting is that there are too few learning samples to train models that can be generalized to new data. Data enhancement is to generate more training data from the existing training samples. The method is to increase the samples using a variety of random transformations that can generate credible images. In the training of the model, we do some operations on the training set, such as random stagger transformation, random scaling, and randomly flipping half of the image horizontally to reduce overfitting, as shown in Figure 5.21.

To further reduce overfitting, we also add dropout layer in the model, and it is added before the dense connection classifier. Dropout is one of the most effective and commonly used regularization methods for neural networks. Another common method to reduce overfitting is to force the model weight to take a smaller value, thus limiting the complexity of the model, which makes the distribution of weight values

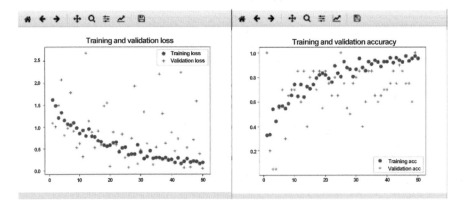

FIGURE 5.20   The loss and accuracy change diagram of the model.

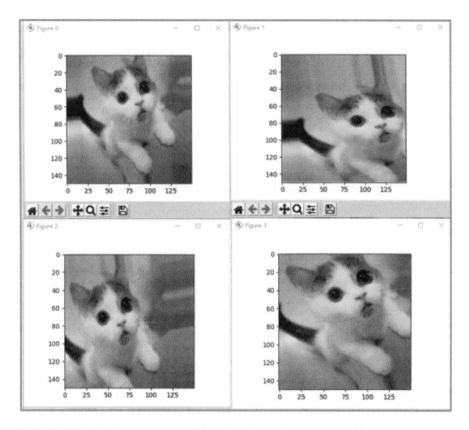

FIGURE 5.21   Cat image generated by random data enhancement.

more regular. It generally has two forms, L1 Regularization and L2 regularization. In our model, we use L2 regularization.

To reduce the interference of background information of images and to ensure the integrity of face feature information as much as possible, this study firstly reformed the data set by cutting the targets after SSD network detection, and finally, for the unbalanced part of the data set, the data set was expanded by flipping, rotating, adjusting the contrast, adjusting the brightness, and adjusting the chromaticity saturation, fancy PCA, to guarantee the integrity and enrichment of its triad. The first convolutional layer of the SSD is VGG-16, the main purpose of which is to extract the low-scale feature-mapping map; the second part is to connect the feature-mapping map output from the previous part of the network and to output four high-scale feature information through the convolutional neural network, the main task being to extract the high-scale feature-mapping map; and the last part is to predict the rectangular box information and the class information of each point in the feature-mapping map. The corresponding loss function consists of the loss of the predicted box position and the loss of the predicted class.

5.5.2.2 Disease Identification Network Optimization

The features of diseases have some similarities, which makes them relatively difficult to identify. To better identify and diagnose diseases, it is very important to improve the feature extraction of the network, so we substitute the bottleneck module with the ShuffleNetV2 basic unit in the network. At the beginning of each unit, the input of c feature channels is split into two branches with $c1$ and $c0$ channels, respectively. And one branch remains as identity. The other branch consists of three convolutions with the same input and output channels to satisfy the "equal channel width minimizes memory access cost." The two 1×1 convolutions are no longer groupwise, unlike, it is partially to follow "excessive group convolution increases MAC," and partially because the split operation already produces two groups. After convolution, the two branches are concatenated. So, the number of channels remains the same. The "channel shuffle" operation is then used to enable information communication between the two branches. After the shuffling, the next unit begins. Elementwise operations such as ReLU and depthwise convolutions exist only in one branch. ShuffleNetV2 is specifically designed for mobile devices with very limited computational power, so it is easy to deploy the model to mobile. It makes use of two new operations, namely, point-by-point grouped convolution and channel shuffle, which significantly reduces computational cost while maintaining accuracy (Figure 5.22).

The lightweight model is more practical and has faster training speed and less computing resources. DSC is used to establish a model in the original network to achieve the model's lightweight. The first layer of DSC is DW, which performs lightweight filtering by applying a convolution filter to each input channel. The second layer is a point-by-point convolution, which is responsible for constructing new

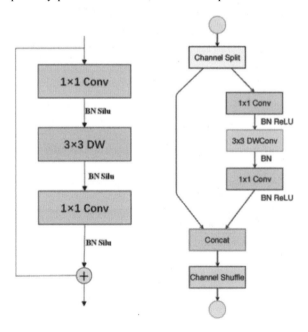

FIGURE 5.22 Bottleneck block and ShuffleNetV2 basic unit.

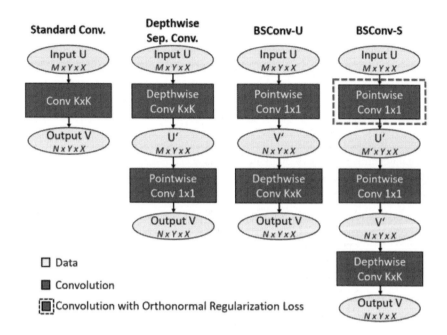

FIGURE 5.23 Computational graphs for the efficient implementation of the different BSConv variants.

features by calculating the linear combination of input channels. To further improve the model without increasing complexity, we use blueprint separation convolution (BSConv) instead of DSC as an effective building block of the backbone network. The explanation of BSConv is shown in Figure 5.23. BSConv focuses on the correlation within the kernel, while DSC strengthens the correlation between the kernels. The results show that the former is dominant and has greater potential for the effective separation of regular convolution. This is because in BSConv, through the previous point-by-point distribution, the depth convolution can make full use of the feature mapping of the previous convolution. In contrast, each kernel of the DSC's first deep convolution can only benefit from a single feature map, resulting in limited expression ability. Therefore, we introduce BSConv as a more effective regular convolution separation.

However, in order to avoid the problem of gradient disappearance and gradient explosion caused by the deeper network structure, the residual neural network was selected for this study, and the network structure was deepened using Shortcut Connection, which effectively solved the above problems. This structure can not only establish connections between adjacent network layers but can also perform cross-layer connections. This neural network is not only less computationally intensive but also allows for a significant increase in the number of depth layers.

5.5.3   Network Model Visualization

To further analyze the model, visualization operations were carried out, which mainly contained a thermal diagram, intermediate activation, and visualization filter. The class-activated thermal map is a two-dimensional fractional grid related to a specific output category; every position of any input image must be calculated, which indicates the importance of each location to the category. The visualization of class-activated thermal map is helpful in understanding which part of an image makes the final classification decision, which is used to debug the decision-making process of the convolutional neural network, especially in the case of classification errors (see Figure 5.24).

The intermediate activation of the convolutional neural network helps to understand how the continuous layer of the convolutional neural network transforms the input and also to preliminarily understand the meaning of each filter in the convolutional neural network (see Figure 5.25). The filter of the convolutional neural network is helpful to understand the visual pattern or visual concept easily accepted by each filter in convolutional neural network (see Figure 5.26).

5.5.4   Face Disease Visualization and Analysis Interface

Through data training, we finally get a model with an accuracy of about 80%. We visualize the trained model and get a UI model as shown in Figure 5.27. Disease

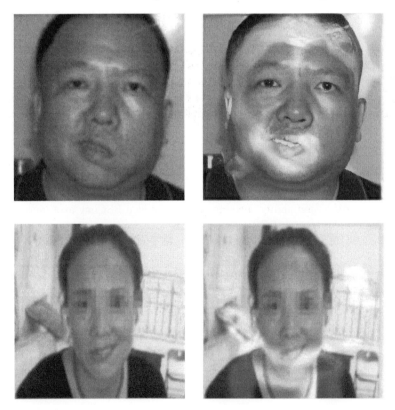

FIGURE 5.24   Overlay the class-activated thermal map to the original image.

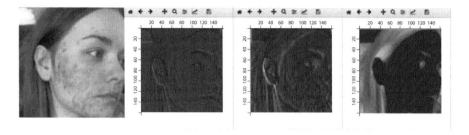

FIGURE 5.25 Visualization of some intermediate activated channels.

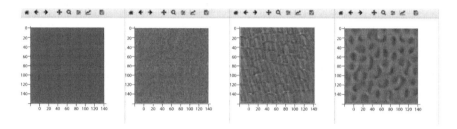

FIGURE 5.26 Filter mode for some layers.

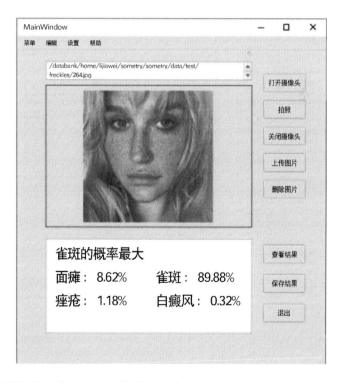

FIGURE 5.27 Face disease analysis UI model.

diagnosis can be done by taking pictures or uploading local pictures to the model, clicking the view result button to diagnose the disease, and the model will output the probability of each disease and determine which disease is most likely. The diagnostic results can be saved by clicking the save result button. Through this interface, we can upload images for disease identification and analysis, which is very interesting and useful.

5.6 SUMMARY

In this chapter, we introduce the present research and work progress related to plant disease identification, livestock management, medical technology, and facial disease detection. For plant disease identification, we propose an improved detection algorithm based on YOLOv5s and design a plant disease detection application system. For livestock management, we propose an improved method of fusion of multiple optimization to verify the high similarity of cashmere goat ID. For medical technology, we propose a cutting-based surface parameterization transfer algorithm that can be used to transfer the surface parameterization attribute. For facial disease detection, we propose a platform to embed deep learning methods, train and generate a network that can recognize and classify facial diseases first, and then embed the network into the system to assist the rural health system.

In the future, computer technology will further assist agricultural development, for example, building a crop monitoring system based on drones, designing robots for automatic pesticide spraying, building an intelligent system for crop grading and sorting, and selecting and classifying crops based on their phenotypic analysis. In addition, computer technology can also be applied to livestock management, identifying and classifying animals for their behavior, predicting their body size and weight, etc. In our study, we combine computer technology with the actual situation in the countryside to promote the development of intensive, factory, modern, and industrialized farming and animal husbandry, which is an effective way to bring the distance between the countryside and the towns closer and to achieve high-quality sustainable development of farming and animal husbandry.

REFERENCES

Berg, A. C., Fu, C. Y., Szegedy, C., Anguelov, D., Erhan, D., & Reed, S. et al. (2015). *SSD: Single Shot MultiBox Detector*. Springer, Cham. https://doi.org/10.1007/978-3-319-46448-0_2.

Bochkovskiy, A., Wang, C. Y., & Liao, H. (2020). *YOLOv4: Optimal Speed and Accuracy of Object Detection*. Cornell University, Canada.

Bock, C. H. et al. (2010). Plant disease severity estimated visually, by digital photography and image analysis, and by hyperspectral imaging. Critical Reviews in Plant Sciences, 29(2), 59–107.

Carion, N. et al. (2020). End-to-end object detection with transformers. In *European Conference on Computer Vision*, pp. 213–229. Springer, Cham: Springer International Publishing.

Chollet, F. (2017). Xception: Deep learning with depthwise separable convolutions. In *IEEE Conference on Computer Vision and Pattern Recognition (CVPR)*. pp. 1251–1258. IEEE, Boston, MA.

Garciaab, J. (2013). Digital image processing techniques for detecting, quantifying and classifying plant diseases. *Springerplus*, 2(1), 660.

Goodfellow, I., Pouget-Abadie, J., Mirza, M. et al. (2014). *Generative Adversarial Nets. Neural Information Processing Systems.* MIT Press, Cambridge, MA.

Haase, D. & Amthor, M. (2020). *Rethinking Depthwise Separable Convolutions: How Intra-Kernel Correlations Lead to Improved MobileNets.* IEEE, Boston, MA. https://doi.org/10.1109/CVPR42600.2020.01461.

Jiang, H. et al. (2020). CNN feature based graph convolutional network for weed and crop recognition in smart farming. *Computers and Electronics in Agriculture*, 174, 105450.

Ma, N., Zhang, X., Zheng, H.T. et al. (2018). *ShuffleNet V2: Practical Guidelines for Efficient CNN Architecture Design.* Springer, Cham.

Qi, J. et al. (2022). An improved yolov5 model based on visual attention mechanism: application to recognition of tomato virus disease. *Computers and Electronics in Agriculture*, 194, 106780

Schroff, F., Kalenichenko, D., & Philbin, J. (2015). *FaceNet: A Unified Embedding for Face Recognition and Clustering.* IEEE, Boston, MA. https://doi.org/10.1109/CVPR.2015.7298682.

Shepley, A. et al. (2020). *Confluence: A Robust Non-IoU Alternative to Non-Maxima Suppression in Object Detection.* Cornell University, Canada.

Simonyan, K. & Zisserman, A. (2014). Very deep convolutional networks for large-scale image recognition. *Computer Science*, 1409, 1556.

Sun, H. et al. (2021). Mean-SSD: A novel real-time detector for apple leaf diseases using improved light-weight convolutional neural networks. *Computers and Electronics in Agriculture*, 189, 106379.

Sun, K., Xiao, B., Liu, D. et al. (2019). *Deep High-Resolution Representation Learning for Human Pose Estimation.* arXiv e-prints.

Szegedy, C. et al. (2016). *Rethinking the Inception Architecture for Computer Vision*, pp. 2818–2826. IEEE, Boston, MA.

Wang, D. et al. (2021). T-CNN: Trilinear convolutional neural networks model for visual detection of plant diseases. *Computers and Electronics in Agriculture*, 190, 106468.

Wojke, N., Bewley, A., & Paulus, D. (2017). *Simple Online and Realtime Tracking with a Deep Association Metric.* IEEE, Boston, MA. https://doi.org/10.1109/icip.2017.8296962.

Zhang, D. et al. (2022). Assessment of the levels of damage caused by fusarium head blight in wheat using an improved yolov5 method. *Computers and Electronics in Agriculture*, 198, 107086.

Zhang, Z. & Sabuncu, M. R. (2018). *Generalized Cross Entropy Loss for Training Deep Neural Networks with Noisy Labels.* Cornell University, Canada.

Zhu, J. Y., Park, T., & Isola, P. et al. (2017). *Unpaired Image-to-Image Translation using Cycle-Consistent Adversarial Networks.* IEEE, Venice, Italy.

6 Sustainable Mental Health Services for Rural Schools

Guozhen Zhao

6.1 INTRODUCTION

6.1.1 Mental Health of Rural Adolescents is Worrying

Recently, the China Children's Center and the Social Sciences Literature Publishing House jointly released the *Blue Book for Children: Report on the Development of Chinese Children* (2021) in Beijing. It pointed out that, under the influence of health management policies, Chinese children's health has continued to improve. However, the mental problems have been getting worse at the same time. According to the 2018 China Youth Development Report, there are about 30 million Chinese children and adolescents under the age of 17 suffering from various emotional and behavioral problems. Incorrect educational methods of parents, intense competition for higher education, bullying in schools, and the complex network environment have brought different degrees of tension and psychological pressure to teenagers.

When investigating adolescents' mental health status in urban and rural areas, we find adolescents in rural areas are more vulnerable to mental problems. Xie (2019) investigated the mental health status of 1,317 rural primary school students in Jiangxi and found that 55.9% of the students had severe learning anxiety. Yu and his colleagues surveyed 7,672 students in grades three to six in 47 primary schools in Guangxi province from September to December 2018 (Yu et al., 2019). The results showed that there were significant differences between urban and rural areas in the scores of the eight subscales of mental health: learning anxiety, loneliness, physical symptoms, fear, impulsiveness, anxiety about others, self-blame, and allergy. Hou (2010) conducted a psychological survey on the children of the rural migrant population in Taicang. The result showed that compared with urban students, rural students are more likely to show early warning on factors such as interpersonal sensitivity, terror, and psychotic symptoms. In addition, rural students performed worse on interpersonal dimension, for they have lower interpersonal support and are hard to get along with others (Yu and Wang, 2018). Apart from higher incidence in mental problems, rural students have lower scores in positive mental characters. According to Li's study (2019), the overall level of positive mental health of rural students is lower than that of urban students.

DOI: 10.1201/9781032686691-6

6.1.2 THE SHORTAGE OF RURAL MENTAL HEALTH RESOURCES

The reason why rural adolescents have worse mental status than their urban peers comes from both family and school.

When considering factors from family, the first that comes into our mind is socio-economic status (SES). It is shown in a study that, according to social cognitive theory of social class, people who are in low SES own fewer socioeconomic resources than people in high SES. Thus, they will be conquered with more threats, negative emotions, and pressure that induced mental problems (Li et al., 2019). Born in low SES families, children are easier to get the risk of developmental problems, because they have little access to material, social resources, and methods in coping with stress (Bradley and Corwyn, 2002). Generally speaking, families in rural areas have fewer access to social resources than families in urban areas, which makes it more difficult for rural adolescents to get enough attention and support when they suffer from psychiatric disturbance.

Another factor from the family is that, in rural areas, a large percentage of students are "left-behind children" (LBC). In China, the rapid development of urbanization and industrialization in the past several decades has made rural-to-urban migration to its largest scale (Wang et al., 2019). In order to make a better life, many rural adults choose to make living in other cities, leaving their children at hometown. The estimated LBC is about 41 million in rural area, meaning that, in rural areas, almost in every three children, there is a left-behind child (Lv et al., 2018). This reality is an obstacle to communication between family members. Ye (2000) conducted a survey on the families of urban and rural junior high school students. He found that urban junior high school students were significantly better than rural junior high school students in terms of family intimacy and family members' communication. The absence of parents in youth development makes youth vulnerable to negative effects in several domains, such as personality, stress-coping strategy, life events, and mental health problems (Qin and Albin, 2010). Besides, LBC are also more likely to receive caregiver's neglect or mental abuse and exposed to delinquent behaviors and victimization (Cheng et al., 2010; Chen et al., 2017).

Because of the long distance to get to school, there are a large number of rural schoolchildren who have to study at boarding schools. Thus, they spend a majority of time at school. From this point of view, school plays an important role in affecting rural students' mental health. However, it seems mental health education in rural school lags behind that in urban school, which also contributes to poor mental health status of rural students.

For one thing, it is not rare for rural schools underestimating the importance of mental health. Compared to urban students, the academic competition for rural school children is more intensive. Education is always the critical path for rural students to have a wider range of career options or to improve the SES. Most of the time, only top students in rural areas have access to this transition. Given that mental health has nothing to do with test scores, mental health courses and activities are often replaced by courses that are conducive to good grades in the entrance exam (e.g., Chinese, Math, and English). Generated from intensive competition, it is too hard for rural students to relieve competitive pressure as they have weak mental health supports.

At the same time, rural schools are in shortage of professional support, both in basic equipment and in human resources.

In order to investigate the current situation of mental health education resource allocation in primary and secondary schools, Xi (2018) took Xingtai as an example, only to find that psychoeducational resources in urban and rural areas are distributed unequally. 78.95% of urban schools carry out mental health education. However, only 40.58% of rural schools offer mental health courses. Among 58 pilot schools with mental health programs, 19 do not have funds earmarked for mental health education, 16 of which are rural primary schools. There were 48 private counseling rooms, among which 18 belong to rural school and 30 belong to urban schools. In addition, only 35 schools have full- or part-time mental health teachers, of which 22 are located in cities and 13 in rural areas. A large number of leaders and teachers in rural areas lack a comprehensive understanding of mental health, because of which mental health education has been put on hold or suspended. Many elite teachers are reluctant to work in rural areas, leading to a wider gap between urban and rural mental health education. In addition, urban teachers regularly receive mental health training from educational psychologists or experts, while rural teachers are less likely to get these resources, making the latter lacking of knowledge regarding professional mental health monitoring, mental health education, and intervention skills. For example, rural teachers might regard symptoms (such as fatigue, silence, or abnormal emotional reactions) displayed by depressed students as normal signs of weariness and thus pay little attention or empathy.

6.1.3   SUSTAINABLE MENTAL HEALTH SERVICE MODEL

Taking all these issues into account, we proposed that there would be a sustainable model, which is run to provide high-quality mental health services to rural areas. There are three components included in the Sustainable Mental Health Services Model: classic mental health screening, multimodal observation, and intervention for students.

The classic mental health screening is designed to get a comprehensive understanding of the mental state of rural students, by carrying out professional psychological assessment. There are many teachers who know little about psychological assessment, so they don't know how to conduct mental screening, what kind of tools could be used for, or what the scores reveal about students' mental status. Meanwhile, the huge number of rural students makes it more difficult to assess general mental health status in rural schools. By making use of Multimodal Human Factors Intelligent Quick Check Box, rural students could have access to mental health screening by which the professional psychological assessment becomes available in rural areas.

Considering the shortage of traditional assessment tools that they could only output "outcome data," we add multimodal observation into our Sustainable Mental Health Services Model. Multimodal observation provides us a view to observe what is happening in rural students' mind during activities. By means of multimodal observation, it is possible for us to continuously update the techniques and make the mental evaluation more precisely, by combining kinds of indices into analyzing mental status, such as eye movement, gestures, and facial expressions.

In addition, we have developed data-driven group-counseling and self-adapted mental course design system so that mental health education would be more in line with the mental status of rural students.

6.2   MENTAL HEALTH SCREENING

6.2.1   DESCRIPTION OF MENTAL HEALTH GENERAL SCREENING AND SPECIAL SCREENING

Considering the difficulties in conducting large-scale mental health assessment in rural areas, we designed an efficient, practical, and comprehensive mental health screening program, with Mental Health General Screening and Special Screening included.

General mental health screening is an extensive screening plan for students in schools, evaluating a wide range of psychological issues of children and teenagers, with a large group of students screened each time.

As for special screening, it is designed to detect certain psychological and behavioral problems of rural students at an early stage and is considered as an evidence for psychiatrist diagnosis. It is aimed at children and adolescents with suspected symptoms as well as those who show high risk at certain dimensions in the general screening.

According to the rank of prevalence, we selected four psychological or behavioral disorders as dimensions for special screening, which are also widely concerned by society, including ADHD, depression, Internet addiction, and aggressive behavior. We briefly introduce these four problems as follows.

Attention-deficit hyperactivity disorder (ADHD) is one of the most common behavioral disorders in childhood. It is reported that the prevalence of ADHD in children and adolescents worldwide is about 7.20% (Wolraich et al., 2019), and that in China it is 6.26%. What should not be ignored is, as with the increase in academic competition and pressure, the prevalence of ADHD shows an upward trend year by year (Liu et al., 2018). Additionally, the patients of ADHD are more vulnerable to other mental disorders such as Oppositional Defiant Disorder or Depression at the same time. What's more, ADHD children usually have learning difficulties; hence, they need more medical consumption and education investment, which aggravates the burden of families and society (Guevara and Mandell, 2003). Several studies have shown that the prevalence of ADHD in rural children is 30% higher than that in urban children (Danielson et al., 2018).

In 2019, the special survey on mental health of young people conducted by China Youth Research Center and the Institute of Psychology of the Chinese Academy of Sciences showed that 7.7% of young people aged 14–18 had high risk of depression. Many studies have reported that the incidence of depressive symptoms of LBC is much higher than that of non-LBC (Wang et al., 2019). Hence, we are supposed to pay more attention to the risk of depression among those LBC in remote counties.

Internet addiction refers to problematic, compulsive use of the Internet, which causes significant impairment in an individual's social, academic, and psychological functions over a prolonged period of time (Chen et al., 2007). Adolescents are at particular risk of developing Internet addiction disorder. There are case studies showing that problematic Internet use will lead to a decline in students' academic performance (Mishra et al., 2014). Internet addiction would also cause health consequences as well, such as loss of sleep, exercise, and increased risks for carpal tunnel syndrome and eye and back strain (Wallace, 2014). A longitudinal study of high school students in China found that students with moderate to severe risk of Internet addiction were 2.5 times more likely to develop depressive symptoms compared to their counterparts without Internet addiction (Lam and Peng, 2010). According to a survey, the number of primary school students' Internet users reached 327 million, of which the proportion of rural primary school students' Internet users was 27.6% (Li and Li, 2017). Since many of them are LBC, lacking care from parents, they would be more likely to depend on surfing the Internet to meet the emotional needs. These findings alerted attention to Internet addiction among rural students.

Studies have shown that 48% of teenagers who commit crimes have aggressive behaviors at the age of nine, and 70% of them have shown aggressive behaviors at the age of 13 (Xu and Zhang, 2016). In rural areas, children do not have a benign communication with their parents and other caregivers. This makes children more prone to mood swings during conflicts with others and show aggressive behaviors (Xu and Zhang, 2016). Research shows that if not corrected in time, the aggressive behavior of these children will deteriorate into a violent crime that put threats on social security (Song et al., 2017). Hence, it is crucial for the security of society and the developments of children to figure out whether children in rural areas have aggressive behaviors.

Early detection and intervention of adolescents' mental health problems can prevent the occurrence of mental disorders to a great extent.

6.2.2 SERVICE PATTERN OF MENTAL HEALTH SCREENING

We formulated a complete service pattern of our mental health screening, which can be used for convenient mental health screening in remote counties.

First, we build a team of experts to select effective measurement tools. We made a list of common psychological problems of primary and secondary school students, which is also an important basis for screening tools. Meanwhile, when selecting these tools, we considered the age range for which the tool is intended. For example, Child Behavior Checklist (CBCL) is suitable for assessing the depressive state of primary school students, while PHQ-9 is more suitable for assessing the depressive state of high school students. When testing the ability of sustained attention, we presented elementary school students with an adapted version of the cognitive task, which seems more like a game for fun. When it comes to middle school students, we presented the classic experimental paradigm. At the same time, given the knowledge level of primary school students (especially in lower grades), they might have difficulty in understanding and answering questionnaires. Therefore, in addition to the self-report questionnaire, we also took the evaluation of parents and teachers into consideration and integrated subjective and objective indicators to evaluate the psychological and behavioral problems of primary school students. What's more, we added polygraph questions to the plan, which can accurately screen for invalid individual assessments and timely target and record students with abnormal assessment processes.

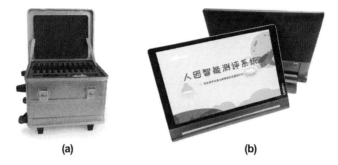

(a) (b)

FIGURE 6.1 Quick Test Box and pad terminals used in mental health screening. (a) Quick Test Box. (b) Pad terminals.

Secondly, during the test, we used self-developed Multimodal Human Factors Intelligent Quick Test Box. Quick Test Box is loaded on the engineering vehicles. Each vehicle can load up to 10 boxes, and each box has 25 pad terminals inside (see Figure 6.1). Two to three scientific research assistants would be on-site to conduct the screening, explain the test instructions, and debug equipment. All assessments can be presented through the pad terminal. Students only need to participate in the assessment in the classroom where they attend daily courses, and there is no need for schools to provide extra classrooms and computers. With this device, we could collect a large number of original data, then analyze the psychological scale and cognitive task data, and monitor the assessment process in real time. Taking advantage of this box, the test administration training for teachers has also become simpler and less time consuming. Quick Test Box and engineering vehicle break the wall of uneven mental health resources in urban and rural areas, making rural schools and families to get mental health screening services easily and quickly.

Finally, the minute the test is over, the evaluation report can be generated immediately, which combines multiple dimensions of the test and norm with a large sample base to comprehensively evaluate the mental health status of students. This is conducive to timely detect students who are under abnormal psychological states. In order to solve the problem that many teachers in rural areas lack mental health knowledge and cannot read the psychological assessment report, we would provide a detailed interpretation about the evaluation results.

In the report analyzing the mental health status of a single student (see Figure 6.2), we labeled the mental health status with three levels: mild warning, moderate warning, and severe warning. The level of warning depends on the degree to which the score exceeds the normal range. The higher the warning level, the greater the gap between the individual's mental health and the normal value. Mild warning indicates that the individual's study, daily life, and interpersonal communication are slightly impacted by mental health status. Moderate warning indicates that the individual has some troubles in study or life, requiring one-to-one psychological counseling. Severe warning indicates that the student might be at higher risk of mental illness, that is, his/her study and daily life are negatively impacted. Teachers and professional psychological counselors can also take the assessment results as a reference to quickly formulate targeted interventions. If a student's mental state is rated as severe

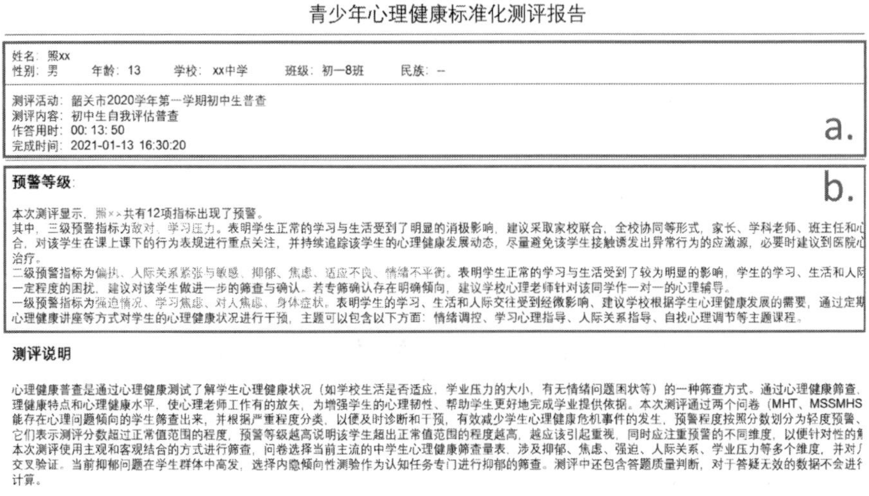

青少年心理健康标准化测评报告

姓名: 熙xx
性别: 男   年龄: 13   学校: xx中学   班级: 初一8班   民族: --

测评活动: 韶关市2020学年第一学期初中生普查
测评内容: 初中生自我评估普查
作答用时: 00: 13: 50
完成时间: 2021-01-13 16:30:20   a.

预警等级: b.

本次测试显示, 熙××共有12项指标出现了预警。
其中, 三级预警指标为放对   学习压力。表明学生正常的学习与生活受到了明显的消极影响, 建议采取家校联合, 全校协同等形式, 家长、学科老师、班主任和心
合。对该学生在课上课下的行为表现进行重点关注, 并持续追踪该学生的心理健康发展动态, 尽量避免该学生接触诱发出异常行为的应激源, 必要时建议到医院心
治疗。
二级预警指标为偏执、人际关系紧张与敏感、抑郁、焦虑、适应不良、情绪不平衡。表明学生正常的学习与生活受到了较为明显的影响, 学生的学习、生活和人际
一定程度的困扰。建议对该学生做进一步的筛查与确认。若专筛确认存在明确倾向, 建议学校心理老师针对该同学作一一对一的心理辅导。
一级预警指标为强迫倾向、学习焦虑、对人焦虑、身体症状。表明学生的学习、生活和人际交往受到轻微影响, 建议学校根据学生心理健康发展的需要, 通过定期
心理健康讲座等方式对学生的心理健康状况进行干预, 主题可以包含以下方面: 情绪调控、学习心理指导、人际关系指导、自我心理调节等主题课程。

测评说明

心理健康普查是通过心理健康测试了解学生心理健康状况 (如学校生活是否适应, 学业压力的大小, 有无情绪问题困状等) 的一种筛查方式。通过心理健康筛查,
理健康特点和心理健康水平, 使心理老师工作有的放矢, 为增强学生心理韧性、帮助学生更好地完成学业提供依据。本次测评通过两个问卷 (MHT、MSSMHS
能在心理问题倾向的学生筛查出来, 并根据严重程度分类, 以便及时诊断和干预。有效减少学生心理健康危机事件的发生, 预警程度按照分数划分为轻度预警、
它们表示测评分数超过正常值范围的程度, 预警等级越高说明该学生超出正常值范围的程度越高, 越应该引起重视, 同时应注重预警的不同维度, 以便针对性的教
本次测评使用主观和客观结合的方式进行筛查, 问卷选择当前主流的中学生心理健康筛查量表, 涉及抑郁、焦虑、强迫、人际关系、学业压力等多个维度, 并对I
交叉验证。当前抑郁问题在学生群体中高发, 选择内隐倾向性测验作为认知任务专门进行抑郁的筛查。测评中还包含答题质量判断, 对于答疑无效的数据不会进行
计算。

FIGURE 6.2   Sample mental health assessment report for individuals. (a) Personal information of the participant. (b) Warning levels and descriptions of the participants' performance
according to the screening process.

warning, the teacher must pay more attention to the student and prevent him/her from
getting exposed to dangerous triggers. And, if necessary, the student needs to go to
the hospital's psychiatric department for treatment.

At the same time, we also provide a group report summarizing the statistics of
all students who participated in the test (see Figure 6.3), which includes ratios of
different stressors and mental health problems in this assessment as well as the ratio
of warnings within each grade. This will be helpful for the school administration
team to obtain a macroscopic understanding of the students' current mental health
conditions and the differences in stressors and mental health issues among students
of different grades so that the school can accordingly adopt targeted teaching and
management plans.

Using engineering vehicles and Quick Test Box, remote rural areas can easily and
quickly get scientific psychological and behavioral evaluation. We may update the
measurements tools, such as scales and cognitive tasks. However, we will keep the
evaluation method by combining subjective and objective indicators and get data of
high reliability.

6.2.3   CASE STUDY OF CONDUCTING MENTAL HEALTH
GENERAL SCREENING IN RURAL AREAS

In this section, we first introduce a standardized procedure of conducting the Mental
Health General Screening of primary and high school students living in rural areas.
Then, we present some statistics and findings from our large-scale mental health
screening projects in two counties, Ruyuan and Shixing.

The Mental Health General Screening program has developed four toolkits for
assessing four psychological and behavioral problems (i.e., ADHD, depression,

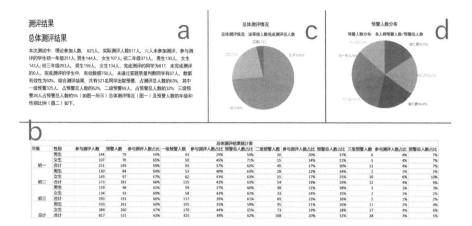

FIGURE 6.3 Sample mental health assessment report for groups. (a) Summarize the assessment results of all students, including the number of students with valid assessment results, and the number of students with three levels of warning. (b) Descriptive statistics that reveals the number and proportion of boys and girls in each grade in the three warning levels. (c) The proportion of students whose mental health status is in normal state, mild warning, moderate warning, and severe warning. (d) The proportion of boys and girls whose results show early warning by grade.

Internet addiction, and aggressive behaviors) that are particularly worrying in school-age individuals. Furthermore, the focus of screening and the specific tools applied differ between individuals of different age groups. The detailed dimensions assessed in the Mental Health General Screening program and tools applied are summarized in Table 6.1.

A typical Mental Health General Screening process consists of five steps, as shown in Figure 6.4. First, the Quick Test Box is carried by trained personnel as they enter the school. To prepare for the subsequent test procedure, they will set up the Quick Test Box and build internal networks connecting the main system and tablets used for evaluation. In the meanwhile, teachers or other relevant persons in charge will organize students to enter a quite classroom to wait for the assessment. After equipment setup is completed, the testers will distribute pads to students, explain instructions, and ask them to complete the questionnaires and cognitive tasks. To reduce indiscriminate or deliberately messed responses, which can affect the accuracy of the assessment, we use indicators such as polygraph questions and reaction time to evaluate the quality of responses for each questionnaire and cognitive task. Students whose responses did not pass the quality assessment will be removed from the data pool. After all students have finished the whole assessment, the testers will take back the pads and generate a group report of the present assessment to show to the teachers or other relevant persons in charge.

We have implemented the Mental Health General Screening program in many rural areas. We will emphasize on the results and statistics collected from two counties, Ruyuan and Shixing, because of the high proportion of LBC population and relatively delayed economic development in these two areas. Since the tools used for

TABLE 6.1

The General Mental Health Test Framework for Elementary, Middle, and High School Students

Educational Stage	Dimensions	Type	Note
Elementary school	Depression	Questionnaire	To get the knowledge about whether children have any sign of depressive disorder.
		Cognitive task	To detect whether children have attention bias to negative facial expressions.
	Attention	Questionnaire	To detect whether children could focus on specific task.
		Questionnaire	Invite parents to evaluate whether their children have any difficulties in keeping attention and controlling impulsive behaviors.
		Cognitive task	To test whether children could focus on a specific target sustainably.
	Internet-addictive behavior	Questionnaire	To detect whether students have an addiction to Internet.
Middle school	Overview	Questionnaire	To evaluate comprehensive mental status from diverse perspectives, including obsessive–compulsive symptoms, paranoia, hostility, interpersonal tension and sensitivity, depression, anxiety, learning pressure, maladaptation, emotional imbalance, and other 10 factors.
	Anxiety	Questionnaire	To test whether adolescents have general or chronic anxiety.
	Depression	Cognitive task	To detect whether adolescents have attention bias to negative facial expressions.
High school	Overview	Questionnaire	To evaluate comprehensive mental status from diverse perspectives, including somatization, obsessive–compulsive symptoms, interpersonal sensitivity, depression, anxiety, hostility, terror, paranoia, psychosis, and other factors.
	Depression	Questionnaire	To test whether adolescents have any sign of depressive disorder.
		Cognitive task	To detect whether adolescents have attention bias to negative facial expressions.

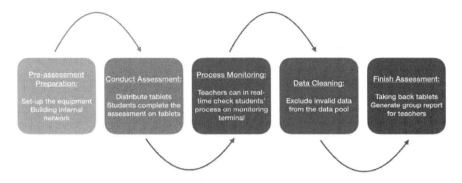

FIGURE 6.4 The Mental Health General Screening process. The whole process starts at preassessment preparation and ends at finish assessment.

Mental Health General Screening program of secondary school students are fully consistent, here we primarily compare data collected in middle and high school students.

As an example, we chose to present the statistics obtained using the Chinese Middle School Student Mental Health Scale (MSSMHS). MSSMHS is a comprehensive mental health assessment questionnaire designed for Chinese students aged between 11 and 20 years, which consists of 10 dimensions, including obsessive–compulsive symptoms, paranoid, hostility, relationship tension and sensitivity, depression, anxiety, academic pressure, maladaptive, emotional imbalance, and mental imbalance. It was used in our General Mental Health Screening program to get a comprehensive knowledge about adolescents' mental states. The detailed interpretations of each dimension are summarized in Table 6.2.

In Ruyuan, a total of 6,475 students completed the assessment. There were 2,045 invalid responses that were excluded, resulting in an effective response rate of 65.93%. The results indicated that a total of 3,634 students reached a warning level in at least one dimension, accounting for 56.12% of the total number of students who completed the assessment. Among middle school students, the number of students who reached a warning level in the emotional imbalance dimension was 1,347, accounting for 62.6% of the total, which was the highest among all dimensions. Figure 6.5 illustrates the total number of middle school students who reached the three warning levels in each dimension.

As we can see in Figure 6.5, the dimension that has the highest number of students who reached the Severe warning level was anxiety, with 149 students in total, accounting for 6.9% of students who completed the assessment. As with the dimension that has the highest number of Moderate warnings was emotional imbalance (343 students, accounting for 15.9% of the total). Obsessive–compulsive symptom and emotional imbalance are two most prominent dimensions in those who reached a Mild warning level, with a total of 927 and 926 students, accounting for 43.1% and 43% of the total, respectively.

Figure 6.6 illustrates the number of high school students in Ruyuan county who reached the three warning levels in each dimension. We can see that among high school students, academic pressure was the most prominent dimension among all

TABLE 6.2

Interpretations of Dimensions of the MSSMHS

Dimensions	Interpretations
Obsessive–compulsive symptoms	Measures obsessive–compulsive behaviors, e.g., repeated, persistent, and unwanted thoughts; worrying about minor problems; and uncontrollably double-check their homework because of worry about making mistakes.
Paranoid	Measures paranoid behaviors, e.g., distrust of most people, irrationally suspecting that they are being intentionally misjudged and excluded by others, and thinking they are being threatened in some way.
Hostility	Persistent anger accompanied by an intense urge to retaliate. Typical behaviors include being difficult to control one's temper, frequently arguing or fighting with others, and being easily agitated.
Relationship tension and sensitivity	Measures feelings of being rejected in interpersonal relationships, such as being misunderstood by others, blame others for hurting their feelings, and feel uncomfortable when interacting with others.
Depression	Measures symptoms related to depression, such as feelings of sadness, tearfulness, emptiness or hopelessness, loss of interest or pleasure in most or all normal activities, and lack of energy.
Anxiety	Measures symptoms related to anxiety, such as difficulty controlling feelings of worry, being easily fatigued, having difficulty concentrating, and being irritable.
Academic pressure	Measures stressful feelings about their academic achievement, such as refusing to go to school or attend class, refusing to complete homework, and excessive anxiety of exams.
Maladaptive	Measures feelings of being ineffective in coping with school life, such as feel uncomfortable in school, refuse to participate in extracurricular activities, and unsuitable to the teacher's teaching methods.
Emotional imbalance	Measures behaviors or feelings related to emotional instability, such as being overemotional, having changeable attitudes toward others, and showing noticeable fluctuations in academic performance caused by emotion swings.
Mental imbalance	Measures feelings of being treated unfairly by others or feelings of anxiety, sadness, and jealousy when peers achieved higher grades than themselves.

warning levels, as a total of 731 students reached a warning level at this dimension, accounting for 52.9% of the total. Emotional imbalance was the second most prominent dimension among all warning levels, with a total of 701 students, accounting for 50.8% of the total.

In the Shixing county, the same program was conducted in a larger sample of students. In this assessment, a total of 19,330 elementary, middle, and high school

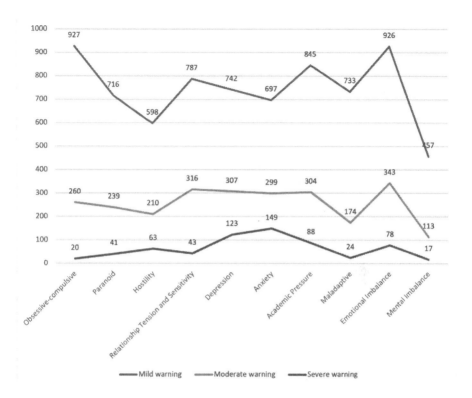

FIGURE 6.5 The number of Ruyuan middle school students reaching the three warning levels at each dimension.

students had completed the whole assessment, and a total of 17,511 valid data were retained, resulting in a final data validity rate of 90.59%. The results showed that a total of 11,739 students reached a warning level in at least one dimension, accounting for 60.73% of the total number of students who completed the assessment.

As we can see in Figure 6.7, statistics obtained from Shixing middle school students share a lot of similarities with that from Ruyuan middle school students. In Shixing, anxiety was also the most prominent dimension for middle school students who reached the Severe warning level (396 students, accounting for 6.1% of the total). There were 829 students who reached the Moderate warnings in emotional imbalance, accounting for 12.8% of the total, which is the highest number of Moderate warnings. The highest number of Mild warnings was obsessive–compulsive symptoms (2,781 students, accounting for 43% of the total).

Figure 6.8 illustrates the number of Shixing high school students who reached warning thresholds in each dimension. Similar to that in Ruyuan high school, academic pressure was still a serious problem for high school students in Shixing county, since 1,827 (37.1%) students received warnings at this dimension. However, it is different from Ruyuan high school that emotional imbalance appeared to be the most prominent issue among high school students in Shixing county, with 2,053 (41.8%) students received warnings at this dimension.

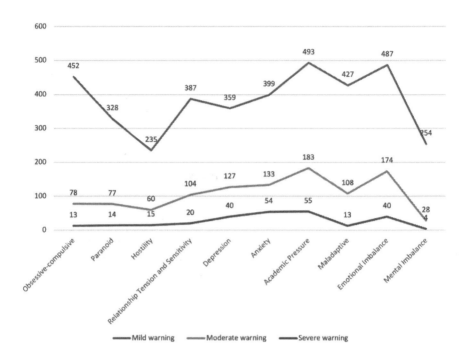

FIGURE 6.6 The number of Ruyuan high school students reaching the three warning levels at each dimension.

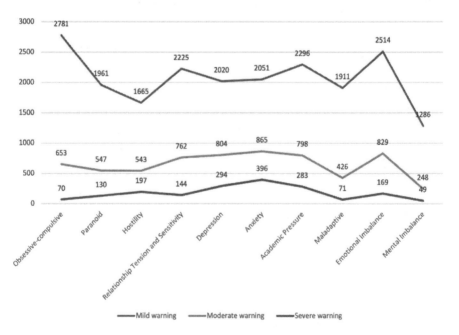

FIGURE 6.7 The number of Shixing middle school students reaching the three warning levels at each dimension.

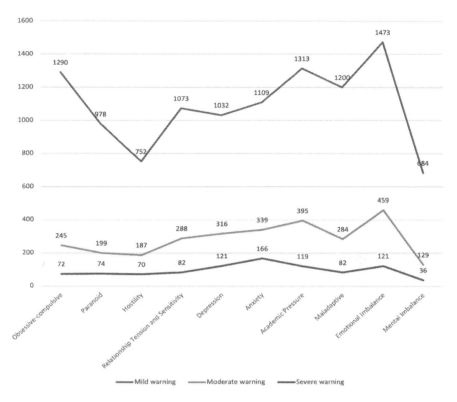

FIGURE 6.8 The number of Shixing high school students reaching the three warning levels at each dimension.

From the statistics described above, we can see that anxiety, academic pressure, emotional imbalance, and obsessive–compulsive symptoms were noticeable dimensions that are impacting middle and high school students' mental health conditions. These findings are consistent with previous research conducted in rural areas. For example, a survey of 1,186 middle school students from a rural area in the western Guangxi using the Mental Health Test (MHT) found that academic anxiety is one of the main factors influencing students' mental health, as 54.55% of them indicated academic anxiety tendencies above the warning threshold (Li et al., 2021). Another study further compared MHT scores of middle school students living in rural and urban areas, and they found that the average total score was significantly higher in rural students, indicating a generally higher prevalence of psychological problems among rural students, and the average score of academic anxiety was also more pronounced in the rural student population (Ye, 2000). One possible explanation could be the idea that "knowledge is the key to change your destiny," which is widely committed by parents in rural areas. Thus, they usually pay more attention to their children's grades and tend to regard high academic achievement as a prerequisite to be admitted to a top university, find a well-paid job, and enjoy life with a high quality in the future. Therefore, rural parents tend to have more restricted requirements for their children's academic performance, which will finally cause higher academic pressure and academic anxiety.

In addition, the proportion of LBC is usually high in rural areas since parent–child separation is regarded as one of the most influential stressors in early childhood experiences (Liu et al., 2020). Prolonged lack of parental care will lead to poorer academic performance, greater academic anxiety, higher levels of emotional imbalance, and more conflict against teachers and peers. Due to the poor mental health educational system in rural areas, many students with psychological and behavior problems cannot receive appropriate care, and sometimes, it is even difficult to find out that they are struggling with mental health problems.

To summarize, the results of our Mental Health General Screening program conducted in rural schools further highlighted prevalent psychological problems for students in rural areas as well as shed light on further interventions. In our programs, we also included follow-up targeted intervention strategies, such as group counseling, which will be further explained in the following sections.

6.3   MULTIMODAL OBSERVATION

6.3.1   Unique Functions of Multimodal Observation

Multimodal observation refers to the collection and fusion of data originated from different data channels, which are subjective and/or objective (Järvelä et al., 2019). Recent advances in the development of commercially available sensing technologies represent an increasing capability of capturing data across modalities of our bodies, brains, languages, and behaviors. These new technologies include eye-movement tracking, wearable electroencephalogram (EEG) technology, and physiological signal-based methods such as measurements of skin conductance and heart rate.

Capturing data across multiple modalities allows researchers and practitioners to go beyond analyzing ontologically flat data of modeling behaviors to multimodal datasets that simultaneously trace cognitive and noncognitive processes in more nuanced ways (Reimann et al., 2014). Combined with advanced computer algorithms, cognitive researchers applied multimodal datasets to trace cognitive states or evaluate complex cognitive processes. For example, a group of Chinese researchers developed a system called the DeepFocus System, which integrates real-time measures of facial expression, behavioral performance, eye-movement tracking, and EEG data to assess students' levels of attention (Chen et al., 2019). The fusion of multimodal data has also been applied to improve the precision of detecting mental disorders. Zhang et al. (2020) integrated eye-movement information into EEG data to identify anxiety disorder and achieved an optimal classification accuracy of 82.7% with machine-learning models. Affective computing is another area where multimodal data fusion is gaining popularity. Affective computing is an emerging field of research that aims to enable AI systems to recognize, feel, infer, and interpret human emotions (Poria et al., 2017). Several studies presented promising results on the development of emotion recognition systems through using wearable devices to collect physiological signals such as EEG and electrocardiogram (ECG) (e.g., Marín-Morales et al., 2018; Chen et al., 2015; AlZoubi et al., 2012).

Multimodal observation technologies are receiving a significant research interest because of their unique advantage in modeling cognitive and noncognitive processes as well as their capability of providing more comprehensive results compared with single modality data. One of the crucial advantages of multimodal datasets relates to their richness in terms of type and volume. Multimodal data can be collected from channels including physiological signals, voice, facial expressions, and even social media posts (Poria et al., 2017; Poria et al., 2016; Poria et al., 2015). Combined with advanced computing algorithms such as machine learning and deep learning, multimodal approaches reveal more promising results compared to single modality approaches (Agarwal et al., 2021). Another crucial advantage of multimodal datasets is that it supports procedural assessments of one's mental state. Thus, in analyzing continuous physiological signals, we can identify the temporal and cyclical processes of regulation and examine different patterns of activation of regulatory processes to see how possible sequences of these processes contribute. Researchers also marked that multimodal datasets support the recognition of mental states to more fine-grained levels. Unimodal analysis usually performs binary classifications of affective states (i.e., positive vs negative), while multimodal analysis aims to classify data according to a large set of affective labels (Poria et al., 2017).

Furthermore, compared with the General Screening and the Special Screening programs described in the previous sections, multimodal observation approaches enable the procedural assessment of students' cognitive and emotional states with greater accuracy and ecological validity. Cognitive states can be assessed using subjective, behavioral, and physiological measures. It is important to bear in mind that since cognitive states are multifaceted and dynamic concepts, self-report or behavioral measures alone can barely represent them. In real-life scenarios, such as in a classroom, those measurements could be limiting if the assessment is disruptive to the ongoing activities. More importantly, humans are not always accurate in making judgments about their cognitive states, such as their levels of attention (Schmidt et al., 2009). The implication of physiological data has been found to significantly improve the accuracy of assessing cognitive states (e.g., Lenneman and Backs, 2010). Physiological responses are almost impossible to be voluntarily concealed or manipulated; thus, they are free of concerns about dishonest responses as sometimes found in self-report measurements. Compared with behavioral measures, physiological measures also demonstrate a greater sensitivity to variations in the attribute they are measuring, for example, cognitive workload (Belyusar et al., 2015).

Multimodal approaches also make their unique contributions to education in rural areas. In rural areas, training of psychology was relatively limited for teachers; thus, it might be difficult for them to appropriately interpret psychological concepts and relevant indicators presented in self-report and cognitive task assessments. However, multimodal approaches support real-time fusion and display of results, so teachers can easily see at a glance, for example, who was distracted during class, without spending extra effort to interpret indicators. The installation of multimodal sensor-based equipment is quite simple; even those without psychological backgrounds could master how to install and use the system after a short training. It is also important to know that there is a high density of students in rural areas, resulting in an unbalanced resource distribution where one teacher may be in charge of 50 or more students, making it difficult for them to pay equal attention to every student in a class. Consequently, our team developed the so-called Multisensory Classroom program, which presents the attention states of all students in the class in a real-time and concise manner, helping teachers reduce their cognitive workloads during class and focus on teaching.

6.3.2   How to Observe Mental Status with a "Wristband"

Offering real-time monitoring of students' mental status in class helps teachers adjust their teaching methods to fit students' cognitive and affective states so as to improve the quality of teaching. For example, if students started to show little interest or suffered from heavy cognitive load in class, their learning performance may be negatively impacted. Additionally, it is necessary to monitor the state synchronization of both students and teachers in real time. As we all know, relationship between teachers and students plays a crucial role in teaching. In real-world settings, the teacher–student relationship is sometimes reflected in the process of classroom interaction, and contains the emotional transmission of both sides, which means that it is difficult to be objectively measured. Therefore, we developed the Multisensory Classroom program, which provides real-time assessment of students' mental status during class by analyzing data collected from multiple modalities such as physiological signals and tablet interaction logs.

Here, we start with a brief introduction of the theoretical background about how physiological data reflect our cognitive and emotional states. The fundamental hypothesis is that external stimuli can cause unconscious, automatic responses of the Autonomic Nervous System (ANS), and these inner alterations can be captured by physiological sensors. In general, the ANS is composed of two branches, the sympathetic nervous system and the parasympathetic nervous system. The sympathetic nervous system increased metabolic reactions such as elevated heart rate, blood pressure, and sweating to prepare the body for dealing with external challenges, while the parasympathetic nervous system promotes restoration and conservation of bodily energy. For example, cardiovascular data can reveal arousal, and heart rate and heart rate variation indices have been applied to measure increment in cognitive load (Jerčić et al., 2020). Galvanic Skin Response (GSR) has strong association with emotional arousal (Boucsein, 1992; Critchley, 2002; Anders et al., 2004). The signals that are produced by the sympathetic nervous system lead to a change in the Skin Conductance Response (SCR), which means in essence that the more emotionally aroused an individual is, the more the SCR amount is increased (Benedek and Kaernbach, 2010).

The ErgoSensing wristband (see Figure 6.9) is developed by our team as a novel, unobtrusive, and convenient device that can capture physiological, behavioral, and environmental information in a synchronized manner. This device is embedded with PPG, EDA, and Acceleration and Gyroscope sensors, supporting simultaneous recording and presentation of a wide range of physical and behavioral indicators, including heart rate, GSR, skin temperature, and actions.

In the Multisensory Classroom program, we conducted a study to monitor the state synchronization of teachers and students by analyzing their emotion convergence. The process of this study is shown in Figure 6.10. First of all, we helped students and teachers wear wristband. Then, they entered the classroom and had a quiet

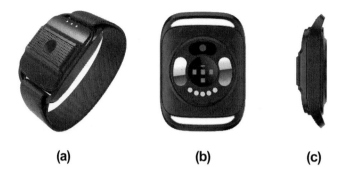

FIGURE 6.9 The ErgoSensing wristband. (a) Stereo view of the wristband. (b) Rear view of the wristband dial. (c) Left view of the wristband dial.

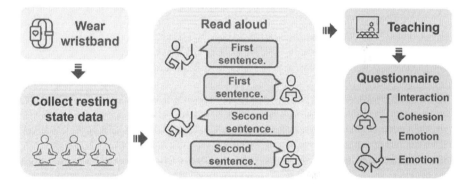

FIGURE 6.10 The process of emotion convergence study.

rest in their seats. After that, there was a reading process, where the teacher led the class to read poetry aloud. Students must pay attention to the teacher's reading, decipher the emotions, and try to express the same emotions exactly through pronunciation and intonation. The process of alternating reading between teachers and students induces positive emotional interaction. Following this part, the teacher started teaching something about poetry. We recorded physiological data during reading session and asked teachers and students to fill out questionnaires at the end of the class.

Emotion convergence in teacher–student interactions is assessed through three pathways:

1. Affective responses synchrony: at the end of the course, both students and teachers conduct a self-report, which includes three items about positive emotional experiences (creativity, empathy, and esteem). This research was based on the category's framework proposed by Zhang's team, where positive emotion categories could be clustered into four major positive categories (fun, empathy, esteem, and creativity) (Zhang et al., 2023). The behavioral indicator of emotion convergence is the difference between student and teacher ratings.

2. Physiological synchrony in general: we adopted the SSI (Single Session Index) as the indicator of physiological synchrony in general. The time window was 15 seconds and slide on the corresponding GSR data with an overlap of 10 seconds. The number of positive and negative correlation windows in the entire data was calculated using the Pearson correlation coefficient between the physiological data of teachers and students in each time window. We divided the number of positive correlation windows by the number of negative correlation windows and then took the natural logarithm to obtain SSI. SSI greater than 0 and less than 0 indicated that the GSR signal exhibited more positive and negative coordination during this period, respectively.

3. Physiological influence: to calculate physiological influence, this study established a time series prediction model of teachers' GSR signals to students' GSR signals. The GSR level of students at a specific time point T was jointly predicted by the GSR level before the student's k-order time point and the GSR level before the teacher's k-order time point. Accordingly, a linear regression model of students' GSR level was developed in this study. And physiological synergy was the indicator of physiological predictability.

After completing data collection, the system will generate an overview report regarding the performance of the whole class and a set of group reports regarding each group's performance. At the top of the report presents a curve graph demonstrating how the degree of teacher–student emotional convergence changed over time. Then, the following section presents descriptive statistics including the average, maximum, and median of teacher–student emotional convergence. Finally, the last section of the overview report provides teachers with suggestions for class design and follow-up recommendations for teaching method.

On the whole, the Multisensory Classroom program investigates the possibility of detecting relationship between teachers and students using GSR in natural classroom. The result has shown that shared emotions between teachers and students, as well as their affective perceptions of each other, could be manifested by their physiological responses synchrony. Specifically, teacher–student interaction was positively related to teacher–student cohesion. In addition, this positive association was mediated by affective responses synchrony and physiological synchrony in general between students and teachers. We further investigated the moderating role of physiological predictability in the indirect relationship and found that physiological predictability moderated the path from teacher–student interaction to affective responses synchrony.

In previous studies, physiological indicators at the individual level are closely related to emotional traits, working as a moderating factor in many behavioral traits and emotion-related outcomes (Blankenship et al., 2018; Makvand et al., 2007). The physiological indicators at the group level, however, are rarely considered to be moderating factors. Our results imply that physiological synergy at the group level can be a trait of dyadic relationships that moderate the relationship between social interactions and interaction outcomes. What's more, this study provides the possibility to monitor real-time social interactions through physiological measurements.

We conducted real-time monitoring of teacher–student emotional convergence and provided a report summarizing the continuous change of cohesion during class. For teachers, this program helps them improve curriculum designs, distribute learning instructions scientifically and sensibly, and adjust teaching methods in response to changes in teacher–student emotional convergence.

6.4 INTERVENTION

6.4.1 GROUP COUNSELING

We carried out targeted group psychological counseling activities for students based on comprehensive and scientific psychological screening results. The data-driven group counseling could amplify the effect of mental health screening, making it easier for psychology teachers in rural regions to provide targeted treatments to students in need. In addition, a closed loop created by routine screening, group counseling, and ongoing care created a model for sustainable mental health services.

In several pilot schools, we first conducted the General Mental Health Screening for junior students and got a list of students who got moderate warning or severe warning. Then, we recruited students who are in high risk of depression and asked them to complete a Special Mental Health Screening, which could evaluate the risk of depression and potential triggers of depression symptoms.

It shows that test anxiety is the most prevalent trigger for these students as about 90% students in high risk for depression are under the pressure of tests. Therefore, we created a group-counseling course to help students overcome their test anxiety and perform better.

It is important to note that we separate these students with high test anxiety into various groups (see Figure 6.11), because they might be too low motivated to participate in activities, which would affect the vibe of group counseling negatively.

FIGURE 6.11 Seating arrangement and dividing groups. We divided students into groups of five and separated the students who showed high test anxiety into different groups. Before the activity started, we wrote each student's name on the labels, respectively, and placed the labels on the table according to the group list. Students are asked to sit where their name labels are.

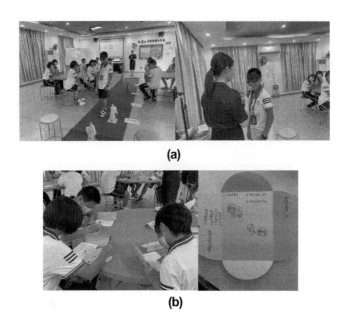

FIGURE 6.12 Games used in group-counseling course. (a) Take another test: We asked students to image that the tests they usually experience as a visible road and take physical obstacles in front of them as the inner self-limitation. It was shown vividly how the inner self-limitation affects their performance in tests. (b) Overcome test anxiety: We gave students a "magic spell" assignment to help them cope with test anxiety. It requires students to be aware of the available psychological resources they possess under test pressure, and learn to mastering test skills, so that it enhances their endurance under intense pressure.

The general idea for this group counseling is to expose students to test-related events and help them find an appropriate way to deal with test anxiety. We developed visualized games (see Figure 6.12) and encouraged students to engage on stage during the group-counseling course. Playing a variety of games can help students learn how their bodies and minds respond under pressure and to practice test-taking tactics. Additionally, these games can lower test anxiety, boost test confidence, and increase students' ability to handle pressure, all of which help students perform better on tests.

During the group counseling, one psychology teacher served as the host, while the other two psychology teachers served as observers, tracking and recording students' behavior throughout the course activities.

After the group counseling, teachers could receive individual reports for each participant (see Figure 6.13), which contain comparison results of the student's test anxiety before and after the group counseling, the student's subjective evaluation of the group counseling, the analysis of students' behavior in the group-counseling process, and comprehensive suggestions for intervention afterward.

Group-counseling courses have an advantage over general mental health courses in that students would have a strongly sense of engagement, so the intervention effect is better. The majority of the students who took our group-counseling course

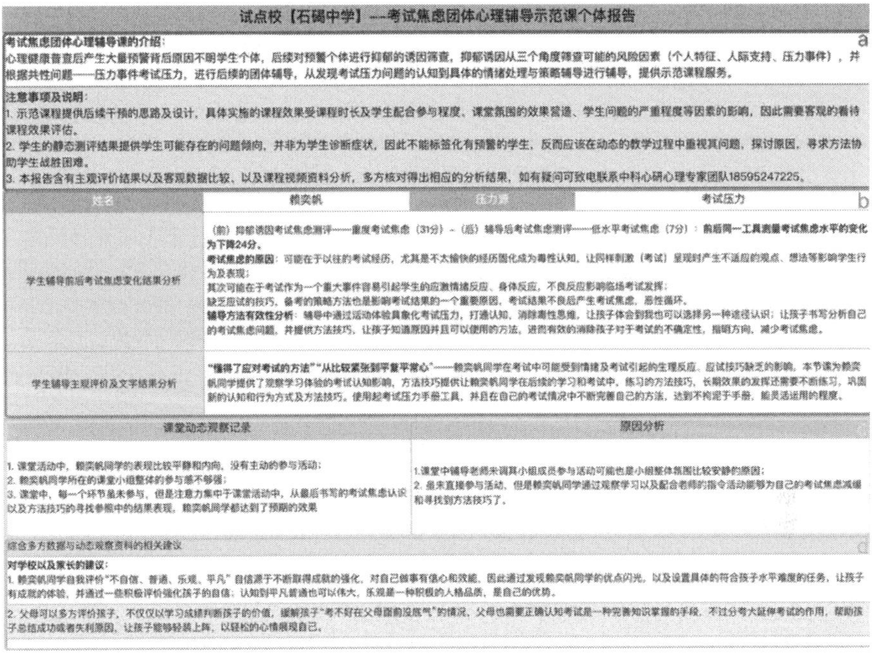

试点校【石碣中学】---考试焦虑团体心理辅导示范课个体报告

a

考试焦虑团体心理辅导课的介绍：
心理健康普查后产生大量预警背后原因不明学生个体，后续对预警个体进行抑郁的诱因筛查，抑郁诱因从三个角度筛查可能的风险因素（个人特征、人际支持、压力事件），并根据共性问题——压力事件考试压力，进行后续的团体辅导，从发现考试压力问题的认知到具体的情绪处理与策略辅导进行辅导，提供示范课程服务。

注意事项及说明：
1. 示范课程提供后续干预的思路及设计，具体实施的课程效果受课程时长及学生配合参与程度、课堂氛围的效果营造、学生问题的严重程度等因素的影响，因此需要客观的看待课程效果评估。
2. 学生的静态测评结果提供学生可能存在的问题倾向，并非为学生诊断症状，因此不能标签化有预警的学生，反而应该在动态的教学过程中重视其问题，探讨原因，寻求方法协助学生战胜困难。
3. 本报告含有主观评价结果以及客观数据比较、以及课程视频资料分析，多方核对得出相应的分析结果，如有疑问可致电联系中科心研心理专家团队18595247225。

b

姓名	赖奕帆	压力源	考试压力
学生辅导前后考试焦虑变化结果分析	（前）抑郁诱因考试焦虑测评——重度考试焦虑（31分）-（后）辅导后考试焦虑测评——低水平考试焦虑（7分）：前后同一工具测量考试焦虑水平的变化为下降24分。 考试焦虑的原因：可能在于以往的考试经历，尤其是不太愉快的经历固化成为毒性认知，让同样刺激（考试）呈现时产生不适应的观点、想法等影响学生行为及表现； 其次可能在于考试作为一个重大事件容易引起学生的应激情绪反应、身体反应，不良反应影响临场考试发挥； 缺乏应试的技巧，备考的策略方法也是影响考试结果的一个重要原因，考试结果不良后产生考试焦虑，恶性循环。 辅导方法有效性分析：辅导中通过活动体验具象化考试压力，打通认知，消除毒性思维，让孩子体会到我也可以选择另一种途径认识；让孩子书写分析自己的考试焦虑问题，并提供方法技巧，让孩子知道原因并且可以使用的方法，进而有效的消除孩子对于考试的不确定性，指明方向，减少考试焦虑。		
学生辅导主观评价及文字结果分析	"懂得了应对考试的方法""从比较紧张到平复平常心"——赖奕帆同学在考试中可能受到情绪及考试引起的生理反应、应试技巧缺乏的影响，本节课为赖奕帆同学提供了观察学习体验的考试认知影响，方法技巧提供让赖奕帆同学在后续的学习和考试中，练习的方法技巧，长期效果的发挥还需要不断练习，巩固新的认知和行为方式及方法技巧。使用起考试压力手册工具，并且在自己的考试情况中不断完善自己的方法，达到不拘泥于手册，能灵活运用的程度。		

课堂动态观察记录	原因分析
1. 课堂活动中，赖奕帆同学的表现比较平静和内向，没有主动的参与活动； 2. 赖奕帆同学所在的课堂小组整体的参与感不够强； 3. 课堂中，每一个环节虽未参与，但是注意力集中于课堂活动中，从最后书写的考试焦虑认识以及方法技巧的寻找参照中的结果表现，赖奕帆同学都达到了预期的效果	1.课堂中辅导老师未调其小组成员参与活动可能也是小组整体氛围比较安静的原因； 2. 虽未直接参与活动，但是赖奕帆同学通过观察学习以及配合老师的指令活动能够为自己的考试焦虑减缓和寻找到方法技巧了。

综合多方数据与动态观察资料的相关建议

d

对学校以及家长的建议：
1. 赖奕帆同学自我评价"不自信、普通、乐观、平凡"自信源于不断取得成就的强化，对自己做事有信心和效能，因此通过发现赖奕帆同学的优点闪光，以及设置具体的符合孩子水平难度的任务，让孩子有成就的体验，并通过一些积极评价强化孩子的自信；认知到平凡普通也可以伟大，乐观是一种积极的人格品质，是自己的优势。
2. 父母可以多方评价孩子，不仅仅以学习成绩判断孩子的价值，缓解孩子"考不好在父母面前没底气"的情况，父母也需要正确认知考试是一种完善知识掌握的手段，不过分夸大甚至考试的作用，帮助孩子总结成功或者失利原因，让孩子能够轻装上阵，以轻松的心情展现自己。

FIGURE 6.13 Sample of postreport generated after group counseling. (a) Introduction to the group-counseling course and precautions. (b) The change in student's test anxiety before and after the group-counseling course, the student's subjective evaluation, and the analysis of the results. (c) Behavior observation records and cause analysis. (d) Suggestions to teachers and parents on how to care for the student.

subjectively reported feeling less stressed afterward. In addition, the test anxiety level of students also decreased significantly. For example, in one of our pilot schools, there are 15 students who participated in our group-counseling course. We compared scores of anxiety test before and after the intervention, and the results revealed that nearly all of the students had seen a considerable decline in test anxiety.

6.4.2 Self-Adapted Mental Course Design System

As mentioned in the Introduction, many teachers in rural areas lack a comprehensive understanding of mental health, so it is challenging for them to conduct mental health teaching. Thus, it seems that the easiest way to work out this problem is teaching according to textbooks.

However, sometimes, textbooks might not fit students well, which makes mental health education in rural areas get half the result with twice effort. For one thing, the update of textbooks does not conform to the psychological development of students. Compared to few years ago, students today enter puberty earlier, where they have heightened self-awareness and more pronounced mood swings. Besides, textbooks for mental health teaching are closely related to living environment. However, it always takes several years to revise a textbook, during which time, the living environment has changed a lot. For example, a few years ago, students were not allowed to use mobile phones; however, in recent years, mobile phones have become an important tool for students to communicate with their parents and teachers. They need to use mobile phones to receive information from the school, take learning videos, and even take classes online. For teachers, it gets harder to teach students to wean themselves off their phones and develop the habit of focusing on their studies, not to mention that teachers can only teach according to the content of old textbooks.

In addition to the problems caused by inappropriate teaching materials, there are also some limitations in the teacher's design of courses. There are few psychology teachers in rural areas, and it happens from time to time that one teacher is in charge of psychological education of multiple grades at the same time. Designing courses takes up a lot of time for teachers, and sometimes, in order to save time, they will present the content of a lesson to students of different grades at the same time.

In order to help psychology teachers in preparing mental health classes that can be continuously updated to suit students' psychological development, we have created a self-adapted mental course design system. This system could provide advice on lesson themes that meet the needs of students' psychological growth as well as automatically generate teaching plans and slides. How does it work?

First of all, we have built a pool for mental health course materials, which contains a huge amount of course topics and interactive games for class. This pool consists of materials that are suitable for students from 6 to 18 years. Based on the *Guidelines for Mental Health Education for Primary and Secondary School Students* (2012) issued by the Ministry of Education of China, we created a collection of lesson themes, all of which are derived from the psychological development goals of the Guidelines for students of all ages. We disassembled these psychological development goals into subgoals, until each subgoal corresponds to a specific behavioral performance, and saved these subgoals into the pool as course topics. Then, experienced professional mental health teachers design interactive games for each course topic. In order to make these games suitable for students at different stages, each topic contains multiple alternative games. Take the course theme of "master learning skills" as an example. The games designed for primary school students focus primarily on time management, habit building, and study planning skills. As students grow older, the focus of games is gradually adjusted to learning strategies, problem solving, metacognition, etc.

Apart from the age difference of students, the prevalence of psychological problems is also one of the main basic for the system to match students with course topics. At the end of each semester, the psychology teacher would distribute questionnaires to students and parents to find the problems existing in the students. Besides, assessment results from General Mental Health Screening and Specific Mental Health Screening are also taken into consideration. Results of these surveys and screenings are stored in online system.

So, if there was any psychology teacher asking help from self-adapted mental course design system, all he/she needs to do is to type in the age of students, total class hours for the semester, and the length of each class. Then, according to the age of the students and the psychological problems in high prevalence manifested in assessment, the system would provide course topics and at least three alternative teaching plans.

Benefiting from the continuously updated material pool and the latest psychological assessment results, this system can provide teaching programs that meet the needs of students' mental health development. It makes sustainable mental health education an available resource in rural areas.

6.5   APPLY ADVANCED TECHNOLOGIES IN RURAL SCHOOLS

6.5.1   IMPROVE TRADITIONAL MENTAL SCREENING WITH ADVANCED INTELLIGENT TECHNIQUES

Smart serving technology helped us conduct professional and comprehensive mental health screening in rural areas. Taking the advantage of Multimodal Human Factors Intelligent Quick Check Box, we have made it easier for rural adolescents to get professional mental health screening. However, several limitations should be considered.

Take a look at the framework for our mental assessment, you would find that questionnaire evaluation accounts for a large proportion of the current psychological evaluation, which means most of our data are focusing on the "outcome." And as a result, students, teachers, and parents make judgments according to their memories of a previous period of time, not real-time reactions or feelings, and there might be a certain deviation between the results of the responses and reality. The current assessment only presents a static mental status at a certain time point, it could reveal neither a dynamic mental processing nor the critical developmental factors of adolescents.

Another stuff in this assessment program that needs to be advanced is to make better use of the data. In the current version, our report mainly described the risk levels of rural students' mental health status. However, it failed to use the information to reveal the development trend and potential threats in the future. What's more, we have only conducted screening in several rural schools located in Guangdong Province, which means our norm for grading mental crises is not representative enough.

In the future, we aim to update mental health screening by two ways.

From the perspective of the measurement method, it is the virtual assessment that comes into our view. Virtual assessment is a kind of novel assessment method that is carried out in a computerized virtual environment, which makes use of the characteristics of the virtual environment (Agard and von Davier, 2018). In virtual assessment, there are many simulated scenes that feel like what happen to students every day, which could also release the anxiety for the assessment. And also, virtual assessment would be more attractive to students and help them to think and behave like usual. Though the scenarios of virtual assessments are illusory, what the data reveals could be closer to reality than that in traditional assessment. Taking this advantage, virtual assessment makes it possible for us to take out tests for personality and sociality factors at classrooms, such as tests for moral development, prosocial behavior, and aggressive behavior.

Apart from the presentation, the data generated in virtual assessment would be another resource worthy to detect. To be compared with the traditional methods, virtual assessment is not only able to collect students' response to assessment items, which is the outcome of their thinking, but could also simultaneously capture their process of assessment items at every time stamp by log files. In other words, the process data of virtual assessment does not limit its focus on "what is the result" but pay more attention on "how this result came about" (Greiff et al., 2015). What's more, during the virtual assessment, there are multiple types of real-time data (multimodel data) that could be recorded automatically, which provides more hints to detect psychological process. For example, Zoanetti (2010) did a study in which he not only recorded the outcome data of participants in problem-solving task but also collected the verbal expressions (such as "I don't understand" at a certain moment) and external behaviors (such as frowning and sighing), which in turn differentiate cognitive processes while they generated similar process data. For example, when different subjects spend similar time before telling their answers, it would be of great help to combine the verbal information to judge whether they spent the time to understand the problem or conceive a solution. Analyzing process data provides us vital clues to explore the psychological processing of students while answering to tests, which plays an important role in accurately diagnosing the psychological status of students (Bergner and von Davier, 2018; Jiao et al., 2019). Benefiting from this advantage, the process data collected in the virtual assessment can reflect the individual's psychological activities and human–computer interaction and human–human interaction during psychological assessment.

From the perspective of data analysis, the data of virtual assessment is so complex that it urges us to make an improvement on analyzing process data. Generally, the analysis methods for process data can be divided into two categories: data mining and statistical modeling. The former is an "explorer," which is based on the data-driven method, to get the result from a bottom-up path, using the existing data to describe, analyze, summarize, and induce knowledge about participants (Fayyad et al., 1996). The latter feels more like a "judge," which is driven by theories, using a top-down method under the routine of generating hypotheses, testing with data, and then accepting or rejecting hypotheses (Bergner and von Davier, 2018). Compared with the statistical modeling, the data mining seems more closer to how we analyze assessment data at the current stage, because both of them are mainly based on observed variables for classification, rather than on individual latent traits. However, classification based on underlying traits is an important indicator, as it could help teachers or counselors to carry out targeted intervention on students whose underlying traits show danger alarms. In view of the fact that statistical modeling method can preconstruct the causes of explicit behavior based on the theoretical model, using statistical modeling makes it easier to interpret students' behavior outcomes, which is particularly important in psychological and educational measures, especially in diagnosis. Thus, we would make full use of statistical modeling at next stage to conduct more detailed, comprehensive, and accurate predictions.

To realize the vision of mental health screening, and make it applicable to rural areas, we consider increasing the number of engineering vehicles, making route plans, and dividing different screening areas. Thus, we could expand rural areas and cities of screening year by year. When the number of cities screened increases, the norm database expands continuously; eventually, it can update to a national norm. In addition, we could gather the needs of families who live in remote rural areas and drive the engineering vehicles to the town center or other places close to these families. In this way, we could collect the data of parents, not just the data of teachers in the school, to make our database more diversified. Besides, we could also put Quick Test Box in the school instead of entering schools by driving engineering vehicles at the fixed time every year and train teachers to conduct more convenient screening, which could also save human resources.

In this way, we could quickly screen out children and adolescents with psychological or behavioral problems and gave follow-up intervention treatment to break the barrier of uneven distribution of resources between urban and rural areas in China.

6.5.2 FUTURE IMPLICATIONS OF MULTIMODAL TOOLS IN MENTAL HEALTH

As described in Section 4.3, the confluence of multimodal data with advanced computational algorithms allows us to monitor teacher–student emotional convergence in real time. Meanwhile, we have also used multimodal observation to trace changes in students' levels of attention over time and successfully differentiate students' states of distraction and concentration during class. We emphasized the contributions this program made to identifying signs of attention-deficit symptoms of ADHD. However, the prospect of multimodal data in the mental health care industry goes far beyond that.

In the future, we are looking forward to applying the ErgoSensing wristband, possibly its combination with other multimodal measurements to areas beyond screening. Our ultimate vision is to build an all-in-one mental health care system covering the assessment of mental health states, interventions for mental health and developmental disorders, and evaluation of treatment effects to form a closed loop. In the present section, we propose three directions of how our ErgoSensing wristband can be applied to mental health care in the future.

First, we are expecting to integrate measurements of other modalities into our programs, such as eye tracking, audio data, or EEG data, to further expand the types of data as well as the variety of attributes we can measure. For example, gaze data measured by eye-movement tracking provides information on attentional cues (Poole and Ball, 2005). Gesture, posture, and motion data can tell us about the way learners interact or communicate with each other or with the system in a certain learning environment (Giannakos et al., 2019). It is important to consider both pros and cons of each method. For example, one of the main drawbacks of using wearable EEG is that regardless of the connection type, movements of cables and electrodes can cause artifacts in the EEG signal that contaminate our data (Soufineyestani et al., 2020). Thus, it may not be wise to apply wearable EEG devices in learning activities requiring high levels of bodily movements, like in an outdoor teaching scenario. A wider range of options leads to an increasing number of possible combinations of measurements. We could choose the combination of modalities depending on different environments and different types of tasks; for instance, in informal collaborative settings such as extracurricular teaching activities in a museum, audio data and motion/posture data can be recorded and analyzed to inform the process of collaboration (Giannakos et al., 2019).

Second, it might be a valuable attempt to move from measuring internal states including emotions and attention to behavioral assessments of how individuals interact with the environment and others. More specifically, the measurements of interpersonal and collaboration skills are considered as making crucial contributions not only to academic success (Lievens and Sackett, 2012; Vargas et al., 2018) but also to general well-being (Segrin and Taylor, 2007; Sun et al., 2014). Multimodal data has been applied to predict students' collaborative will, collaborative learning product, and dual learning gain (Pijeira-Díaz et al., 2016). Our ErgoSensing wristbands support the collection and fusion of group-level physiological signals; thus, they can be applied to evaluate students' collaboration skills in teamwork, through tracing their microlevel behaviors during collaboration tasks, including help-seeking and -giving behaviors, problem solving, reasoning, and decision-making.

Third, we are working on expanding functions that our multimodal tools can achieve. At present, three main directions are proposed:

1. Feedback for learning and teaching: Prieto and colleagues (2016) reported reasonable accuracy using multimodal data features to predict teachers' activities in the classroom, which was later used as a reflection tool for teachers. Real-time feedback was also achieved by a system that can adapt the type of formative feedback and the way it should be presented based on students' affective states, consequently reducing boredom and off-task behavior in class (Grawemeyer et al., 2017). Similarly, we are working on an add-on function of the Multisensory Classroom program: when teachers found atypical physiological response patterns in students, which implies they might be distracted, in an abnormal emotional state, or in other unusual cognitive status, they could send a command to make the student's wristband vibrate to remind them.

2. Feedback on students' cognitive states can also be provided to students themselves with suggestions for future improvement. For example, Ochoa and colleagues (2018) proposed a system utilizing audio and video data for providing feedback to avoid common errors in oral presentations. The survey revealed a relatively high level of student satisfaction with the system, with scores ranging from 6 to 10 on a 10-point scale in terms of overall experience, usefulness, and learnability. In the future, we might be able to provide personalized learning materials and learning plans based on the combination of multimodal datasets and big data analysis technologies. Furthermore, we could provide children with developmental disorders with learning resources that fit their levels of cognitive development to help them with their academic achievements, since developmental disorders, ADHD for example, usually have a negative influence on academic achievement (Scholtens et al., 2013). Some researchers have preliminarily explored this field. Asiry and colleagues (2015) explored the design of a system aiming to evaluate a gaze-based attentive user interface that monitors children's eyes, which can be used to manipulate the content of educational materials based on the level of attention the child keeps with the material. Researchers also envisaged a future learning system that can adapt educational activities with machine-learning algorithms through analyzing emotional states to reduce

the level of frustration and maintain students' engagement with learning activities (Cornejo and Martinez, 2016).

3. Identification of mental health and developmental disorders: So far, the Multisensory Classroom program supports only the identification of children with potential attention-deficit symptoms. In the future, we might be able to use multimodal data to inform the diagnosis of developmental disorders in children. Recent research findings are in support of this idea. For instance, Jiang and colleagues (2020) developed WeDA, a wearable diagnostic assessment system for ADHD with an accuracy higher than 90%, consisting of wearable motion sensors, 3D printed interactive devices, and a computer machine.

4. Similarly, some preliminary works have been done to identify individuals with emotional disorders such as depression or anxiety disorders. Williamson and colleagues (2016) constructed a model for predicting depression through integrating physiological signals, voice information, facial expression, and dialogue semantics. Haque and colleagues (2018) from Stanford University applied a machine-learning method to analyze 3D facial expressions and spoken language, ultimately achieving an accuracy of around 80% in predicting depression. Furthermore, we can manipulate task designs to evoke affective states in students using video clips (Domínguez-Jiménez et al., 2020) or virtual reality games (Marín-Morales et al., 2018) and achieve initial screening of emotional disorders through the analysis of multimodal physiological datasets collected during the tasks.

5. Feedback on intervention strategies: The collection of continuous multimodal datasets during the process of mental health treatment may help us to further acquire information from patients regarding, for example, their engagement in treatment, skill acquisition, and currently perceived stress to determine whether or not it is appropriate to move to the next treatment stage. Ahani and colleagues (2013) applied EEG and respiration data to successfully differentiate whether or not participants are engaged in mindfulness meditation, and they noted that future studies should work on quantifying different levels of meditation depth and meditation experience using their classifier. Other applications of multimodal physiological signals to psychotherapy include assessing skill utilization and skill acquisition of patients receiving CBT (Juarascio et al., 2018) as well as recognition of anxiety levels during virtual reality exposure therapy for anxiety disorders (Šalkevicius et al., 2019).

Novel approaches of using multimodal data collected via smartphone or smartwatch to augment psychotherapy or behavioral interventions, known as mobile health technologies (mHealth), have received a broad research interest (Juarascio et al., 2018). A meta-analysis found that mHealth technologies boosted the effectiveness of mental health treatment (Lindhiem et al., 2015). Ecological momentary interventions (EMIs), as one promising application of mHealth technologies, enable the delivery of personalized interventions as patients go about their daily lives, such as delivery through text messages, phone calls, and smartphone apps (Heron and Smyth,

2011). EMIs' functions can be further improved through multimodal data collection technologies, as to determine the timing and content of EMIs depending on real-time data analysis results, known as just-in-time adaptive interventions (JITAIs) (Spruijt-Metz and Nilsen, 2014). In the near future, we expect to further explore the implementation of a just-in-time adaptive intervention system for rural students with mental health disorders.

6.5.3　Implement Psychological Intervention by Telepsychology

Telepsychology is a growing prevalent approach for the psychological intervention aside from the traditional face-to-face method. It uses telecommunication technology to provide psychological services, such as email, interactive videoconferencing, and self-help websites (American Psychological Association, 2013). Telepsychology is feasible for using among people of varied ages (from the youth to the old) and for differing mental illnesses (e.g., depression, anxiety, and insomnia). Hilty et al. (2013) have found that telepsychology could take similar effects as face-to-face counseling. In addition, telepsychology makes it more convenient for rural residents to get professional psychological intervention. As long as they have a mobile terminal that can connect to the network, no matter it is a computer, laptop, or mobile phone, they would get in touch with psychological counselor from 1,000 miles away. And in this way, they could also save a lot of travel expenses. Sometimes, there are chances for them to get access to free telepsychology paid by the government.

For rural students who are in poor mental health status, telepsychology is a good choice. In addition to advantages mentioned above, the application of smart service technology can amplify the effect of remote psychological counseling.

We have developed a portable wristband, which looks like a watch and could be used to track mental status without interfering with daily activities. Moreover, this watch can simultaneously collect a variety of physiological signals and behavioral data in real-life scenarios. The collected indicators such as PPG, TEMP, and ACC/GYRO can be used to calculate the visitor's sleep quality, circadian rhythm, exercise index, and peripheral physiological changes in system tension. Peripheral physiological signal is difficult to conceal, which makes it one of the most direct indicators of the internal emotional state. At the same time, the watch has unlimited data communication capabilities and interactive operation capabilities, which allow us to monitor the physical and mental health of visitors for a long time. Therefore, even if there is a long geographical distance with the client, the counselor can pay attention to the real mental status of the client in time.

For rural students at low risk for psychological problems, telepsychology will mainly focus on online group counseling. Online group counseling of students must be led or responsible by a professional psychological counselor who can keep topic on mental problem solving (Pickett et al., 1998). Members could exchange information via emails or online messages. To make communication more direct and synchronized, chat room or video meeting could be built. Online group counseling makes it possible for sharing experience among students across the spanning space.

However, there are still some precautions for online counseling. For example, it is important to ensure that students' privacy is well protected. From a study of a telepsychology service, only 18% websites have taken measures to protect personal health information (Fiene et al., 2020). Besides, a quiet and cozy environment is necessary for an effective online students counseling, while some students might take it as informal, so they might take part in the counseling in a noisy room or even lie in bed or eat during the session (Perrin et al., 2020).

The construction of the sustainable mental health service model in rural areas should adopt a strategy, where different evaluation perspectives, multimodal observation, and group-based intervention are fully integrated. It is to build a closed-loop service for continuous self-service update and improvement. There are several kinds of integration that should be included in the model: an integration of perspectives of adolescents, parents, and teachers; an integration of traditional psychological test paradigm and advanced intelligent techniques; an integration of mental problem screening and mental literacy improvement; and the most important, an integration of academic theory and social applications. To build a sustainable mental health service model, it is essential to make use of big data and smart serving technology. It needs to take the development of people and technology as the perspective and should explore psychological methods for mental health development of rural adolescents.

REFERENCES

Agard, C. & von Davier, A. (2018). The virtual world and reality of testing: Building virtual assessments. In H. Jiao & R. Lissitz (Eds.), *Technology Enhanced Innovative Assessment: Development, Modeling, and Scoring from an Interdisciplinary Perspective* (pp. 1–30). Charlotte, NC: Information Age Publishing.

Agarwal, A., Graft, J., Schroeder, N., & Romine, W. (2021). Sensor-based prediction of mental effort during learning from physiological data: A longitudinal case study. *Signals*, 2(4), 886–901. https://doi.org/10.3390/signals2040051.

Ahani, A., Wahbeh, H., Miller, M., Nezamfar, H., Erdogmus, D., & Oken, B. (2013). Change in physiological signals during mindfulness meditation. *2013 6th International IEEE/ EMBS Conference on Neural Engineering (NER)*, pp. 1378–1381. California, United States https://doi.org/10.1109/NER.2013.6696199.

AlZoubi, O., D'Mello, S. K., & Calvo, R. A. (2012). Detecting naturalistic expressions of nonbasic affect using physiological signals. *IEEE Transactions on Affective Computing*, 3(3), 298–310. https://doi.org/10.1109/T-AFFC.2012.4.

American Psychological Association. (2013). *Guidelines for the Practice of Telepsychology*. Washington, DC: American Psychologist.

Anders, S., Lotze, M., Erb, M., Grodd, W., & Birbaumer, N. (2004). Brain activity underlying emotional valence and arousal: A response-related fMRI study. *Human Brain Mapping*, 23(4), 200–209.

Asiry, O., Shen, H., & Calder, P. (2015). Extending attention span of ADHD children through an eye tracker directed adaptive user interface. *Proceedings of the ASWEC 2015 24th Australasian Software Engineering Conference*, pp. 149–152. Adelaide, Australia https://doi.org/10.1145/2811681.2824997.

Belyusar, D., Mehler, B., Solovey, E., & Reimer, B. (2015). Impact of repeated exposure to a multilevel working memory task on physiological arousal and driving performance. *Transportation Research Record*, 2518(1), 46–53. https://doi.org/10.3141/2518-06.

Benedek, M. & Kaernbach, C. (2010). A continuous measure of phasic electrodermal activity. *Journal of Neuroscience Methods*, 190(1), 80–91. https://doi.org/10.1016/j.jneumeth.2010.04.028.

Bergner, Y. & von Davier, A. (2018). Process data in NAEP: Past, present, and future. *Journal of Educational and Behavioral Statistics*, 44(6), 706–732. https://doi.org/10.3102/1076998618784700.

Blankenship, T. L., Broomell, A. P., & Bell, M. A. (2018). Semantic future thinking and executive functions at age 4: The moderating role of frontal brain electrical activity. *Developmental Psychobiology*, 60(5), 608–614.

Boucsein, W. (Eds). (1992). *Electrodermal Activity*. London: Plenum University Press.

Bradley, R. H. & Corwyn, R. F. (2002). Socioeconomic status and child development. *Annual Review of Psychology*, 53, 371–399. https://doi.org/10.1146/annurev.psych.53.100901.135233.

Chen, X., Li, F., Long, L., Zhao, Y., Feng, S., & Li, Y. (2007). Prospective study on the relationship between social and internet addiction. *Chinese Mental Health Journal*, 21(4), 240–243.

Chen, M., Zhang, Y., Li, Y., Hassan, M. M., & Alamri, A. (2015). AIWAC: Affective interaction through wearable computing and cloud technology. *IEEE Wireless Communications*, 22(1), 20–27. https://doi.org/10.1109/MWC.2015.7054715.

Chen, X., Liang, N., & Ostertag, S. F. (2017). Victimization of children left behind in rural China. *Journal of Research in Crime and Delinquency*, 54(4), 515–543. https://doi.org/10.1177/0022427816660145.

Chen, M., Cao, Y., Wang, R., Li, Y., Wu, D., & Liu, Z. (2019). DeepFocus: Deep encoding brainwaves and emotions with multi-scenario behavior analytics for human attention enhancement. *IEEE Network*, 33(6), 70–77. https://doi.org/10.1109/MNET.001.1900054.

Cheng, P. X., Da, C. J., Cao, F. L., Li, P., Feng, D., & Jiang, C. (2010). A comparative study on psychological abuse and neglect and emotional and behavioral problems of left-behind children and non-left-behind children in rural areas. *Chinese Journal of Clinical Psychology*, 18(2), 250–251.

Cornejo, R. & Martinez, F. (2016). Exploring digital and manual modalities in educational activities for children with ADHD. *Research in Computing Science*, 129, 37–44.

Critchley, H. (2002). Review: Electrodermal responses: What happens in the brain. *The Neuroscientist*, 8(2), 132–142.

Danielson, M. L., Bitsko, R. H., Ghandour, R. M., Holbrook, J. R., Kogan, M. D., & Blumberg, S. J. (2018). Prevalence of parent-reported ADHD diagnosis and associated treatment among US children and adolescents, 2016. *Journal of Clinical Child & Adolescent Psychology*, 47(2), 199–212.

Domínguez-Jiménez, J. A., Campo-Landines, K. C., Martínez-Santos, J. C., Delahoz, E. J., & Contreras-Ortiz, S. H. (2020). A machine learning model for emotion recognition from physiological signals. *Biomedical Signal Processing and Control*, 55, 101646. https://doi.org/10.1016/j.bspc.2019.101646.

Fayyad, U., Piatetsky-shapiro, G., & Smyth, P. (1996). Knowledge discovery and data mining: Towards a unifying framework. *Shapiro*, 96, 82–88.

Fiene, S. L., Stark, K. S., Kreiner, D. S., & Walker, T. R. (2020). Evaluating telehealth websites for information consistent with APA guidelines for telepsychology. *Journal of Technology in Human Services*, 38(2), 91–111.

Giannakos, M. N., Sharma, K., Pappas, I. O., Kostakos, V., & Velloso, E. (2019). Multimodal data as a means to understand the learning experience. *International Journal of Information Management*, 48, 108–119. https://doi.org/10.1016/j.ijinfomgt.2019.02.003.

Grawemeyer, B., Mavrikis, M., Holmes, W., Gutiérrez-Santos, S., Wiedmann, M., & Rummel, N. (2017). Affective learning: improving engagement and enhancing learning with affect-aware feedback. *User Modeling and User-Adapted Interaction*, 27(1), 119–158. https://doi.org/10.1007/s11257-017-9188-z.

Greiff, S., Wüstenberg, S., & Avvisati, F. (2015). Computer generated log-file analyses as a window into students' minds? A showcase study based on the PISA 2012 assessment of problem solving. *Computers & Education*, 91, 92–105.

Guevara, J. P. & Mandell, D. S. (2003). Costs associated with attention deficit hyperactivity disorder: Overview and future projections. *Expert Review of Pharmacoeconomics & Outcomes Research*, 3(2), 201–210.

Haque, A., Guo, M., Miner, A. S., & Li, F. (2018). Measuring depression symptom severity from spoken language and 3D facial expressions. Machine Learning for Health (ML4H) Workshop at NeurIPS, Montréal, Canada.

Heron, K. E. & Smyth, J. M. (2011). Ecological momentary interventions: Incorporating mobile technology into psychosocial and health behaviour treatments. *British Journal of Health Psychology*, 15(1), 1–39. https://doi.org/10.1348/135910709X466063.

Hilty, D. M., Ferrer, D. C., Parish, M. B., Johnston, B., Callahan, E. J., & Yellowlees, P. M. (2013). The effectiveness of telemental health: A 2013 review. *Telemedicine and e-Health*, 19(6), 444–454.

Hou, G. (2010). The investigation and research on the mental heath state of flowing children in rural junior middle schools of Taicang City (Master dissertation). Soochow University.

Järvelä, S., Malmberg, J., Haataja, E., Sobocinski, M., & Kirschner, P. A. (2019). What multi-modal data can tell us about the students' regulation of their learning process. *Learning and Instruction*, 72(7), 4. https://doi.org/10.1016/j.learninstruc.2019.04.004.

Jerčić, P., Sennersten, C., & Lindley, C. (2020). Modeling cognitive load and physiological arousal through pupil diameter and heart rate. *Multimedia Tools and Applications*, 79(5), 3145–3159.

Jiang, X., Chen, Y., Huang, W., Zhang, T., Gao, C., Xing, Y., & Zheng, Y. (2020). WeDA: Designing and evaluating a scale-driven wearable diagnostic assessment system for children with ADHD. *Proceedings of the 2020 CHI Conference on Human Factors in Computing Systems*, pp. 1–12. New York: Association for Computing Machinery.

Jiao, H., Liao, D., & Zhan, P. (2019). Utilizing process data for cognitive diagnosis. In M. von Davier & Y. S. Lee (Eds.), *Handbook of Diagnostic Classification Models: Models and Model Extensions, Applications, Software Packages* (pp. 421–436). Cham: Springer International Publishing.

Juarascio, A. S., Parker, M. N., Lagacey, M. A., & Godfrey, K. M. (2018). Just-in-time adaptive interventions: A novel approach for enhancing skill utilization and acquisition in cognitive behavioral therapy for eating disorders. *International Journal of Eating Disorders*, 51(8), 826–830. https://doi.org/10.1002/eat.22924.

Lam, L. T. & Peng, Z. W. (2010). Effect of pathological use of the internet on adolescent mental health: A prospective study. *Archives of Pediatrics & Adolescent Medicine*, 164(10), 901–906.

Lenneman, J. K. & Backs, R. W. (2010). Enhancing assessment of in-vehicle technology attention demands with cardiac measures. *Proceedings of the 2nd International Conference on Automotive User Interfaces and Interactive Vehicular Applications, 20–21. AutomotiveUI '10*. New York: Association for Computing Machinery. https://doi.org/10.1145/1969773.1969777.

Li, L. (2019). A comparative study on the family dynamics and the positive mental health of urban and rural students in junior high school (Master dissertation). Tianjin Normal University.

Li, X. & Li, X. (2017). The relationship of self-concept, internet addiction and life satisfaction in rural adolescents. *Chinese Journal of Behavioral Medicine and Brain Science*, 26(4), 370–373.

Li, X., Ren, Z., Hu, X., & Guo, Y. (2019). Why are undergraduates from lower-class families more likely to experience social anxiety? --The multiple mediating effects of psychosocial resources and rejection sensitivity. *Journal of Psychological Science*, 42(6), 1354–1360.

Li, X., Yao, J., & Zhang, Q. (2021). Research on the implementation status and countermeasures of mental health education for rural middle school students: Taking D middle school in an autonomous county in western Guangxi as an example. *Decision Exploration*, 2(08), 23–25. https://doi.org/10.16324/j.cnki.jcts.2021.08.013.

Lievens, F. & Sackett, P. R. (2012). The validity of interpersonal skills assessment via situational judgment tests for predicting academic success and job performance. *Journal of Applied Psychology*, 97(2), 460–468. https://doi.org/10.1037/a0025741.

Lindhiem, O., Bennett, C. B., Rosen, D., & Silk, J. (2015). Mobile technology boosts the effectiveness of psychotherapy and behavioral interventions: A meta-analysis. *Behavior Modification*, 39(6), 785–804. https://doi.org/10.1177/0145445515595198.

Liu, A., Xu, Y., Yan, Q., & Tong, L. (2018). The prevalence of attention deficit/hyperactivity disorder among Chinese children and adolescents. *Scientific Reports*, 8(1), 1–15.

Liu, Z., Zhou, Y., & Wang, J. (2020). Mental health status of left-behind children in rural poverty-stricken areas. *Mental Health Blue Book: Report on the Development of Mental Health in China (2019-2020)*, pp. 165.

Lv, L., Yan, F., Duan, C., & Cheng, M. (2018). Changing patterns and development challenge of child population in China. *The Journal of Population Research*, 42, 65–78.

Makvand, H. S., Azad, F. P., Rasoulzadeh, T. S., Ghanadian, L. S., Heise, C., & Heysi, C. (2007). Brain activity, personality traits and affect: Electrocortical activity in reaction to affective film stimuli. *Journal of Applied Sciences*, 7(23), 3743–3749.

Marín-Morales, J., Higuera-Trujillo, J. L., Greco, A., Guixeres, J., Llinares, C., Scilingo, E. P., Alcañiz, M., & Valenza, G. (2018). Affective computing in virtual reality: Emotion recognition from brain and heartbeat dynamics using wearable sensors. *Scientific Reports*, 8(1), 13657. https://doi.org/10.1038/s41598-018-32063-4.

Mishra, S., Draus, P., Goreva, N., Leone, G., & Caputo, D. (2014). The impact of internet addiction on university students and its effect on subsequent academic success: A survey based study. *Issues in Information Systems*, 15(1), 344.

Ochoa, X., Domínguez, F., Guamán, B., Maya, R., Falcones, G., & Castells, J. (2018). The RAP system: Automatic feedback of oral presentation skills using multimodal analysis and low-cost sensors. *Proceedings of the 8th International Conference on Learning Analytics and Knowledge, 360–364. LAK '18*. New York: Association for Computing Machinery. https://doi.org/10.1145/3170358.3170406.

Perrin, P. B., Rybarczyk, B. D., Pierce, B. S., Jones, H. A., Shaffer, C., & Islam, L. (2020). Rapid telepsychology deployment during the COVID-19 pandemic: A special issue commentary and lessons from primary care psychology training. *Journal of Clinical Psychology*, 76(6), 1173–1185.

Pickett, S. A., Heller, T., & Cook, J. A. (1998). Professional-led versus family-led support groups: Exploring the differences. *The Journal of Behavioral Health Services & Research*, 25(4), 437–445.

Pijeira-Díaz, H. J., Drachsler, H., Järvelä, S., & Kirschner, P. A. (2016). Investigating collaborative learning success with physiological coupling indices based on electrodermal activity. *Proceedings of the Sixth International Conference on Learning Analytics & Knowledge*, pp. 64–73. Edinburgh, Scotland, United Kingdom https://doi.org/10.1145/2883851.2883897.

Poole, A. & Ball, L. J. (2005). Eye tracking in human-computer interaction and usability research: Current status and future prospects. In C. Bailenson & Blascovich, J. (Eds.), *Encyclopedia of Human Computer Interaction*. Lancaster: Psychology Department, Lancaster University.

Poria, S., Cambria, E., & Gelbukh, A. (2015). Deep convolutional neural network textual features and multiple kernel learning for utterance-level multimodal sentiment analysis. *Proceedings of the 2015 Conference on Empirical Methods in Natural Language Processing*, pp. 2539–2544. Lisbon, Portugal: Association for Computational Linguistics. https://doi.org/10.18653/v1/D15-1303.

Poria, S., Chaturvedi, I., Cambria, E., & Hussain, A. (2016). Convolutional MKL based multimodal emotion recognition and sentiment analysis. *2016 IEEE 16th International Conference on Data Mining (ICDM)*, pp. 439–448. Barcelona, Spain https://doi.org/10.1109/ICDM.2016.0055.

Poria, S., Cambria, E., Bajpai, R., & Hussain, A. (2017). A review of affective computing: From unimodal analysis to multimodal fusion. *Information Fusion*, 37, 98–125. https://doi.org/10.1016/j.inffus.2017.02.003.

Prieto, L. P., Sharma, K., Dillenbourg, P., & Jesús, M. (2016). Teaching analytics: Towards automatic extraction of orchestration graphs using wearable sensors. *Proceedings of the Sixth International Conference on Learning Analytics & Knowledge*, pp. 148–157. Edinburgh, Scotland, United Kingdom https://doi.org/10.1145/2883851.2883927.

Qin, J. & Albin, B. (2010). The mental health of children left behind in rural China by migrating parents: A literature review. *Journal of Public Mental Health*, 9(3), 4–16. https://doi.org/10.5042/jpmh.2010.0458.

Reimann, P., Markauskaite, L., & Bannert, M. (2014). E-research and learning theory: What do sequence and process mining methods contribute? *British Journal of Educational Technology*, 45(3), 528–540. https://doi.org/10.1111/bjet.12146.

Šalkevicius, J., Damaševičius, R., Maskeliunas, R., & Laukienė, I. (2019). Anxiety level recognition for virtual reality therapy system using physiological signals. *Electronics*, 8(9), 1039. https://doi.org/10.3390/electronics8091039.

Schmidt, E. A., Schrauf, M., Simon, M., Fritzsche, M., Buchner, A., & Kincses, W. E. (2009). Drivers' misjudgement of vigilance state during prolonged monotonous daytime driving. *Accident Analysis & Prevention*, 41(5), 1087–1093. https://doi.org/10.1016/j.aap.2009.06.007.

Scholtens, S., Rydell, A.-M., & Yang-Wallentin, F. (2013). ADHD symptoms, academic achievement, self-perception of academic competence and future orientation: A longitudinal study. *Scandinavian Journal of Psychology*, 54(3), 205–212. https://doi.org/10.1111/sjop.12042.

Segrin, C. & Taylor, M. (2007). Positive interpersonal relationships mediate the association between social skills and psychological well-being. *Personality and Individual Differences*, 43(4), 637–646. https://doi.org/10.1016/j.paid.2007.01.017.

Song, M., Chen, C., Liu, S., Li, J., Hou, Y., & Zhang, L. (2017). Effects of parenting styles on aggression of junior school students: Roles of deviant peer affiliation and self-control. *Psychological Development and Education*, 33(6),675–682.

Soufineyestani, M., Dowling, D., & Khan, A. (2020). Electroencephalography (EEG) technology applications and available devices. *Applied Sciences*, 10(21), 7453. https://doi.org/10.3390/app10217453.

Spruijt-Metz, D. & Nilsen, Wendy. (2014). Dynamic models of behavior for just-in-time adaptive interventions. *IEEE Pervasive Computing*, 13(3), 13–17. https://doi.org/10.1109/MPRV.2014.46.

Sun, P., Jiang, H., Chu, M., & Qian, F. (2014). Gratitude and school well-being among Chinese university students: Interpersonal relationships and social support as mediators. *Social Behavior and Personality: An International Journal*, 42(10), 1689–1698. https://doi.org/10.2224/sbp.2014.42.10.1689.

Vargas, D. L., Bridgeman, A. M., Schmidt, D. R., Kohl, P. B., Wilcox, B. R., & Carr, L. D. (2018). Correlation between student collaboration network centrality and academic performance. *Physical Review Physics Education Research*, 14(2), 020112. https://doi.org/10.1103/PhysRevPhysEducRes.14.020112.

Wallace, P. (2014). Internet addiction disorder and youth: There are growing concerns about compulsive online activity and that this could impede students' performance and social lives. *EMBO Reports*, 15(1), 12–16.

Wang, F., Lin, L., Xu, M., Li, L., Lu, J., & Zhou, X. (2019). Mental health among left-behind children in rural China in relation to parent-child communication. *International Journal of Environmental Research and Public Health*, 16(10), 1855. https://doi.org/10.3390/ijerph16101855.

Williamson, J. R., Godoy, E., Cha, M., Schwarzentruber, A., Khorrami, P., Gwon, Y., & Quatieri, T. F. (2016). Detecting depression using vocal, facial and semantic communication cues. *Proceedings of the 6th International Workshop on Audio/Visual Emotion Challenge*, pp. 11–18. Amsterdam, The Netherlands. https://doi.org/10.1145/2988257.2988263.

Wolraich, M. L., Hagan, J. F., Allan, C., Chan, E., Davison, D., Earls, M., & Zurhellen, W. (2019). Clinical practice guideline for the diagnosis, evaluation, and treatment of attention-deficit/hyperactivity disorder in children and adolescents. *Pediatrics*, 144(4), e20192528.

Xi, M. (2018). Resource allocation of mental health education in primary and secondary schools under the background of urban-rural integration. *Journal of Xingtai University*, 33(3), 61–63.

Xie, F. (2019). Status of mental health of primary school student in rural areas of Jiangxi Province. Nanchang University. Master Dissertation.

Xu, D. & Zhang, Y. (2016). Study on aggressive behavior and intervention strategy of left behind children: Based on family perspective. *Journal of Jilin Normal University (Humanities & Social Science Edition)*, 44(2), 104–107.

Ye, Y. (2000). A comparative study on mental health state of the rural and urban middle-school students in Guizhou Province (Master dissertation). Guizhou Normal University.

Yu, G. & Wang, Q. (2018). Social transformation: A study on the structure and characteristics of mental health of junior middle school students. *Journal of Southwest Minzu University (Humanities & Social Science Edition)*, 39(1), 219–225.

Yu, X., Wang, J., & Yang, J. (2019). Analysis on mental health status among Grade 3–6 students in Guangxi Province. *Chinese Journal of Health Education*, 35(12), 1089–1093. https://doi.org/10.16169/j.cnki.issn.10029982.2019.12.008.

Zhang, X., Pan, J., Shen, J., Din, Z. U., Li, J., Lu, D., & Hu, B. (2020). Fusing of electroencephalogram and eye movement with group sparse canonical correlation analysis for anxiety detection. *IEEE Transactions on Affective Computing*, 13(2), 958–971. https://doi.org/10.1109/TAFFC.2020.2981440.

Zhang, Y., Zhao, G., Shu, Y., Ge, Y., & Sun, X. (2023). CPED: A Chinese positive emotion database for emotion elicitation and analysis. *IEEE Transactions on Affective Computing*, 14(2), 1417–1430.

Zoanetti, N. (2010). Interactive computer-based assessment tasks: How problem-solving process data can inform instruction. *Australasian Journal of Educational Technology*, 26(5), 585–606.

7 Smart Building

Hongan Wang

7.1 INTRODUCTION TO SMART BUILDING

7.1.1 DEFINITION OF SMART BUILDING

The concept of smart building was born in the United States. In 1984, in Hartford, Connecticut, the United States, the "City Place Building" transformed from an old financial building was considered as the world's first smart building. This building has a total floor area of more than 100,000 m² and 38 floors. The United Technologies Building System Co (UTBS) contracted the elevators, air conditioners, etc. and connected them with computers and communication equipment, providing computing and communication services to the users of the building in the meantime. In 1986, the United States established a research institution engaged in smart building to promote the development of building intellectualization. In 1991, the American National Standards Institute issued the "Standard for Smart Building Telecommunications Cabling Channel and Space", which provides a standard basis for the design and construction of integrated cabling systems for smart building. "Hakozaki Building" was the first smart building built in Japan in 1985. After that, "Tokyo Honda Aoyama Building", "NTT Shinagawa Building", etc. all have perfect equipment systems. With the vigorous development of building intellectualization in the United States and Japan, the United Kingdom, Germany, Singapore, and other countries have gradually begun to pay attention to the theoretical research of smart building.

China began to introduce the concept of smart building in the 1990s. In 1995, the "Building and Building Integrated Cabling System and Design Specifications" was issued by the Committee of Information and Communication, China Association for Engineering Construction Standardization. Then the "Interim Regulations on Engineering Design and Management of smart Building Systems" was issued by the Ministry of Construction in 1997. Such a series of norms and regulations provide a basis for the planning, design, and construction of smart buildings, and promote the development of the same. Subsequently, a large number of smart buildings with a high degree of intelligence were built in China, such as Beijing Development Building, Shenzhen Diwang Tower, CITIC Plaza, and Shanghai Jinmao Tower. The proportion of smart buildings in China only accounted for 26% of new buildings in 2012, far lower than the 70% in the United States, and only 40% in 2018, but the data is expected to maintain an annual growth rate of about 3%.

Since 1980, the definition of smart building has been continuously developed, and people continue to improve this definition by drawing on new knowledge and experience (Brooks, 2011). In 1983, smart building was first defined as "a building with a fully automatic *service control* system." Then, in 1988, it was defined as "a building that integrates multiple subsystems and manages resources through a collaborative model to

DOI: 10.1201/9781032686691-7

maximize technical performance, investment, operational cost reduction, and flexibility" (Wong et al., 2005). In 1998, the European Smart Building Organization defined it as "creating a building that maximizes performance, minimizes environmental impact and reduces resource waste for building owners" (So et al., 1999).

There are various definitions of smart building in countries and regions. The United States believes that a smart building should be a building that can provide an efficient, comfortable, and convenient environment with a reasonable investment by optimizing its structure, systems, services, and management as well as their inherent relationships. Japan believes that a smart building is a building that has the functions of information communication, office automation services, and building automation services and facilitates the needs of intellectual activities. Europe proposes that creating a building environment that enables users to achieve optimum efficiency, while managing their resources most effectively and with minimum maintenance costs, to enable users to achieve their business quickly, is fundamental to smart buildings.

China released three editions of "Smart Building Design Standards" (GB/T50314-2000, GB/T50314-2006, and GB/T50314-2015) in 2000, 2006, and 2015, respectively. The definitions of smart building in these standards are listed in Table 7.1.

The latest definition of smart building appears in the "Assessment Standard for Smart Building" released by the Architectural Society of China in 2021. This standard proposed that smart buildings that build a comprehensive service platform are based on common buildings with smart applications as the goal. They achieve comprehensive perception, reasoning, judgment, and self-determination of building data, and also a harmonious integration of people, facilities, and environment through self-evolution and adaptive control of facilities and environmental space, so as to provide buildings with a safe, efficient, energy-saving, comfortable, and humanized functional environment.

TABLE 7.1
The Definition of Smart Building in "Smart Building Design Standards"

2000	It uses building as the platform and owns equipment, automated office, and communication network system; it provides people with a safe, efficient, comfortable, and convenient building environment by integrating the structure, systems, services, management, and their optimized combination.
2006	It uses building as the platform and owns information facility system, information application system, building equipment management system, public security system, etc.; it provides people with a safe, efficient, convenient, energy-efficient, environmentally friendly, and healthy building environment by optimally integrating the structure, systems, services, management, and their optimized combination.
2015	It uses building as the platform and is based on the integrated application of various types of intelligent information; it integrates structure, system, application, management, and their optimized combination; it has an integrated command capability of perception, transmission, memorizing, reasoning, judgment, and decision-making; it achieves a harmonious integration of people, buildings, and environment; it provides people with a safe, efficient, and convenient building with sustainable development of functional environment.

7.1.2 Features of Smart Buildings

Smart building is the product of modern science and technology. As the basic element of the urban smartness, it provides people with places to live, work, and play and is closely related to the development of society. Based on the research conducted on the buildings that have been built and used, a smart building is supposed to have the following characteristics:

Smartness of equipment and construction. From design to construction, a smart building integrates various tech equipment, and the idealization of construction is achieved through the integration of new technologies such as Building Information Modeling (BIM), Internet of Things (IoT), cloud computing, and artificial intelligence. Every step of the development of a smart building is inseparable from the support of technology.

Huge sensor network, large-scale data collection, and massive data storage. Only with a large amount of building equipment data to support data mining, analysis, and self-learning can artificial intelligence be used to control and manage buildings more efficiently and safely.

Having an efficient and smart integrated management system. There are at least thousands of data nodes in an ordinary office building. Without such a management system, they cannot be effective and reliable, and the efficiency of operation and maintenance will be greatly reduced. For example, when one of the data nodes goes wrong, the faults will be difficult to detect and locations will be difficult to locate as well.

A more complete actuator network. In smart buildings, there will be more number of systems capable of automatic operation. According to the habits analysis and learning of the people in the building, combined with environmental parameters and preset indicators, the "brain" of smart buildings can adjust the operation status of equipment in time to achieve a better result.

Stronger safety requirements. In terms of safety and disaster resistance, more high-security and high-reliability intelligent security systems are deployed to protect the life and property safety of people in the building and the asset safety of enterprises.

Normalization of learning and innovation. Users who work or live in smart buildings can easily complete the data interaction with other people, machines, and objects through the Internet and enjoy intelligent services at any time. People can work, study, and do other stuff without leaving the building.

High investment in the early stage and large payback later. Compared with traditional buildings, smart buildings use a large number of integrated systems and new technologies during construction, but the advanced control system can greatly improve resource utilization and reduce the cost of maintenance after completing the construction. In general, the cost of smart buildings during the construction period accounts for a large part of the total cost. However, the total investment is much less than that of traditional buildings, and the benefits can be guaranteed due to a longer lifespan.

High requirements for energy saving. In the early stage of design, smart buildings adopt reasonable building structure design and use new energy-saving equipment to avoid energy waste. Through the deployment of various intelligent subsystems, high efficiency, low energy consumption, and low pollution are achieved, which is proposed to meet the need of ecological sustainability. They also constantly revise the building operation algorithm based on the feedback from user and environment to achieve the best balance between user satisfaction and low energy consumption.

People oriented. Meeting the needs of human social activities is the driving force for the development of buildings. Smart buildings should be built with the goal of providing every user with a safe, comfortable, efficient, and manageable working and living environment.

7.1.3 Development of Smart Buildings

The intelligent development of buildings can be divided into three stages: traditional buildings, intelligent buildings, and smart buildings.

The concept of intelligent building originated in the 1980s. Compared with traditional buildings, intelligent buildings are deeply integrated with information and automation technology and provide people with a safer, more comfortable, and more convenient building environment. However, although intelligent buildings have made many improvements in equipment management, energy saving, security management, etc., they still cannot be called smart.

Although smart buildings and intelligent buildings are different in one word, whether there is a "smart brain" is the essential difference. The concept of "integrated service platform for smart building" (China Building Energy Conservation Society, 2021) is given in the "Assessment Standard for Smart Building", the first smart building–related standard in China, which is a management platform built on the basis of technologies such as the IoTs, big data, and artificial intelligence and with building data acquisition, data processing, data services, and intelligent operation of the whole building life cycle. This platform is undoubtedly the "smart brain." Its existence makes the building a "living body" that can be fully perceived and always online. Through the brain, all the data collected in the building can be processed in time. At the same time, artificial intelligence provides excellent data analysis and decision-making capabilities. The building continues to learn and evolve, ultimately providing people with better services and greatly improving user experience.

Table 7.2 shows the specific differences between smart building and intelligent building (Wong et al., 2005).

The architecture of smart building should be constructed based on IoT technology, including perception layer, network transmission layer, data platform layer, and smart application layer, as shown in Figure 7.1.

The key technologies of smart building mainly include the following parts:

IoT technology: IoT refers to "rely on the network for computing, processing, transmission, and interconnection to achieve the information interaction and seamless connection of people-objects and objects-objects; use perception technology, expansion, network extension, and intelligent devices to perceive and identify communication networks and the Internet; achieve precise management, real-time control, and scientific decision-making in turn for the physical world" (Zhang and Chen, 2021). It is an information carrier based on the Internet, traditional telecommunication

TABLE 7.2

Differences between Smart Building and Intelligent Building

Comparative Content	Intelligent Building	Smart Building
System architecture	It is based on automation technology and information and uses distributed architecture.	It is based on big data and artificial intelligence and uses Open IoT architecture.
Subsystem relationship	Subsystems are independent of each other.	Subsystems are interconnected and operate collaboratively.
Data platform	There is no unified data platform, and each subsystem forms isolated data island.	There is a unified data platform to build and run big data.
Data processing and sharing	Data is not shared across systems.	Artificial intelligence technology is used to process data and achieve data sharing.
System characteristic	It is equipment-centric and operates with locally optimization.	It is an integration of human, machine, and object and is human-centric. It uses global optimization and operates and maintains intelligently.
Remote storage and access	Remote access is not available.	Cloud deployment, remote access, and remote operation and maintenance are supported.

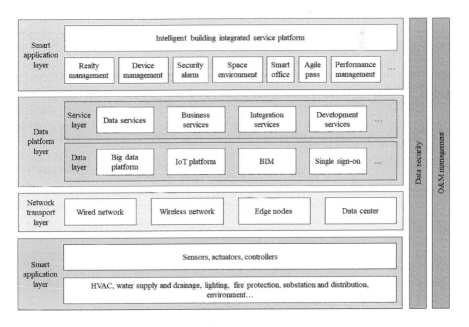

FIGURE 7.1   Smart building structure diagram.

network, etc. and enables all common physical objects that can be independently addressed to form an interconnected network (Wong et al., 2011).

Smart buildings are the foundation of smart cities, and the combination with the IoT is an inevitable trend in the development of science and technology. The IoT technology has a unified data management strategy and open interface protocol, which can encode the sensors inside the building, remove the network boundary, and make the building subsystems interconnected. Applying the IoT technology in smart building can steadily promote the intelligent construction of cities, especially in energy consumption monitoring, equipment management, smart home, energy management, safety management, and environmental monitoring.

BIM technology: building information model, which integrates all relevant construction information together through three-dimensional digital technology, is a detailed expression of the full-cycle information of the engineering project. Moreover, BIM is the application of digital visualization technology in construction engineering. It provides early warning and analysis of various problems in advance of the project so that all parties involved in the project can understand and respond. At the same time, it provides a solid foundation for collaborative work.

BIM is a revolutionary platform for the construction industry. BIM provides the necessary basic data for construction projects and at the same time brings great assurance of responsiveness and speed in decision-making. Different from the traditional 2D, once the building information model is established, the user can enter any space of the virtual building and roam while being able to watch the process of building growth. The combination of the IoT and BIM technology has broad prospects and great value and can promote the evolution of intelligent building into smart building.

Artificial intelligence technology: Artificial intelligence is a new technical subject that studies and develops theories, methods, technologies, and application systems for simulating, extending, and expanding human intelligence.

A smart building with a "brain" has the skills of self-learning and self-evolution, which are honed on the gradually mature artificial intelligence theory and technology. Through these skills, the building can self-learn personalized needs according to the user habits, and it mines, calculates, analyzes, and integrates real-time data from various subsystems. It finally achieves the purpose of autonomous control, comprehensive decision-making, self-organization, collaboration, and so on. As a representative of the development of modern artificial intelligence, deep reinforcement learning shows promising perception and decision-making ability in complex tasks and environments and will bring new ideas for situational awareness and comprehensive decision-making in the process of smart building management (Liu et al., 2011).

7.2   TOWARD A MORE PERCEPTIVE SMART BUILDING

7.2.1   Overview

Since the 1990s, the functional design of buildings to meet the needs of specialized building structures, services, and application equipment management has increasingly emphasized the need for a complete smart perception system in the actual smart building construction process to provide users an efficient, comfortable, and humanized architectural design scheme. Various advanced human perception technologies have been adopted to design the building's perception system inside the building in the architectural design process. On the other hand, there are two core systems that consume more than 70% of energy in commercial office buildings (Boonekamp, 2007; Pérez-Lombard et al., 2008; Nguyen and Aiello, 2013) – lighting system and heating–ventilation–air-conditioning, namely, HVAC Systems – whose operating state and energy consumption dynamics are directly related to environmental context and occupant behavior. Thus, understanding fine-grained building environment occupancy information is important in efficient energy use. Different types of sensors can be deployed and used to achieve fine-grained knowledge of occupant behavior patterns in the built environment (Andersen et al., 2015).

The health and productivity status of occupants in indoor environments depends on indoor environmental quality (IEQ) (Navada et al., 2013; Choi, 2016; Jin et al., 2018; Ekwevugbe et al., 2012; Tetlow et al., 2014). Various sensors can be used to sense indoor environmental quality and individual occupant satisfaction, which can be used to improve energy savings, thermal comfort, and indoor air quality conditions (Dong et al., 2018; Spataru and Gauthier, 2013; Christensen et al., 2014). Thermostats, smart meter sensors, and heart rate sensors (Cheng and Lee, 2014; Cheng and Lee, 2016; Sim et al., 2016; Goyal et al., 2015; Kim et al., 2018) have all been deployed to sense heat distribution and the environmental quality of living spaces and to make occupants more productive and healthier. At the same time, using occupant behavior sensors to analyze occupants' behavior patterns can also improve the building environment's energy efficiency (Nguyen and Aiello, 2013; Li et al., 2012). Different types of sensors are used in the built environment to understand indoor environmental characteristics and occupant behavior. Table 7.3 classifies the sensors used for smart building operations into three main types: the first category includes occupant detection sensors in the built environment, the second category includes various types of sensors used to measure indoor building environment parameters, and the last category represents sensors used to perceive fine-grained human behavior. The scope of smart building perception discussed in this chapter includes the utilization scheme of building-level and building environment-related information obtained by the most advanced sensing acquisition methods and no longer includes access to the last category of fine-grained information on the personal status of occupants.

With the development of IoT technology, sensors have been able to empower smart building management systems in the form of densely embedded network systems in data collection, information processing, decision-making, and supporting potential spatiotemporal solutions, enabling monitoring and regulation applications to produce tangible economic, environmental, and social benefits. Several modern technologies

TABLE 7.3

List of Sensors Deployed in Smart Buildings

Smart Building–Related Sensors	Sensor Type
Occupancy sensors	Image-based sensor, Passive infrared sensor, Radio-based sensor, Threshold and mechanical sensors, Chair sensors, Pressure Mats, Camera sensor, Photosensor, Ultrasonic doppler, Microwave doppler, Ultrasonic ranging
Building environment measurement sensors	CO_2 sensor, Air temperature sensor, Humidity sensor, Thermofluidic sensor, Sound sensor, Light sensor, Volatile organic compound sensor, Particulate matter sensor, and Air velocity sensor
Human behavior sensors	Wearable sensor, IoT-based sensor, Smart Phones, Heart Rate sensor, Fingerprint sensor, Mobile pupilometer, and Skin Temperature sensor

Note: The sensor type classification criteria are referenced from Dong et al. (2019).

provide technical support for building regulation for energy management, building resource utilization detection/prediction, and safety.

Many smart sensors on the IoT adopt different communication protocols and interface standards, and the timing data from each sensor across scales lacks unified storage and management. The analysis and application of these timing data are limited to the internal independent (autonomous) subsystems. No data is shared among these subsystems, which leads to the whole IoT system unable to achieve joint operation. In smart buildings, there are many subsystems inside, such as lighting systems, elevator systems, water-supply systems, parking management systems, intrusion alarm systems, access control systems, power-monitoring systems, and automatic fire alarm systems. There is no interconnection and interoperability of information between each subsystem as well as no data fusion and sharing. Thus, it is challenging to achieve linkage and collaboration between the systems.

To address the above challenges, this chapter presents a data fusion scheme that integrates the time-series correlation information extracted from multiple sensing data sources. With this scheme, the time-varying data from multiple sources generated by the system operation can be aggregated from the distributed deployment of sensors in the building, and then the information-rich sensing features can be extracted by fusion processing. This chapter introduces a real-time data–distributed integration method which can perform multiarea resource scheduling and linkage control based on the real-time integrated sensory information.

7.2.2 A Solution to Multisource Sensing Data Fusion for Smart Building

7.2.2.1 Cross-Scale Multisensors Data Fusion System for Smart Buildings

A smart building platform with complete sensing capability usually consists of dozens of subsystems, such as air-conditioning system, heat-exchange system, water-supply system, elevator system, and electric window system. Its characteristics are listed as follows:

- The complexity of the system makes it challenging to complete pure mechanistic modeling.
- There are various types of sensors and subsystems; their data collection and operation rules are heterogeneous.
- The control strategy of environment parameters is complex. Equipment information and operation laws with cross-node correlation and situational awareness are adaptive needs.
- The modes of operation are diverse. There are classification and linkage requirements from data storage to system applications.

In view of the above status quo, this chapter proposes a bottom-up six-layer fusion system architecture. The fusion technology is researched and developed in the data collection layer, fusion component layer, interface protocol layer, data model layer, rule configuration layer, and system application layer to achieve a top-down integration of information fusion, knowledge fusion, and decision fusion. We can collect, extract, and characterize high-quality data information; reduce the generation and distribution of redundant data using hierarchical data collection requirements; and improve network transmission efficiency (Figure 7.2).

7.2.2.1.1 Information Fusion Technology for Multisource Building Data

The hierarchical information fusion route includes: the venue data are collected and stored according to the type of equipment operation real-time and historical data,

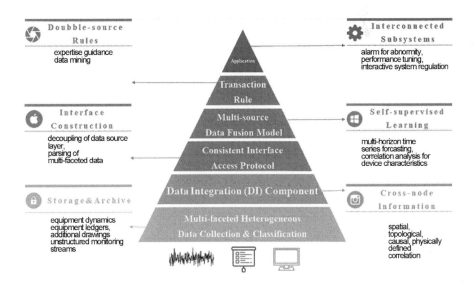

FIGURE 7.2 Schematic diagram of the cross-scale multisource heterogeneous data fusion architecture.

equipment ledgers, additional drawings, monitoring streams, and other unstructured data and then integrated with cross-node information using self-developed data fusion components provided for real-time data collection, including spatial, topological, causal, and physically defined cross-node association of fusion rules; consistent access protocol interface enables multiple sources of heterogeneous information for upper-level reasoning with a unified information conversion format; the multidimensional time-series data model custom-accessed by scenario-aware adaptive integration applications, fusing cross-cycle temporal and feature associations in the system's operational history information; and further extraction of sequential patterns of arena equipment operation based on data mining techniques.

7.2.2.1.2   Cross-Scale Knowledge Fusion Technology

In order to meet the need of reasoning and decision-making for smart building operation and control, cross-scale knowledge fusion method which integrates information from the fusion component layer to the rule reasoning layer has been investigated. The generated high-quality knowledge representations and reasoning rules are eventually used for building operation and control. The main technical routes include knowledge representation and knowledge base entry obtained by transforming cross-node association data (spatial, topological, causal, and physically defined fusion rules) of the fusion component layer by a consistent interface protocol; feature representation of cross-cycle temporal correlation and dependency between device-scenario information captured based on multidimensional time-series data modeling; and factual and triggered inference rules combining business expert knowledge and data mining.

7.2.2.1.3   System Operation Decision Fusion Technique Combined with Real-Time Rule Reasoning

Decision fusion is a decision and response based on the fusion of the operation process of the building system (associated operation of linked subsystems and scenario change and other processes). The decision fusion for the smart operation of the venue includes two technical points: firstly, multivariate predictive control decision based on a time-series model of equipment operation, which realizes the overall regulation and optimization with the change of perceived scenarios through process prediction; secondly, real-time rule inference engine compatible with real-time data acquisition ensures operational safety and efficiency by dynamically adjusting decisions in response to sudden events or contextual changes.

7.2.2.2   Dense to Sense: A Feature-Extraction Model for Data Fusion in Smart Building

Based on the technologies mentioned above, a more maturely sensing data platform for buildings has the ability to aggregate a large volume of system feature data and manage and store a rich set of system device association rules, which also brings unprecedented challenges to the exploration of system-level application in management, operation, maintenance, etc.

The platform for building management has the characteristics of covering rich dimensions of data features and a large number of heterogeneous associations such as topology, spatial associations, and physical relations of operation states.

The observable state variables during the operation of many types of building sub-systems reach over a thousand or even ten thousand levels, which not only brings a wide range of redundant information and noise pollution to the perceived state but also makes it difficult for the limited regulation measures to grasp the core regulation characteristics and objectives.

On the other hand, various machine learning methods that have emerged in the past decade possess the dimensionality reduction capability of transforming and extracting low-dimensional, dense feature vectors from a sparse, high-dimensional feature space. The extracted low-dimensional key features can be used for efficient subsequent monitoring or conditioning tasks. Based on the dimensionality reduction and modeling capabilities of the above machine learning methods, this chapter introduces a mechanism that can dynamically identify and extracts critical features to achieve transformation from high-dimensional multisource data to a small number of core features.

As shown in Figure 7.3, the proposed feature-extraction model takes M-dimension temporal data as the input and the output as m-dimension data after dimensionality reduction and filtering, where $m \ll M$ indicates that the purpose of feature dimensionality reduction is achieved. The blocks and element descriptions of this model are elaborated as follows.

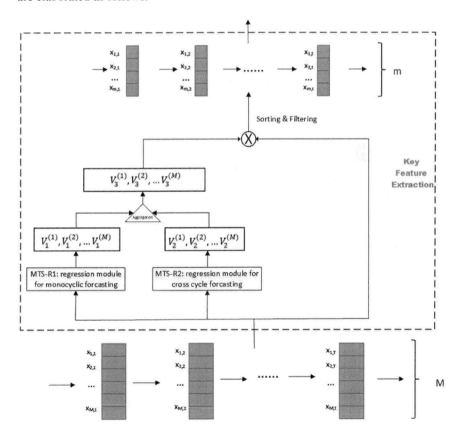

FIGURE 7.3 Schematic diagram of the feature-extraction model structure.

7.2.2.2.1   Timing Alignment of Data

Because the building data originate from distributed asynchronous sensors, the raw sensing data cannot be fully guaranteed to be the reported data from all collection points under synchronous trigger timestamps. Therefore, this step performs prepro-cessing based on historical data records and complements each dimensional attribute under each synchronous sampling moment within the time window by interpolation fitting, nearest neighbor, or other interpolation methods to form a multivariate time series represented as two-dimensional data:

$$
X = \begin{bmatrix}
X_{1,1} & X_{1,2} & \cdots & X_{1,t} \\
X_{2,1} & X_{2,2} & \cdots & X_{2,t} \\
\vdots & \vdots & \vdots & \vdots \\
X_{M,1} & X_{M,2} & \cdots & X_{M,t}
\end{bmatrix}
\tag{7.1}
$$

where $X_{i,j}$ denotes the sampled data of the ith sensor at the jth moment; the process-ing time window length of the sampled data is t; and the total number of IoT sensors included in the model is M. The dimensional units and measurement ranges of $X_{i,j}$ may vary due to the heterogeneity of data X, and the varying sampled values of $X_{i,j}$ at different sampling instants j demonstrate the temporal nature of X.

7.2.2.2.2   Dual-Module Integrated Downscaling

The effectiveness of the extracted low-dimensional features varies significantly depending on the specific application goals or downstream tasks, when compared to other feature-extracted models. This chapter attributes these differences to the diver-sity of assessment framework. In order to alleviate the differences in feature-extrac-tion effectiveness caused by various application tasks and to achieve the maximum decoupling between feature extraction and downstream tasks, this chapter proposes a compromise solution by introducing two types of modules to establish two sets of evaluation criteria for feature importance and considering feature effectiveness in order to increase the adaptability of extracted features to different application goals.

Module 1 focuses on the prediction performance of short-term data after dimen-sionality reduction; i.e., a single-step prediction target fitting model is used as the module's structure. Module 2 focuses on the evaluation of the recovery or prediction ability of long-term data after dimensionality reduction; i.e., a fitting model with a cross-period objective is used as the module's structure. By considering the dimen-sionality reduction features' ability to reconstruct both short- and long-term data, the more critical data features are finally selected using a comprehensive evaluation criterion. The construction process of the two types of modules and the evaluation scheme are described below.

The single-step prediction target fitting model receives multivariate time-series X as input and the following k prediction targets for the next step (moment $t + 1$) as the model learning task:

$$\left[y_{t+1}^{(1)}, y_{t+1}^{(2)}, \ldots y_{t+1}^{(k)} \right] \tag{7.2}$$

When $k = 1$, a single-objective prediction task is conducted, such as predicting only the system's electricity consumption in the following period. When $k > 1$, a multiobjective prediction task is conducted, such as predicting both the system electricity consumption and the deviation of the environmental monitoring index from the ideal state.

After completing training, the described single-step predictive target fitting model outputs the importance coefficients of the corresponding features for each dimensional sensor:

$$\left[v_1^{(1)}, v_1^{(2)}, \ldots, v_1^{(M)} \right] \tag{7.3}$$

The described cross-period prediction target fitting model focuses on system signals with periodic fluctuations, such as days, weeks, and quarters. The multivariate time-series data X is received as input, and the following k prediction targets after multiple cycles ($t + s$ moments) are used as the model learning task:

$$\left[y_{t+s}^{(1)}, y_{t+s}^{(2)}, \ldots, y_{t+s}^{(k)} \right] \tag{7.4}$$

where a single-objective prediction task is learned when $k = 1$, and a multiobjective prediction task is learned when $k > 1$.

The cross-period prediction target fitting model outputs the importance coefficients of the corresponding features for each dimensional sensor after training:

$$\left[v_2^{(1)}, v_2^{(2)}, \ldots, v_2^{(M)} \right] \tag{7.5}$$

Combining the evaluation results of the described single-step prediction target fitting model and the cross-period prediction target fitting model, the importance of the features corresponding to the first to M sensors was converted to

$$\left[v_3^{(1)}, v_3^{(2)}, \ldots, v_3^{(M)} \right] = \left[\max\left\{ v_1^{(1)}, v_2^{(1)} \right\}, \max\left\{ v_1^{(2)}, v_2^{(2)} \right\}, \ldots, \max\left\{ v_1^{(M)}, v_2^{(M)} \right\} \right] \tag{7.6}$$

In order to facilitate the quantitative comparison standard, further normalization is performed to obtain the final importance coefficient of each dimension feature:

$$\left[v^{(1)}, v^{(2)}, \ldots, v^{(M)} \right] = \frac{1}{\sum_{i=1}^{M} v^{(i)}} \left[v_3^{(1)}, v_3^{(2)}, \ldots, v_3^{(M)} \right] \tag{7.7}$$

Arrange $v^{(1)} \sim v^{(M)}$ in descending order and select top m-dimensional features or filter features by threshold value directly according to the system characteristics and actual requirements (e.g., retain all the corresponding features with importance coefficient > 0.05). The final retained feature dimension is denoted as m, indicating the preservation of data records from m sensors out of M, where $m \gg M$.

7.2.2.2.3 *Discussion of Module Structure Design*

Theoretically, the requirements of the two modules described above for the internal functionality of the module include (1) a multivariate serial data structure that can be accepted as module inputs, (2) machine learning models with the capability of short- and long-term data reconstruction, respectively, and (3) the ability to quantitatively evaluate the feature importance of each input dimension.

There are many modified machine learning models that can satisfy the above requirements, such as a deep neural network model with multivariate time series as input, where the importance corresponding to each variable dimension can be evaluated by the extent to which the missing input of that dimension leads to a decrease in the accuracy of the fit on the training set.

In this chapter, the authors, involved in the modification of an entire building management system, have adopted a more efficient model for training. In this model, both modules $R1$ and $R2$, which are mechanically identical, take two-dimensional data in the form of $\{X\}_{M \times t}$ as input and the k-dimensional vector $\vec{Y} \in \mathbb{R}^k$ as the fitting target and obtain $\{X\}_{M \times t}$ per one-dimensional row vector $[X_{i,1}, X_{i,2}, ..., X_{i,t}]$ to fit $\vec{Y}$ contribution of the feature importance $v^{(i)}$, $i = 1, 2, ..., M$. The construction process of the two stages is described as follows:

Data vectorization. The data $\{X\}_{M \times t}$ is transformed into a vector format that can be handled by the Gradient Boosting Regression Tree (GBRT) model by spreading each row of the two-dimensional $\{X\}_{M \times t}$ as

$$\vec{X}_{\text{flat}} = \left[X_{1,1}, X_{1,2}, ..., X_{1,t}, X_{2,1}, X_{2,2}, ..., X_{2,t}, ..., X_{M,1}, X_{M,2}, ..., X_{M,t}\right] \tag{7.8}$$

GBRT fitting. For each dimensional objective Y_j of the fitted objective $\vec{Y} \in \mathbb{R}^k$, an integrated GBRT model of $\vec{X}_{\text{flat}} \to Y_j$ is built, and after the boosted tree of GBRT is created, the importance score of each attribute is obtained relatively easily based on the improved performance metric of each attribute split point in the decision tree (e.g., split node Gini purity or other metric functions) for each attribute in the decision tree. Then, the weighted average of the attributes in all boosting trees is used as the importance score of the attribute.

Let $X_{i,\tau}$ in $\vec{X}_{\text{flat}}$ have an importance score of $v_{i,\tau}^{(j)}$ for Yj, and the ith-dimensional sensor feature has t importance scores $[v_{i,1}^{(j)}, v_{i,2}^{(j)}, ..., v_{i,t}^{(j)}]$ for Y_j. Here, the combined importance score of the ith-dimensional sensor feature on Y_j is defined as

$$v_i^{(j)} = \max_{\tau=1,...,t} \left\{v_{i,\tau}^{(j)}\right\} \tag{7.9}$$

Further, the ith-dimensional sensor feature has k importance scores $\left[v_i^{(1)}, v_i^{(2)}, ..., v_i^{(k)}\right]$. Define the combined importance score of the ith-dimensional sensor feature on $\vec{Y}$ as

$$v_i = \frac{\max\limits_{j=1,...,k}\left\{v_i^{(j)}\right\}}{\sum\limits_{i=1}^{M} \max\limits_{j=1,...,k}\left\{v_i^{(j)}\right\}} \tag{7.10}$$

7.2.2.2.4   Discussion of Feature Enhancement Options

Based on the steps mentioned above, the *m* original features are believed to be retained to the maximum after the original feature dimensionality reduction. On the other hand, in addition to the original features, some associative features are combined to form new features, which often become the critical features with richer feature discriminative power. This is also the key for many deep learning models to obtain performance improvement.

For this reason, it is necessary to find a new combination scheme of the features. Visual analysis of real data revealed that many time-series signals recorded in the system have multiscale periodic approximations (e.g., air-conditioning systems highly correlated with outdoor weather show mixed fluctuations of daily, seasonal, and even potential annual cycles. Units in automatic control mode show reciprocal signal oscillations between high and low thresholds, and data recorded from equipment related to building operation and maintenance show fluctuations based on working mode, environment as a cycle, etc.). Inspired by this phenomenon, a combination of information in terms of time- and frequency-domain channels is introduced to extract and transform information-rich system characteristics.

- Time-domain feature extraction. Based on the preserved temporal signal in each system dimension, the project design mechanism makes reference to the convolutional units in convolutional neural networks to bring performance gains for downstream recognition tasks. It adds a one-dimensional window convolution (also called 1-Dimensional Convolution or $1 \times D$ Conv) unit to the data model, which can extract time-domain features within local time segments. Depending on the convolution parameters, the potential roles also include local time-domain signal smoothing (to overcome local high-frequency interference) and the function of measuring the coincidence relative to the reference signal fragment (shapelet) (Figure 7.4).
- Frequency-domain feature extraction. As mentioned earlier, the time-series signals collected by the devices in the building do not present a single-scale periodicity, so the multiscale frequency-domain characteristics presented by the multidimensional data need to retain the data features of a more

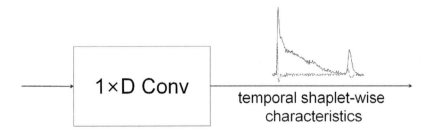

FIGURE 7.4   Schematic of the time-domain feature-extraction channel.

FIGURE 7.5   Schematic of the frequency-domain feature-extraction channel.

comprehensive spectral range. Based on this requirement, this chapter designs a branching channel for frequency-domain feature extraction and performs frequency-domain transformation on the time-series data within the window period using the discrete Fourier transform separately. The anomalies of each single-dimensional signal band that clearly exceed the threshold are filtered, and the signal quantities within the remaining window spectrum are retained. Further, a $1 \times D$ convolution unit is appended to identify the local frequency-domain signal patterns, following the design of the time-domain channel (Figure 7.5).

The final correlated feature-extraction module output features consist of automatically evaluated m-dimensional significant raw features, time-domain convolved features, and frequency-domain convolved features for downstream application tasks. It is worth noting that the retained m-dimensional raw features can be directly separated from the data modeling during the features obtained from the time- and frequency-domain convolution because they contain internal channel parameters and eventually need to be combined with other modules into an overall model structure for end-to-end model training together.

7.2.3 Leveraging the Perception in Real Time

In the field of smart buildings, the real-time data communication of the underlying smart devices is a significant difficulty. On the one hand, there are many types of underlying smart devices. Smart buildings contain video, fire, access control, security, air conditioning, equipment automation control, and many other subsystems; each subsystem has its unique function. These devices come from different manufacturers, using different communication protocols. Each subsystem not only has inconsistent data format, but its communication rate response speed is also different. The data collected from these devices cannot be unified for storage and access. Therefore, it is necessary to develop a robust data platform for data analysis and resource scheduling. On the other hand, the magnitude of real-time data in smart buildings is large. For example, in a smart building of $10,000\,m^2$, the magnitude of multiple subsystems data can reach 10,000. The number of data increases dramatically with the expansion of the building scale, which can reach millions for the building complex. Therefore, it is necessary to introduce real-time database technology to realize data integration of heterogeneous subsystems of smart buildings and resource scheduling of smart buildings.

At present, there are ways to integrate local systems before unified collection in the market. First, the same type of smart equipment of the same manufacturer is integrated into a subsystem; then, the subsystem of a region is integrated; and finally, the data of the regional subsystem is collected in the upper system. This data integration method is multilayered, cumbersome to deploy, complex to implement, and does not have enough openness. In practice, the stability and real-time response of the system have potential severe problems, and a new deployment plan is required additionally for scenarios with high real-time requirements. Besides, the scale of real-time data points of the above solutions is limited under 10,000, which is only suitable for small smart buildings. There is no mature solution in the market for real-time data integration of large- and medium-sized smart building groups.

This section proposes a method for integrating distributed real-time data in smart buildings, which employs a distributed architecture with real-time database and protocol conversion deployment and demonstrates significant improvements in scalability, stability, and real-time performance compared to traditional integration methods. It is a simple, reliable, and efficient way to solve the problem of real-time data interaction of large-scale, multi-protocol-type smart devices in smart buildings.

7.2.3.1   Distributed Integration Methods for Real-Time Data

As shown above, this method consists of the following key components: protocol conversion, distributed real-time data storage service, distributed data collection service, distributed interregional logic linkage and control service, Web API Server, and configuration center (Figure 7.6). The main components are:

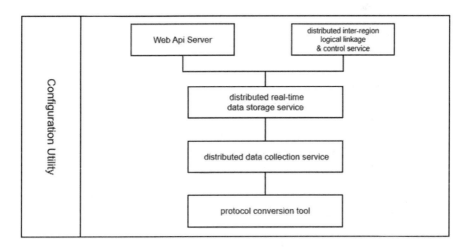

FIGURE 7.6 Principles of distributed and integrated control methods for real-time data for smart buildings.

- The conversion protocol of the underlying smart devices converts the real-time data of different protocol types into a uniform data format for subsequent storage;
- Deploy a distributed real-time data storage service for storing the converted real-time data;
- Deploy the distributed data collection service to deliver the converted real-time data to the real-time data center in real time to complete the unified storage of data;
- Deploy the distributed interregion logical linkage and control service to handle the data linkage relationship between multiarea smart devices;
- Deploy Web API Server to provide an upper-level data access interface for distributed real-time data storage service;
- Complete some configuration work.

The key elements of the above steps are further explained below:

- Protocol conversion of the underlying smart devices: It mainly includes the application of a protocol conversion gateway, which connects the smart devices conforming to the current standard communication protocols in smart buildings to the protocol conversion gateway. It outputs the real-time data in the uniform protocol format by the protocol conversion gateway.
- Distributed data collection service: It mainly includes data communication between the protocol conversion gateway and the real-time database to collect real-time data from the underlying smart devices to the real-time database. At the same time, the internal interface provided by the real-time database is used to listen to the write-back events of the real-time database. When the user controls a device through the upper-layer application, the upper-layer application passes the control information to the real-time database, and the real-time database will trigger the write-back event. In the write-back event, the control information passed is sent to the protocol conversion gateway, which converts the control information into control commands and sends them to the underlying smart device, thus controlling the underlying device to complete the user's control requirements once.
- Distributed real-time data storage service: It mainly includes the application of a distributed real-time database, which is deployed using a distributed architecture as a data center for real-time data of smart buildings.
- Web API Server: It mainly includes a real-time database interface, implementing Web API Server to provide the upper-layer service interface. It also provides support for data analysis and processing applications and other redevelopment applications.
- Distributed interregional logic linkage and control services: It mainly includes using real-time database data integration tools to realize the linkage logic between the control points of smart devices in different areas. The implemented program can be used to manage the logic linkage and control between smart devices.

- System configuration: It includes the configuration of the point information and the internal logic using the configuration tool of the protocol conversion gateway and the configuration of the point information using the configuration tool of the real-time database. In particular, the data collection service and Web API Server can be configured by modifying the configuration file, which adopts XML file format.

Compared with the existing technology, this method provides many improvements. The distributed integrated control method for real-time data in smart buildings has a simpler architecture, is more convenient to deploy, and has good scalability. For new access devices, if the device protocol is a known standard protocol, it can be directly connected to the protocol conversion gateway, and the corresponding points are added without modifying other content or adding other modules; if the device protocol is private or protocols are not supported by the protocol gateway, independently implementing the data acquisition program and logic control program is only needed for the device, without affecting the existing system. In addition, this method can integrate real-time data and linkage control of smart devices in smart buildings with large-scale and multiprotocol types.

7.2.3.2   Implementation Scheme of Real-Time Data–Distributed Integrated Control Technology

The technical implementation steps of real-time data distributed integrated control method as described above include (1) dividing the smart building into a plurality of regions and setting one or more protocol conversion gateways in each region; (2) based on the protocol conversion gateway in each area, the real-time data collected by the smart devices in the area is converted into a uniform format and sent to the data center of the smart building; and (3) the said data center, according to the deployed distributed interregional logical linkage and control services, processes the data linkage relationship between multiarea smart devices. The technical implementation points covered therein are described below:

- Logic linkage and control service: It is based on the linkage control of data points in the real-time database, serving and storing all the logic of logic linkage and control between multiple areas. Each logic is stored as a logic object, which includes a logic name, a logic event, a logic condition, and a logic action. The logic name is the globally unique identification of the logic; the logic event is the event that needs to happen to trigger the logic; the logic condition is the condition that needs to be satisfied when the logic event of logic occurs to execute the action defined by the logic; the logic action is the predefined action to be executed by each logic.
- Data Center: It includes multiple real-time databases deployed in a distributed architecture and interaction with the upper-layer application interface Web API Server; each real-time database corresponds to a Web API Server service interface.
- Configuration of the real-time database: It includes the construction of the real-time database point table for each point configuration point name,

source node name, device name, point type, data collection flag, and related alarm information.

- Configuration of distributed logic linkage and control services: It includes configuring the connection properties of multiple real-time databases and the corresponding logical properties of points based on the point properties in the real-time database.
- The configuration of protocol conversion gateways: It includes configuration of IP for each protocol translation gateway, connection channel attributes, and each input serial port of the protocol conversion gateway corresponding to a channel. Each channel corresponds to a protocol, and each channel connects multiple smart devices of the same protocol. Configure device attributes for each channel connected to the smart devices. Add data collection points for each smart device and configure the corresponding attributes.
- Upper-layer application interface: It is used to receive the input control information and pass it to the corresponding real-time database, which triggers a write-back event based on the control information. The write-back event sends the control information to the protocol conversion gateway, which converts the control information into control commands and sends them to the corresponding smart device to control the said smart device to complete the corresponding control requirements.
- Local area network interconnection: According to the target demand, the protocol conversion gateway is connected to form multiple LANs; each LAN is connected to form the smart building network.

7.2.3.3   Implementation Method

The above real-time data–distributed integration control method accomplishes a more comprehensive deployment of resources for distributed storage management of building-aware information through the specific implementation process shown in Figure 7.7.

7.2.3.3.1   Protocol Conversion

First of all, the protocol conversion gateway is introduced, and smart devices of various protocol types are connected to the protocol conversion gateway through the physical bus using integrated wiring technology. The lower input port of the protocol conversion gateway is generally a multiplexable RS232/RS485 bus interface, and the upper output port is an Ethernet interface. In particular, the protocol conversion gateway generally has multiple Ethernet ports, and smart devices with Ethernet ports can be directly connected to the protocol conversion gateway via network cables. In addition, according to the specific (building group size limit, regional isolation, physical deployment, etc.) needs to divide the smart building into multiple regions for protocol conversion, each region sets one or more protocol conversion gateway.

7.2.3.3.2   Network Access

The protocol conversion gateway is connected to the LAN through a network switch. In the case of a single LAN, multiple protocol conversion gateways are connected to the same LAN. In particular, the network can be divided into multiple LANs

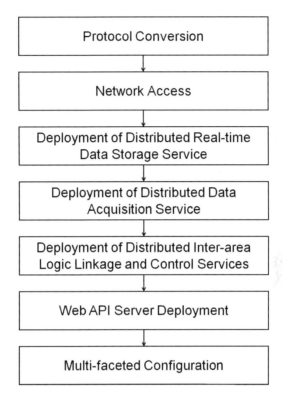

FIGURE 7.7 Process for implementing a distributed integration method for real-time data.

according to specific (physical deployment restrictions, regional isolation, device isolation, etc.) needs, and protocol conversion gateways in different regions in step (1) can choose to access different LANs.

7.2.3.3.3 Deployment of Distributed Real-Time Data Storage Service

First, we introduce a distributed real-time database and deploy the real-time database in a distributed architecture. At the same time, ensure the network interoperability between this distributed data storage service and each LAN in step (2). In particular, the deployment size of the distributed real-time database depends on the size of the building complex. It is also related to the performance of the real-time database. Generally speaking, the larger the size of the building complex, the larger the deployment scale of the real-time database, and the better the performance of the real-time database, the smaller the deployment scale. The scale of real-time database deployment can be decided according to the actual situation and specific needs.

7.2.3.3.4 Deployment of Distributed Data Acquisition Service

The data acquisition service is a data communication middleware between the protocol conversion gateway and the real-time database. Its internal is a data acquisition program or service that can be distributed based on the TCP protocol. In particular, the data acquisition service is a data acquisition program based on the secondary development interface of the real-time database and the protocol conversion gateway.

A data acquisition program corresponds to a combination of a real-time database and a protocol conversion gateway, and the corresponding data acquisition program should be selected (real-time database with data acquisition program) or developed (real-time database without data acquisition program) according to the real-time database and protocol conversion gateway used in the actual project.

7.2.3.3.5   Deployment of Distributed Interarea Logic Linkage and Control Services

The interarea logical linkage and control service is responsible for the logical linkage and control between smart devices located in different zones. The logical linkage and control service is based on the linkage and control of data points in the real-time data storage service. For example, in a pilot project, when it is 9:00 a.m., and the personnel detector detects the staff activity, the lights of the workstation, HVAC, and curtains will be turned on automatically. Lighting and air conditioning can be divided into different areas, but to ensure synchronization and linkage will require a service to support them. Logic linkage and control service stores all the logic of logic linkage and control between multiple areas, and each logic is stored in the form of a logic object, consisting of four main components: logic name, logic event, logic condition, and logic action. Among them, the logic name is the globally unique identification of the logic; a logical event refers to the event required to trigger the logic, including point update events, periodic events, timed events, rule execution failure events, etc.; logical conditions indicate the conditions that need to be met for executing the actions defined by the logic when the logical event occurs; logic action is the logic to perform the predefined actions. Logic linkage and control services will listen to each logical object when the service is started. When a logical event occurs in a logical object, if the logical conditions of the logical object are met, the logical action of the logical object will be executed.

7.2.3.3.6   Deploy Web API Server

Web API Server is a data interface service for upper-layer applications based on data storage service package, relying on Microsoft's IIS service and providing data access and control interface in the form of RESTful architecture, which perfectly solves the cross-platform requirements of redevelopment applications.

7.2.3.3.7   Configuration

The distributed integration method of real-time data in smart buildings involves a protocol conversion gateway, real-time database, data collection service, logical linkage, control service, Web API Server, etc. All these components require the corresponding configuration work:

- Protocol conversion gateways require configuration work that includes: first, configuring the IP access address of each protocol conversion gateway to identify the network location of each protocol conversion gateway; second, configuring the connection channel properties of each gateway, each input serial port of the protocol conversion gateway corresponds to a channel, a channel corresponds to a protocol, and each channel can be connected to multiple devices of the same protocol; then, for each channel to add Then, add devices to each channel and configure the device properties; finally, add device data collection points to each device and configure the corresponding point properties.

- The configuration work required for the distributed real-time database includes building the real-time database point table. Each point needs to be configured with a point name, source node name, device name, point type, data collection flag and related alarm information, history storage, and other attributes.

- The configuration work required for the distributed data collection service includes first, configuring the connection attributes of the protocol conversion gateway, including the IP address and port of the gateway and the user name and password of the connection; then, configuring the connection attributes of the real-time database, including the IP address and port of the real-time database, the user name and password of the connection, and the connected devices.

- The configuration work required for the distributed logical linkage and control services includes first, configuring the connection properties of multiple real-time databases, including the unique identification name of each real-time database, the type, version, IP address, and port of the real-time database as well as the authentication user name and password. Then, based on the point properties in the real-time database, configure the corresponding logical properties of the point, including the logical name, logical events, logical conditions, and the corresponding logical actions. In particular, the connection conversion properties of the real-time database and the relational database can be configured according to the requirements, and the point information of the real-time database can be transferred to the relational database.

- The configuration work required for the Web API Server includes: Web API Server service is deployed synchronously with the real-time database, and each database corresponds to a Web API Server service. This deployment method only needs to configure the real-time database connection information in the Web API Server, including the real-time database IP address and port, and authentication user name and password. In particular, Web API Server relies on IIS service, so you can configure some services for Web API Server through IIS service configuration according to your needs.

Based on the above implementation, this method can enable real-time data integration and linkage control of smart devices in large-scale, multiprotocol smart buildings.

7.3 NATIONAL SPEED SKATING OVAL: A CASE STUDY

7.3.1 Overview

The National Speed Skating Oval, also known as the "Ice Ribbon", is one of the main venues for the 2022 Beijing Winter Olympics and the only new ice competition venue. With a total construction area of $126,000\,m^2$ and seating capacity of 12,000, the venue adopts the world's largest two-way orthogonal saddle-shaped cable-net roof with single layer and is the world's first Winter Olympic speed skating venue that uses carbon dioxide transcritical cooling technology. Figures 7.8 and 7.9 show the exterior and interior views of the National Speed Skating Oval, respectively.

FIGURE 7.8   Exterior views of the National Speed Skating Oval.

FIGURE 7.9   Interior views of the National Speed Skating Oval.

In response to the slogan "High-tech Winter Olympics", all parties involved in the construction of the National Speed Skating Oval have worked with scientific institutions and high-tech enterprises to conduct research from various perspectives such as spectator experience, ice surface maintenance, intelligent operation and maintenance, and energy consumption management. The purpose is to enhance the spectator experience, accurately control the temperature, improve operation and maintenance efficiency, and reduce energy consumption. Based on the purpose and characteristics of the speed skating oval, the intelligent system design of the venue should follow the following basic principles (Liu, 2022):

Stability and reliability. The core system of the venue should have strong fault tolerance, self-test, and automatic faulty alarm functions; independent operation of each system when network fails; and the need to reply to the system operation within the specified time limit.

Standardization and normalization. The venue design is modularized and combined. The import of models and data is strictly implemented in accordance with various standards to ensure consistency.

Advanced nature and practicality. The venue adopts international advanced artificial intelligence, edge computing, big data mining, and image analysis technologies. The basic support parts (database, middleware, etc.) are also chosen from stable and reliable software with practical functions.

Ease of use and intelligence. Various systems of the venue need to ensure a friendly operation interface, clear module classification, and easy to understand, operate, and control. It also needs to establish a complete response mechanism as well as automatic analysis and early warning functions. And it can be displayed in combination with the map, which is convenient for judgment and decision-making.

Expandability and openness. The system should have good scalability to future expansion, upgradation, and secondary development. And it should open peripheral interfaces to facilitate quick connection to other facilities, systems, and platforms.

Compatibility and efficiency. The system should have excellent compatibility and be able to fully access submodule systems with different functions, different manufacturers, and different data formats, which effectively integrates multidimensional perception information. The data center is introduced, and then advanced models and algorithms are used to efficiently mine and analyze massive data.

According to the requirements of the Olympic Organizing Committee, the demand analysis of the speed skating pavilion, and the reference to GB 50314-2015 "Intelligent Building Design Standard", the building equipment management system, information facility system, public safety system, and sports-specific facility system in the venue have various upgrades in system architecture and hardware configuration. The information application and intelligent integration system responds to the topic "High-tech Winter Olympics", which builds a "super brain" with Chinese intellectual property rights – the intelligent integration management platform of the National Speed Skating Oval. It achieves the combination of building technology and information technology (Figure 7.10).

Figure 7.11 is the "super brain" platform architecture of the National Speed Skating Oval.

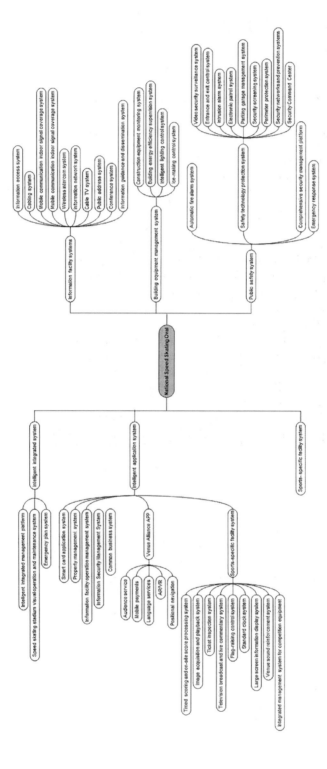

FIGURE 7.10 Architecture diagram of the National Speed Skating Oval intelligent system.

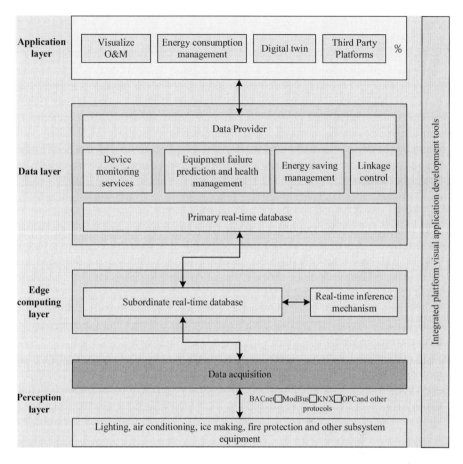

FIGURE 7.11 "Super brain" platform architecture of the National Speed Skating Oval.

7.3.2 MULTISENSORY DATA COLLECTION AND STORAGE

As a huge and technologically advanced venue, the National Speed Skating Oval has more than 30 electromechanical subsystems with different functions such as ice making, air-conditioning system, elevator, video monitoring, fire alarm, lighting, and power monitoring working at the same time. Each subsystem is unable to communicate within the system in order to achieve its independent function. This results in information silo and creates difficulties for operation and maintenance management and data sharing. In order to make the venue convenient for operation and maintenance, unified management of data and information, efficient data sharing, and to make it "sense, breathe, and remember", multisource heterogeneous data collection and real-time database are essential.

Multisource heterogeneous data collection is one of the core functions of the entire platform, which directly interacts with many devices. It is the data portal of the whole data management platform. There are more than 30 subsystems in the speed skating oval working at the same time (including ice-making system, chiller system, dehumidification system, humidification system, seat air supply system, air-conditioning system, heat-exchange system, water-supply system, lift system, electric window system, electric shading system, roof weather station system, air quality detection system, entrance/exit control system, video-monitoring system, intrusion alarm system, venue lighting control system, intelligent lighting control system, façade lighting control system, intelligent power distribution system, site sound reinforcement system, electric power-monitoring system, water, electricity, cooling, and heating online monitoring system, fire alarm system, fire door-monitoring system, fire power-monitoring system, electrical fire alarm system, residual pressure-monitoring system, fire emergency evacuation system, etc.) The current data source of the platform is mainly the data sent by the subsystem devices after connecting to the gateway. These subsystems have a wide variety of data and very different communication protocols. The data acquisition program needs to perform TCP/IP protocol conversion according to the different types of devices and their corresponding industrial control protocols. And it needs to convert the different data formats into a unified standard and store them in the real-time database through the data acquisition interface. The data acquisition architecture is shown in Figure 7.12.

The data acquisition program needs to run four different threads simultaneously once the acquisition has started (as shown in Figure 7.13). The functions of each thread are as follows.

In multisource heterogeneous data acquisition, real-time performance is the most important. The data acquisition system needs to respond quickly with good real-time performance and data-processing capabilities. It shouldn't affect the internal system of the building while having high real-time performance. Secondly, a large amount of real-time data should be stored in a timely manner without affecting

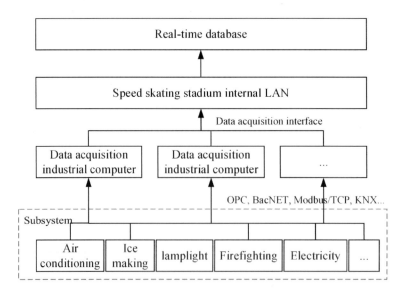

FIGURE 7.12   Data acquisition architecture.

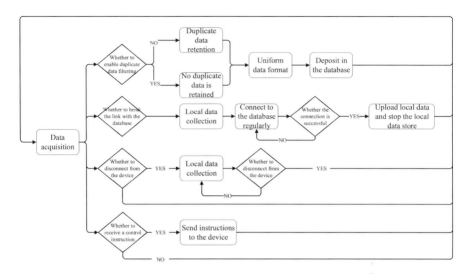

FIGURE 7.13   Data acquisition based on multiple threads.

the high frequency of data collection of the building's substrate equipment. Finally, to ensure timeliness, many transactions need to be completed within the deadline. The relational database sets up synchronous and mutually exclusive operations in order to ensure the ACID characteristics of the data. However, this also results in the loss of the real-time element of the data. In order to complete the synchronous data collection and real-time interaction of massive terminal equipment, the platform adopts Agilor real-time database system as the real-time data collection platform to ensure synchronous data collection and real-time transactions. The main differences between the real-time database and the traditional relational database are shown in Table 7.4 (Hu, 2015).

Agilor real-time database system is a large distributed real-time database system with fully independent intellectual property rights, which has been independently developed by the Institute of Software Chinese Academy of Sciences for more than 20 years. It combines real-time technology with database technology to achieve efficient storage and management of large amounts of real-time data. It is mainly used to collect, store, and manage status and process data from various control systems and field devices. And it provides a unified real-time data management platform for enterprises. The system adopts several unique and advanced patented technologies, including real-time transaction scheduling algorithms, adaptive historical data compression algorithms, multiserver dynamic redundancy technology and active rule inference technology, real-time and fast interthread data-exchange methods, and efficient sensor historical data archiving methods. It provides services such as hot standby, data mirroring, and automatic backup, and the data acquisition program provides breakpoint reconnection, data caching, and other functions. The single server system supports data management of more than 10 million points and historical data storage of more than 10 years. Its main functional features are as follows:

TABLE 7.4

Difference between Real-Time Database and Relational Database

Compare Content	Real-Time Database	Relational Databases
Concurrent processing speed	It can process tens of thousands or even millions of data read and write requests in 1 second	It can process thousands of data read and write requests in 1 second
Storage structure	It is stored with a measuring point structure	Relational table structure
Storage policy	Adopts certain storage policies to ensure long-term stable operation	There is no storage policy
Data compression	The data is compressed using a compression algorithm	No compression and store all your data
Object relationship description	Computational description by mathematical model	Relational model description by primary and foreign keys
Object information definition	Not supported	Supported

- Supports millisecond data acquisition
- High performance: 1 million points per second real-time data updates
- Compression ratio: data compression ratio greater than 50:1
- Retrieval rate: retrieval of historical data up to 200,000 items per second
- Concurrency: simultaneous support for data collection from hundreds of devices and concurrent access by more than 1,000 clients
- Large scale: single database node supports more than 10 million points and more than 32 nodes at the same time
- Reliability: hot standby, 24/7 stable operation, and system redundancy backup mechanism
- Security: supports one-way GAP of the mirror service and data collection interface
- Cross-platform: supports Windows, Linux, and some Chinese operating systems.

The system is structured in three main parts: data collection, data management, and data presentation and application, as shown in Figure 7.14.

The sensor data of all subsystems in the speed skating oval are converted into the standard data format of Agilor real-time database and stored in the database through the data collection program. The situation of multiple applications to multiple subsystems becomes a multiapplications to data management platform, which makes it faster and more convenient for third parties to obtain data. Moreover, it eases the overall network congestion. The specific data formats are shown in Table 7.5.

7.3.3 DEVICES MONITORING AND VISUALIZATION

The monitoring and visualization of the National Speed Skating Oval is mainly achieved by the visualization of O&M and the digital twins.

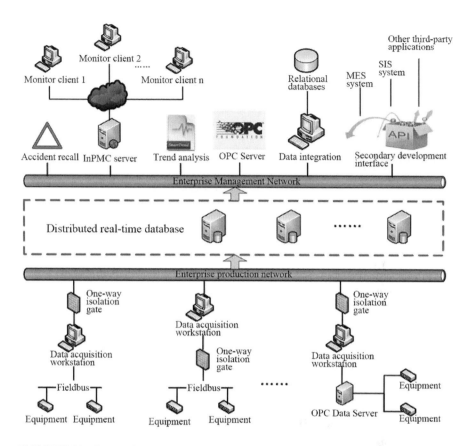

FIGURE 7.14   System functions architecture of Agilor real-time database.

TABLE 7.5
Data Structure of Agilor Real-Time Database

ID	The Unique ID Number of the Data Point
Point name	Globally unique
Description	An explanatory description of the data point
Type	The point value data type
Unit	The unit name of the point data
The current value	The current value of the data point
Timestamp	The timestamp of the current value of the data point
State	The status bit of the current point
Alarm	The current alarm state of the data point
Source device station	The name of the device to which the data point belongs

(*Continued*)

TABLE 7.5 (*Continued*)
Data Structure of Agilor Real-Time Database

ID	The Unique ID Number of the Data Point
The source node group	The name of the point group to which the data point belongs
Source node	The station number corresponding to the data point is globally unique
Collect the mark	Whether it is possible to control the flag
Typical values	The initial value of the data point
Minimum interval between data processing (seconds)	The minimum time interval for data acquisition and processing
Maximum data-processing interval (seconds)	The maximum time interval during which data processing takes place
Data processing sensitivity (seconds)	Variable sensitivity of real-time data processing
Upper range	Corresponds to the upper range of the physical point device
Lower range	Corresponds to the lower range of the physical point device
Alarm type	Predefined data alarm types
Alarm high high	Predefined alarm high high
Alarm high	Predefined alarm high
Alarm low	Predefined alarm low
Alarm low low	Predefined alarm low low
Priority of AHH	Priority of alarm high high
Priority of AH	Priority of alarm high
Priority of AL	Priority of alarm low
Priority of ALL	Priority of alarm low low
Historical data storage	Flags whether the data point is historically stored
Historical data compression	Flags whether the data point is compressed for historical data storage
Historical data interpolation form	What type of compression is performed on historical data and the corresponding type of interpolation when decompressed
Minimum interval between compression (seconds)	The minimum time interval for historical data compression
Maximum compression interval (seconds)	The maximum time interval for historical data compression
Compression sensitivity (seconds)	The compression sensitivity at which historical compression is performed
Historical index	The ID number used by the data point in the history library
Last data archive value	The last time historical data was stored, the value stored
Last data archive time	The last time historical data was stored
The data point creation time	The time the data point was created

Visualization of O&M is based on BIM, GIS, and configuration technology and integrates functions such as operation and maintenance management, faulty alarm, energy analysis, and O&M assurance. This is shown in Figure 7.15.

Supervisory control and data acquisition (SCADA) is a specific software for data acquisition and process control. It is a software platform in the monitoring layer of the field control system. According to the working phase of the SCADA (from the user's point of view), it is composed of two major parts: the configuration design environment and the configuration runtime environment. The configuration design environment is the working environment that the automation design engineer must rely on in order to implement the control solution and to carry out the system generation of the application program under the support of the SCADA (Figures 7.16 and 7.17). By creating a series of user data files, the final graphical target application is generated for

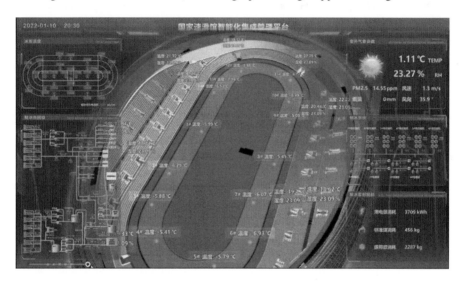

FIGURE 7.15   Visualization of O&M.

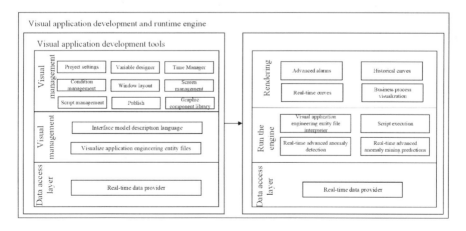

FIGURE 7.16   Structure of SCADA.

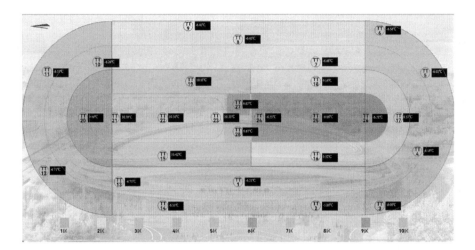

FIGURE 7.17   Real-time temperature zone of the ice surface of the speed skating oval produced by SCADA.

use during the operation of the system runtime environment. It consists of several configuration programs, such as graphical interface configuration program and real-time database configuration program. The system configuration environment provides a platform for automation design engineers to build applications. In the system runtime environment, the target application is loaded into the computer memory to achieve real-time operation. The system prototype environment consists of several runtime programs, such as graphical interface runtime programs and real-time database runtime programs. The system runtime environment interprets and runs the applications developed by the automation design engineers. It provides an interactive interface between the industrial site and the user and performs tasks such as storing the necessary data (Cheng, 2010). The architecture of the configuration and monitoring software is shown in Figure 7.18.

Digital Twin (also known as "digital mapping", "digital object mapping", etc.) enables comprehensive perception, simulation, prediction, and feedback of real-world systems by creating a digital virtual system that contains all the information of a "real physical device or system", as shown in Figure 7.19.

Digital modeling based on technologies such as CAD and BIM, virtual–real mapping based on IoT sensing devices, and intelligent analysis based on big data and artificial intelligence are the three main steps to reach the digital twin application system, as shown in Figure 7.20.

The key technologies involved in the above process include:

- Three-dimensional modeling: use professional modeling software for three-dimensional modeling of buildings, spaces, facilities, and other object entities. BIM is currently the best and most important way for three-dimensional modeling of digital twin systems in venues because of having the modeling function of both geometric objects and associated attributes.

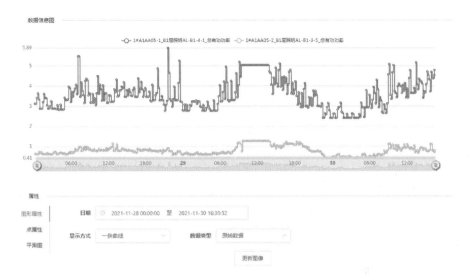

FIGURE 7.18 Visual energy analysis.

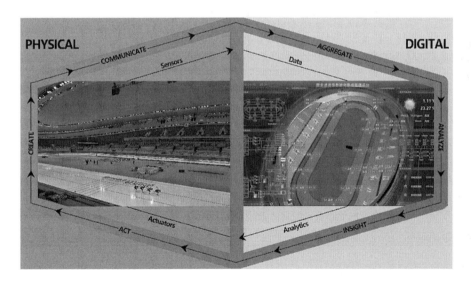

FIGURE 7.19 Principle of digital twin.

FIGURE 7.20 Main stages for digital twin system.

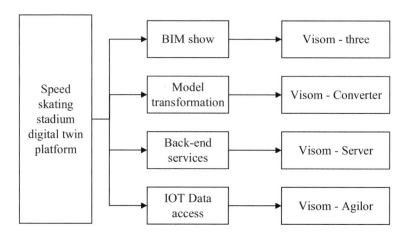

FIGURE 7.21   Main technical components of the platform.

- IoT perception: it mainly includes various types of sensing equipment and facilities such as security, environment, and energy consumption as well as their communication and data transmission technologies. Among them, the new generation of communication technologies represented by LoRa, NB-IoT, and 5G are hotspots in related fields in recent years.
- Data aggregation and fusion sharing: achieve consistent access and aggregation of rich IoT perception data through dedicated real-time databases. And it realizes data fusion applications based on fuzzy logic, neural network, cluster analysis, etc.
- Data intelligent analysis: use rule-based reasoning, data mining, machine learning, and other technologies to achieve intelligent analysis that can successfully collect and fuse shared data to meet the operational and maintenance needs of different digital twin application scenarios such as security, environment, and energy consumption.
- Data visualization: visualization of the digital twin model is achieved in a three-dimensional, dynamic, and real-time manner, of which Web 3D based on WebGL is currently the most used technique.
- The digital twin platform of the National Speed Skating Oval is mainly managed intelligently through the intelligent aggregation of BIM models and IoT data. The system is based on a BS architecture and is designed and developed using the front- and back-end separation approach, as shown in Figure 7.21.

The overall technical architecture of the digital twin platform is shown in Figure 7.22.

7.3.4   Improvements on Ice State and Energy Predicting

In the ice-making system of the speed skating oval, the regulated variables including elements such as the carbon dioxide supply flow rate of the barrel pump refrigerant used directly for ice making and the temperature of the supply fluid. And they also

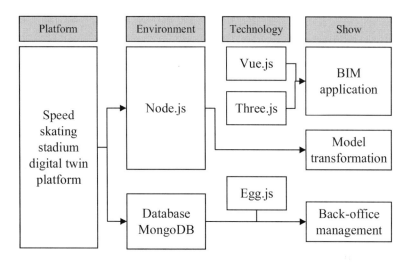

FIGURE 7.22 Technical architecture of the digital twin platform.

contain the surrounding environment temperature and humidity, ice-making north and south pipe ditch, courtyard, ice-making machine room, and other associated equipment or space elements. Constrained by the volume of data collected for indicators such as temperature and humidity of the venue above the ice surface, and the clear correlation between the temperature of the venue itself and the outdoor air conditions, further outdoor temperature and humidity data was incorporated as the original features for the task of analyzing the ice production system.

Those ice-making data integration solutions based on venue time-series data currently use ice surface temperature regulation and energy consumption of ice production as two types of evaluation criteria for ice-making systems. Therefore, with reference to the feature selection channel in Section 6.2, the above features and their historical feature data within 1 hour are retained to construct XGBoost integrated learning models that take ice surface temperature and energy consumption of ice production as the fitting targets. The feature importance evaluation obtained after training is used as an important reference for feature selection (Figure 7.23).

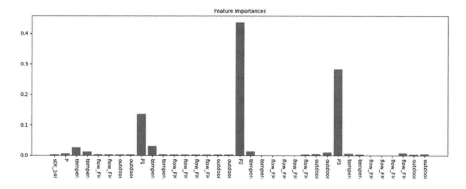

FIGURE 7.23 The evaluation of the importance of data features for ice production systems.

Based on the above experimental results, the power history of the ice surface which is corresponding to the ice drum pump is the most important data characteristic. In addition to this, other relatively important characteristics include ice supply outlet temperature > outdoor temperature > outdoor air humidity > carbon dioxide flow rate of the drum pump. In an attempt to explain this phenomenon through post-mortem analysis, the historical energy consumption recorded by the ice system under continuous ice-making conditions provides an important benchmark for the current status of ice consumption and cooling capacity and therefore becomes the most important raw feature within the assessment methodology. The supply temperature of the ice-making bucket pump and the refrigerant delivery volume together directly determine the amount of heat exchange with the ice surface. However, as the regulation of the carbon dioxide delivery volume is almost constant or within a small range under current operating conditions, the influence of the supply outlet temperature on the energy consumption of the ice production and the ice surface temperature is more obvious in comparison. In addition, the temperature and humidity of the outdoor air also affect the amount of cooling required for ice production and the temperature of the ice layer in the venue because of the circulation of the outdoor air and the heat exchange between the venue and the external environment.

After selecting the above features, the historical time series generated in their corresponding dimensions were used to train multidimensional time-series data models with total energy consumption of ice production and cold layer temperature as learning targets, respectively. This project designs a combined temporal model that incorporates time-domain, frequency-domain, and filtering original system features. The aim of overcoming noisy data interference is achieved by training the recovery task of short-term prediction of data and medium- and long-term data distributions. The combination improves the accuracy of long-term prediction of multidimensional time-series data. The learning framework for the multidimensional time-series data of the venue is established as shown in Figure 7.24. The key mechanisms are:

- Temporal correlation recognition mechanisms. There has been a great deal of research toward modeling time-series data for the recognition of temporal correlation, ranging from differential regression and autoregressive

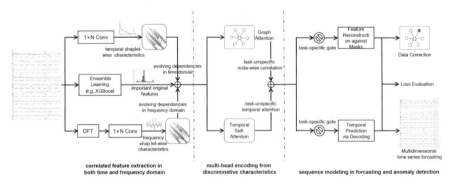

FIGURE 7.24 Learning framework for multidimensional time-series data models for venues.

integrated sliding average (ARIMA) models of sequences to recurrent neural networks in deep learning and code-and-decode models of sequences that introduce attention mechanisms. This project has all been tested using actual data from the speed skating oval and other similar publicly available energy consumption datasets. In the current attempts to combine with other modules, the sequence model introduced with the self-attention mechanism can consider the accuracy of the modeling output and the anti-interference of data defects at the same time when the stadium data has been extracted for more than 2 months. Therefore, the temporal correlation recognition module used in the final delivered version of this project is the time-series self-attention unit.

- Feature space correlation recognition mechanism. Since the platform treats the correlation of topological, spatial, and operational physical properties between data as feature space correlation, the correlation between multidimensional time series constitutes a heterogeneous graph under the condition that each dimensional feature itself is regarded as an entity. After finding that shallow graph embedding and graph convolution are not effective for heterogeneous graphs, the platform finally adopts Multihead Graph Attention to effectively capture the correlation properties between features.

- Gating mechanism. A gating unit is set before accessing downstream modeling tasks after the above two channels recognize the implicit vector of temporal and spatial correlation properties. A focus on temporal or spatial correlations is selectively output to the modeling task.

- Joint training of dual downstream tasks. The loss evaluation target of the data reconstruction unit is combined into the final loss evaluation function together with the main downstream tasks such as time-series prediction in a result-weighted manner. The feature representation generated by the end-to-end channel of time-series data and the important features selected by the original feature are both used in the learning process for modeling. In the intelligent integrated application of the National Speed Skating Oval based on the IoT, the modeling technology driven by multisource heterogeneous time-series data is widely used in the management and operation and maintenance work such as equipment operation, safety monitoring, energy prediction, and ice surface element analysis, which provides important reference indicators for subsequent optimization strategies and system management.

In order to evaluate the validity and advancement of the modeling techniques designed and implemented in this project, three other classical models and the latest advances in the current research field are selected in this section as the baseline methods for comparison – ARIMA, LSTM, and the StemGNN model that combines time–frequency-domain feature recognition. The results of both mean error (MAE) and root mean square error (RMSE) evaluations on two types of tasks, ice production energy prediction after 1 hour and ice surface temperature prediction after 10 minutes, are shown in Table 7.6. The bolded blue markings represent the best results under this evaluation criterion.

TABLE 7.6

Comparation of Time-Series Data Modeling for Ice Production Systems

Predictive Models	ARIMA		Univariate LSTM		StemGNN		Modeling Methods for This Project	
Forecast category	Energy consumption for ice making	Ice surface temperature	Energy consumption for ice making	Ice surface temperature	Energy consumption for ice making	Ice surface temperature	Energy consumption for ice making	Ice surface temperature
MAE	32.12°C 9.18%	0.0412	19.14°C 5.47%	0.0238	10.86°C 3.10%	0.0178	8.09°C 2.31%	0.0136
RMSE	38.95°C 11.12%	0.0952	21.23°C 6.07%	0.0552	12.40°C 3.54%	0.0342	12.83°C 3.66%	0.0294

From the comparison of the above evaluation results, the multisource heterogeneous data modeling method designed in this project has reached a leading level in the prediction accuracy of the ice-making system. By adding nonlinear units such as neurons to the model, the fitting ability of the model is significantly higher than the traditional method based on mathematical statistics and difference models (ARIMA). At the same time, because the multidimensional features are selected from the linkage subsystem, and the correlation between the data is captured, the model accuracy also exceeds the independent variable prediction (Univariate LSTM) which lacks consideration of the linkage. The comprehensive evaluation of the modeling method design of this project is better than the latest StemGNN model. Moreover, the time domain, frequency domain, and important original features are captured through multiple feature-extraction channels, and the attention to each feature is calculated, thereby enhancing the interpretability of the model.

7.3.5 REGULATION STRATEGY FOR ICE-MAKING AND COOLING SYSTEM

The internal and inter-subsystems of the National Speed Skating Oval are complicated in cascade. There are a lot of physical dependencies in the operation and debugging of the equipment, and the location and extension space of the devices are adjacent or even overlapped. These situations cause the ice-making state to be directly or indirectly affected by the changes in the scene inside and outside the venue. For example, changes in outdoor meteorological conditions affect natural lighting conditions and the changes in air temperature and humidity. This should cause dynamic response regulations to the venue's shading, air conditioning, and other systems, thereby affecting the heat exchange between the space and ice surface and cooling demand.

Therefore, the management, operation, and maintenance of the ice-making system of the National Speed Skating Oval need to be adaptively adjusted with the changes in the situation. Therefore, this project designs a scenario-aware system with adaptive regulation mechanism to cope with the system-level regulation solutions caused by real-time changes in the internal and external environments of the arena, as shown in Figure 7.25.

A dynamic evaluation of the linkage update of the ice-making system forms because of the changes in scenarios such as light conditions, outdoor temperature and humidity, and event start and finish, which lead to valid data changes that are detected by the multisource heterogeneous data-integrated terminal, as well as the trend prediction for each subsystem triggered by real-time data at the system level and the time-series data, and continuous iteration of anomaly detection models. Moreover, the system-level adaptive regulation solution is composed of two types of optimized adjustment strategies: (1) Predictive regulation, which takes the prediction results of the ice-making dynamics generated by the above models as the evaluation criteria and generates prediction/prevention by solving the optimization problem. It focuses on the "advance" adjustment action and considers the control scheme of high efficiency, energy saving, stability, and safety. (2) Real-time transaction regulation, which is designed to provide direct access to the real-time reasoning engine and realize a regulation solution that uses trigger rules to instantly respond to real-time events.

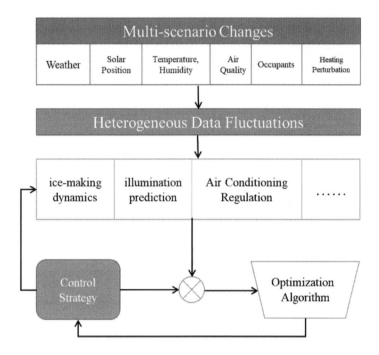

FIGURE 7.25   Structure of scenario-aware system with adaptive regulation mechanism.

According to the significant characteristics that affect the energy consumption of ice production and ice surface temperature mentioned in the previous section, and the comparison between the model predicted value and the actual value through modeling, the trends of energy consumption of ice production and ice surface temperature with the two-dimensional data features that are most significantly associated with them (except for their own characteristic historical values, such as past power consumption and ice layer temperature) are visualized as scatter plots, respectively. The purpose is to obtain the trends of energy consumption of ice production versus outdoor temperature/refrigerant temperature and ice surface temperature versus refrigerant temperature/outdoor temperature, see Figures 7.26–7.29.

Energy consumption of ice production. When the outdoor temperature reaches above 23°C, the power consumption of the three ice-making units per hour may exceed 300 kW·h. However, the energy consumption of ice production is slightly inversely proportional to the temperature of the refrigerant. This can be explained by the decrease in temperature difference when the refrigerant reacts with the outside world, which results in a reduction in cooling capacity and less energy consumption. While increasing the temperature of the refrigerant reduces the energy consumption of ice making, it also makes the ice-making process longer. Similarly, the temperature of the ice surface is largely determined by the feed temperature setting. The representative threshold for ice measurement temperatures that currently can be used as a marker of ease of melting (or water vapor transpiration) in ice maintenance has not yet been fully determined. If the measured temperature in the ice layer is higher than −4.8°C, the ice surface is prone to melting or fogging in a large area. Then, the setting of the ice-making liquid temperature is recommended not to be higher than

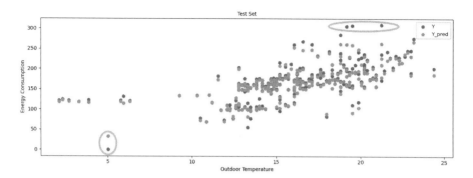

FIGURE 7.26   Energy consumption versus outdoor temperature.

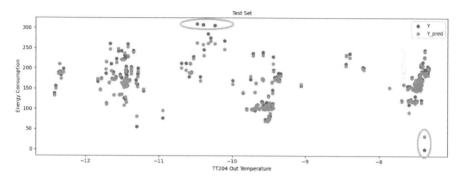

FIGURE 7.27   Energy consumption versus refrigerant temperature.

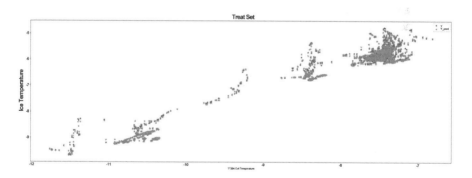

FIGURE 7.28   Ice surface temperature versus refrigerant temperature.

−7.7°C. In addition, the outdoor temperature has a weak positive effect on the ice surface temperature, but it is not as obvious as the outdoor temperature on the energy consumption of ice production.

The above figures plot the actual value of energy consumption of ice production/ ice temperature (blue dots) and the predicted values from autonomous modeling (yellow dots) on the same graph. It can be recognized that the data model used in this project is ideally in line with the real data distribution. And under the same scenario

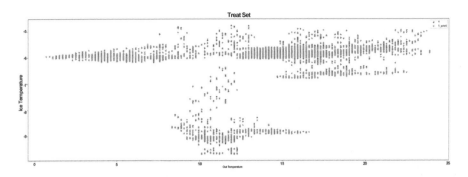

FIGURE 7.29 Ice surface temperature versus outdoor temperature.

conditions, the predicted value of the model tends to predict the average meaningful state; that is, the distribution is more concentrated. Therefore, this has inspired an idea for the monitoring of ice-making energy consumption status – the abnormal detection of monitoring data is judged from the degree of deviation of the predicted value from the actual value by depicting correlations in different data feature dimensions. Taking Figures 7.25–7.28 as an example, the sample points circled in yellow represent energy consumption records with a large deviation from the predicted situation, so they are marked as highly suspected abnormal energy consumption data. Further investigation is needed to determine whether the data has been reported incorrectly, or whether other conditions have caused the energy consumption data to deviate.

Based on the above predictions and analysis of the energy consumption of ice production and the state of the ice surface, the following recommendations can be made for the operation and management of the ice production system:

- Energy consumption of ice production is significantly positively affected by outdoor temperature. At present, the integrated extraction of ice-making data is still limited to autumn and winter (below 25°C). Based on the trend of energy consumption curve/distribution of energy consumption, once the ice-making system needs to be operated in summer (above 30°C), the consumption will increase rapidly compared with autumn and winter. So, in summer, special attention should be paid to heat insulation that closes the doors and windows of the venues and halls.
- Raising the temperature of the refrigerant within a certain threshold can effectively reduce the energy consumption of ice making, but at the same time, attention should be paid to the obvious risk of melting ice surface or evaporation of water. With the current operation mode of ice making in the speed skating oval, if the measured temperature of the cold layer on the ice surface is not higher than −5°C this quarter, it is recommended to set the temperature of the refrigerant not higher than −7.8°C while maintaining the current carbon dioxide supply flow rate.
- If the venue needs to make ice in summer, according to the current model, it is estimated that water vapor will be generated above the ice surface due to the temperature of the ice surface and the temperature inside the venue.

Then, after the dehumidification system is turned on for a long time, the feature selection results of the current data model are likely to be significantly different. Therefore, it is necessary to update and iterate the model after incorporating new data.

7.4   DISCUSSION ON SMART HOME FOR RURAL AREAS

As smart buildings and smart homes become realities in urban areas, it is inevitable that such technologies will eventually trickle down to the rural homes. The key question of transforming this technology from urban areas to rural areas is how to design smart homes that are suitable for the rural environments and users' needs. The future research in this filed needs to investigate (1) what guidelines and standards are suitable for rural smart homes? (2) do we design for the same ethnographic issues as those in urban centers? (3) how do we evaluate the different settings and infrastructures to inform our designs and construction (Anijo, 2005)?

REFERENCES

Andersen, M., Fierro, G., Kumar, S., Kim, J., Arens, E., Zhang, H., Raftery, P., Culler, D. Well-connected microzones for increased building efficiency and occupant comfort. *Proceedings of the 2nd ACM International Conference on Embedded Systems for Energy-Efficient Built Environments* (2015, pp. 121–122), held in Seoul, South Korea.

Anijo, M. Smart homes for the rural population: new challenges and opportunities. *ACADIA05: Smart Architecture*, 2005. https://papers.cumincad.org/data/works/att/acadia05_024.content.pdf.

Boonekamp, P.G. Price elasticities, policy measures and actual developments in household energy consumption - A bottom up analysis for the Netherlands. *Energy Economics*, 2007, 29(2):133–157.

Brooks, D.J. Intelligent buildings: an investigation into current and emerging security vulnerabilities in automated building systems using an applied defeat methodology, *Australian Security and Intelligence Conference, Security Research Institute Conferences*, Perth, Western Australia, 2011, pp. 16–26.

Cheng, G. *Research on the Framework and Real-Time Database of the Configuration Software.* Hubei, China: Wuhan University of Technology, 2010, pp. 7–8.

Cheng, C.C., Lee, D. Smart sensors enable smart air conditioning control. *Sensors (Basel)*, 2014, 14(6):11179–11203.

Cheng, C.C., Lee, D. Enabling smart air conditioning by sensor development: a Review. *Sensors (Basel)*, 2016, 16(12):2028.

China Building Energy Conservation Society. Smart building evaluation standard. 2021, 2(021):6. Standard number is T/CABEE002—2021, and Effective from May 1, 2021.

Choi, J.H. Investigation of human eye pupil sizes as a measure of visual sensation in the workplace environment with a high lighting colour temperature. *Indoor and Built Environment*, 2016, 26(4):488–501.

Christensen, K., Melfi, R., Nordman, B., Rosenblum, B., Viera, R. Using existing network infrastructure to estimate building occupancy and control plugged-in devices in user workspaces. *International Journal of Communication Networks and Distributed Systems*, 2014, 12(1):4.

Dong, B., Yan, D., Li, Z., Jin, Y., Feng, X., Fontenot, H. Modeling occupancy and behavior for better building design and operation-a critical review. *Building Simulation*, 2018, 11(5):899–921.

Dong, B., Prakash, V., Feng, F. et al. A review of smart building sensing system for better indoor environment control. *Energy and Buildings*, 2019, 199:29–46.

Ekwevugbe, T., Brown, N., Fan, D. A design model for building occupancy detection using sensor fusion. *6th IEEE International Conference on Digital Ecosystems and Technologies (DEST)*, Campione d'Italia, Italy, 2012.

Goyal, S., Barooah, P., Middelkoop, T. Experimental study of occupancy-based control of HVAC zones. *Applied Energy*, 2015, 140:75–84.

Hu, F. *Design and Implementation of Building Automation System Based on Real-Time Database*. Dhaka: Southeast University, 2015, pp. 14

Jin, M., Liu, S., Schiavon, S., Spanos, C. Automated mobile sensing: towards high granularity agile indoor environmental quality monitoring. *Building and Environment*, 2018, 127:268–276.

Jin, X., Wang, G., Song, Y. et al. Smart building energy management based on network occupancy sensing. *Journal of International Council on Electrical Engineering*, 2018, 8(1):30–36.

Kim, J., Schiavon, S., Brager, G. Personal comfort models-a new paradigm in thermal comfort for occupant-centric environmental control. *Building and Environment*, 2018, 132, 114–124.

Li, N., Calis, G., Becerik-Gerber, B. Measuring and monitoring occupancy with an RFID based system for demand-driven HVAC operations. *Automation in Construction*, 2012, 24:89–99.

Liu, Y. *Simulation Study of Energy Saving Optimization for Cooling Water System of Central Air Condition Based on TRNSYS*. GuangZhou: South China University of Technology, 2013.

Liu, J. Discussion on intelligent venue design of national speed skating oval. *Building Electricity*, 2022, 41(2):3–10.

Liu, C., Jing, X.H., Dong, G. Talking about the technical characteristics of the internet of things and its wide application. *Scientific Consulting*, 2011, 86(9):86.

Navada, S.G., Adiga, C.S., Kini, S.G. A Study on daylight integration with thermal comfort for energy conservation in a general office. *International Journal of Electrical Energy*, 2013, 1(1):18–22.

Nguyen, T.A., Aiello, M. Energy intelligent buildings based on user activity: a survey. *Energy and Buildings*, 2013, 56:244–257.

Pérez-Lombard, L., Ortiz, J., Pout, C. A review on buildings energy consumption information. *Energy and Buildings*, 2008, 40(3):394–398.

Sim, S.Y., Koh, M.J., Joo, K.M., Noh, S., Park, S., Kim, Y.H., Park, K.S. Estimation of thermal sensation based on wrist skin temperatures. *Sensors (Basel)*, 2016, 16(4):420.

So, A.T.P., Wong, A.C.W., Wong, K. A new definition of intelligent buildings for Asia. *Facilities*, 1999, 17(12/13):485–491.

Spataru, C., Gauthier, S. How to monitor people 'smartly' to help reducing energy consumption in buildings? *Architectural Engineering and Design Management*, 2013, 10(1–2):60–78.

Tetlow, R.M., Beaman, C.P., Elmualim, A.A., Couling, K. Simple prompts reduce inadvertent energy consumption from lighting in office buildings. *Building and Environment*, 2014, 81:234–242.

Wong, J.K.W., Li, H., Wang, S.W. Intelligent building research: a review. *Automation in Construction*, 2005, 14(1):143–159.

Wong, J.K.W., Li, H., Wang, S.W. A review research on automation in construction of intelligent building. *Artificial Intelligence Research*, 2011, 14(4):143–159.

Zhang, G.Q., Chen, H. Building brains make intelligent buildings move towards intelligent buildings. *Journal of Shandong Jianzhu University*, 2021, 10:3–24.

8 Natural and Emotional Interaction Techniques with AI for Smart Services

Cuixia Ma

8.1 INTRODUCTION

Rural areas are at the heart of many global issues. From increased mechanization of agriculture to migration, migration puts pressure on resources and municipal infrastructure, while creating problems of outmigration of youth from rural areas. Rural areas often lack many of the advantages of cities: sparse populations, inadequate infrastructure (e.g., no Internet access), few economic resources, and low access to expertise. HCI researchers have begun to study the use and design of natural and user-oriented human–AI interaction technology in rural areas, which has revealed significant differences in how rural areas are defined, what types of communities are studied, and what methods are used to study them. Therefore, the study and use of natural human–computer interaction in rural areas is very conducive to the integrated development of the rural area, as it is a productivity enhancement at the technological level.

Human–computer interaction (HCI) is generally known as a multidisciplinary field of study that focuses on designing and optimizing computer interfaces that satisfy human users' need. Users communicate with the computer through the HCI interface. The design of the HCI interface is a highly potential topic which decides the effectiveness of the system and the efficiency of information sharing. It is relevant to multiple disciplines, which include computer science, cognitive psychology, sociology, and designing.

To construct the smart city, HCI helps to convey information between urban and rural communities and encourage the participation of people, which is beneficial for the unified management of the city. Due to the proportion of the elderly in the rural area being high, the service system based on HCI can design simple operations for natural and efficient interaction including communication of young people in urban area and elderly in rural area, health counseling, diagnosis and care for elderly, and convenient information sharing. Thus, the HCI service system will narrow down the gap between urban and rural communities and promote the progress of the intelligent city management.

DOI: 10.1201/9781032686691-8

With the development of HCI, computer becomes more adaptive to human. Traditional HCI relies on manual operation and command language, which are inconvenient for humans to operate. The graphical user interface (GUI) enables common unskilled users to use a computer. It is user-friendly and promotes the development of the network. To further enhance the naturalness of HCI, multimodal interaction such as sketch interaction, emotional interaction, and gesture interaction has emerged, which immensely improves the efficiency of interaction and becomes a hot spot in recent researches.

The goal of natural interaction and smart service is to allow users to easily and effectively express their interaction intentions. In recent years, the field of human–computer interaction has been continuously investigating various natural interaction techniques with low learning costs that enable computers to accurately recognize users' intent. Among all these proposed methods, user action understanding and processing are the most critical. User motions, including finger, hand, head, and body movements, are the main channels through which users express their interaction intentions. Accurate identification of users' interaction intent is the basis for the computer to make correct decisions and responses and is the key to complete interaction tasks efficiently. User modeling is essentially a computational approach to portray the behavioral capabilities of users and is scientifically important for understanding user intent and exploring the computational principles of natural interaction.

As we know, interactions involve lots of cognition activities, which means there are intentional reasoning existing during interactions between human and computers. In order for computers to interact naturally and effectively with humans, a common cognitive foundation also needs to be established. This includes both common-sense knowledge reasoning and personalized knowledge updating, where computers can not only automatically update the knowledge graph with the perceived information but also adopt active interaction strategies to confirm unreliable reasoning results. Using the relevant knowledge from the knowledge graph, the computer develops a holistic understanding of the people, objects, and environment involved in the interaction situation. Sketch intuitively describes an object's appearance and spatial layout. It is a natural interaction tool to convey users' intention and innovative ideas at any time.

At the same time, pleasure and emotion can be used to help illustrate design approaches to deliver a positive experience for the necessary emotional connection between the product and the user (Mallin and Carvalho, 2015). Emotional design can generate values in the corresponding fields such as multimedia learning (Tien et al., 2018), medical caring (Mao et al., 2017), and intelligent assistance system (Hao et al., 2015). Moreover, the emotional factor can't be neglected in the field of human–computer interaction (Ayanoğlu and Duarte, 2019). HCI designs follow four principles, namely, safety, performance, comfort, and aesthetics. In addition, it is required to be promoted based on four human factors, namely, physical, cognitive, social, and emotional (Boy, 2017). Therefore, analyzing the emotion evoked by the emotional design or intelligent systems is relatively critical.

Emotion recognition is a key research topic in the field of affective computing and has attracted widespread attention in the field of human–computer interaction, emotional intelligence-assisted robots, etc. Generally, human emotions are expressed as behavioral signals, and the most commonly used behavioral signals include facial expression, body language, hand gestures, and speeches (Adolphs, 2002; Kleinsmith and Bianchi-Berthouze, 2013). Compared with behavioral signals used for emotion recognition, physiological signals, i.e., electroencephalography (EEG), galvanic skin response (GSR), and electrocardiogram (ECG), are more desirable due to their objectivity in emotion recognition (Guo et al., 2015; Picard et al., 2001; Wen et al., 2014). Among the physiological signals, EEG is the main type of input signals for emotion recognition, as it can directly capture the brain activities via the electrodes attached to the scalp with high temporal resolution (Bekkedal et al., 2011; Davidson et al., 2007). Therefore, EEG-based emotion recognition provides an efficient and feasible way to recognize user's emotion feedback.

8.2 USER-ORIENTED SERVICE WITH AFFECTIVE COMPUTING

8.2.1 OVERVIEW

Emotions, highly generalized from a series of subjective cognitive experiences, are physiological states arising from a variety of feelings, thoughts, and behaviors. People convey a large amount of emotional information all the time during communication. From the perspective of cognitive neuroscience, emotions are also a classical type of cognition. Emotions are significant in human-to-human communication; thus, understanding emotions is an essential part of human–computer interaction to achieving humanization.

Meanwhile, a recent report published by the Social Science Press and the Institute of Psychology of the Chinese Academy of Sciences indicates that anxiety and depressive disorder have now become a serious social problem; most people in the rural areas are more anxious than we think. Therefore, how to detect, visualize, and regulate emotions promptly in daily life has become an imminent problem, which can be dealt with user-oriented HCI technology.

At present, research on computer-related technologies mainly focuses on object detection and object recognition. In order to improve the intelligence of human–computer interaction, it is also necessary to correctly understand the emotional needs and intentions of users so as to better set up emotional regulation schemes. The current emotion recognition algorithm can only identify the emotion category corresponding to the emotion content in the data and can only identify the emotional state of the human in the human–computer interaction scene and does not involve the understanding of emotional intention. Natural human–computer interaction requires emotion understanding technology to continuously deepen the understanding of emotional content and improve the harmony of human–computer interaction on the basis of user emotion recognition and reasoning. Therefore, in the in-depth study of emotion understanding technology, it is necessary to further study how to use interpretable ways to reason emotions in interactive scenes, that is, to understand the reasons behind the content, the intention, and the user's behavioral motivation. Emotion recognition and visualization should be carried out in the human-centered human–computer interaction scene. Only by placing people in a specific situation can we make full use of the multimodal information in the interaction process, complete the understanding of emotions, and then deduce the multiple aspects involved in emotions.

In general, two widely used emotion models exist for characterizing the emotional space: one is the discrete model and the other is the dimension model. In the discrete model, the emotional space is described by a few basic discrete emotions. Although there is no consensus on what constitutes a "basic" emotion, many studies use at least six basic emotions: joy, sadness, surprise, fear, anger, and disgust. In the dimension model, the emotional space is characterized with continuous coordinates in two or three dimensions, i.e., the valence–arousal or valence–arousal–dominance dimensions. Specifically, the valence dimension ranges from negative to positive; the arousal dimension ranges from calm to peaceful, then to active, and finally to excited; and the dominance dimension characterizes an individual's status ranging from in control to being controlled.

The concept of affective computing was first proposed by Professor Picard of the MIT Media Lab, who defined in his book (Picard, 2000) that *"affective computing is computing about, from, or capable of influencing emotions"*. The purpose of affective computing is to achieve full computer intelligence by giving computers the ability to recognize, understand, express, and adapt to human emotions to create a harmonious human–computer environment (Picard, 2000). Affective computing brings new application prospects for the development of artificial intelligence and allows humans to perceive the world from a different perspective. It is gradually evolving into a key technology for advanced human–computer interaction.

8.2.1.1 Multimodal Affective Computing

In recent years, with the continuous development of artificial intelligence and portable noninvasive human sensor technology, multimodal emotion recognition has become a research hotspot in the field of affective computing at home and abroad. At present, research of multimodal emotion recognition mainly focus on multiple external behavioral modalities and multiple neurophysiological modalities.

As opposed to unimodal, multimodal sentiment analysis aims to understand the sentiment conveyed by the user through information from multiple modalities such as audio, text, and visual. Sun et al. (2018) proposed a cascaded structured model consisting of two recurrent neural networks (RNNs) to recognize emotions in videos using multimodal contextual information and the facial expression information of the characters. Lee et al. (2019) designed a deep neural network to recognize emotions by integrating facial expression features of characters and contextual information in an aggregated and boosted manner. Qi et al. (2021) proposed a multimodal transformation network that unifies visual and auditory representations mapped to the same feature space for multimodal emotion recognition.

Based on behavioral performance, Professor Wu Min's affective computing team at the China University of Geosciences has conducted research on multimodal emotion recognition based on external behaviors such as voice emotion and facial expressions (Liu et al., 2018), and on this basis, it has also conducted more in-depth research on multidimensional emotional intent understanding and human–computer emotional interaction. The Multimedia Computing Laboratory of the Renmin University of China fuses two modalities, audio and visual, and adopts a conditional attention fusion strategy for continuous dimensional emotion prediction research (Chen and Jin, 2016). It also focuses on exploring the fusion mechanisms of effective substitution, complementarity, and interference of multiple channel interaction information to achieve the naturalness of human–computer interaction.

The Pervasive Perception and Intelligent Systems team at Lanzhou University focuses on multimodal knowledge modeling and applications based on human physiological signals and behavioral performance modalities such as eye movements and expressions (Zhang et al., 2019). By organizing and modeling the physiological signals and other modalities, the team investigates models applicable to different populations (depression patients and psychological hypertension patients) for accurate, objective, and real-time monitoring of abnormal emotional and psychological state changes. The emotion information processing team of Southeast University has carried out research on emotion analysis based on modalities such as EEG, expression, voice, and body movement (Zong et al., 2016) and has achieved certain results in both basic exploration and practical application of emotion analysis.

In terms of research on emotion recognition based on neurophysiological signals, Prof. Lu Baoliang's team at Shanghai Jiaotong University has established a public emotion dataset SEED and has done a lot of basic research on the most relevant signal frequency bands and brain regions for emotion and the temporal stability of EEG. In addition, He Huiguang's research team at the Institute of Automation, Chinese Academy of Sciences and Liu Guangyuan's team at Southwest University have conducted more in-depth research on emotion recognition by physiological signals.

In addition, among the many emotion recognition tasks, emotion identified from facial expressions or speech may not be accurate, since they as we know are easy to distinguish but also easy to disguise. In contrast, emotion obtained from physiological signals-based classification model is less artifactual because of their objectivity. Besides, physiological signals always contain more information than other modalities. For example, electroencephalography (EEG) reflects the electrophysiological activity of brain nerve cells in the cerebral cortex or scalp surface with high temporal resolution. With the advantages of accessibility, low cost (compared with other neuroimaging techniques such as PET and fMRI), and effectiveness, EEG-based emotion recognition is gaining more and more attention.

8.2.1.2 Emotion Visualization and Interaction

As "human–machine interaction" gradually increases, people put forward higher requirements for human–machine interaction technology, i.e., emotional needs. Communication between human beings is natural and emotional, so people expect the machines they interact with to have the ability to observe, understand, and generate emotional characteristics similar to those of humans. With the continuous development of affective computing technology, emotional interaction has become the main trend of human–computer interaction in the advanced information era. Emotional interaction is to make human–computer interaction as natural, intimate, vivid, and emotional as human–human interaction.

When people communicate with each other, they can perceive each other's feelings through facial expressions, voice emotions, body movements with feelings, and textual emotional information. Therefore, emotional interaction can be explored in terms of facial expression interaction, voice emotion interaction, body behavior emotion interaction, physiological signal emotion recognition, and text information emotion interaction. Moreover, previous studies have shown the importance and urgent need for emotion regulation and management. Boekaerts et al. (2011) used a set of video clips to elicit emotions in student subjects and interviewed students' reactions in certain situations. The study noted that how students handled stress during a math exam affected their engagement and possibly their performance. Huang et al. (2015) consulted a university counseling center and found that college students were poorly self-aware of their emotions and lacked self-analysis skills.

Emotions, as internal psychological and physiological responses, are invisible. Semertzidis et al. (2020) designed a geometric fractal to represent different types of emotions, using graphical information to represent complex emotional dimensions. This emotion visualization model can be applied to distance learning and online meeting scenarios. For example, in online education, teachers cannot fully perceive the learning status of each student. If the emotional state of each student is displayed in a graph, teachers can grasp the emotional state of students through the distribution of the graph in real time and adjust the online teaching method in time. Just as the geometric fractal mentioned above should be as simple and intuitive as possible, the key issue in the study of emotion visualization is the design of the visual form, which should follow the following three main requirements:

Intuitive: Most of the current emotion visualizations use charts or rigid geometric fractals. An intuitive emotion visualization design should allow users to easily establish the connection between the visualization and the emotion dimension or category, thus reducing the cognitive load on the user and making the user experience better.

Timeliness: Current sentiment visualization systems usually take historical data as the main subject of analysis, but visualization of current sentiment states is also an important aspect. A highly time-sensitive sentiment visualization system can reflect users' sentiment states and their changes in real time so that users can adjust their sentiment in time.

Continuity: Most of the current real-time emotion visualization systems only show the emotion state at a certain moment. A system with continuity can reflect the context of emotion in the design and show the process of emotion change, thus providing users with more scale information, making users' understanding of emotion from "point" to "surface".

8.2.2   EEG-BASED AFFECTIVE COMPUTING

Emotion recognition, which aims at identifying human emotion, plays an important role in human–computer interaction and brain–computer interaction. Recently, the research on emotion recognition from multichannel EEG recordings has attracted great interest from a vast number of interdisciplinary fields from psychology to engineering, which includes basic studies on emotion theories and applications to affective Brain–Computer Interaction (aBCI) (Mühl et al., 2014), which enhances the BCI systems with the ability to detect, process, and respond to users' emotional state using physiological signals.

As a complex psychological and physiological expression, human emotional state produced by cognitive processes, subjective feelings, motivational tendencies, behavioral reactions, and physiological arousal is associated with mood, temperament, personality, and motivation (Koelstra et al., 2012). Studies that focus on modeling emotion recognition network often adopt implicit features of human communication, such as speech, facial expressions, and gestures in different experiment settings (Kleinsmith and Bianchi-Berthouze, 2013). However, the features mentioned above are easy to disguise and thus are probably not the ideal features for emotion recognition task. Currently, physiological measurements such as electroencephalography (EEG) is introduced as it contains rich information about the underlying neural activities and is closely associated with the mental states (Lotfi and Akbarzadeh, 2014).

Many emotion recognition methods have been proposed based on EEG signals. A more comprehensive overview can be found in Zheng (2017). Most of these research works utilize traditional machine learning algorithms to recognize or predict emotional states. For example, Liu et al. (2017) adopted support vector machines (SVM) to recognize seven discrete emotions and neutrality. Piho and Tjahjadi (2020) compared the classification performance of three supervised learning algorithms – SVM, K-nearest neighbors (KNN), and naive Bayes (NB) – and KNN achieves the best accuracy when recognizing valence.

Recently, deep neural networks have been successfully introduced into EEG-based emotion recognition and achieved the state-of-the-art performance. Zheng and Lu fed PSD, DE, the differential asymmetry feature (DASM), the rational asymmetry feature (RASM), and the differential causality feature (DCAU) into a Deep Belief Network (DBN) for extracting high-level emotional features, and the features are used for emotion classification. Tang et al. proposed a bimodal deep denoising autoencoder and a bimodal-LSTM model that uses wavelet EEG features as input. A deep framework that adopted a convolutional neural network (CNN) kernel to extract emotion-related features using the input of time, frequency, and electrode location features was proposed in Zheng et al. (2015).

While many existing deep models can perform well in EEG-based emotion recognition, less attention is paid to extract the EEG feature that optimizes the functional relations among different EEG channels/electrodes. A few pioneering research works (Li et al., 2017; Zheng et al., 2019; Zheng and Lu, 2015) attempted to address this issue. Li et al. (2017) proposed a preprocessing method that uses wavelet and scalogram transform to encapsulate the multichannel EEG signals into grid-like frames and hybrid CNN and RNN to extract task-related features. By solving a group feature selection problem from raw EEG frequency features, Zheng et al. (2019) proposed a group sparse canonical correlation analysis for simultaneous selection from EEG multichannels. A state-of-the-art work (Zheng and Lu, 2015) characterized the 2D topographical map of EEG electrodes on the scalp with an adjacency matrix. The matrix was further fed into a graph CNN for optimizing weights in the matrix entities. However, the adjacency matrix can only characterize linear relations, and these models have many other disadvantages.

8.2.2.1 ATDD-LSTM Model for Emotion Recognition Based on Multichannel EEG Data

Exploring practical EEG features for emotion recognition is vital. Although the EEG measurements usually have sufficient density to sample the brain electrical field (i.e., generally more than 30 electrodes are placed on the scalp), the spatial feature that optimally characterizes the functional relations among different EEG channels is rarely considered. Recently, a few pioneering works (Song et al., 2020; Yang et al., 2018; Zheng, 2017) have been proposed that explore such spatial features through multichannel EEG signals. Among these methods, the state of the art (Song et al., 2020) introduced a dynamic graph convolutional neural network (DGCNN) to learn the optimal adjacency matrix M automatically. However, M can only represent linear relations, which characterizes the strengths of connections between pairs of EEG channels.

Therefore, by studying the relation among different EEG electrodes, a deep learning method is proposed to automatically extract the spatial features that characterize the functional relation between EEG signals at different electrodes. The deep model is called Attention-based LSTM with Domain Discriminator (ATDD-LSTM), a model based on Long Short-Term Memory (LSTM) for emotion recognition that can characterize nonlinear relations among EEG signals of different electrodes. To achieve state-of-the-art emotion recognition performance, the architecture of ATDD-LSTM has two distinguishing characteristics: (1) By applying the attention mechanism to the feature vectors produced by LSTM, ATDD-LSTM automatically selects suitable EEG channels for emotion recognition, which makes the learned model concentrate on the emotion-related channels in response to a given emotion; (2) To minimize the significant feature distribution shift between different sessions and/or subjects, ATDD-LSTM uses a domain discriminator to modify the data representation space and generate domain-invariant features.

In the ATDD-LSTM model, the input for a given temporal sample is a channel sequence representing the EEG signal from different electrodes, and the output is the emotion label corresponding to the input EEG channel sequence. Unlike most previous research, the model focuses on addressing the following two challenges: (1) selecting effective emotion-related channels and (2) building domain-invariant features to ensure robust recognition across subjects and different sessions of a subject.

Channel selection. Not all EEG signals are related to emotion. The EEG signals collected from different electrodes on the scalp reflect a variety of information, and it is well known that the electrodes located in the prefrontal cortex are associated with the emotional process (Harmon-Jones, 2004; Liu et al., 2017; Zhao et al., 2018; Zhao et al., 2018). In the study, in addition to making use of existing neurophysiological research for establishing the relations among multichannels, it is expected that the data-driven approach can also help explore more subtle relations.

Domain-invariant features. Many previous studies build the emotion recognition model on the basis of each individual person's brain responses, due to the data distribution shift between different persons. Despite the popularity of subject-dependent models in EEG-based emotion recognition (Zheng et al., 2019; Zheng and Lu, 2015), some recent studies (Li et al., 2018; Pan et al., 2011; Pandey and Seeja, 2019; Schölkopf et al., 1998; Tripathi et al., 2017; Zheng et al., 2015) suggest building models specially designed for subject-independent evaluation. To address the data distribution shift problem, ATDD-LSTM incorporates a domain discriminator in this model to constrain the features extracted from training (source) data and test (target) data to have similar distributions.

Five EEG features – differential entropy (DE), power spectral density (PSD), differential asymmetry (DASM), rational asymmetry (RASM), and differential causality (DCAU) – are evaluated in Zheng and Lu (2015) for multichannel EEG signal analysis in which DE is reported to achieve the best overall performance in emotion recognition. Following Zheng and Lu (2015), the DE features of multichannel EEG signals are used as input to the ATDD-LSTM model.

As shown in Figure 8.1, the ATDD-LSTM consists of three modules: a sequential feature extractor, a domain discriminator, and an attention-based encoder–decoder. The sequential feature extractor utilizes a two-layer LSTM to capture the sequential feature of multichannel EEG recordings. The domain discriminator is designed to reduce the effect of the distribution shift between features of training and test sets and help the feature extractor to produce domain-invariant features. The attention-based encoder–decoder includes two parts. One uses the attention mechanism to focus on emotion-related channels and construct an integrated representation and then predicts the classification probability. The other combines the above feature and probability to perform reconstruction, which leads to an encoder–decoder. The encoder–decoder adds further constraints to facilitate learning. By operating the encoder–decoder module m times, one for each emotion category, where m is the number of emotion categories, a prediction probability for emotion recognition is obtained.

The experimental results on three public EEG emotional databases (DEAP, SEED, and CMEED) for emotion recognition demonstrate that ATDD-LSTM model achieves superior performance on subject-dependent (for the same subject), subject-independent (for different subjects), and cross-session (for the same subject) evaluation.

To better understand how attention mechanism learns to solve emotion recognition tasks, illustration of the functional aspects of attention mechanism and feature maps will be helpful. The visualization of attention allocation in Figure 8.2 shows the qualitative results. In the heat map, the horizontal axis represents the number of channels, and each grid represents the attention weight on this channel, and the vertical axis shows arousal dimension and valence dimension. The scalp map represents

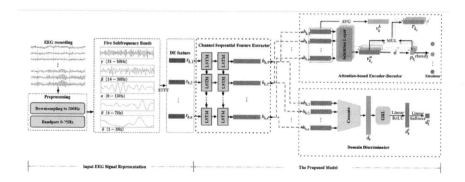

FIGURE 8.1 ATDD-LSTM model for emotion recognition based on multichannel EEG data.

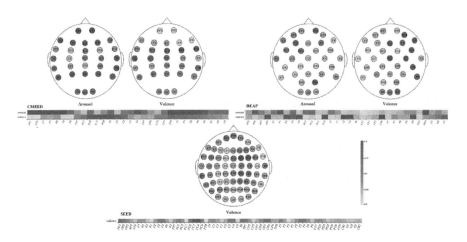

FIGURE 8.2   Visualization of attention allocation.

the contribution of all electrodes to the binary classification on the arousal dimension or the valence dimension of emotion, with the electrode location corresponding to the grid in the heat map. Notably, since the SEED database is only annotated with the valence dimension of emotion (positive, neutral, and negative), only the scalp map associated with the valence dimension is shown.

In order to analyze the effectiveness of attention mechanism more intuitively, ATDD-LSTM maps the attention weights to the electrode location on scalp. For the binary classification task on the arousal dimension or valence dimension, different channels may not contribute equally. From the scalp map, the frontal lobe and occipital lobe are correlated with the arousal dimension of emotion, and the parietal lobe and temporal lobe reflect obvious lateral partial phenomenon for the valence dimension of emotion. Moreover, the right hemisphere activity is more related to the emotional states on the valence dimension. This visualization result demonstrates the effectiveness of attention mechanism in ATDD-LSTM for capturing emotion-related channels.

8.2.2.2   Co-attention-based Label Distribution Learning Model for Positive Emotions

Existing EEG-based emotion recognition research mainly classify the EEG signals into one single emotional label. However, due to the complex nature of human emotion, one emotional image rarely expresses a single emotion but a mixture of multiple emotions. Emotions conveyed by videos can be even more complicated, as emotional information contained in video clips is much more complicated. Emotion expression in video is related to the characters' facial expression and context information, such as gesture and place. Therefore, the emotional arousal to people while watching videos is often a mixture of multiple emotions. Besides, people with diverse social and cultural backgrounds may have different emotional reactions to the same video clip. Therefore, this model learns multiple emotion labels via continuous emotion distribution from input EEG signals. Figure 8.3 illustrates emotion distribution learning.

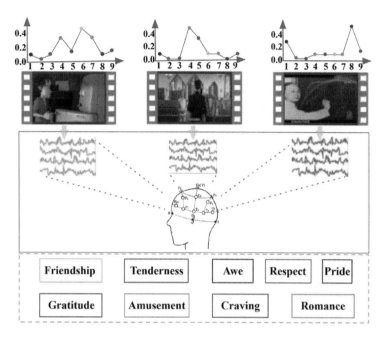

FIGURE 8.3   Emotion distribution learning.

Therefore, a deep neural network is proposed integrating coattention mechanism and the LSTM to learn the positive emotion distributions, as shown in Figure 8.4. The input feature matrix is composed of the PSD feature of each EEG signal, and it uses the fully connected layer to further obtain the EEG features. Then, the coattention mechanism is used to learn the interaction between pairs of brain regions by aligning and combining the pairwise EEG features of regional electrodes. To encode the EEG PSD features, the model adopted a two-layer LSTM module to learn the temporal correlation on temporal sequence. Then, the attention scores and EEG representation are multiplied as the input of classifier. The SoftMax is used to predict the emotion distribution, and the KLDivLoss function is applied to train the model.

8.2.2.2.1   EEG Feature Extractor

To build the emotional EEG representation, the frequency domain of EEG features is used from the CPED database. The PSD is one of the most widely used EEG features in EEG-based emotion recognition tasks. The CPED database provides the PSD feature of multichannel EEG signals, and the dimension of PSD feature for each EEG signal at one unit time step is 5. All electrodes are split into five parts according to the division of brain regions, namely, Frontal (seven electrodes), Temporal (eight electrodes), Central (nine electrodes), Parietal (three electrodes), and Occipital (three electrodes). Note that the number of electrodes of each brain region is not equal, like the number of electrodes of Frontal is 7, and the number of electrodes of Occipital is 3. For the brain region, it is assumed that the number of the electrodes (i.e., EEG channels) is c, and the PSD dimension is $c \times 5$. Therefore, this model adopted the fully connected layer to map the EEG PSD features into the same dimension space:

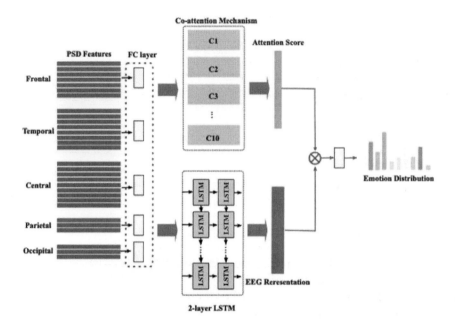

FIGURE 8.4 Co-attention-based label distribution learning model for positive emotions.

$$f_i^{1:T} = FC\left(s_i^{1:T}\right) \tag{8.1}$$

where $f_i^{1:T} \in \mathbb{R}^{T \times d}$ for $i = 1, 2, \ldots,$ n is the ith brain regional feature obtained by the fully connected layer, FC is the fully connected layer, and $s_i^{1:T}$ is the ith brain regional PSD feature matrix. Thus, the $f_i^{1:T}$ is the input of the subsequent modules, coattention mechanism, and LSTM module.

8.2.2.2.2 *Coattention Mechanism*

The interaction between the pairs of brain regions is obtained through the coattention mechanism. The input of each coattention module is the pairwise brain regional features. For example, the first coattention module learns the correlation between Frontal and Temporal, and the second one learns the correlation between Frontal and Central. After the operation of coattention modules, m values of α_k are obtained, in which $k = 1, 2, \ldots, m$ corresponds to each pairwise coattention operation:

$$\alpha_k = \text{CoA}\left(f_{k1}^{1:T}, f_{k2}^{1:T}\right) \tag{8.2}$$

where $k1, k2$ denote the indexes of the five brain regional feature matrix, and CoA(·) represents the operation of the coattention mechanism. The coattention mechanism learns the correlation between two inputs by calculating the similarity of two input features. The coattention method is as follows:

$$\alpha_k = SoftMax\left(w_{\alpha_k}, z_k\right) \tag{8.3}$$

$$z_k = \varnothing\left(w_{k1}f_{k1}^{1:T} \oplus w_{k2}f_{k2}^{1:T}\right) \tag{8.4}$$

where w_{α_k}, w_{k1}, and w_{k2} are the learnable parameters during training procedure, $\varnothing$ $(\cdot)$ is the tanh activation function for both inputs, and $\oplus$ denotes the concatenation operation between two brain regional features. Thereafter, the α_k is concatenated to obtain the attention score distribution α:

$$\alpha = \text{concate}[\alpha_1, \alpha_2, \ldots, \alpha_m] \tag{8.5}$$

Then, the attention distribution is applied to EEG representation to learn the attended/relevant parts for emotion distribution learning in experiments.

8.2.2.2.3 EEG Representation Learning

The EEG feature is encoded using a two-layer LSTM method. The LSTM method is a variation of RNN, which is mainly designed to solve the gradient disappearance and gradient explosion problems during the training of long sequences. LSTM is able to learn the dependencies between contextual information on the longer sequence of data. The LSTM cell consists of input gate, forget gate, output gate, and cell state. The formulas of each unit are as follows:

$$f_t = \sigma\left(W_f \cdot [h_{t-1}, x_t] + b_f\right) \tag{8.6}$$

$$i_t = \sigma\left(W_i \cdot [h_{t-1}, x_t] + b_i\right) \tag{8.7}$$

$$\tilde{C}_t = \tanh\left(W_C \cdot [h_{t-1}, x_t] + b_C\right) \tag{8.8}$$

$$C_t = f_t * C_{t-1} + i_t * \tilde{C}_t \tag{8.9}$$

$$o_t = \sigma\left(W_o \cdot [h_{t-1}, x_t] + b_o\right) \tag{8.10}$$

$$h_t = o_t * \tanh(C_t) \tag{8.11}$$

where $\sigma(\cdot)$ denotes the Sigmoid function, W_f, W_i, W_C, W_o, b_f, b_i, b_C, and b_o are the learnable parameters during training process, h_{t-1} is the hidden layer output of the $(t-1)$th time step, x_t denotes the input EEG features at tth time step, and C_{t-1} is the cell state of the $(t-1)$th time step.

LSTM is used to learn the dependent correlation among temporal dimensions. The input of LTSM is $S^{1:T} = \text{concat}[\ f_1^{1:T},\ f_2^{1:T}, \ldots,\ f_i^{1:T}\ ]$, and $i = 5$. Thereafter, the stacked EEG features are encoded by the LSTM module; the formally definition is as follows:

$$R = LSTM\left(S^{1:T}\right) \tag{8.12}$$

After obtaining the attention score distribution α and the EEG representation R, α and R are multiplied to obtain the weighted average of the EEG features.

8.2.2.2.4 Emotion Distribution Learning

The sample in CPED is denoted by $s \in R^{T \times c \times d_{psd}}$, where T denotes the temporal length of the sample, c denotes the number of EEG channels, and d_{psd} represents the dimension of PSD EEG features. The corresponding emotion label is illustrated by $Y = \{y_1, y_2,..., y_e\}$, $e = 9$. If emotion e exists, $y_e = 1$, otherwise, $y_e = 0$ and $0 \leq d_s^{y_e} \leq 1$ to be the degree of the emotion e of the EEG sample s, and $d_s^{y_e}$ satisfies the constraint $\sum_{y_e} d_s^{y_e} = 1$.

Therefore, a training set can be formulated as $S = \{(s_1, D_1), (s_2, D_2),...,(s_N, D_N)\}$, where s_i is the ith sample, and $D_i = \{d_{s_i}^{y_1}, d_{s_i}^{y_2},...,d_{s_i}^{y_e}\}$ is the label distribution of the sample s_i.

The emotion distribution is predicted via applying SoftMax to the weighted average of EEG features:

$$\hat{D}_i = \text{SoftMax}\left(\alpha \otimes R\right) \tag{8.13}$$

where $\otimes$ denotes the multiplication between matrix and vector, the SoftMax output is assigned to the predict emotion distribution $\widehat{D}_i = \{d_{s_i}^{\hat{y}_1}, d_{s_i}^{\hat{y}_2},...,d_{s_i}^{\hat{y}_e}\}$, and the d_{si} denotes the predicted probability of emotion e for sample s_i.

Following the work from Huang et al. (2015), Inventado et al. (2011), and James and Collomosse (2014), this model uses the Kullback-Leibler divergence loss as the overall loss function:

$$L = \frac{1}{n} \sum_{i=1}^{n} \left(\sum_{j=1}^{e} d_{s_i}^{y_j} \ln \frac{d_{s_i}^{y_j}}{d_{s_i}^{\hat{y}_j}} \right) = \frac{1}{n} \sum_{i=1}^{n} \sum_{j=1}^{e} d_{s_i}^{y_j} \ln d_{s_i}^{y_j} - \frac{1}{n} \sum_{i=1}^{n} \sum_{j=1}^{e} d_{s_i}^{y_j} \ln d_{s_i}^{\hat{y}_j} \tag{8.14}$$

where n represents the number of samples in the training dataset, and $d_{s_i}^{\hat{y}_j}$ represents the probability that the label of the ith input sample is the emotion category j. With the above loss function, the parameters of the model can be optimized until convergence.

The experiments on the Chinese Positive Emotion Database (CPED), which is the first multilabel emotional EEG database, demonstrate that this method outperforms the state-of-the-art approaches.

Emotion is an essential role in human-centered design, especially the positive emotion evoked by the designs in products and intelligent assistant systems. This method is considered as the foundation of the emotional design, and it tried to explore an efficient method to recognize user's emotion state in real time when they are engaging in the products or are served by the intelligent systems. These applications can help designers learn the user's preferences and therefore design the user-centered products in a better way. Moreover, the applications based on these works can recognize user's emotion precisely in time, and the real-time feedback on emotions can assist the refinement of the product design.

8.2.3 AFFECTIVE VISUALIZATION IN HCI

8.2.3.1 Introduction of Visual Analytics on Emotions

The visualization of emotion is an externalization of the internal emotional states. Various approaches have been explored to visualize emotion. The most basic representation is diagrams, such as histograms, bubble charts, and boxplot charts (Ruiz et al., 2016; Zhang et al., 2010), which are easy to understand but hard to convey the complex emotional context. A geometric fractal is usually designed for more creative representation, and several visual properties have been assigned to distinguish different emotional dimensions or categories. Pinilla et al. (Palacios et al., 2020) used properties to present the audiovisual emotional cues, including shape, color, brightness, speed, direction, and path curvature. Expressing emotion with different colors has been widely examined in academia (Bartram et al., 2017; Labrecque and Milne, 2012; Valdez and Mehrabian, 1994). For example, blue indicates peacefulness and calmness (Madden et al., 2000), while red, green, and blue indicate negative valence, positive valence, and arousal, respectively (Cernea et al., 2013; Inventado et al., 2011). Speed naturally relates to arousal that a lower speed suggests more calmness (Feng et al., 2017), and a higher speed suggests more excitement and urgency (Feng et al., 2014). Regarding path curvature, a jerky path indicates higher arousal than a straight path in linear motion (Lockyer et al., 2011).

Visual analytics enables effective understanding, reasoning, and decision-making with automated data analysis and interactive visualizations on large and complex datasets (Keim et al., 2008). Because emotions are complex and not intuitive, visual analytics tools are necessary to assist in the analysis of emotions. A timeline-based visual analytic tool was proposed to discover and examine personal emotional style derived from social media text (Zhao et al., 2015). Novel visual analysis techniques for presenting emotional data have been created to provide meaningful insights. New visual forms were developed to show changing group emotion (Zeng et al., 2021) and multimodal emotional coherence (Zhang et al., 2010) in an intuitive way. Due to the weak interpretability of multimodal sentiment analysis techniques, some work (Wang et al., 2022) has used visual analysis techniques to improve the understanding and analysis of multimodal sentiment.

In summary, multimodal visual analytics on emotions still needs to be further explored in more intuitive visualization forms, more explainable analysis methods, and more user-oriented applications.

8.2.3.2 Spiral-based Visual Analysis Technique

Spiral-like visualization is "appropriate for presenting many events within a single dense display" (Brehmer et al., 2017). It has advantages for displaying certain kinds of information, but its potential may not have been exhausted. The changes in emotion, for example, are important to consider in the analysis of emotion and can be combined into typical spirals in a visually dramatic way. Clockwise and counterclockwise turns in the spiral indicate shifting negative and positive emotions, with sharp angles of the visualization showing the emotional turning points. Due to the compact structure, a large-scale comparison is also possible.

The type of emotion and the valence and arousal of emotion are considered as the input of visualization. In Figure 8.5, each small circle appears in chronological order, starting at the center of the spiral. Significant shifts in the valence of speeches are reflected in the change of direction. The color of the circle is indicated as the emotional type of the interval. The circle radius represents the arousal of emotions, while the transparency represents the probability of the emotion being labeled correctly.

The spiral is generated in polar coordinates with $\theta_n = \theta_{n-1} + 2 * \pi * \Delta_r * p_i$. θ_n is the polar angle of the center of the nth circle, and $\Delta_r = r_n - r_{n-1}$ is the variation of the polar radius between the nth circle and the $(n-1)$th circle, which is a constant value since the spiral expands at a constant variation of radius.

The emotional turning points are generated based on the positive and negative changes of accumulated emotions in intervals. $E_i = \sum a_n$ is the accumulative emotion in an interval of 5 seconds in which a_n is one of the valence data in interval i. The spiral turns clockwise when $p = 1$, while it turns counterclockwise when $p = -1$. The changing of p decides the emotional turning points in spirals, which is calculated in Equation (8.16). The initial value of p is defined by the emotion in the first interval, shown in Equation (8.15).

$$p_0 = \begin{cases} 1, E_0 \geq 0 \\ -1, E_0 < 0 \end{cases} \tag{8.15}$$

$$p_{i \geq 1} = \begin{cases} -p_{i-1}, E_i \times E_{i-1} < 0 \text{ and } |E_i - E_{i-1}| \geq 10 \\ p_{i-1}, \text{otherwise} \end{cases} \tag{8.16}$$

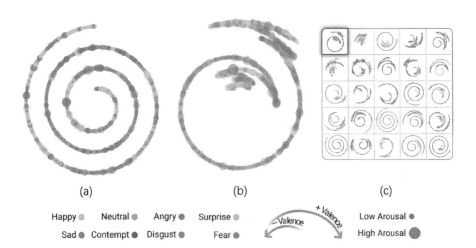

(a)   (b)   (c)

Happy ○ Neutral ○ Angry ● Surprise ○   Low Arousal ●

Sad ● Contempt ● Disgust ● Fear ●   Valence + Valence   High Arousal ●

FIGURE 8.5 E-spiral: a novel spiral-type visualization of time-series emotion data. A comparison is given: (a) spiral without turning points, (b) spiral with turning points, and (c) spirals in a collection.

With the help of the spiral-based visualization, the changes in emotion can be clearly seen via the turning spiral.

8.2.3.3 Text-based Visual Analysis Technique

Emotion expressed through text or speech is an important source. There exists a need and necessity to analyze these emotions in relation to textual content. No previous work has been found in visual analytics that involves letter shape adjustment in order to convey quantitative emotion. Brath et al. (Brath and Banissi, 2016) survey existing text visualizations, noting only one case of quantitative glyphs being used to indicate prosodic song qualities such as pitch and duration.

The text-based visual analysis technique aims to provide an audience with ordinary visualization literacy with an intuitive way of understanding script emotional data by changing letter shapes to encode quantitative information (quantitative glyphs), indicated in Figure 8.6. It allows fine-grained understanding of multimodal text emotion, speech emotion, word speed, and pauses. The word speed is indicated by the tracking between letters in a word, while the pauses as the spaces between words.

FIGURE 8.6 A novel visualization allowing key information about the text expression and emotional trends.

The text-based visual form highlights emotionally intense (high-arousal) moments by directly mapping with the line shape. Sievers et al. (2019) found that the shape of lines can visually encode emotion and is closely related to arousal and can be seen as independent of valence. The size of the text was also changed in order to highlight emotionally intense moments in the speech. The color corresponds to the valence and arousal in the speech script, as promoted by Gross (1998).

8.2.4 APPLICATION OF AFFECTIVE COMPUTING IN SMART SERVICE

8.2.4.1 Biofeedback System for Negative Emotion Regulation

Emotion regulation (ER), defined as "how we try to influence which emotions we have, when we have them, and how we experience and express these emotions" (Rieffe et al., 2008), is a noteworthy approach to fostering the emotional well-being of people. The effects of existing ER systems are hard to be reflected in a short time. It is of certain significance to develop ER systems that can responsively help regulate emotions in the moment, preventing emotional breakdown. Based on the theory of ER success, "immediate emotion regulation" can be defined as a responsive ER process of current emotion, achieving a target emotional state in a short period of time. Compared with normal ER, which improves physical and mental health from a long-term perspective, immediate ER focuses more on the dynamic awareness of current emotion and attention to target emotion.

Aiming at immediate ER, Emocean, a biofeedback system for negative emotion regulation, and its interactions are designed based on two factors: emotional awareness and emotional goal setting. Prior works have examined their relationships with ER. Firstly, being aware of one's emotion is an attentional process that enables an individual to monitor and identify emotions and locate their antecedents (Mauss and Tamir, 2014). Thus, emotional information availability in a proper form is a necessary condition for ER. Secondly, considering ER is a motivated process; setting an emotional goal can activate the process and motivate individuals to strive for the emotion goal.

In Emocean (Figure 8.7), a closed loop of biofeedback is constructed between a user and Emocean. On the one hand, the EEG recordings of a user are collected in

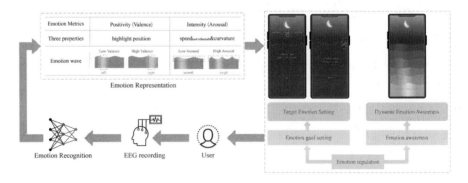

FIGURE 8.7 The overall framework of Emocean.

real time and fed into the emotion recognition algorithm. The continuous output metrics control the generation of wave representations and further support the visualization system of Emocean. On the other hand, Emocean encodes the boring numbers into vivid visual languages and provides the user with multimodal stimuli that support ER process. The interaction design is motivated by two factors correlated to ER. A user can get instant feedback concerning emotional states. Considering the privacy of emotional regulatory process, Emocean is presented as a mobile web application.

Blue and white are the main color schemes of the application interface, creating a peaceful and pure atmosphere (Figure 8.8). Wave is the core of the visualization design. Each wave can be regarded as an emotional state, which is a short-term internal experience. The wave continually occurs at the bottom of the interface every 10 seconds and moves upward as time goes by. The color changes from light blue to deep blue over time. The retention time of a wave is one minute, which means there coexist at most six waves in one interface. Parameter equations and trigonometry are utilized to simulate the upper bound of the wave. The value of valence linearly varies with the horizontal position of the highlight. With the position from left to center and then to right, the emotional positivity changes from negative to neutral and then to positive. Arousal is double encoded by the curvature and the transverse speed. In fact, these two properties are correlated; high speed always leads to a rough wave, and low speed leads to a smooth one. The higher the arousal, the curvier the wave shapes.

The moon has two properties: position and brightness. The position represents the valence of the target emotion, which has the same implication as the highlight of waves. One can set the position of moon manually at the beginning, and it will be fixed once confirmed. Brightness indicates the overall similarity between target emotion and current emotion. The brightness of the moon is refreshed every 10 seconds (the frequency of real-time emotion recognition). The larger the similarity is, the brighter the moon looks, which can be a motivation to the pursuit of goal.

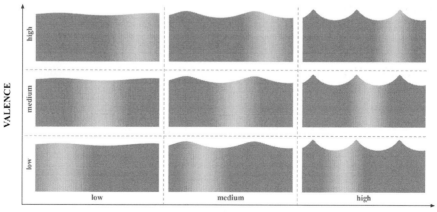

FIGURE 8.8 Wave representations.

Similar to the moon, the sea level is an indicator of target arousal. It is a wave holding the qualities of arousal in essence. Once the target arousal is set, the sea level will turn darker to act as a reference in the subsequent interface. According to the difference between the target and current emotions, the textual feedback is generated automatically. It gives user suggestions such as "Calm down...", "Cheer up!!", or "Well done! Keep in mood". In terms of the two audio sources, one is the background music of the sound of waves. It is played automatically as long as the waves move, which aims at enhancing the immersion of Emocean. The other is voice guidance of abdominal breathing in which the speech agent tells instructions in a gentle voice.

8.2.4.2   Emotion-based Speech Visualization and Analysis System

Effectiveness in speeches has long been a controversial subject. Aristotle began his work Rhetoric by criticizing contemporary experts in the field "the framers of the current treatises on rhetoric have constructed but a small portion of that art" (Quoidbach et al., 2014). While Aristotle focused on persuasive speaking, the effectiveness of other kinds of public speaking remains to be understood on a large scale. Today, organizations and public speaking experts train and coach people to improve their public speaking ability in various contexts. Recently published works in analytical systems have focused on describing the speaking strategies of high-level speeches. However, there is a lack of analytical systems that support evaluation of the effectiveness of speaking strategies. Additionally, existing works cannot determine what strategies are effective and what are not, since they lack a clear metric of effectiveness.

E-ffective, a visual analytic system for speech experts and novices to evaluate the effectiveness of speaking strategies, is proposed to analyze the speech factors that take into account the relative success of speeches (Figure 8.9).

The dataset for analysis includes 203 videos from the World Championship of Public Speaking published online, including YouTube and WeChat channels. In order to acquire the speech factors, features are extracted from image frames, voice, and text scripts from the original video, see Figure 8.10. The voice and text are aligned at the sentence level, while the images remain at the frame level.

The raw data extracted from videos are time series of multimodal valence and arousal data. As it is not intuitive for users to explore the data, speech factors are calculated based on the raw data extracted. The time series of multimodal valence or arousal data is represented as $D = \left\{ d_t^m \right\}_{t=1}^{T}$, where d_t^m indicates the tth sample of the time-series data in the modality of m. Similarly, the time series of multimodal emotion type data is represented as $E = \left\{ e_t^m \right\}_{t=1}^{T}$. The average factor represents the average value of a specific data modality over time:

$$average = \frac{\sum_{t=1}^{T} d_t^m}{T} \tag{8.17}$$

Volatility represents the change of data over time. The data is first normalized and then computed into volatility according to Equations (8.18) and (8.19):

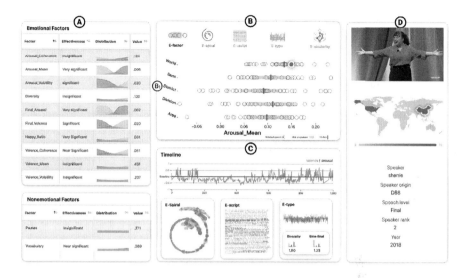

FIGURE 8.9 E-ffective system supports understanding and exploring the effectiveness of different factors in public speaking in four views: the view of factors (a), the view of all speeches (b), the view of the selected speech (c), and the view of the selected speech context (d).

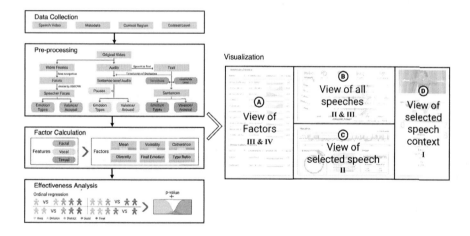

FIGURE 8.10 An overview of the analytic system.

$$D_{diff} = \left\{ d_t^m - d_{t-1}^m \right\}_{t=2}^{T} \qquad (8.18)$$

$$\text{volatility} = \sqrt{D_{\text{diff}} \cdot D_{\text{diff}}} \qquad (8.19)$$

Diversity represents the variety and relative abundance of the emotions. It is calculated as in Equation (8.20):

$$\text{diversity} = \sum_{i=1}^{e} (r_i \times \ln r_i) \tag{8.20}$$

Here, e equals the total number of emotion types in E, and r_i equals the proportion of E that contains the ith emotion.

Zhang et al. (2010) explore the effect of emotion coherence across facial, text, and audio modalities. Similarly, the values of arousal and valence coherence are calculated as defined in Equation (8.21), where std and mean indicate functions of calculating the standard deviation and the mean value, respectively. The superscripts represent the modalities of data, where w, v, and f mean the textual, vocal, and facial modalities:

$$\text{coherence} = \frac{1}{T} \sum_{t=1}^{T} \frac{\text{std}\left(d_t^w, d_t^v, d_t^f\right)}{\text{mean}\left(d_t^w, d_t^v, d_t^f\right)} \tag{8.21}$$

In interviews, experts estimate the last 20% of a speech to be more important than other parts. So, the final valence and arousal are calculated with Equation (8.22):

$$\text{final ratio}_{\text{emotion}} = \frac{\sum_{t=0.8T}^{T} i}{T} \tag{8.22}$$

8.2.4.2.1 Views

E-ffective consists of four views: (A) the view of factors, (B) the view of all speeches, (C) the view of the selected speech, and (D) the view of the selected speech context. In view A, the table displays the factors and p-values obtained from the factor calculation and effectiveness analysis steps. It helps users to understand the relation between speech effectiveness and various speech factors as well as the connection of emotional data to other speech factors. Given the range of factors of interest to the audience, a visualization system that provides an overview of all factors would be ideal for understanding their relation to effectiveness. View B provides a panel to view all speeches for comparison, navigation, and exploration with five novel subviews: E-factor, E-similarity, E-spiral, E-script, and E-type. The raw arousal and valence data from preprocessing phase and factor values from factor calculation phase are utilized to generate visualizations. View C contains four subviews showing the data and visualizations of selected individual speech. It helps users analyze a selected speech in more detail. View D contains information about the dataset and detailed context information of the speaker. The four views of the system assist users to explore dataset and find the factors that affect the effectiveness of speech.

8.2.4.2.2 Subviews

Views B and C contain some subviews. The subviews in view B are set to assist users to analyze the overall trends, navigate, and locate speeches of interest in the dataset. E-factor and E-similarity show the distribution of all speeches. E-spiral, E-script, and E-type aggregate the visualizations of all speeches. The subviews in view C are set to help users to observe the visualization of a selected individual speech in more detail using visualization tools such as E-spiral, E-script, and E-type.

8.2.4.2.3   Interaction

The interaction design of the system follows Schneiderman's information-seeking mantra as a guideline: "overview first, zoom and filter, then details-on-demand" (Yu et al., 2016). The views are organized from left to right in terms of the level of abstraction of the data. Some interactions are provided to support the overview-to-detail exploration process. Upon selection of an effectiveness factor, E-factor will show the distribution of the factor values with all speeches. Users can also hover the mouse over the speeches to see the individual speech data and click to change the view of the selected speech. This interaction is supported by each of the subviews in the view of all speeches (B). These subviews aggregate all the visualizations of speeches and organize them by level. For deep exploration, users can click the subviews in view (C) to generate a bigger visualization in a floating window. In E-similarity, upon clicking the dot representing an individual speech, a radar-like chart will be displayed in the right to show the predicted level of the critical factors of the selected speech.

8.3   SKETCH-BASED INTERFACES IN SMART SERVICE

8.3.1   Overview

As claimed in Lin et al. (2020), "a sketch speaks for a 'hundred' words", sketching is a simple and effective way to express user intents in a straightforward way. Contrast to traditional interaction technologies, sketch interaction is more efficient in two aspects. First, free-hand sketch is a kind of flexible visual recollection which can intuitively provide fine-grained information of objects or scenes by depicting their approximate appearance and layout. Second, free-hand sketch has the advantage of conveniency; that is, it can be easily obtained with the aid of popular sketching interfaces on various touch devices. Therefore, sketch has become a highly desired tool for intelligent applications, such as computer-assisted designing (Chen et al., 2009; Li and Zhang, 2022; Suleri et al., 2019) and human–AI cocreation tasks (Li et al., 2017; Zou et al., 2018).

The studies of sketch including scene-level sketch semantic segmentation and sketch-based image or video retrieval benefit intelligent interaction performance in smart services. Specifically, scene-level sketch semantic segmentation is considered a fundamental task for many downstream applications, such as scene sketch colorization. Sketch-based image or video retrieval provides a natural and accurate interaction tool to help users get desired images or videos from massive multimedia data.

8.3.2   Multimodal Semantics Modeling for Sketch

8.3.2.1   Sketch Semantic Segmentation

Sketch semantic segmentation (SSS) is a fundamental problem in sketch understanding. SSS aims to assign strokes in sketch with certain semantic labels. According to the segmentation granularity and types of semantic labels, SSS can be classified into two categories: scene- and object-level segmentation. In scene-level segmentation, prior art methods (Gennari et al., 2005) migrated the models in image domain to sketch domain for feature extraction. However, directly using image semantic segmentation for sketch ignores the strong temporal sequential context among strokes in hand-drawn sketch, as strokes belonging to the same object are likely to be drawn in close proximity. Besides, contrast to normal image, sketches are of sparsity, which is pretty suitable for features extracted using encoder model. In order to address the above two issues, a stroke-based method is utilized for scene-level semantic segmentation. The input of the method is stroke sequences that are stored in a term of vector.

Early efforts often use low-level geometric features (Graves and Schmidhuber, 2005) and traditional machine learning methods (Wang et al., 2020) to predict the categories that strokes in a sketch belong to. While some results could be achieved, these methods highly rely on specific input format and are time consuming. Following the flourishing of deep learning, various neural network architectures are proposed for SSS, including CNN-based methods (Wu et al., 2018) and RNN-based methods (Yang et al., 2021). CNN-based models treat SSS as an image segmentation task and pay more attention to the edge and outline features. Since a sketch is drawn by stroke sequences, sequence modeling of sketch strokes is a promising solution for SSS. RNN-based models extract the sequential features of stroke points. Besides the above visual and sequential features, the spatial relationship between strokes is also useful for SSS. Since graph-based networks can learn structural relationships effectively, some efforts use graph neural networks for single-object SSS (Sangkloy et al., 2016). Recently, a hybrid architecture of CNN, RNN, and GCN, Stroke-based Sequential-Spatial Neural Network (S^3NN), is proposed to capture multiscale sketch features and conduct stroke-based multiobject SSS. Compared to images, sketches are highly sparse, and their appearance is dominated by outlines and edges. The key challenges of SSS lie in the sparseness and diversity of sketches. The stroke sequence representation of scene sketch reduces the sparsity issue of sketch. In order to extract the diverse feature of sketch, visual, sequential, and spatial information are integrated in S^3NN. Specifically, a pretrained CNN is utilized to extract the overall visual feature of each stroke. The sequential relationship of strokes and the spatial connection between neighboring strokes are then learned by a RNN and a graph convolutional network (GCN).

The overview of S^3NN is illustrated in Figure 8.11. Given an input scene sketch, statistical parameters (i.e., length, drawing duration, and bounding box) are first

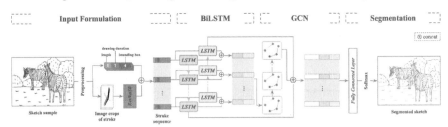

FIGURE 8.11   The framework of S^3NN. For a sketch sample, the preprocessing includes computing statistic features and capturing visual features of each stroke via ResNet50. The concatenated sequence feature is cascadingly fed into the Sequential Encoder (SeqE) for temporal relationship extraction and Spatial Encoder (SpaE) for spatial connection learning. Finally, the fusion of spatial and global sequential features is mapped to 40 categories. Classification is conducted by the SoftMax probabilities.

computed for each stroke as its global features. Then, the image patch corresponding to the bounding box of each stroke is fed into a pretrained CNN to extract the primary visual features of the stroke. The above two stroke features are concatenated and fed to subsequent modules, Sequential Encoder (SeqE) and Spatial Encoder (SpaE). SeqE utilizes Bidirectional LSTM (BiLSTM) to extract temporal features, and SpaE leverages the spatial context modeling ability of GCN to extract spatial features. Finally, the extracted temporal/spatial features are fed into a fully connected layer with SoftMax to predict the class label of each stroke.

8.3.2.1.1   Input Representation

A scene-level sketch contains a certain number of strokes. Each stroke S can be represented by a point sequence $(x_1, y_1), (x_2, y_2), \cdots, (x_n, y_n)$, where (x_k, y_k) are the coordinates of the kth point, and n is the number of points in a stroke. The feature of the ith stroke $\mathbf{f}_i = \text{concat}\left(f_i^{len}, f_i^{dur}, \mathbf{f}_i^{box}, \mathbf{f}_i^{cnn}\right)$ can be obtained by concatenating four types of features: (1) a scalar of stroke length f_i^{len}, i.e., the sum of Euclidean distances between each pair of adjacent points; (2) a scalar of drawing duration f_i^{dur}; (3) 4D vector of stroke bounding box $\mathbf{f}_i^{box}$; and (4) 256D visual feature $\mathbf{f}^{cnn}$ obtained by converting each stroke into an image and feeding it into a pretrained CNN for feature extraction. Finally, the sketch features F can be obtained by $F = [\mathbf{f}_1, \mathbf{f}_2, \cdots, \mathbf{f}_m]$, where m is the number of strokes in the scene sketch.

8.3.2.1.2   Sequential Encoder

Strokes belonging to the same object are found likely to be drawn in close proximity, so it is a key problem to effectively incorporate this sequential context into feature learning of strokes. Since BiLSTM has been proved to be effective to extract both forward and backward temporal features, it is utilized for the sequential encoder of strokes. Although other RNNs can be alternatives, experiments demonstrate that BiLSTM is more effective. The forward and backward modules of BiLSTM can be formulated as follows:

$$\mathcal{L}_f\left([\mathbf{f}_1, \mathbf{f}_2, \ldots, \mathbf{f}_m]\right) = \left[\overrightarrow{\mathbf{h}_1}, \overrightarrow{\mathbf{h}_2}, \cdots, \overrightarrow{\mathbf{h}_m}\right] \in \mathbb{R}^{d_h \times m} \tag{8.23}$$

$$\mathcal{L}_b\left([\mathbf{f}_m, \mathbf{f}_{m-1}, \ldots, \mathbf{f}_1]\right) = \left[\overleftarrow{\mathbf{h}_1}, \overleftarrow{\mathbf{h}_2}, \cdots, \overleftarrow{\mathbf{h}_m}\right] \in \mathbb{R}^{d_h \times m} \tag{8.24}$$

where $\mathcal{L}_f$ and $\mathcal{L}_b$ denote the forward and backward LSTM operations, and d_h is the hidden unit dimension. The output of BiLSTM is $\mathbf{H}_t = [\mathbf{h}_1, \mathbf{h}_2, \cdots, \mathbf{h}_m]$, where $\mathbf{h}_i = \text{concat}\left(\overrightarrow{\mathbf{h}_i}, \overleftarrow{\mathbf{h}_{m-i+1}}\right)$. The hidden states will be used as the feature vector of nodes in the subsequent modules for spatial encoder and temporal features for stroke segmentation.

8.3.2.1.3   Spatial Encoder

There is uncertainty in the reliability of sequential features; e.g., two temporally adjacent strokes may belong to the end of one object and the start of another object, respectively. In order to compensate for the probability of wrong classification caused by SeqE, further consider spatial information in this module.

SpaE mainly learns the correlations between different strokes at spatial level by GCN. Given a scene sketch, construct a scene sketch graph $G = (V, E)$ to extract the spatial features of strokes, where $V = \{v_i\}$ and $E = \{e_{ij}\}$ are vertices and edges of graph G, respectively. Vertex v_i denotes stroke S_i, and an edge e_{ij} links each pair of vertices and denotes the spatial correlation between strokes S_i and S_j.

Given two vertices v_i and v_j of the graph, define an edge $e_{ij} \in \{0,1\}$ according to their spatial proximity; i.e., $e_{ij} = 1$ if the bounding box $B(S_i)$ of stroke S_i contains part of stroke S_j or vice versa:

$$
e_{ij} = \begin{cases} 1 & \left| B(S_i) \bigcap b(S_j) \neq \varnothing \text{ or } B(S_j) \bigcap b(S_i) \neq \varnothing \right. \\ 0 & \left| \text{otherwise} \right. \end{cases} \tag{8.25}
$$

where $B(\cdot)$ is the bounding box of a stroke, and $b(\cdot)$ is the set of points in a stroke. $\mathbf{E}$ is the matrix that represents edges.

For each vertex, get a fused feature $\mathbf{h}_i$ by concatenating forward and backward sequential features of stroke S_i. To extract the spatial features among strokes, adopt four graph convolution layers similar to (Zheng, 2017) to learn spatial features $\mathbf{P}^{(l+1)}$ by propagating features between adjacent vertices, where input the feature $\mathbf{P}^{(l)}$ of the previous layer and the adjacency matrix. Formally,

$$
\mathbf{P}^{(0)} = \{\mathbf{h}_i\}_{i=1}^m \tag{8.26}
$$

$$
\mathbf{P}^{(l+1)} = \text{ReLU}\left(\tilde{\mathbf{A}} \mathbf{P}^{(l)} \mathbf{W}^{(l)}\right) \tag{8.27}
$$

where $\tilde{\mathbf{A}} = \mathbf{E} + \mathbf{I}$ is the adjacency matrix, $\mathbf{I}$ is an identity matrix, and $\mathbf{W}^{(l)}$ is a learnable weight matrix.

8.3.2.1.4   Stroke Segmentation

After conducting the above two encoders, fuse the learned sequential and spatial features of strokes, which can be used to predict the class label of each stroke. Specifically, first get the fused feature $\mathbf{R}_i$ by concatenating the output feature of the GCN's last layer and two global features of BiLSTM since the transformation of GCN may lead to loss of sequential information. Then, $\mathbf{R}_i$ is further fed into a fully connected layer and SoftMax for stroke classification. Formally,

$$
\hat{Y}_i = \text{softmax}\left(fc(\mathbf{R}_i)\right) \tag{8.28}
$$

$$\mathbf{R}_i = \mathrm{concat}\left(\mathbf{P}, \overrightarrow{\mathbf{h}_m}, \overleftarrow{\mathbf{h}_m}\right) \tag{8.29}$$

where $fc(\cdot)$ is the fully connected layer.

8.3.2.1.5 Loss Function

Adopt a cross-entropy loss function for sketch stroke segmentation as follows:

$$\mathrm{Loss} = -\frac{1}{m}\sum_{i=1}^{m} w_c \cdot Y_i \cdot \log\left(\hat{Y}_i\right) \tag{8.30}$$

where Y_i is the ground truth label, and $\hat{Y}_i$ denotes the probability of the stroke segmentation prediction. In order to address the long-tailed distribution of each class, adopt a different weight w_c for each class c.

8.3.2.2 Fine-grained Image Retrieval Based on Sketch

With the growing popularity of touch-screen devices, Sketch-Based Image Retrieval (SBIR) has become an important research topic. People prefer to use more natural manners, such as sketching on the touch screen, to press their intention when retrieving images or videos.

Most existing SBIR methods are category or object level, as illustrated in Figure 8.12, which aim at retrieving the images belonging to a specific category or containing the target objects given a sketch query. However, a large portion of real-world images are scene level, while very few studies have concentrated on scene-level SBIR problem.

Existing scene-level SBIR works aim at retrieving an image of the same scene category (e.g., bedroom, forest, and ballroom) as the query scene sketch (Szegedy et al., 2016) (see the bottom left part of Figure 8.12). These methods, together with those

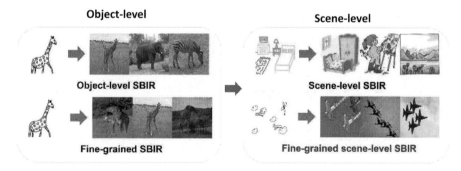

FIGURE 8.12 Illustration of the whole spectrum of SBIR problems. The proposed method, focusing on retrieving the fine-grained scene-level images satisfying the user's specific requirements via a free-hand sketch, is in stark contrast to those of object-level SBIR methods (Castrejon et al., 2016; Lin et al., 2020) and those focusing on retrieving scene-level images of the same scene class (Xie et al., 2019).

text- or image-based retrieval methods, are not able to efficiently retrieve image with specific scene content that user desires, such as searching a target image having a few airplanes with specific poses and relative size, as shown in the bottom right part of Figure 8.12. Therefore, an SBIR method focusing on fine-grained scene-level image retrieval is required. Recently, Zou et al. (2018) conducted a preliminary study of fine-grained scene-level SBIR (Gennari et al., 2005). However, the retrieval method used is largely a pilot study, which is built upon an object-level SBIR model, and the images are all cartoon images.

In this chapter, a new GCN-based architecture named SceneSketcher-v2 is introduced for fine-grained scene-level SBIR, where multimodal scene information is utilized, including global layout, category-level semantic attributes, and instance-level visual features. The GCN model is trained in an end-to-end manner through a triplet training process. Then, an adaptive graph convolutional module is adopted to model the spatial and semantic correlations between object categories, which increases the flexibility of the model for graph feature learning.

The framework of this network is illustrated in Figure 8.13, which mainly consists of a graph generation module, an adaptive graph convolution module, and a triplet similarity module. The overall network extracts feature embeddings of scene sketches and images and feeds them to a triplet ranking loss to enforce that the distance in the feature space reflects how close scene sketches and images are in terms of global layout, appearance, and semantic information. In order to model the key scene context in fine-grained scene-level SBIR, adopt adaptive GCNs as the graph encoders, which integrate the hierarchical information in scene sketches and images, including global scene visual features, global layout, semantic correlations between object categories, and projected features of visual and location features of each object category.

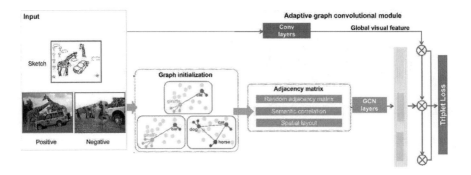

FIGURE 8.13 Framework of the proposed SceneSketcher-v2. The network mainly consists of a graph generator, an adaptive graph encoder module, and a triplet loss for training. First, construct graphs for the input scene sketch and the images and then utilize the adaptive GCNs to encode the graph features. Finally, use triplet loss to train the network.

8.3.2.2.1 Graph Initialization

Employ a weighted, undirected scene graph to model the multimodal scene information, including global layout, the semantic correlation, and the visual appearance of the object instances. The scene graph can be formulated as $G = (N, E)$, where $N = \{n_i\}$ is the node set, $E = \{e_{i,j}\}$ is the edge set, and $e_{i,j} = (n_i, n_j)$ is the edge connecting nodes n_i and n_j. The category set of the nodes in the graph is denoted as $C = \{c_i\}$, where c_i is the category label of node n_i.

8.3.2.2.1.1 Node Construction

Figure 8.14 illustrates the graph node initialization process. Given an object category c_i, construct a corresponding node n_i by integrating the characteristics of all the instances $\{o_{ij}\}$ from the same object category c_i. There are two types of information in each node n_i, i.e., the visual features v_i and the spatial position p_i. Specifically, resize the bounding boxes of the instances to a fixed size of 128×128 and adopt Inception-V3 (Kipf and Welling, 2017) to extract a 2,048-d visual feature v_{ij} for each instance. Then, concatenate the visual feature v_{ij} of instance o_{ij} with its spatial position p_{ij} (i.e., the coordinates of the upper left and bottom right corners of its bounding box). Finally, for each graph node n_i representing an object category, get a 2,052-d fused feature x_i by fusing the characteristics of instances $\{o_{ij}\}$ with the same category c_i via a perception layer (see Figure 8.14). In the experiment, when the number of instances in a certain category is more than three, choose the top three instances with the max sizes to construct the node for this category.

8.3.2.2.1.2 Edge Construction

For each category node n_i, define its position p_i by computing the coordinates of the center point of the bounding boxes of all instances in the category c_i. Each node position p_i is denoted as a 2-d vector, and the coordinates are normalized to $(0, 1)$. Given two nodes n_i and n_j with positions p_i and p_j, define the edge weight $A_{i,j} \in (0, 1)$ between them based on the normalized Euclidean distance as follows:

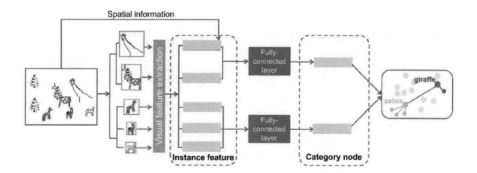

FIGURE 8.14 Illustration of the graph node construction, where each node represents an object category. For each object instance from the same category, concatenate the extracted visual feature and its spatial position. Then, get a graph node with a 2,052-d fused feature for each object category by integrating the features of all the object instances from the same category through a fully connected layer.

$$A_{i,j} = 1 - D_{i,j} \tag{8.31}$$

where $D_{i,j} = p_j - p_{i2}$ is the Euclidean distance of the spatial positions of nodes n_i and n_j.

8.3.2.2.2 Graph Convolutional Networks

After graph construction, adopt GCNs to learn node-level representations. The lth layer of a GCN takes a feature matrix $\mathbf{H}^{l-1}$ and the corresponding adjacency matrix $\mathbf{A} = \{A_{ij}\}$ as inputs and learns a function $f(\cdot, \cdot)$ to extract features on a graph $G = (N, E)$. The lth layer of the GCN can be formulated as

$$\mathbf{H}^{(0)} = \{x_i\}_{i=1}^n \tag{8.32}$$

$$\mathbf{H}^{(l)} = f\left(\mathbf{H}^{(l-1)}, \mathbf{A}\right), \, l > 1 \tag{8.33}$$

Then, adopt the propagation rule introduced in Hu et al. (2022), and the feature extraction function $f(\cdot, \cdot)$ can be written as

$$f\left(\mathbf{H}^{(l)}, \mathbf{A}\right) = \sigma\left(\hat{\mathbf{D}}^{-\frac{1}{2}} \hat{\mathbf{A}} \hat{\mathbf{D}}^{-\frac{1}{2}} \mathbf{H}^{(l)} \mathbf{W}^{(l)}\right) \tag{8.34}$$

where $\sigma(\cdot)$ is the leaky ReLU activation function, $\hat{\mathbf{A}} = \mathbf{A} + \mathbf{I}$, $\hat{\mathbf{D}}$ is the diagonal node degree matrix of $\hat{\mathbf{A}}$, and $\mathbf{W}^{(l)}$ is a weight matrix to be learned.

8.3.2.2.3 Adaptive Graph Convolutional Module

Inspired by the spatial attention module in 2SA-GCN (Zhang et al., 2020) and the temporal attention module in STA-GCN, use an adaptive graph convolution module with a powerful attention mechanism for the fine-grained scene-level SBIR task. In order to integrate different aspects of graph structures, use the sum of three adjacency matrices as the adjacency matrix $\mathbf{A}$. The construction process of the adjacency matrices is as follows:

1. Use the original spatial graph adjacency matrix as $\mathbf{A}_1$, which denotes the category-level characteristics and spatial layout of the scene sketch;
2. $\mathbf{A}_2$ represents the semantic correlation of the category labels. Specifically, the category label c_i of each node is encoded as a 300-d vector $\tilde{c}_i$ by Word2Vec (Collomosse et al., 2009). Use the cosine distance between them to model the correlation of the two nodes;
3. $\mathbf{A}_3$ is a trainable matrix. During training, the model can learn a specific graph that can help achieve better performance of fine-grained scene-level task on a particular dataset.

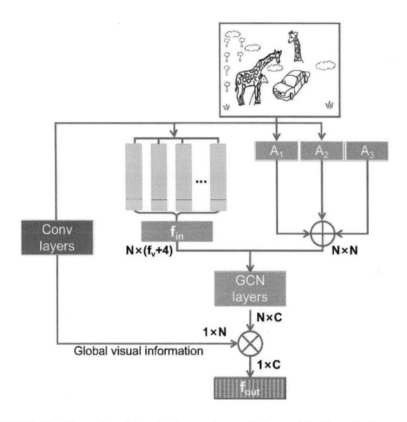

FIGURE 8.15 Illustration of the adaptive graph convolution module. Given the input scene sketch, embed it into a $1 \times C$ feature f_{out} with the adaptive graph convolution module by integrating the global visual feature, the fused feature f_{in} of each category, and the graph adjacency matrices $\{A_i\}_{i=1}^3$ of categories. N is the number of nodes in the graph, C is the output dimension of the GCN layers, and f_v is the size of instances' visual feature extracted by the convolutional layers.

Figure 8.15 illustrates the architecture of the adaptive graph convolutional layer. Given the input scene sketch, first get a graph feature map f_{in} of $N \times (f_v + 4)$-d via the node construction module, where f_v denotes the size of the extracted feature of the visual feature extraction network, and extract a $1 \times N$ global visual feature of the whole scene sketch using Inception-V3. Then, use graph convolutional layers to embed f_{in} with the sum of the proposed three adjacent matrices into an $N \times C$ graph feature. Finally, the $N \times C$ graph feature and the $1 \times N$ global visual feature are multiplied into a scene-level feature vector of the size $1 \times C$.

8.3.2.2.4 Loss Function

Use triplet loss to update the fine-grained scene-level SBIR framework. The input of the SceneSketcher-v2 is a triplet (S, I^+, I^-), where S is a scene sketch, I^+ is the corresponding image of S, and I^- is an image of a different scene. The triplet loss L_{tri} of a given triple (S, I^+, I^-) can be computed by

$$L_{tri} = \max\left(d\left(S,I^{+}\right) - d\left(S,I^{-}\right) + m, 0\right) \qquad (8.35)$$

where $d(\cdot, \cdot)$ is the Euclidean distance in the embedding space, and m is a margin between the anchor-positive distance and the anchor-negative distance, which is set to 0.4 in the experiments.

8.3.2.3   Scene-Level Video Retrieval Based on Sketch

Free-hand sketches are effective of describing fine-grained and intuitional information and have been used to search videos since 2009 (Hu and Collomosse, 2010), where the sketches were combined with motion vectors to model the appearance and motion features in videos. Traditional sketch-based video retrieval (SBVR) works (Hu et al., 2012, 2013; James and Collomosse, 2014) study the coarse-grained video retrieval task using sparse lines and vague contours as queries, and video details (e.g., object size, appearance and pose, and background elements) are neglected (see Figure 8.16a). More recently, Xu et al. (Xu et al., 2021) carried out the instance-level Fine-Grained (FG) SBVR task, which still overlooked the presence of multiple objects and scene context of background information in the real-world videos (see Figure 8.16b).

Scene-level fine-grained SBVR problem is first studied. It aims at retrieving a target video with a hand-drawn scene sketch called storyboard sketch, which contains multiple foreground instances that appear in different video frames and background elements. The sketch is depicted with more fine-grained details (i.e., appearance, size, and pose) to support fine-grained scene-level SBVR (see Figure 8.16c). This is challenging for two aspects: (1) The inherent domain gap becomes even larger between sketches and videos, as sketches only contain sparse strokes, and there are dense color and spatial information in videos. (2) A mechanism has to be delicately

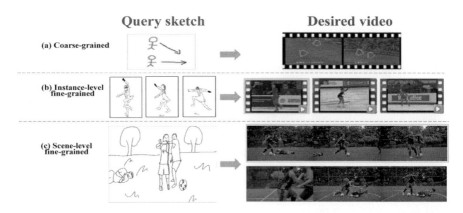

FIGURE 8.16   The comparison of different types of sketch-based video retrieval (SBVR): (a) coarse-grained sketch without appearance details, infeasible for accurate retrieval; (b) fine-grained sketch(es) without background elements, limited to single instance; (c) fine-grained scene-level sketch, providing sufficient visual descriptions for accurate video match.

designed to model the dynamic temporal information in videos using static scene sketches.

Therefore, a novel fine-grained scene-level video retrieval solution is introduced, which uses a single storyboard sketch as query input and designing a SQ-GCN (Sketch Query Graph Convolutional Network) structure to model semantic and visual correlation between two modalities of videos and sketches. Then, an adaptive video sampling strategy is used to reduce the computational cost and improve the efficiency of video encoding.

Firstly, the keyframe-level sketch–video pairs are extracted and used to train a sketch–image correlation model, which can be used for selecting the most relevant video frames, given a storyboard sketch query. Afterward, category and appearance graphs are constructed for both sketch and video, where position features are also encoded. Through GCN for sketch encoding and ST-GCN for video encoding, fine-grained cross-modal triplet loss is used to train the model. Figure 8.17 shows the overview of the model, which consists of three modules: storyboard sketch encoding, video encoding, and feature matching.

8.3.2.3.1   Storyboard Sketch Encoding

- Graph Construction. Construct a category graph $G_{s,c}$ and an appearance graph $G_{s,a}$ for a storyboard sketch S. Both graphs contain n instance nodes g_s^i $(i = 1, 2, ..., n)$ to represent instance-level information. Additionally, the appearance graph $G_{s,a}$ has a scene node $g_s^{(0)}$ to represent the global appearance. The scene node is separated from the instance nodes during feature updating via graph convolutions. Use normalized Distance-IoU (Xiao, n.d.) computed with their bounding boxes to define the edge weight $A_{i,j} \in (0,1)$.
- Node Representation. The node features in $G_{s,c}$ are initialized with category features and positional embeddings, while those in $G_{s,a}$ are appearance features with positional embeddings. Appearance features f_a are obtained into

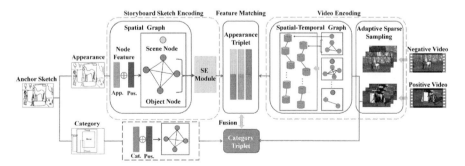

FIGURE 8.17   The pipeline of the SQ-GCN for fine-grained scene-level SBVR with storyboard sketches. The network includes three components, i.e., storyboard sketch encoding, video encoding, and feature matching. Firstly, use an adaptive video frame sampling strategy to select relevant video samples. Then, construct appearance graphs (appearance and position features) and category graphs (category and position features without scene node) for both sketch and video. Through GCN for sketch encoding and ST-GCN for video encoding, embed sketch and video into a common feature space and use a triplet network for training.

2,048-d by pretrained GoogLeNet Inception-V3, and category features f_c are encoded into 768-d via pretrained Bert model (Vaswani et al., 2017). For layout information encoding, use sine and cosine functions of different frequencies (Carion et al., 2020; Hu et al., 2018) to obtain absolute position features f_p and then add it to f_a and f_c, respectively.

- Graph Encoding. Use a two-layer GCN (Hu et al., 2022) for feature embedding; the node features F_s^{l+1} of graph Gs (including $G_{s,c}$ and $G_{s,a}$) are updated in the lth layer as follows:

$$F_s^{l+1} = ReLU\left(AW^l F_s^l\right) \tag{8.36}$$

where A is the normalized adjacency matrix, and W^l is the trainable weights of the lth layer.

Then, use the Squeeze-and-Excitation (SE) module to obtain the encoded local features by treating all the instance nodes' features as different channels:

$$F_s^l = \frac{1}{n}\sum_{i=1}^{n}\sigma\left(W_{se}^{(1)}ReLU\left(W_{se}^{(0)}F_s^{(i)}\right)\right) \tag{8.37}$$

where σ is the Sigmoid activation function, and W_{se} is the weight matrix of the SE module.

Finally, concatenate $F_{s,a}^l$ with the scene node's features $F_{s,a}^{(0)}$ to get appearance features $F_{s,a}$ of the appearance graph:

$$F_{s,a} = \left(F_{s,a}^{(0)}; F_{s,a}^l\right) \tag{8.38}$$

8.3.2.3.2   Video Encoding

- Adaptive Video Frame Sampling. One of the most challenging part of video encoding is the massive temporal redundancy of video data. To avoid frame-by-frame processing, which requires huge computational cost, propose an adaptive video frame sampling method (see Figure 8.18). Specifically, train a sketch–image correlation model for cross-modal semantic similarity analysis, which contains two fully connected layers. Utilize the sketch–image correspondence to train the model with triplet loss, where each keyframe sketch uniquely corresponds to a single video frame. During inference, the correlation model uses the extracted appearance features of storyboard sketches as input and predicts the most relevant k frames in a video.

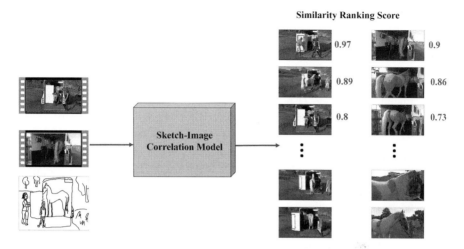

FIGURE 8.18 Illustration of adaptive video sampling module. The module can adaptively sample the most visually relevant frames, given a storyboard sketch as query.

- Graph Construction. Given k sampled video frames, extract the spatial and temporal features by constructing spatial–temporal graphs. Extract appearance features f_a by a ResNet-152 (Sun et al., 2018) network and construct spatial graphs similar with the storyboard sketch for each frame. For the appearance stream, fuse the spatial instance features through SE module into a single temporal instance node and build two temporal graphs G_T^S and G_T^I, which consist of each frame's scene node $v_t^s (t = 1,...,T)$ and temporal instance node $v_t^I (t = 1,...,T)$, respectively. The nodes are connected in temporal order. For the category stream, only construct a temporal graph with instance nodes.
- Video Graph Encoding. Encode each spatial and temporal video graph with the Storyboard Sketch Encoder and obtain the category and appearance embeddings $F_{v,c}$ and $F_{v,a}$ of the video.

8.3.2.3.3 Feature Matching

- Loss Function. After obtaining storyboard sketch features F_s and video features F_v, adopt a fine-grained cross-modal triplet loss where an input triplet contains the features of the query sketch F_{s_i}, the features of the corresponding video F_{v_i}, and the features of the hard negative video $F_{v_{i,h}}$. The loss function is denoted as

$$L = \frac{1}{b} \sum_{i=1}^{b} L_{s_i}^{v_i,v_{i,h}}$$ (8.39)

$$L_{s_i}^{v_i,v_{i,h}} = \max\left(0, d\left(F_{s_i}, F_{v_i}\right) - d\left(F_{s_i}, F_{v_{i,h}}\right) + \Delta\right)$$ (8.40)

$$v_{i,h} = \operatorname{argmin}_{v_j} d\left(F_{s_i}, F_{v_j}\right), \ i \neq j \tag{8.41}$$

where $d(\cdot, \cdot)$ is the Euclidean distance function, Δ is the margin between the positive and negative pairs, and b is the batch size.

- Inference. During testing, sort the candidate video pools based on the Euclidean distance D between sketch features F_s and video features F_v. Utilizing both category and appearance information, fuse the two distances D_c and D_a with appropriate weights:

$$\alpha D_c + (1 - \alpha) D_a \tag{8.42}$$

where α is determined during experiments.

8.3.3 Case Study – Sketch-based Interactive Application in Smart Service

8.3.3.1 Interactive Sketch Segmentation System

The scene sketch segmentation method can divide the objects with different drawing levels robustly in the sketch. Each extracted sketch object provides material for the user's painting creation. In this work, we built a prototype application to support users to quickly obtain sketch instance materials from scene sketches. As shown in Figure 8.19, both high and low drawing level sketches can achieve good segmentation results, and different color sketch instances can be copied and combined to form a new scene sketch.

8.3.3.2 Sketch Extraction and Reuse for Interactive Scene Sketch Composition

For most of the users with no sketching skills (nonprofessional users), it is difficult to draw an object sketch in a short time, and the obstacles become even greater when drawing a scene containing multiple objects. Thus, effective reuse of existing sketches and quick composition of input sketches for sketch-related applications bring a new perspective, which is an important problem for investigation. Large amounts

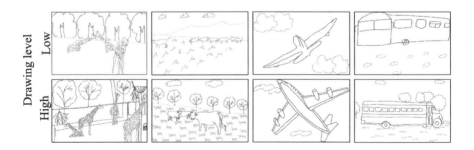

FIGURE 8.19 Visualization of representative segmentation results at different drawing skill levels.

of object sketches exist as parts of scene sketches, e.g., in storyboards, animations, comics, or illustrations in story books, where overlapping and occlusion often occur, making direct reuse difficult.

To address the problem mentioned above, an interactive scene sketch processing and composition system, named SketchMaker, is introduced here. SketchMaker can extract and reuse the existing sketch data to help nonprofessional users create new scene sketches, providing a convenient way to generate input sketch for sketch-oriented applications such as SBIR. With SketchMaker, users can easily create scene sketches and make full use of the existing sketch data.

The user interface of the SketchMaker contains two pages (see Figure 8.20), the Sketch Data Extraction Page and the Scene Sketch Composition and Image Retrieval Page. Users are able to conduct sketch extraction or scene sketch composition by switching between the two pages (Figure 8.20a). The interface is developed based on a website that can be adapted to various devices such as mobile phone, laptop,

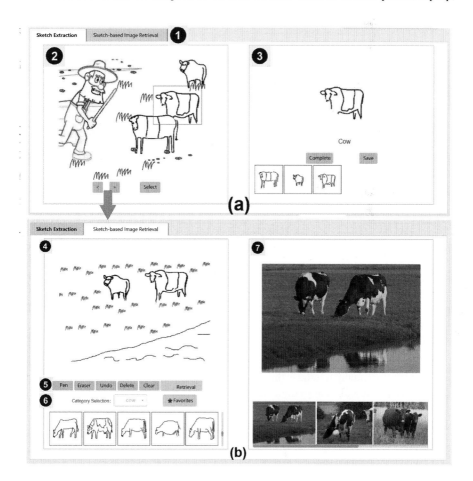

FIGURE 8.20 The user interface of the SketchMaker contains two pages, the Sketch Data Extraction Page and the Scene Sketch Composition and Image Retrieval Page.

and digital whiteboard. SketchMaker supports inputs with fingers or pen on touch screens as well as mouse on desktops.

In the Sketch Data Extraction Page, when users are reading a list of scene sketches in a storyboard, the scene sketch display panel displays the current scene sketch, and users are able to select their interested sketch object elements via drawing a rectangular box surrounding the object (Figure 8.20b). Sketch objects selected by users may exist occlusion or overlapping; then, the sketch object extraction tools panel (Figure 8.20c) can automatically complete the sketch and save it to the users' personal favorites.

In the Scene Sketch Composition and Image Retrieval Page, the scene sketch composition canvas (Figure 8.20d) supports user operations of compositing scene sketches, where dragging, moving, zooming in /out, and rotating operations of sketch elements are offered.

The scene sketch editing tools panel (Figure 8.20e) contains Pen, Eraser, Undo, Delete, Clear, and Retrieval (from left to right), supporting creation and editing of sketch elements. Users can query an image with the created scene sketch by clicking the Retrieval button.

The sketch object browsing and selection panel lists sketch object elements selected or suggested by the system (Figure 8.20f).

The image retrieval result display panel (Figure 8.20g) shows the retrieved images of the system, where the Top 1 result is shown at the top, and other similar images are listed at the bottom.

As illustrated in Figure 8.21, the main functions of the SketchMaker system are as follows:

1. Extracting objects from existing scene sketches: This function enables SketchMaker to help users obtain and save their interested object sketches from scene sketches in an interactive manner. This is done by the user selecting an interested sketch element from an existing scene sketch, and then the system completes the corrupted sketch object.
2. Scene sketch composition: This function enables users to create new scene sketches in a fast and convenient way. Users are allowed to reuse existing sketch objects through dragging, moving, zooming in/out, rotating operations, etc. Several drawing tools, e.g., pen, eraser, and undo, are also offered for drawing new objects.
3. Image retrieval using scene sketch inputs: This function allows users to query images using their composited scene sketches as inputs. Users can also continuously adjust the scene sketch to get a more appropriate image consistent with that in their mind.

8.3.3.3   Interactive Sketch-based Video Retrieval System

Compared to images, videos are more complex with abundant temporal information and high redundant content. It is necessary to develop an accurate retrieval system for videos.

FIGURE 8.21   An example drawing scenario of using SketchMaker. When the user browses a scene sketch, SketchMaker enables sketch object extraction via sketch completion (a) operations. Then, the user can compose a sketch scene by selecting from personal favorites or database of sketch elements (b). The user can further use the created scene sketch as query input to retrieve an image (c). Moreover, users are able to continuously adjust the sketch composition via selecting different sketch elements from the database for further image retrieval (d and e).

Sketch is a natural input modal that facilitates great creative freedom; thus, fine-grained scene-level SBVR has a wide range of applications, such as finding videos in a cellphone album and collecting video materials for video creation. This section briefly introduces a prototype system that supports interactive fine-grained scene-level SBVR on a PC or a tablet.

The user interface (Figure 8.22) provides two ways of sketch creation, including sketch composition and sketch drawing. For sketch composition, users change the category options (Figure 8.22b) and select sketch materials existing in the dataset from the sketch element gallery (Figure 8.22c). Then, they can compose refined scene sketches by resizing, dragging, and rotating sketch materials on the sketch canvas (Figure 8.22a). For sketch drawing, users use pen and eraser (Figure 8.22d) to depict the desired scene content. The retrieval results are displayed (Figure 8.22e), and users can watch the retrieved videos by clicking them.

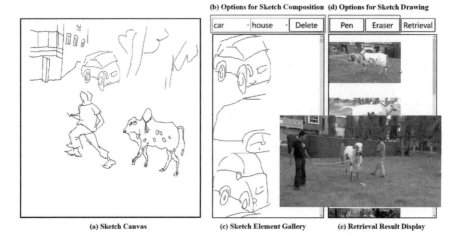

(a) Sketch Canvas   **(c) Sketch Element Gallery**   **(e) Retrieval Result Display**

FIGURE 8.22 The user interface of the fine-grained video retrieval system with scene sketch, which supports storyboard sketch depiction (including sketch composition and sketch drawing) and retrieval results display.

8.3.4 SUMMARY

As sketching is a natural and intuitive form of communication for a human being to express their concepts or ideas, and scene-level images and videos exist in a large portion of the image and video data in real world, this chapter studies the scene-level sketch semantic segmentation, sketch-based image retrieval, and sketch-based video retrieval tasks. These methods are beneficial for sketch-based intelligent interaction and greatly promote the development of smart services.

REFERENCES

Adolphs, R. (2002). Recognizing emotion from facial expressions: Psychological and neurological mechanisms. *Behavioral and Cognitive Neuroscience Reviews, 1*(1), 21–62. https://doi.org/10.1177/1534582302001001003

Ayanoğlu, H., & Duarte, E. (2019). *Emotional Design in Human-Robot Interaction.* Chem: Springer.

Bartram, L., Patra, A., & Stone, M. (2017). Affective color in visualization. *Proceedings of the 2017 CHI Conference on Human Factors in Computing Systems, Denver, Colorado, USA, 2017-May,* pp. 1364–1374. https://doi.org/10.1145/3025453.3026041

Bekkedal, M. Y. V., Rossi, J., & Panksepp, J. (2011). Human brain EEG indices of emotions: Delineating responses to affective vocalizations by measuring frontal theta event-related synchronization. *Neuroscience and Biobehavioral Reviews, 35*(9), 1959–1970. https://doi.org/10.1016/j.neubiorev.2011.05.001

Boekaerts, M. (2011). Emotions, emotion regulation, and self-regulation of learning: Center for the study of learning and instruction, Leiden university, the Netherlands, and Ku Leuven. In *Handbook of Self-Regulation of Learning and Performance* (pp. 422–439). London: Routledge.

Boy, G. A. (2017). The handbook of human-machine interaction. In G. A. Boy (Ed.), *The Handbook of Human-Machine Interaction: A Human-Centered Design Approach*. Boca Raton, FL: CRC Press. https://doi.org/10.1201/9781315557380

Brath, R., & Banissi, E. (2016). Using typography to expand the design space of data visualization. *She Ji: The Journal of Design, Economics, and Innovation*, 2(1), 59–87. https://doi.org/10.1016/j.sheji.2016.05.003

Brehmer, M., Lee, B., Bach, B., Riche, N. H., & Munzner, T. (2017). Timelines revisited: A design space and considerations for expressive storytelling. *IEEE Transactions on Visualization and Computer Graphics*, 23(9), 2151–2164. https://doi.org/10.1109/TVCG.2016.2614803

Carion, N., Massa, F., Synnaeve, G., Usunier, N., Kirillov, A., & Zagoruyko, S. (2020). End-to-end object detection with transformers. In *Lecture Notes in Computer Science (including subseries Lecture Notes in Artificial Intelligence and Lecture Notes in Bioinformatics): Vol. 12346 LNCS* (pp. 213–229). https://doi.org/10.1007/978-3-030-58452-8_13

Castrejon, L., Aytar, Y., Vondrick, C., Pirsiavash, H., & Torralba, A. (2016). Learning aligned cross-modal representations from weakly aligned data. *Proceedings of the IEEE Computer Society Conference on Computer Vision and Pattern Recognition, Las Vegas, NV, USA, 2016-December*, pp. 2940–2949. https://doi.org/10.1109/CVPR.2016.321

Cernea, D., Weber, C., Ebert, A., & Kerren, A. (2013). Emotion scents: A method of representing user emotions on GUI widgets. In P. C. Wong, D. L. Kao, M. C. Hao, C. Chen, & C. G. Healey (Eds.), *Visualization and Data Analysis 2013* (Vol. 8654, p. 86540). France: SPIE https://doi.org/10.1117/12.2001261

Chen, S., & Jin, Q. (2016). Multi-modal conditional attention fusion for dimensional emotion prediction. *Proceedings of the 24th ACM International Conference on Multimedia, Amsterdam, The Netherlands*, pp. 571–575. https://doi.org/10.1145/2964284.2967286

Chen, T., Cheng, M. M., Hu, S. M., Tan, P., & Shamir, A. (2009). Sketch2Photo: Internet image montage. *ACM Transactions on Graphics*, 28(5), 1–10. https://doi.org/10.1145/1618452.1618470

Collomosse, J. P., McNeill, G., & Qian, Y. (2009). Storyboard sketches for content based video retrieval. *Proceedings of the IEEE International Conference on Computer Vision, Kyoto, Japan* pp. 245–252. https://doi.org/10.1109/ICCV.2009.5459258

Davidson, P. R., Jones, R. D., & Peiris, M. T. R. (2007). EEG-based lapse detection with high temporal resolution. *IEEE Transactions on Biomedical Engineering*, 54(5), 832–839. https://doi.org/10.1109/TBME.2007.893452

Feng, C., Bartram, L., & Riecke, B. E. (2014). Evaluating affective features of 3D motionscapes. *Proceedings of the ACM Symposium on Applied Perception, Vancouver, British Columbia, Canada*, pp. 23–30. https://doi.org/10.1145/2628257.2628264

Feng, C., Bartram, L., & Gromala, D. (2017). Beyond data: Abstract motionscapes as affective visualization. *Leonardo*, 50(2), 205–206. https://doi.org/10.1162/LEON_a_01229

Gennari, L., Kara, L. B., Stahovich, T. F., & Shimada, K. (2005). Combining geometry and domain knowledge to interpret hand-drawn diagrams. *Computers & Graphics*, 29(4), 547–562. https://doi.org/10.1016/j.cag.2005.05.007

Graves, A., & Schmidhuber, J. (2005). Framewise phoneme classification with bidirectional LSTM networks. *Proceedings of the International Joint Conference on Neural Networks*, 4(5–6), 2047–2052. https://doi.org/10.1109/IJCNN.2005.1556215

Gross, J. J. (1998). The emerging field of emotion regulation: An integrative review. *Review of General Psychology*, 2(3), 271–299. https://doi.org/10.1037/1089-2680.2.3.271

Guo, H. W., Huang, Y. S., Chien, J. C., & Shieh, J. S. (2015). Short-term analysis of heart rate variability for emotion recognition via a wearable ECG device. *2015 International Conference on Intelligent Informatics and Biomedical Sciences (ICIIBMS), Okinawa, Japan*, pp. 262–265. https://doi.org/10.1109/ICIIBMS.2015.7439542

Hao, Y., Wang, D., & Budd, J. G. (2015). Design of intelligent emotion feedback to assist users regulate emotions: Framework and principles. *2015 International Conference on Affective Computing and Intelligent Interaction (ACII)*, Xi'an, China, pp. 938–943. https://doi.org/10.1109/ACII.2015.7344687

Harmon-Jones, E. (2004). Contributions from research on anger and cognitive dissonance to understanding the motivational functions of asymmetrical frontal brain activity. *Biological Psychology, 67*(1–2), 51–76. https://doi.org/10.1016/j.biopsycho.2004.03.003

Hu, R., & Collomosse, J. (2010). Motion-sketch based video retrieval using a trellis levenshtein distance. *2010 20th International Conference on Pattern Recognition*, Istanbul, Turkey, pp. 121–124. https://doi.org/10.1109/ICPR.2010.38

Hu, R., James, S., & Collomosse, J. (2012). Annotated free-hand sketches for video retrieval using object semantics and motion. In *Lecture Notes in Computer Science (including subseries Lecture Notes in Artificial Intelligence and Lecture Notes in Bioinformatics): Vol. 7131 LNCS* (pp. 473–484). https://doi.org/10.1007/978-3-642-27355-1_44

Hu, R., James, S., Wang, T., & Collomosse, J. (2013). Markov random fields for sketch based video retrieval. *Proceedings of the 3rd ACM Conference on International Conference on Multimedia Retrieval - ICMR '13*, Dallas, Texas, USA, pp. 279. https://doi.org/10.1145/2461466.2461510

Hu, J., Shen, L., & Sun, G. (2018). Squeeze-and-excitation networks. *Proceedings of the IEEE Conference on Computer Vision and Pattern Recognition (CVPR)*, Salt Lake City, UT, USA, pp. 7132–7141.

Hu, Z., Pan, Z., Wang, Q., Yu, L., & Fei, S. (2022). Forward-reverse adaptive graph convolutional networks for skeleton-based action recognition. *Neurocomputing, 492*, 624–636. https://doi.org/10.1016/j.neucom.2021.12.054

Huang, Y., Tang, Y., & Wang, Y. (2015). Emotion map. *Proceedings of the 18th ACM Conference on Computer Supported Cooperative Work & Social Computing*, Vancouver, BC, Canada, pp. 130–142. https://doi.org/10.1145/2675133.2675173

Inventado, P. S., Legaspi, R., Numao, M., & Suarez, M. (2011). Observatory: A tool for recording, annotating and reviewing emotion-related data. *2011 Third International Conference on Knowledge and Systems Engineering*, Hanoi, Vietnam, pp. 261–265. https://doi.org/10.1109/KSE.2011.48

James, S., & Collomosse, J. (2014). Interactive video asset retrieval using sketched queries. *ACM International Conference Proceeding Series*, London, UK, 2014-November, pp. 1–8. https://doi.org/10.1145/2668904.2668940

Keim, D., Andrienko, G., Fekete, J.-D., Görg, C., Kohlhammer, J., & Melançon, G. (2008). Visual analytics: Definition, process, and challenges. In *Information Visualization* (pp. 154–175). Berlin Heidelberg: Springer. https://doi.org/10.1007/978-3-540-70956-5_7

Kipf, T. N., & Welling, M. (2017). Semi-supervised classification with graph convolutional networks. *5th International Conference on Learning Representations, ICLR 2017-Conference Track Proceedings*, Toulon, France.

Kleinsmith, A., & Bianchi-Berthouze, N. (2013). Affective body expression perception and recognition: A survey. *IEEE Transactions on Affective Computing, 4*(1), 15–33. https://doi.org/10.1109/T-AFFC.2012.16

Koelstra, S., Muhl, C., Soleymani, M., Jong-Seok, L., Yazdani, A., Ebrahimi, T., Pun, T., Nijholt, A., & Patras, I. (2012). DEAP: A database for emotion analysis using physiological signals. *IEEE Transactions on Affective Computing, 3*(1), 18–31. https://doi.org/10.1109/T-AFFC.2011.15

Labrecque, L. I., & Milne, G. R. (2012). Exciting red and competent blue: The importance of color in marketing. *Journal of the Academy of Marketing Science, 40*(5), 711–727. https://doi.org/10.1007/s11747-010-0245-y

Lee, J., Kim, S., Kim, S., Park, J., & Sohn, K. (2019). Context-aware emotion recognition networks. *Proceedings of the IEEE/CVF International Conference on Computer Vision*, Seoul, Korea (South), pp. 10143–10152.

Li, Q., & Zhang, T. (2022). Research on multi-source data fusion technology of energy internet. *Electric Drive, 52*(15), 68–73.

Li, X., Song, D., Zhang, P., Hou, Y., & Hu, B. (2017). Deep fusion of multi-channel neurophysiological signal for emotion recognition and monitoring. *International Journal of Data Mining and Bioinformatics, 18*(1), 1–27.

Li, Y., Luo, X., Zheng, Y., Xu, P., & Fu, H. (2017). SweepCanvas: Sketch-based 3D prototyping on an RGB-D image. *UIST 2017- Proceedings of the 30th Annual ACM Symposium on User Interface Software and Technology*, Québec City, Canada, pp. 387–399. https://doi.org/10.1145/3126594.3126611

Li, Y., Zheng, W., Cui, Z., Zhang, T., & Zong, Y. (2018). A novel neural network model based on cerebral hemispheric asymmetry for EEG emotion recognition. *Proceedings of the Twenty-Seventh International Joint Conference on Artificial Intelligence*, Stockholm, 2018-July, pp. 1561–1567. https://doi.org/10.24963/ijcai.2018/216

Lin, Y., Guo, J., Chen, Y., Yao, C., & Ying, F. (2020). It is your turn: Collaborative ideation with a co-creative robot through sketch. *Proceedings of the 2020 CHI Conference on Human Factors in Computing Systems*, Honolulu, HI, USA, pp. 1–14. https://doi.org/10.1145/3313831.3376258

Liu, Y.-J., Yu, M., Zhao, G., Song, J., Ge, Y., & Shi, Y. (2017). Real-time movie-induced discrete emotion recognition from EEG signals. *IEEE Transactions on Affective Computing, 9*(4), 550–562.

Liu, Z. T., Wu, M., Cao, W. H., Mao, J. W., Xu, J. P., & Tan, G. Z. (2018). Speech emotion recognition based on feature selection and extreme learning machine decision tree. *Neurocomputing, 273*, 271–280. https://doi.org/10.1016/j.neucom.2017.07.050

Lockyer, M., Bartram, L., & Riecke, B. E. (2011). Simple motion textures for ambient affect. *Proceedings - CAe 2011: International Symposium on Computational Aesthetics in Graphics, Visualization, and Imaging*, Vancouver, British Columbia, Canada, pp. 89–96. https://doi.org/10.1145/2030441.2030461

Lotfi, E., & Akbarzadeh, T. M. R. (2014). Practical emotional neural networks. *Neural Networks, 59*, 61–72. https://doi.org/10.1016/j.neunet.2014.06.012

Madden, T. J., Hewett, K., & Roth, M. S. (2000). Managing images in different cultures: A cross-national study of color meanings and preferences. *Journal of International Marketing, 8*(4), 90–107. https://doi.org/10.1509/jimk.8.4.90.19795

Mallin, S. S. V., & Carvalho, H. G. de. (2015). Assistive technology and user-centered design: Emotion as element for innovation. *Procedia Manufacturing, 3*, 5570–5578. https://doi.org/10.1016/j.promfg.2015.07.738

Mao, J., Horan, B., Forbes, H., Smilevski, S., Bucknall, T., Nagle, C., Phillips, D., & Gibson, I. (2017). Application of emotional design to the form redesign of a midwifery training aid. *KnE Engineering, 2*(2), 44. https://doi.org/10.18502/keg.v2i2.594

Mauss, I. B., & Tamir, M. (2014). Emotion goals: How their content, structure, and operation shape emotion regulation. In *Handbook of Emotion Regulation*. New York: Guilford Press.

Mühl, C., Allison, B., Nijholt, A., & Chanel, G. (2014). A survey of affective brain computer interfaces: Principles, state-of-the-art, and challenges. *Brain-Computer Interfaces, 1*(2), 66–84. https://doi.org/10.1080/2326263X.2014.912881

Palacios, A. P., Garcia, J. A., Raffe, W. L., Voigt-Antons, J.-N., Spang, R. P., & Möller, S. (2020). Emotion visualization in virtual reality: An integrative review. CoRR abs/2012.08849.

Pan, S. J., Tsang, I. W., Kwok, J. T., & Yang, Q. (2011). Domain adaptation via transfer component analysis. *IEEE Transactions on Neural Networks, 22*(2), 199–210. https://doi.org/10.1109/TNN.2010.2091281

Pandey, P., & Seeja, K. R. (2019). Subject-independent emotion detection from EEG signals using deep neural network. *Lecture Notes in Networks and Systems*, *56*, 41–46. https://doi.org/10.1007/978-981-13-2354-6_5

Picard, R. W. (2000). *Affective Computing*. Cambridge, MA: MIT Press. https://mitpress.mit.edu/9780262661157/

Picard, R. W., Vyzas, E., & Healey, J. (2001). Toward machine emotional intelligence: Analysis of affective physiological state. *IEEE Transactions on Pattern Analysis and Machine Intelligence*, *23*(10), 1175–1191. https://doi.org/10.1109/34.954607

Piho, L., & Tjahjadi, T. (2020). A mutual information based adaptive windowing of informative EEG for emotion recognition. *IEEE Transactions on Affective Computing*, *11*(4), 722–735. https://doi.org/10.1109/TAFFC.2018.2840973

Qi, F., Yang, X., & Xu, C. (2021). Zero-shot video emotion recognition via multimodal protagonist-aware transformer network. *Proceedings of the 29th ACM International Conference on Multimedia*, Virtual Event, China, pp. 1074–1083.

Quoidbach, J., Gruber, J., Mikolajczak, M., Kogan, A., Kotsou, I., & Norton, M. I. (2014). Emodiversity and the emotional ecosystem. *Journal of Experimental Psychology: General*, *143*(6), 2057–2066. https://doi.org/10.1037/a0038025

Rieffe, C., Oosterveld, P., Miers, A. C., Meerum Terwogt, M., & Ly, V. (2008). Emotion awareness and internalising symptoms in children and adolescents: The emotion awareness questionnaire revised. *Personality and Individual Differences*, *45*(8), 756–761. https://doi.org/10.1016/j.paid.2008.08.001

Ruiz, S., Charleer, S., Urretavizcaya, M., Klerkx, J., Isabel, F. C., & Duval, E. (2016). Supporting learning by considering emotions: Tracking and visualization. A case study. *ACM International Conference Proceeding Series*, Edinburgh, UK, 25–29-April, pp. 254–263. https://doi.org/10.1145/2883851.2883888

Sangkloy, P., Burnell, N., Ham, C., & Hays, J. (2016). The sketchy database. *ACM Transactions on Graphics*, *35*(4), 1–12. https://doi.org/10.1145/2897824.2925954

Schölkopf, B., Smola, A., & Müller, K.-R. (1998). Nonlinear component analysis as a kernel eigenvalue problem. *Neural Computation*, *10*(5), 1299–1319. https://doi.org/10.1162/089976698300017467

Semertzidis, N., Scary, M., Andres, J., Dwivedi, B., Kulwe, Y. C., Zambetta, F., & Mueller, F. F. (2020). Neo-Noumena: Augmenting emotion communication. *Proceedings of the 2020 CHI Conference on Human Factors in Computing Systems, Honolulu, HI, USA*, pp. 1–13. https://doi.org/10.1145/3313831.3376599

Sievers, B., Lee, C., Haslett, W., & Wheatley, T. (2019). A multi-sensory code for emotional arousal. *Proceedings of the Royal Society B*, *286*(1906), 20190513.

Song, T., Zheng, W., Song, P., & Cui, Z. (2020). EEG emotion recognition using dynamical graph convolutional neural networks. *IEEE Transactions on Affective Computing*, *11*(3), 532–541. https://doi.org/10.1109/TAFFC.2018.2817622

Suleri, S., Sermuga Pandian, V. P., Shishkovets, S., & Jarke, M. (2019). Eve: A sketch-based software prototyping workbench. *Extended Abstracts of the 2019 CHI Conference on Human Factors in Computing Systems, Glasgow, Scotland, UK*, pp. 1–6. https://doi.org/10.1145/3290607.3312994

Sun, M.-C., Hsu, S.-H., Yang, M.-C., & Chien, J.-H. (2018). Context-aware cascade attention-based RNN for video emotion recognition. *2018 First Asian Conference on Affective Computing and Intelligent Interaction (ACII Asia)*, Beijing, China, pp. 1–6. https://doi.org/10.1109/ACIIAsia.2018.8470372

Szegedy, C., Vanhoucke, V., Ioffe, S., Shlens, J., & Wojna, Z. (2016). Rethinking the inception architecture for computer vision. *Proceedings of the IEEE Computer Society Conference on Computer Vision and Pattern Recognition*, Las Vegas, NV, USA, 2016-December, pp. 2818–2826. https://doi.org/10.1109/CVPR.2016.308

Tien, L.-C., Chiou, C.-C., & Lee, Y.-S. (2018). Emotional design in multimedia learning: Effects of multidimensional concept maps and animation on affect and learning. *EURASIA Journal of Mathematics, Science and Technology Education, 14*(12), 128–140. https://doi.org/10.29333/ejmste/94229

Tripathi, S., Acharya, S., Sharma, R., Mittal, S., & Bhattacharya, S. (2017). Using deep and convolutional neural networks for accurate emotion classification on DEAP data. *Proceedings of the AAAI Conference on Artificial Intelligence, 31*(2), 4746–4752. https://doi.org/10.1609/aaai.v31i2.19105

Valdez, P., & Mehrabian, A. (1994). Effects of color on emotions. *Journal of Experimental Psychology: General, 123*(4), 394–409. https://doi.org/10.1037/0096-3445.123.4.394

Vaswani, A., Shazeer, N., Parmar, N., Uszkoreit, J., Jones, L., Gomez, A. N., Kaiser, L., & Polosukhin, I. (2017). Attention is all you need. *Advances in Neural Information Processing Systems*, Long Beach, CA, USA, 2017-December, pp. 5999–6009. https://arxiv.org/abs/1706.03762

Wang, F., Lin, S., Li, H., Wu, H., Cai, T., Luo, X., & Wang, R. (2020). Multi-column point-CNN for sketch segmentation. *Neurocomputing, 392*, 50–59. https://doi.org/10.1016/j.neucom.2019.12.117

Wang, X., He, J., Jin, Z., Yang, M., Wang, Y., & Qu, H. (2022). M2Lens: Visualizing and explaining multimodal models for sentiment analysis. *IEEE Transactions on Visualization and Computer Graphics, 28*(1), 802–812. https://doi.org/10.1109/TVCG.2021.3114794

Wen, W., Liu, G., Cheng, N., Wei, J., Shangguan, P., & Huang, W. (2014). Emotion recognition based on multi-variant correlation of physiological signals. *IEEE Transactions on Affective Computing, 5*(2), 126–140. https://doi.org/10.1109/TAFFC.2014.2327617

Wu, X., Qi, Y., Liu, J., & Yang, J. (2018). Sketchsegnet: A RNN model for labeling sketch strokes. *2018 IEEE 28th International Workshop on Machine Learning for Signal Processing (MLSP)*, Aalborg, Denmark, 2018-September, pp. 1–6. https://doi.org/10.1109/MLSP.2018.8516988

Xiao, H. (n.d.). Bert-as-Service. https://github.com/hanxiao/bert-as-service

Xie, Y., Xu, P., & Ma, Z. (2019). Deep zero-shot learning for scene sketch. *2019 IEEE International Conference on Image Processing (ICIP)*, Taipei, Taiwan, 2019-September, pp. 3661–3665. https://doi.org/10.1109/ICIP.2019.8803426

Xu, P., Liu, K., Xiang, T., Hospedales, T. M., Ma, Z., Guo, J., & Song, Y.-Z. (2021). Fine-grained instance-level sketch-based video retrieval. *IEEE Transactions on Circuits and Systems for Video Technology, 31*(5), 1995–2007. https://doi.org/10.1109/TCSVT.2020.3014491

Yang, Y., Wu, Q., Qiu, M., Wang, Y., & Chen, X. (2018). Emotion recognition from multi-channel EEG through parallel convolutional recurrent neural network. *2018 International Joint Conference on Neural Networks (IJCNN)*, Rio de Janeiro, Brazil, 2018-July, pp. 1–7. https://doi.org/10.1109/IJCNN.2018.8489331

Yang, L., Zhuang, J., Fu, H., Wei, X., Zhou, K., & Zheng, Y. (2021). Sketchgnn: Semantic sketch segmentation with graph neural networks. *ACM Transactions on Graphics (TOG), 40*(3), 1–13.

Yu, Q., Liu, F., Song, Y.-Z., Xiang, T., Hospedales, T. M., & Loy, C. C. (2016). Sketch me that shoe. *2016 IEEE Conference on Computer Vision and Pattern Recognition (CVPR)*, Las Vegas, NV, USA, 2016-December, pp. 799–807. https://doi.org/10.1109/CVPR.2016.93

Zeng, H., Shu, X., Wang, Y., Wang, Y., Zhang, L., Pong, T.-C., & Qu, H. (2021). Emotion cues: Emotion-oriented visual summarization of classroom videos. *IEEE Transactions on Visualization and Computer Graphics, 27*(7), 3168–3181. https://doi.org/10.1109/TVCG.2019.2963659

Zhang, S., Huang, Q., Jiang, S., Gao, W., & Tian, Q. (2010). Affective visualization and retrieval for music video. *IEEE Transactions on Multimedia, 12*(6), 510–522. https://doi.org/10.1109/TMM.2010.2059634

Zhang, X., Shen, J., Din, Z. U., Liu, J., Wang, G., & Hu, B. (2019). Multimodal depression detection: Fusion of electroencephalography and paralinguistic behaviors using a novel strategy for classifier ensemble. *IEEE Journal of Biomedical and Health Informatics*, *23*(6), 2265–2275. https://doi.org/10.1109/JBHI.2019.2938247

Zhang, W., Lin, Z., Cheng, J., Ma, C., Deng, X., & Wang, H. (2020). STA-GCN: Two-stream graph convolutional network with spatial-temporal attention for hand gesture recognition. *Visual Computer*, *36*(10–12), 2433–2444. https://doi.org/10.1007/s00371-020-01955-w

Zhao, J., Gou, L., Wang, F., & Zhou, M. (2015). PEARL: An interactive visual analytic tool for understanding personal emotion style derived from social media. *2014 IEEE Conference on Visual Analytics Science and Technology, VAST 2014- Proceedings*, Paris, France, pp. 203–212. https://doi.org/10.1109/VAST.2014.7042496

Zhao, G., Zhang, Y., & Ge, Y. (2018). Frontal EEG asymmetry and middle line power difference in discrete emotions. *Frontiers in Behavioral Neuroscience*, *12*, 225. https://doi.org/10.3389/fnbeh.2018.00225

Zhao, G., Zhang, Y., Ge, Y., Zheng, Y., Sun, X., & Zhang, K. (2018). Asymmetric hemisphere activation in tenderness: Evidence from EEG signals. *Scientific Reports*, *8*(1), 8029. https://doi.org/10.1038/s41598-018-26133-w

Zheng, W. (2017). Multichannel EEG-based emotion recognition via group sparse canonical correlation analysis. *IEEE Transactions on Cognitive and Developmental Systems*, *9*(3), 281–290. https://doi.org/10.1109/TCDS.2016.2587290

Zheng, W. L., & Lu, B. L. (2015). Investigating critical frequency bands and channels for EEG-based emotion recognition with deep neural networks. *IEEE Transactions on Autonomous Mental Development*, *7*(3), 162–175. https://doi.org/10.1109/TAMD.2015.2431497

Zheng, W. L., Zhang, Y. Q., Zhu, J. Y., & Lu, B. L. (2015). Transfer components between subjects for EEG-based emotion recognition. *2015 International Conference on Affective Computing and Intelligent Interaction, ACII 2015*, Xi'an, China, pp. 917–922. https://doi.org/10.1109/ACII.2015.7344684

Zheng, W. L., Zhu, J. Y., & Lu, B. L. (2019). Identifying stable patterns over time for emotion recognition from EEG. *IEEE Transactions on Affective Computing*, *10*(3), 417–429. https://doi.org/10.1109/TAFFC.2017.2712143

Zheng, Z., Wang, P., Liu, W., Li, J., Ye, R., & Ren, D. (2020). Distance-IoU loss: Faster and better learning for bounding box regression. *Proceedings of the AAAI Conference on Artificial Intelligence*, *34*(07), 12993–13000. https://doi.org/10.1609/aaai.v34i07.6999

Zong, Y., Zheng, W., Huang, X., Yan, K., Yan, J., & Zhang, T. (2016). Emotion recognition in the wild via sparse transductive transfer linear discriminant analysis. *Journal on Multimodal User Interfaces*, *10*(2), 163–172. https://doi.org/10.1007/s12193-015-0210-7

Zou, C., Yu, Q., Du, R., Mo, H., Song, Y. Z., Xiang, T., Gao, C., Chen, B., & Zhang, H. (2018). Sketchyscene: Richly-annotated scene sketches. In *Lecture Notes in Computer Science (including subseries Lecture Notes in Artificial Intelligence and Lecture Notes in Bioinformatics): Vol. 11219 LNCS* (pp. 438–454). https://doi.org/10.1007/978-3-030-01267-0-26

9 Home-based Electric Generator Design for Remote Rural Areas with Thermoelectric Generation Technology

Song Qiu and Xiao Zhang

9.1 INTRODUCTION

9.1.1 RESEARCH BACKGROUND

9.1.1.1 Energy Development Trend from the Perspective of Sustainable Development

In recent years, due to the depletion of fossil energy, the energy situation faced by mankind has become increasingly severe. At the same time, the overexploitation of resources and the subsequent environmental deterioration have sounded the alarm for mankind more than once. It can be said that although human beings have written a glorious history of modern civilization, they have also led to problems such as environmental degradation. In order to maximize the benefits in the process of industrialization, human beings exploit and utilize natural resources uncontrollably and destructively, which has severely damaged the living environment of human beings and brought a serious threat to the sustainable development of human civilization. In the face of severe energy scarcity and environmental crisis, many countries have carried out research on "green and clean energy" (including solar energy, wind power, geothermal energy, tidal energy, and biomass energy) and have made considerable achievements. At present, "green and clean energy" accounts for about 15%–20% of the global energy structure. The long-established energy structure in which nonrenewable energy such as coal, oil, and natural gas dominates is expected to change in the future.

In the past 40 years, China's economy has achieved tremendous development, but at the same time, China's energy situation and living environment are becoming more and more precarious. However, China has formed a coal-dominated energy use structure for a long time, and the energy utilization rate is low, which has caused the growth rate of energy supply to lag behind the growth of energy demand, and there is a shortage in the supply of many important energy sources. In order to achieve

DOI: 10.1201/9781032686691-9

sustainable development, energy conservation and emission reduction are imminent, and it is necessary to carry out research on improving new energy development and resource reuse and further reduce greenhouse gas emissions, fossil fuel use, and ozone consumption.

Compared with traditional energy, new energy has many significant advantages, but there are various technical defects. At present, there is no new energy that can replace the dominant position of fossil energy in the energy consumption structure. Switching between energy systems and different energy system operation modes also causes a lot of inconvenience in management and operation. It can be said that the way to comprehensively utilize new energy to achieve efficient coordination between different energy systems and complementary advantages between different energy sources is an important issue facing the sustainable development of human society at present. Thermoelectric power generation is another new energy utilization method after nuclear energy, solar energy, and wind energy, which has attracted the attention of all countries in the world. The thermoelectric power generation equipment has a simple structure, no moving components, no noise during operation, long service life, and no waste discharge. It can rationally utilize solar thermal energy, geothermal energy, industrial waste heat, and other low-grade energy into electrical energy, which is recognized by the world, green and environmentally friendly way of power generation. Due to its remarkable advantages, thermoelectric power generation technology has been widely used in military, aviation, and other fields. With the decreasing oil reserves, developed countries pay more attention to the application research of thermoelectric power generation technology in the civil field.

With the advancement in material science and fabrication technology, great progress has been made in the research on some low-cost high-performance materials. At present, the figure of merit of semiconductor materials that can be used for thermoelectric power generation has been significantly improved. Now, many manufacturers can produce various specifications of thermoelectric power generation sheets with long service life and high-power generation capability, and the cost of thermoelectric power generation is gradually decreasing, which effectively promotes the popularization and application of thermoelectric power generation technology. The high-end field provides a huge opportunity for popularization in the civilian field.

9.1.1.2 Modern Energy Security to Support the Living Habits of Remote Ethnic Minorities

Electricity is a necessity for human life and a guarantee for economic development. Almost all cities and towns can now enjoy sufficient electricity supply. However, a considerable number of ethnic groups cannot integrate into cities due to their special living patterns and still live in low-density areas without electricity supply. According to the latest World Energy Outlook 2018 released by the International Energy Agency, although the number of people without access to electricity fell to less than 1 billion for the first time in 2017, it is expected that there will still be more than 700 million people by 2040. The lack of electricity accounts for 10% of the world's total population, and the popularization of electricity will still be a major challenge faced by all countries in the world for a long time in the future. For example, in northwestern China, especially in Inner Mongolia, Qinghai, Tibet, and other provinces, the electricity consumption problem in many rural and pastoral areas has not yet been resolved: there are still about 28,000 villages, 7 million households, and more than 30 million rural and pastoral populations. The electricity problem needs to be solved urgently. For solving the problem of electricity consumption in remote areas, it is debatable to adopt a single mode of grid extension, and it is more reasonable to use natural resources to establish a relatively independent power supply system on the spot. The specific reasons are as follows:

a. The difficulties in the popularization of electricity in the western region of China are mainly concentrated in the rural and pastoral areas in the west, and the rural and pastoral areas in the west are mostly the areas where ethnic minorities are most widely distributed. Due to lifestyle and other reasons, users in these areas are scattered, the traffic is blocked, and the electricity load is small. As a result, the construction and maintenance of the power grid is difficult, and the construction cost is high.

b. The remote areas in western China are rich in natural resources, which provides conditions for new energy power generation systems.

Among the relatively independent new energy power supply systems, solar photovoltaic power generation and small wind power generation systems are currently widely used (Figure 9.1). However, these two power generation methods also have their limitations. In the winter season when the sunshine time is insufficient and the wind resource is unstable, the working efficiency of the power supply system will be greatly affected.

The thermoelectric power generation technology only needs a stable heat source to start working, and the stable heat source will be generated in the process of

FIGURE 9.1 Wind–solar hybrid power generation system. Image source: provided by the research group ©Xiao Zhang.

cooking, heating, etc., and the thermoelectric power generation technology has reliable performance, less maintenance, and can work for a long time in extremely harsh environments. The advantages of the system perfectly fit the application environment in remote rural and pastoral areas without electricity. It is more feasible to solve the problem of electricity consumption in areas with scattered users, traffic congestion, and small electricity load without electricity. The reasons for this are as follows:

a. Thermoelectric power generation technology only needs a stable heat source and a reasonable temperature difference to work stably in extremely harsh environments.

b. Residents living in areas without electricity in China still need to burn biomass fuel for food cooking, lighting, and heating. The high temperature generated by the combustion of biomass fuel can be used as an ideal (recirculating and reused) heat source for thermoelectric power generation after cooking and heating.

c. With the development of material science, materials with higher and higher thermoelectric conversion efficiency are constantly being discovered and created. The unit thermoelectric power generation sheet (Figure 9.2) is made of bismuth telluride as the material to make a 40 mm * 40 mm sheet-like unit. The heat-resistant temperature of the hot end reaches 300°C. When the temperature difference between the cold and hot ends reaches 140°C, the open circuit voltage that can be generated is 8.4 V, and the power generation current is 969 mA. The thermoelectric power generation device made with multiple pieces of this type of thermoelectric power generation sheet can generate enough electricity to meet the lighting needs of a family or to charge and supply energy for small electrical appliances.

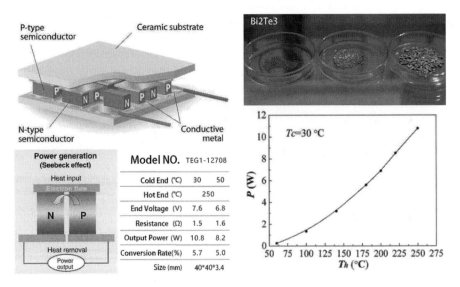

FIGURE 9.2 Introduction of thermoelectric power generation sheet. Image source: provided by the research group ©Xiao Zhang.

9.1.2 RESEARCH CONTENT AND INNOVATION

9.1.2.1 Design Morphology Based on Heat Transfer Research

Usually, the "forms" we mentioned are mostly visible to the naked eye, and more forms are not visible to the naked eye, but they need to be presented through some description methods such as heat transfer. The "Mechanical Theory of Heat" is a theory for explaining thermal phenomena, introduced by Benjamin Thompson in 1798 and further developed by the French physicist Nicolas Léonard Sadi Carnot. This doctrine states that heat and mechanical work are equivalent in changing internal energy. In the 19th century, with the second law of thermodynamics proposed by Rudolf Clausius in 1850, this theory was further developed into a relatively complete thermodynamic theory. In 1851, in his book *On the Dynamical Theory of Heat, Kelvin*, based on the experiments of James Prescott Joule and others at the time, generalized the doctrine: "Heat is not a substance, but a motion phenomenon, and we believe that there must be an equal relationship between mechanical work and heat, like cause and effect."

Subsequently, the term "thermodynamic theory" was gradually replaced by the new term "thermodynamics." For example, in 1876, Richard Sears McCulloh mentioned in his monograph on thermodynamics: "Thermodynamic theory, also known as thermodynamics, is a branch of science that treats thermal phenomena as the motion of matter." Thermodynamics is a discipline that studies the properties and laws of thermal motion of matter from a macroscopic perspective. Thermodynamics does not investigate the microscopic structure of matter composed of a large number of microscopic particles but only cares about the thermal phenomena exhibited by the system as a whole and the basic laws that must be followed for its change and development. However, the object of this chapter is the transfer of heat in different media or at different locations of the same medium. This process is a dynamic one, and it takes time for it to happen. In the process of heat transfer, changes in shape, color, and mechanical properties of objects often occur, which is the focus of this study.

For example, Keenan Crane from Carnegie Mellon University calculated the shortest distance between two points on a three-dimensional geometric surface by means of heat source diffusion (Figure 9.3) (Crane et al., 2017). Before this method was proposed, it took a lot of time to search and calculate with traditional computer graphics methods. However, this method greatly reduces the amortized calculation cost through the diffusion method, which increases the calculation speed by an order of magnitude. The innovation of calculating three-dimensional geometric geodesics by heat conduction simulation method provides the basis for fabric technology innovation. Traditional fabric technology can only weave flat fabrics, but through the equidistant expansion of three-dimensional geometry, flat looms can also weave three-dimensional geometry (Figure 9.4) (Yige et al., 2019). It can be seen that the study of heat transfer behavior can not only solve temperature-related problems, through the analysis of heat transfer phenomena, we can have more innovations in design morphology.

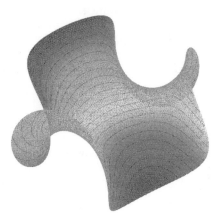

FIGURE 9.3   Geodesic calculation method of 3D mesh based on heat method. Image source: provided by the research group ©Xiao Zhang.

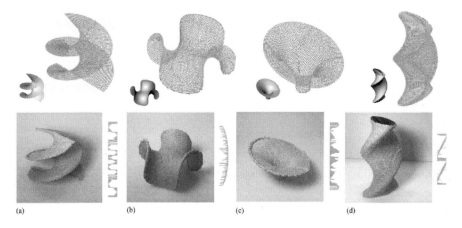

FIGURE 9.4   Three-dimensional fabric made by flat loom based on heat method. Image source: "A Computational Approach for Knitting 3D Composites Preforms" ©Yige Liu.

9.1.2.2 Exploration of Intelligent Thermal Environment Intervention Based on Materials

In the traditional sense, most of the materials in artificial form have a long service life but lack intelligent features and also bring many problems such as pollution. With the development of phase-change material technology, materials exhibit the characteristics of interacting with the surrounding environment. The appearance of phase-change materials not only brings more interesting responsiveness and passivity to man-made objects but also gives the form a certain lifespan. In some short-cycle application scenarios, the biointelligent characteristics of materials will produce huge advantages, especially in the interaction with the thermal environment. How to construct a suitable shape based on thermal environment-responsive materials is a long-term topic of this research. At the same time, the responsive relationship between materials and the environment also requires sufficient attention in design. A large number of interactive devices still rely on various sensors; the results of such a design method are often mechanical and even biased toward the field of robotics. Cleverly solving real-world problems or meeting needs at a fraction of the cost could be based on material intelligence.

9.1.2.3   Exploration of Collaborative Innovation Methods for Disciplines

When initially conducting technical research in the field of thermoelectric power generation, the research team treated this topic as a traditional industrial design project. But during the design process, they found that the designing shape can have a huge impact on the power of the final product. With the gradual promotion of the research, they found that there are a large number of interaction designs based on temperature differences at the forefront of design science. These designs are related to both robotics and materials studies. Therefore, they returned to the basics of design, reanalyzed the core of thermoelectric power generation design in terms of geometry, technology, and structure, and formed a research report. Thermoelectric power generation technology has great application prospects in its application fields, the research and development of thermoelectric materials, and the improvement of thermoelectric power generation efficiency. Relevant research starts from one point, summarizes the general law, and obtains a wide range of unexpected results.

9.2   RESEARCH METHOD

9.2.1   Performance-based Design

9.2.1.1   Geometricalization of Structures: From Constant to Dynamic

"Structure" refers to the arrangement and organization of interrelated elements in a system or material. The way the atoms are arranged in a material can be called structure, and the way different materials are combined in the macroscopic world can also be called structure. In this section, we mainly discuss the latter, the structure in the macroscopic world. Structure is a form construction method based on materials. When trying to combine different materials, the material needs to bear a variety of stress conditions. At this time, it is necessary to optimize the distribution of the material and change the morphological structure based on the external force. The ideal structure should take full advantage of the mechanical properties of the material, avoid its weaknesses, and have no redundancy. In order to generate an efficient structure, it is an indispensable process to understand the transmission of force in the form; the optimization thinking of the form based on the force flow and material is a classic method of structural design. With the deepening of structural cognition, people's application of mechanical knowledge has changed from constant to dynamic, from explicit to implicit, and from result to process.

In a temperature-related study, Lining Yao's team at Carnegie Mellon University investigated thermally denatured spaghetti structures, designed by introducing stress into the plane, usually by exploiting the isotropic and anisotropic differences in the structure (Figure 9.5) (Ye et al., 2021). Her research team identified a simple and

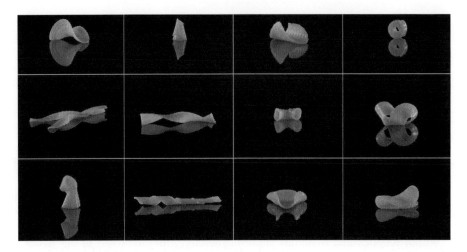

FIGURE 9.5 Yao Lining's team realized the deformation structure design of spaghetti based on temperature changes. Image source: "Morphing pasta and beyond" (https://hcii. cmu.edu/people/lining-yao) ©Lining Yao.

general device based on a diffusion-based mechanism: achieving transient deformation effects in heated states with parametric surface groove structures. The device can be realized from a single material and fabricated using low-cost fabrication methods. Quantitative experiments and multiphysics simulations demonstrate that temporally asynchronous expansion or de-expansion of dough can be induced by parametric surface grooving, and planar objects can be transformed into designed 3D shapes. Yao Lining's team further studied the deformation characteristics of thermally deformed structures and achieved nonzero Gaussian curvature geometry by adjusting the groove pattern.

9.2.1.2 Interactive Functionalization of Materials: From Inhibition to Activation

In the process of heat conduction, thermal expansion and contraction of materials and thermochromic discoloration are very interesting natural phenomena. These phenomena will transform information that can only be felt by touch into visual information or bring about other mechanical changes. Therefore, the deformation or color change of the temperature-dependent material is also in our study. Phase-change material (PCM) in a narrow sense refers to a substance that changes its state of matter and can provide latent heat under the condition of constant temperature, while "phase change" in a broad sense can refer to a material that changes its physical properties due to changes in the external environment (Guseinov et al., 2020). The ability of a material to change its properties depending on the environment can have a major impact on the construction of form. Movable control of form through material properties is often closer to design than mechanical driving. The response of materials to the environment is often passive, but compared with mechanical driving, it is often

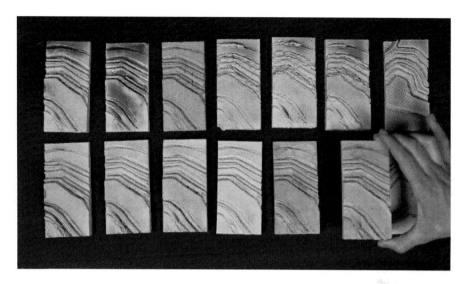

FIGURE 9.6 Morphological and geometric studies through thermochromic materials. Image source: "Thermochromic Animation Thermally-informed and colour-changing surface-configurations" (https://www.youtube.com/watch?v=wOxPYLzzCMs) ©Andreas Körner.

relatively lagging and cannot achieve the characteristics of instantaneous response. Based on the study of the environmental performance of materials, researchers need to control the phase transition process by understanding the microstructural characteristics behind the phase transition.

Taking thermochromic materials as an example, their ability to change color with changes in ambient temperature brings great convenience for researchers to observe temperature changes in some forms. Thermochromic materials act as colorants during thermal studies (Figure 9.6). In order to study the relationship between the thermal transfer phenomenon and the geometric surface texture, in 2021, a related research team from the University of Innsbruck visualized the thermal transfer phenomenon with thermally variable materials (Andreas, 2021). In recent years, thermotropic materials have also been used in clothing and art installations. For example, at MIT, the Self-Assembly Lab blends plastic fibers into clothing and heats them later to make them fit the human body better (Lavender et al., 2019). Similarly, some metals will be deformed by curling and other deformations due to temperature changes. In recent years, a large number of movable structure laboratories control the local temperature of metal sheets through electric currents, thereby driving robots (Guanyun et al., 2018). Such actuation combines the passivity principle of materials with the sensitivity of manual control, while avoiding complex mechanical structures. The research team plans to use thermochromic materials on subsequently improved thermoelectric stoves to allow users to observe changes in furnace temperature or hot water coils from a distance without having to look at a thermometer at close quarters.

9.2.1.3 Manufacturing Performance of Processes: From Execution to Perception

Craft is the process of materializing form. In traditional design science, craftsmanship is often considered to be a job that needs to be considered by development positions and a topic that needs to be studied at the factory side. However, based on certain processes, designers may only be able to use certain materials, which limits the design geometry. Therefore, the designer needs to understand the essential process and participate in the design of the process, rather than just compromising with the existing factory equipment. At present, the dependence on mechanical equipment in the process system is often too large, and the intelligent characteristics of artificial processes are ignored. With the discovery of machine vision and machine touch, machines can gradually feel similar to human hands. Therefore, "craft" may return to the relationship between "human hand" and "object" and return to the essence of craftsmanship.

In the process of shaping the design, humans gradually invented tools to assist. In the process of modern industrial processing, the shaping process of artificial objects can be roughly divided into two steps: (1) The designer expresses the shape of the design through drawings and models and (2) the engineer converts the model geometry into the price path of the equipment and processes the workpiece and achieve a high degree of similarity to the model. In this process, the "people" of man-made objects are actually divided into two categories: designers and engineers. But when humans first made "artificial objects," there was no clear distinction between designers and engineers. Early humans could use sight, touch, and even hearing to sense changes in materials during processing and to make decisions about the next step in construction. With the continuous improvement in sensors, cameras, and 3D scanning technology, machinery has gradually gained the ability to recognize processing objects so as to decide the degree of its own output "strength (power)." It is a return of "artificial objects" to allow machines to create behaviors based on "vision" and "tactile." This return is mainly reflected in two aspects: (1) The improvement in the degree of freedom of the creation tools. (2) The perception of the creation tools. With the help of 3D scanning sensors, the machine can grasp the 3D information of the shape in real time. In 2016, research and experiments were carried out on the adaptive robot weaving structure process. The research team of the University of Stuttgart obtained design inspiration from the behavioral manufacturing logic of weaving birds during the nesting process and combined the design of the three-dimensional weaving structure and robotic manufacturing to explore the feasibility of the robotic weaving process (Figure 9.7) (Brugnaro et al., 2016). Because the results of the behavioral weaving process cannot be determined in advance in a digital model, they are generated in a negotiation between design intent, manufacturing constraints, performance criteria, material behavior, and site-specific conditions. This puts forward higher requirements for immediacy and responsiveness in the process of morphological construction.

FIGURE 9.7 Robotic arm weaving process based on mechanical perception capability. Image source: "Robotic Softness-An Adaptive Robotic Fabrication Process for Woven Structures" ©Giulio Brugnaro.

9.2.2 FORM-FINDING DESIGN

9.2.2.1 Physical Form Finding

In many morphological construction practices, Frei Otto's achievements are characterized by the close combination of natural reason and artificial will. Otto described in "Natural Structure, Future Conception" that we should explore the very common process of artificial object change and self-generation, and what we need to find are those structures and essential characteristics that can clearly show the process of object production. Based on the observation and recording of the changes in natural forms under artificial conditions, Otto summarized the construction methods of many forms, which is also called "Finding Form" (Frei and Bodo, 1996). This type of design method is based on the material system in nature, and the form is generated by simulating the complex "self-organization" process of nature through experiments. In the experiments, each "material machine" was realized through the interaction of "material elements" over a period of time. The design of each "material machine" attempts to find a specific form among a large number of internal interactions. And these "material elements" are solid or liquid mixtures based on elastic or changeable material behavior characteristics, such as sand, wool thread, paper, and soap bubbles (Figure 9.8). Otto's life-long form construction practice seems to have no clear purpose, covering the scope of network structure, inflatable structure, suspension structure, etc., but these practices are all design practices dominated by his unique view of nature.

FIGURE 9.8 Sand model experiment based on "form-finding" design theory. Image source: Sandworks: Material Research © Ahmed Abouelkheir, Behdad Shahi, JI-AH Lee and Peter Wang.

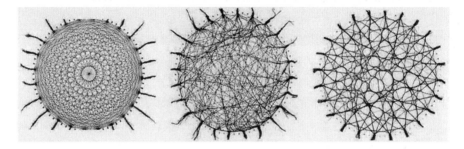

FIGURE 9.9 Experiment of wool-thread bonding form construction. Image source: "Form-Finding - Towards Few Architecture" ©Frei Otto.

Among Frei Otto's many form-finding experiments, the most influential is the "Wool-thread Machine" experiment, whose purpose is to construct the most efficient path in a certain area. During the experiment, Otto used wool threads in a certain area to connect each point and then immersed the entire model in water, took it out after a slight vibration, and found that the wool threads were gradually bonded to each other (Figure 9.9). After the whole device is dried and shaped, the total path length of the entire system is greatly shortened, which is only 30%–50% of the initial shape. The shape generated based on this mechanical and physical principle often has strong internal rationality. Otto's method innovation of morphological construction is based on the mechanical view of nature, which integrates nature with subjective creative will.

9.2.2.2 Digital Form Finding

It is precisely because of such sages' physical exploration of natural forms that a large number of scholars later combined with the advent of the computer age to write mechanical algorithms as plug-ins for designers to use. Most of these software are based on the geometric description method of discrete grids, which convert the original physical experiments into computer simulations. In the process of transforming physical experiments into digital simulations, materials can be abstracted into mechanical relationships between points; for example, the elastic properties of materials can be abstracted according to Hooke's law, and the flexural properties of materials can be abstracted according to angular constraints.

The significance of "digital form finding" lies not only in the simulation of the real form but also in the reshaping of the digital form. For example, in industrial production, parametric surfaces are often used to describe geometry, such as continuous surfaces based on NURBS or efficient mesh modeling. With the advent of the era of computational design, the relationship between design and data has become more and more close. Whether it is the import of external data or the finite element analysis of the model, it is necessary to convert the polysurface (B-rep) into a mesh file (Mesh). Although there are many existing retopology tools in the market, most of them are concentrated in the field of computer animation or digital sculpture, and it is difficult to match the existing manufacturing modeling level. With the digital form-finding method, an ideal physical model can be used to convert the parametric surface model into a mesh model to complete the topology reconstruction of digital geometry.

The physical simulation plug-in of Kangaroo in the visual programming platform Grasshopper under the Rhino platform can be used to construct a comprehensive force system of the spring particle system and the collision system (Figure 9.10). Dynamic simulation effects cannot be accomplished by traditional physical form-finding design systems. Compared with the traditional topology reconstruction algorithm, the digital form-finding method is fundamentally different; it is based on the nature of the mechanical nature view, which makes it better understood by designers, and can also have more variable applications. For example, in the geometric optimization of special-shaped building curtain walls, it is often difficult to solve all problems with a unified algorithm, and digital tools based on physical principles can achieve better universality. It can be seen that the mechanical view of nature always plays a role in making us return to reason and respect nature in design, and through understanding from a mechanical point of view, nature also changes from "perceivable" to "knowable" and then "available."

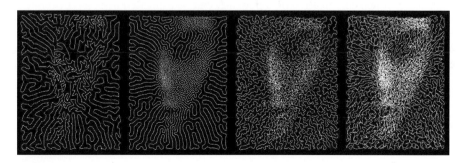

FIGURE 9.10   One-stroke portrait based on spring particle system and collision simulation. Image source: provided by the research group ©Xiao Zhang.

9.3 DESIGN METHOD

9.3.1 Digital Geometry

In design work, we usually use CAD software such as rhino for modeling and finally for manufacturing. Most B-rep surfaces used in industrial design documents define their parametric surfaces by continuous curves on the shape edges. Continuous surfaces are good for manufacturing but not for simulation. The performance-based finite element analysis via CAE software typically requires a mesh model, which is a description of geometry in a discrete manner. In this section, we design digital tools that designers can use by studying the representation of digital geometric models. At the same time, in order to facilitate the planar processing of stoves in the manufacturing stage, this section also describes in detail the flattenable optimization of discontinuous geometries. An understanding of digital geometry is the foundation for proper design.

9.3.1.1 Digital Description of Geometry

In early geometry study, the convex regular polyhedron, as a representative of an ideal shape, was given a Natural Philosophy meaning beyond the shape itself. In a practical sense, geometry also represents the human ideal of form itself. For example, the concept of "continuous": to make the transition between two intersecting lines smooth, the drawing software will use a circular curve to chamfer them; to make the two curves connect smoothly, you can also use the blending command. In order to achieve different degrees of continuity, the concept of curvature is proposed to describe and achieve higher-order smoothing of the "curve" shape. Therefore, geometry can be used as a reduction of functions, and functions can be used as a definite description method for human beings to ideal shapes. In real life, through the description of nature by ideal geometry, human's cognition of objective nature has more subjective certainty.

The ideal geometry is often used in the design process, and it is difficult to restore it when it needs to fit the natural form realistically. Therefore, the concept of discrete geometry was proposed, that is, fitting of nature with the help of elements such as grids, point clouds, and voxels. It can be seen that discrete geometry is a way for humans to intuitively describe nature. "Discretization" refers to taking a curve as an example, which can be fitted by a polyline, that is, expressed by several continuous line segments. The more segments of the polyline, the higher the fitting degree. By analogy, the discretization of continuous surfaces can be represented by triangular planes, because triangles are the basic shape of two-dimensional shapes (three points define a plane). And when a solid needs to be discretized, a regular tetrahedron can be used as the basic shape to fill it. For example, to express the isotropic characteristics of a material, a uniform grid can be used to abstract it, while to express the different properties of a material in the latitude and longitude, it can be described by a quadrilateral grid, and different parameters can be set for the grid edges in different directions. With the help of meshes, the geometry can be given all kinds of information.

9.3.1.2 Conversion of Continuous and Discontinuous Geometry

Converting discrete geometry to continuous geometry is necessary to understand the impact of manufacturing processes on the shape of a design. Taking draping as an example, the process is actually to restore the three-dimensional space geometry to the two-dimensional plane. And how to find a balance between the highest degree of fit and the least suture length requires graphics research based on discrete geometry. Professor Keenan Crane and his team have conducted extensive research on discrete geometry topology optimization for manufacturing (Figure 9.11) (Oded et al., 2018). At the same time, not only on the physical manufacturing side but also in the field of computer graphics, in order to facilitate the definition of grid cells around a grid surface, algorithms such as "half edge data structure" have been invented, providing a mathematical explanation for the concept of "adjacent." In animation and other fields, there are countless mathematical abstractions for natural phenomena such as rendering and halo, and their research goals are to fit natural forms.

Using manufacturing files for numerical analysis requires converting surfaces to meshes. A mesh with an elastic physical model can be used by digital physics simulation software, by attaching it to the surface of the target geometry and avoiding mesh self-intersection through the particle collision model, and by anchoring the model to fix the mesh edges, the target can be changed. The geometric topology makes its shape almost undistorted. For example, during topological reconstruction of a closed surface shape, you can first draw a corresponding basic mesh shape to surround the target shape according to the characteristics of the target shape and then use the "digital form-finding" method to adsorb the mesh to the target shape – mesh reconstruction. Based on the reconstructed mesh, designers can easily perform operations such as texturing and numerical analysis on the mesh. For example, in the case of Figure 9.12, the mechanical model constraints we need to apply are (1) spring force constraints on each line on the drawn mesh, (2) adsorption constraints from all vertices on the mesh to the target surface and (3) volume collision constraints for all vertices of the mesh to avoid mesh self-intersections.

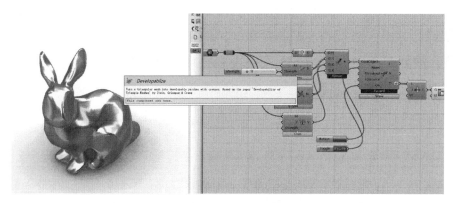

FIGURE 9.11 A scalable optimization study for discrete geometry. Image source: "Developability of Triangle Meshes" ©Chao Yuan.

FIGURE 9.12   The closed polysurface (left); the drawn mesh wraps the target shape after subdivision (middle); and the mesh shape after the retopology process (right). Image source: provided by the research group ©Chao Yuan.

9.3.2   Digital Geometry Materialization

9.3.2.1   Process-based Geometric Dimensionality Reduction

The dimensionality reduction of the process in the manufacturing process is reflected in many aspects, such as the CNC milling process; the dimensionality reduction is reflected in the transformation of the geometry of the workpiece into a tool path, such as the 3D printing process; and the dimensionality reduction is reflected in slicing the workpiece and then outline for material curing. These processes are all spatial dimensionality reduction of the geometry of the form. From the perspective of design morphology, the process needs to put forward expectations for the geometry of the product shape and at the same time consider whether it can be shaped closer to the ideal geometry by optimizing the process.

For example, in the processing of wire, the dimensionality reduction of geometry does not only exist in space but also in the dimension of time. For example, Tongji University, in cooperation with University College London, has emphasized the dimension of time in the research on the 3D concrete widening printing method for robots (Figure 9.13) (Qiang et al., 2021). The maximum printing resolution of the traditional 3D printing technology is limited by the nozzle diameter. Therefore, if a method of controlling the traveling speed of the nozzle is proposed to control the width of the printing path, it provides convenience for the morphological processing

FIGURE 9.13   Variable width concrete printing process and finished product. Image source: "3D Concrete Printing with Variable Width Filament" ©Qiang Zhan.

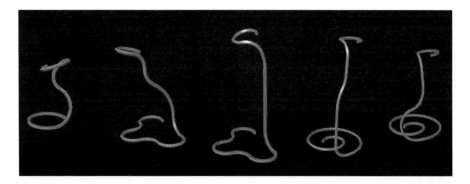

FIGURE 9.14 Linear hot-melt printing practice of variable-speed disguised printing. Image source: "A-line: 4D Printing Morphing Linear Composite Structures" ©Lining Yao.

of nonequal wall thickness (Figure 9.14). Furthermore, in the study of 3D printing process by Wang and his team (Wang et al., 2019), the researchers found that due to hot-melt drawing, the printed plastic often has an excessively stretched prestress, and when it is heated, it shrinks along the printing direction, while the printing speed will affect the amount of stretching, which in turn affects the amount of shrinkage.

9.3.2.2 Material-based Geometric Dimensionality Reduction

Craft is also reshaping of materials. Taking metal as an example, by understanding the melting point of metal, it can be melted into a liquid state in the factory to complete the infusion process; at the same time, using the ductility of metal, the factory can carry out the stamping process. Some forms can be shaped to eliminate their internal force after remodeling, and some forms need to be remodeled to have internal force inside to maintain the stability of the form. Therefore, the reshaping of materials can be roughly divided into two categories: one is reshaping based on the properties of the material itself, and the other is the editing of the macrostructure of the material.

Taking Auxetic Materials as an example, its material feature is that the realization of geometry is accomplished through the elastic deformation of the material. This research process is composed of materials that abstract microgeometry with macrogeometry. Through the geometric editing of the uniform elastic material, its deformation will appear nonuniform under stress conditions to meet our macroscopic geometry requirements (Figure 9.15) (Olga et al., 2017). At the same time,

FIGURE 9.15 Nonlinear buckling tension deformation material. Image source: "Non-Linear Matters: Auxetic Surfaces" ©Olga Mesa.

the internal force of the stretched material enables the elastic material to be tightly wrapped on the target geometric surface due to its internal prestress intended to restore the deformation. In the traditional field of design, the cognitive basis of craftsmanship is often based on "material is constant," but it is not. The mechanical properties of the material should be fully stimulated during the process so that the structure has more efficient properties.

9.4 CASE STUDY: THERMOELECTRIC POWER GENERATION FURNACE DESIGN

9.4.1 BASIC DESIGN

9.4.1.1 Thermoelectric Power Generation Technology

Thermoelectric power generation is the conversion of thermal energy and electric energy realized by thermoelectric effect of thermoelectric power generation materials, produced by temperature difference through the combination of semiconductor materials. When there is a temperature difference between the front and back sides of the thermoelectric power generation sheet, the free electrons inside it will circulate and move from one side to the other side, thereby converting the voltage difference into a potential difference.

However, the conversion efficiency of thermoelectric power generation technology is low, generally only 5%–7%. Moreover, in order to maintain the power of thermoelectric power generation, the user must pay attention to maintaining the temperature difference between the two sides of the thermoelectric power generation sheet; especially, the temperature of the cold end needs to be maintained. To maintain the temperature of the cold end, other energy sources are often required. Thus, the thermoelectric power generation technology can only maintain a very low efficiency. If the power obtained by thermoelectric power generation technology is to be stored, the losses during the conversion process need to be considered; thus, this technology can only serve a narrower application scenario. The working temperature difference between the cold and hot ends of a thermoelectric power generation device directly affects its power generation efficiency and output power. Therefore, maintaining a suitable working temperature difference is also a key factor to improve the efficiency of thermoelectric power generation. In order to maintain a high working temperature difference, it is often necessary to maintain a high temperature at the hot end and at the same time add a heat sink at the low-temperature end of the thermoelectric generator to dissipate heat in time. This involves the thermal design of the thermoelectric generator. Excellent thermal design can use the heat dissipation method and structure matching the thermoelectric generator, so that the equipment can reach a better working state, so as to give full play to the best performance of the generator. Therefore, the thermoelectric power generation device needs to carry out a reasonable and optimized thermal design to ensure its high thermoelectric power generation efficiency.

9.4.1.2 Power Generation Experiment

Since most of the thermoelectric power generation equipment adopt air cooling to maintain the temperature difference, the research used is in the same way (Experiment A). However, during the experiment, the research team found that the efficiency of air cooling is really low and energy wasting. Thus, they decided to change the original thermoelectric refrigeration mode from air cooling to water cooling (Experiment B). In thermoelectric power generation, cooling water with waste heat can be used as heating water for the whole house in winter, while electricity can be stored. At the same time, in further experiments, researchers found that water cooling can improve the efficiency of large temperature difference power generation three times more than air cooling. Moreover, due to the good heat storage performance of water, even if we stop the heating process, warm water can continue to generate electricity for more than 2 hours. The change in refrigeration mode greatly improves the feasibility of the project.

In Figure 9.16a, we used four thermoelectric power generation units in series to generate power and attached an independent fan to the cold end of each thermoelectric power generation unit for cooling. In this experiment, the cooling effect of the fan was not ideal, and the temperature of the cold end could still reach 125.6°C, which means that even if the hot end reached a peak of 250°C, the temperature difference of the entire device was less than 100°C. And in order to achieve the cooling effect, the fan must operate at full power. This process consumes a large amount of produced electricity, and the final voltage obtained is only 5.16 V.

In Figure 9.16b, we use a whole piece of water-cooled aluminum coil unit pasted on the cold ends of the four thermoelectric generators and then circulated the cooling

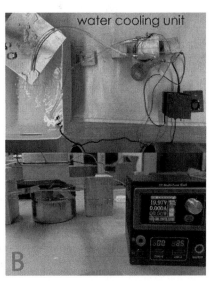

FIGURE 9.16 Experiment A: Air-cooled thermoelectric power generation; Experiment B: Water-cooled thermoelectric power generation. Image source: provided by the research group ©Xiao Zhang.

water through a small water pump. Meanwhile, we used a plastic box as a small water station. Since the water temperature will not exceed 100°C under a normal atmospheric pressure, in the actual test, we have also confirmed that the water temperature is always maintained at around 56°C due to the heat dissipation of the small water station through the measurement with the thermometer. As a result, the temperature difference between the hot and cold ends of the entire device can reach 200°C. At the same time, since the small water pump only needs to ensure the flow of the water body, it does not require excessive power and will not consume too much power. The peak voltage obtained by the whole device can reach 19.97 V.

9.4.1.3   Design Solutions

Based on the choice of the water-cooled thermoelectric power generation technology, the research team decided to use the herdsmen's winter heating water as the cooling refrigerant for the cold end of the semiconductor power generation sheet. The water that has completed the cooling work and carried the waste heat will be circulated throughout the house through the pipes, and the heat exchange with the indoor air will be completed. When the hot water is circulated and cooled to room temperature, it can be reused to cool the power generation device. At the same time, the hot water in the pipeline can also be used for the daily washing of the herdsmen and can be considered to add a local temperature difference power generation unit in the heat exchange between the heating coil and the indoor air, which can be used for lighting or charging at any time. Part of the electricity obtained through thermoelectric power generation will be used to maintain water-circulation pumps, and the excess electricity can be used or stored (Figure 9.17).

Based on the above strategies, this design can be divided into two parts, one is the design of the thermoelectric stove itself, and the other is the design of the heating system in the herdsmen's home. According to the surveying and mapping of our previous research, we have modeled the user's home: the herdsman's house consists of two independent buildings, which are powered by two independent wind and solar hybrid power generation systems. In a house, there are four places where the stove needs to be used. Two are in the two kitchens, and the other two are in the two bedrooms. Kitchen stoves are often only lit when cooking. The kitchen on the left in the picture is not used in winter, and the entire house on the left is only used in spring and summer. Therefore, only two thermoelectric stoves are needed, which are, respectively, located in two bedrooms. The geothermal pipes need to be arranged uniformly. In order to make the two independent houses have the possibility of living in order to meet the future needs of the increasing population of herdsmen, we will lay heating pipes in both the living room and the bedroom (Figure 9.18).

9.4.1.4   Design of the Stove-heating System

Stove design: After investigation, the research team decided to use a cylindrical stove with a diameter of 45 cm and a depth of 30 cm as the first-generation sample based on the usage habits of the herdsmen. In order to take into account both the thermal conductivity and heat resistance, the inner liner of the stove is made of aluminum alloy material. A cylindrical semiconductor thermoelectric power generation device will be customized on the periphery of the stove, and its expansion area will reach

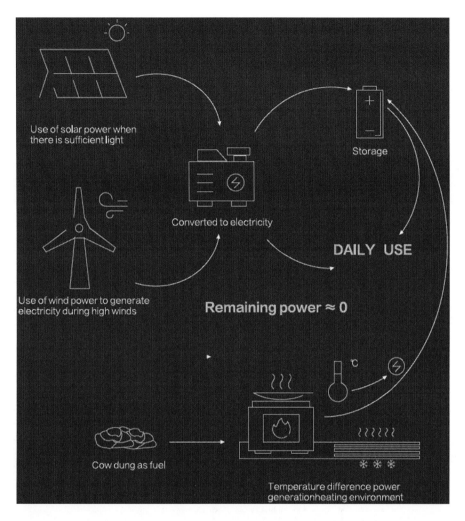

FIGURE 9.17 Herdsmen's comprehensive energy equipment combining thermoelectric power generation stoves and whole-house heating systems. Image source: provided by the research group ©Jiayu Zheng.

4,239 cm². When the temperature difference reaches 100°C, the power generation will reach 1.36 kW. The periphery of the stove will be tightly coiled with aluminum tubes, and cold water will be passed through the tubes to cool the thermoelectric sheet (Figure 9.19).

Pipeline design: We have enumerated many possibilities to conduct research on how to make hot water pipes evenly cover the entire room. We evenly distributed 10*10 points for the room and stipulated the entrance and exit. Our goal is to draw a non-self-intersecting line through each point in the image below. If corners are encountered, chamfering is performed. We found that due to the difference in the number of corners in different arrangements of the pipes, the total length will also

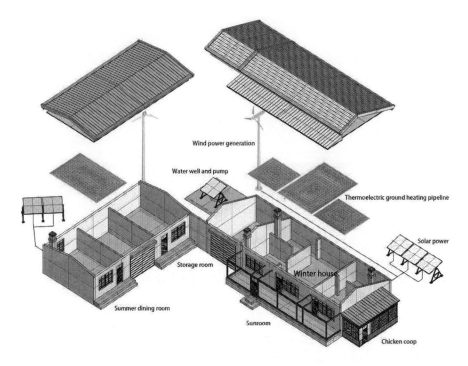

FIGURE 9.18 Whole-house energy system planning. Image source: provided by the research group ©Xiao Zhang.

FIGURE 9.19 Primary design of thermoelectric power generation furnace. Image source: provided by the research group ©Jiayu Zheng.

vary. In order to maximize heating, we need to choose the longest pipe length. After selection by the research team, the indoor hot water coils for heating will be arranged in concentric circles. The shape of concentric circles will effectively avoid the four corners of the room and the ineffective waste of heat. At the same time, the research

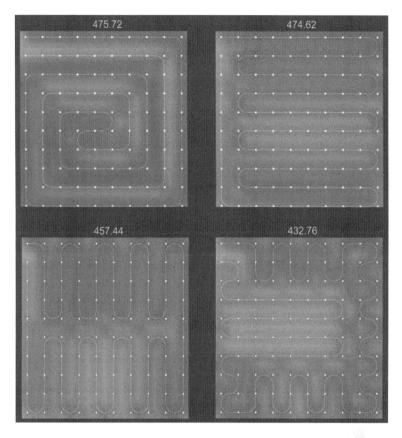

FIGURE 9.20 Four basic arrangements of hot water pipes. Image source: provided by the research group ©Xiao Zhang.

team also carried out parametric optimization of the local density of the pipeline. The ducts will be of two different materials, with good thermal conductivity in the room and insulation on the other paths (Figure 9.20).

9.4.2 Design Optimization

9.4.2.1 Radiation Heat Transfer Simulation of Thermal Coils

Through mathematical analysis, we subdivide the ideal plane of a room into discrete grids. By calculating the position of each grid center point and each point of the coil, the inverse proportional function is used to calculate the amount of thermal radiation received by each point of the floor heating coil, and by accumulating it, the amount of heat radiation of each point on the floor of the room is obtained. As for the heating value size, the researchers also conducted qualitative simulations of the heat in different locations of the hot water coil: the closer the location to the incoming water pipe, the stronger the heat radiation ability. The simulation is constructed by an inverse proportional function from the corresponding point on the hot water coil to the initial point. Finally, the researchers obtained a qualitative floor-level thermal

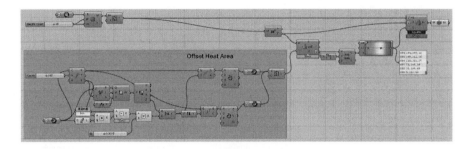

FIGURE 9.21   Simulation algorithm for radiant heat transfer of thermal coil. Image source: provided by the research group ©Xiao Zhang.

performance map of the house through a mesh shading algorithm (Figure 9.21). During this process, the entire simulation algorithm is done in the design software without switching to other simulation software. Although this work sacrifices accuracy, it greatly speeds up the design process.

9.4.2.2   Graph Theory-based Coil Path Optimization Method

In the optimization of floor heating coil design, there are two goals to consider. The first is to minimize the number of corners of the coil, and the second is to optimize the heat density at the required location according to user needs. According to the first type of optimization objective, we propose a design method based on Euler diagram (one stroke). Here, we use a grasshopper plug-in called "LEAFVEIN," which is widely used in graph theory and urban planning (Figure 9.22). Here, we firstly distribute the required heating positions on the indoor plane. In this scheme, we adopt the uniform distribution method. Secondly, we start from a 2*2 lattice and derive it all the way to a 5*5 lattice to solve all possible one-stroke paths. When our simulations reached a scale of 6*6, the computer experienced up to 30 minutes of computation time (Figure 9.23). The research team also designed the number of discontinuous points for judging the curvature of the hot water pipeline and sorted them to find the optimal solution we need. This design method is based on an ergodic algorithm, so the resulting solution is guaranteed to be optimal.

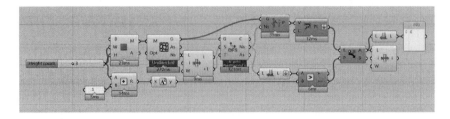

FIGURE 9.22   Hot water coil routing algorithm based on DFS graph theory. Image source: provided by the research group ©Xiao Zhang.

2*2

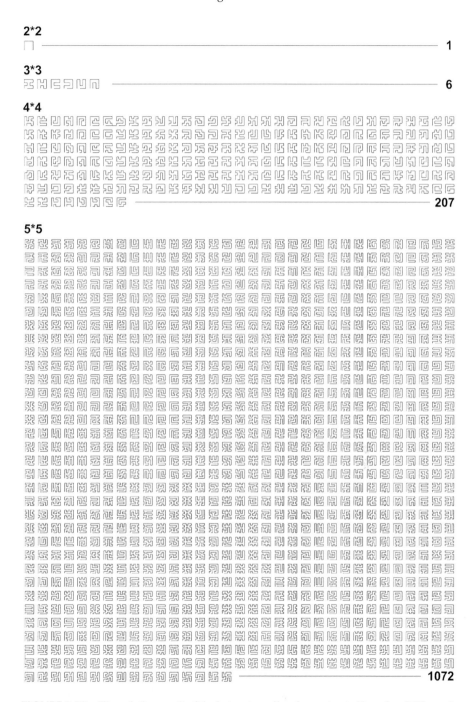

FIGURE 9.23 The solution result of the hot water coil path constructed based on DFS graph theory. Image source: provided by the research group ©Xiao Zhang.

9.4.2.3　Form-finding-based Coil Path Optimization Method

In Figure 9.24, we explain the principle of form finding: first, we draw a closed curve in the plane, discretize it, and divide it into several line segments connected end to end. Secondly, we iterate it "growth." If the length of each segment is greater than a standard value, take the midpoint of the line segment, split a line segment into two line segments, and double the length. When the length doubles, the digital physics engine kicks in, and the line segments are squeezed against each other to get an even arrangement. Such a cycle is a form-finding process. With several iterations of the cycle, the length of the pipeline is extended, and uniform distribution in a certain area is obtained.

The coil path is generated based on the digital form-finding design method (Figure 9.25), which will bring better results to the distribution optimization of the hot zone. Here, we iterate the digital physical model based on a basic coil shape: the spring particle model and the collision model are used, respectively, and the iterative growth method needs to be written in a basic Python script. A segmentation occurs when each section of pipeline grows beyond a certain length. This iterative loop requires the use of the "Anemone" plug-in to control the number of iteration steps according to requirements. If the iteration step size is too long, it will cause excessive looping and pipeline overlap; if the iteration step size is too small, the total pipeline length will not meet the requirement. In order to interfere with the density of the coil, it is also necessary to make a black and white mesh gradient map according to the user's needs. The designer can define the black area to be denser or sparser. When

FIGURE 9.24　Hot water coil routing algorithm based on digital form finding. Image source: provided by the research group ©Xiao Zhang.

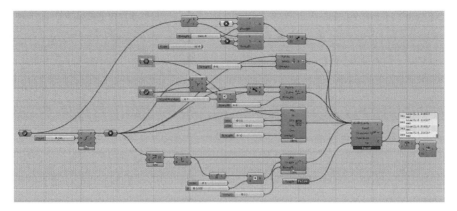

FIGURE 9.25　Algorithm program for optimal finding of hot water pipes. Image source: provided by the research group ©Xiao Zhang.

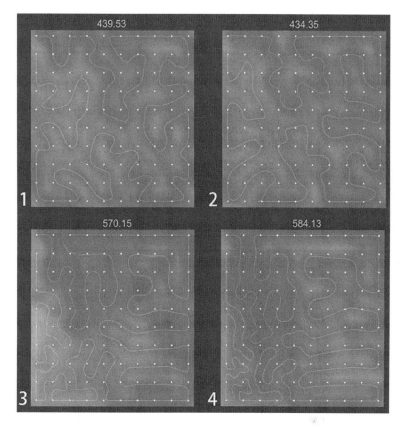

FIGURE 9.26 Optimization results of hot water coil path based on digital form-finding construction. Image source: provided by the research group ©Xiao Zhang.

this simulation process is over, we can form a heat map through the thermal radiation simulation algorithm mentioned above.

The optimal path (Figure 9.26) is obtained by the DFS graphics method, and the path is obtained by the form-finding design method, which have their own advantages and disadvantages. The path obtained by the DFS graphics method is more suitable for the heating mode provided by the hot water coil. However, the disadvantage of this method is as obvious; that is, the operation efficiency is low. The shape obtained by the form-finding design method has high universality, but because the shape is irregular, it is not suitable for direct application at present. But it works well when used as a 3D printing pathway for other forms of production, such as printing thermally conductive materials.

9.5   SUMMARY AND FUTURE WORK

9.5.1   RESEARCH SUMMARY

In this study, the research team proposed a herdsman energy security system based on thermoelectric power generation technology: by converting the waste heat generated by combustion into electricity and using the cooling water that maintains the temperature difference for the whole-house heating system. The research team took thermoelectric power generation technology as the research object and carried out research from three aspects, working principle, technical advantages, and technical limitations, and had a more comprehensive interpretation of thermoelectric power generation technology. The influencing factors of the thermoelectric power generation efficiency are summarized, and starting from the influence factor of the working temperature difference between the cold and hot ends of the thermoelectric power generation device, the relationship between the shape and structure on the thermal design of the thermoelectric power generation device is explored, and the shape and structure are revealed. Regarding the influence on thermoelectric power generation efficiency, in the design and application stage, the design form and structural law of improving the thermoelectric power generation efficiency summarized in the power generation experiment are applied to the design of the thermoelectric power generation device based on the waste heat of the furnace as the heat source. To provide solutions to electricity problems in areas without electricity, through the design of the conceptual scheme, the entire research process is perfected and closed, reflecting the complete design morphology methodology and process. The biggest highlight of this research is the research and summary of the form of improving the efficiency of thermoelectric power generation and the application in product design to solve the problem of electricity consumption in areas where electricity is scarce, reflecting its good practicability. In the design method, the research team mainly proposed a method based on form finding to optimize the pipeline route arrangement.

The difficulties in project research mainly include the following aspects. One is interdisciplinary research, which needs to break the boundaries of disciplines. Through the mutual reference and penetration of knowledge of physics and materials science, the innovation of knowledge and technology can be achieved. The second is that the finite element analysis method and fluid thermodynamic simulation experiments are not fully used, and the final extraction laws are also some relatively simple laws. At the same time, there are many interesting points in the subject research work that can be further deepened. Due to the impact of the epidemic, the research process cannot be fully advanced, but the research team will use this as a platform to continue to complete the physical on-site experiments.

9.5.2 FUTURE WORK FOR OPTIMIZATION

During the research process, the research team always maintains the cutting-edge discipline of combining heat conduction and design. The research team found that the size of the air inlet of a stove can lead to the size of its flame and thus affect the temperature of the stove. In a typical design, the designer can use electronic sensing devices to adjust the size of the air inlet. However, this kind of active adjustment often has unreliable mechanical hidden dangers, and the design integration degree is low. Therefore, the research team has carried out extensive research in the field of thermos-deformable materials. There are two ways to develop the entire thermoelectric power generation furnace in a more intelligent direction: Based on research by the research team, we have discovered a 3D printing-based approach to the design of

Experiment Analysis

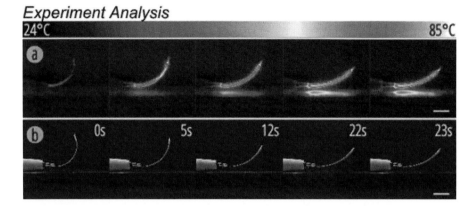

FIGURE 9.27 Deformation effect of conductive PLA material when heated. Image source: "Printed Paper Actuator: A Low-cost Reversible Actuation and Sensing Method for Shape Changing Interfaces" ©Lining Yao.

thermosensitive paper actuators by simply printing a single layer of conductive poly-lactic acid, PLA (Conductive Graphene PLA Filament, Black Magic 3D), on a piece of plastic to make the actuator work (Figure 9.27). Printing on a flat surface with a desktop FDM 3D printer allows the printing material to be drawn to produce residual stress. By applying heat, its residual stress can be activated and cause the flat material to bend in the direction of the print. When the flat material is heated again, the flat state can be restored. This behavior can be powered by electricity (Olga et al., 2017). The research team hopes that electrothermally driven conductive PLA can be driven by furnace temperature, enabling passive furnace temperature adjustment.

REFERENCES

Andreas, K. (2021). Thermochromic animation: Thermally-informed and colour-changing surface-configurations [Paper presentation]. *Proceedings of the 39th International Conference on Education and Research in Computer Aided Architectural Design in Europe (eCAADe)*, Novi Sad, Serbia, Vol. 2, pp. 453–462.

Brugnaro, G., Baharlou, E., Vasey, L., & Menges, A. (2016). Robotic softness: An adaptive robotic fabrication process for woven structures [Paper presentation], Michigan, USA, *ACADIA*, pp. 154–163. https://papers.cumincad.org/data/works/att/acadia16_154.pdf

Crane, K., Weischedel, C., & Wardetzky, M. (2017). The heat method for distance computation [Paper presentation]. *Communications of the ACM*, USA, pp. 90–99. https://doi.org/10.1145/3131280

Frei, O. & Bodo, R. (1996). *Finding Form: Towards an Architecture of the Minimal Hardcover.* Germany: Edition Axel Menges.

Guanyun, W., Tingyu, C., Youngwook, D., Humphrey, Y., Ye, T., Jianzhe, G., Byoungkwon, A., & Lining, Y. (2018) Printed paper actuator: A low-cost reversible actuation and sensing method for shape changing interfaces [Paper presentation]. *Proceedings of the 2018 CHI Conference on Human Factors in Computing Systems*, Montreal, QC, Canada. https://doi.org/10.1145/3173574.3174143

Guseinov, R., McMahan, C., Pérez, J., Daraio, C., & Bickel, B. (2020). Programming temporal morphing of self-actuated shells. *Nature Communications*, 11(1), 1–7. https://doi.org/10.1038/s41467-019-14015-2

Lavender, T., Carmel, D., Bjorn, S., Schendy, K., Jared, L., & Skylar, T. (2019). Active textile tailoring. *SIGGRAPH*. Article No.: 6, Pages 1–2. Los Angeles California, USA. https://doi.org/10.1145/3305367.3327995

Oded, S., Eitan, G., & Keenan, C. (2018). Developable surface flow [Paper presentation]. *ACM Transactions on Graphics*, New York City, USA, Vol. 4, pp. 4. https://doi.org/10.1145/3197517.3201303

Olga, M., Milena, S., Saurabh, M., Jonathan, G., Sarah, N., Allen, S., & Martin, B. (2017). Non-linear matters: auxetic surfaces [Paper presentation]. *ACADIA, 2017*, Cambridge, USA, pp. 392–403.

Qiang, Z., Hao, W., Liming, Z., Philip, F. Y, & Tianyi, G. (2021). 3D concrete printing with variable width filament [Paper presentation]. *eCAADe*, Novi Sad, Serbia, Vol. 2, pp. 153–160.

Wang, G., Tao, Y., Capunaman, O.B., Yang, H., & Yao, H. (2019). *CHI '19: Proceedings of the 2019 CHI Conference on Human Factors in Computing Systems*, May 2019, Paper No.: 426, Pages 1–12. https://doi.org/10.1145/3290605.3300656

Ye, T., Yi-Chin, L., Haolin, L., Xiaoxiao, Z., Jianxun, C., Catherine, M., Mahnoush, B., Jasio, S., Guanyun, W., Danli, L., Di, L., Humphrey, Y., Youngwook, D., Lingyun, S., Wen, W., Teng, Z., & Lining, Y. (2021). Morphing pasta and beyond. *Science Advances*, 7, 19. https://doi.org/10.1126/sciadv.abf4098

Yige, L., Li, L., & Philip, F. Y. (2019). A computational approach for knitting 3D composites preforms [Paper presentation]. *CDRF, Proceedings of the 2019*, Shanghai, China, pp. 232–246. https://doi.org/10.1007/978-981-13-8153-9_21

Index

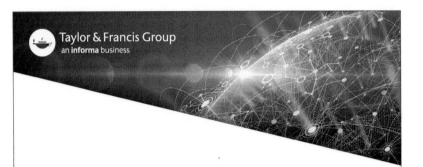

Printed in the United States
by Baker & Taylor Publisher Services